What Ifs of Jewish History

What if the Exodus had never happened? What if the Jews of Spain had not been expelled in 1492? What if Eastern European Jews had never been confined to the Russian Pale of Settlement? What if Adolf Hitler had been assassinated in 1939? What if a Jewish state had been established in Uganda instead of Palestine? Gavriel D. Rosenfeld's pioneering anthology examines how these and other counterfactual questions would have affected the course of Jewish history. Featuring essays by sixteen distinguished scholars in the field of Jewish Studies, *What Ifs of Jewish History* is the first volume to systematically apply counterfactual reasoning to the Jewish past. Written in a variety of narrative styles, ranging from the analytical to the literary, the essays cover three thousand years of dramatic events and invite readers to indulge their imaginations and explore how the course of Jewish history might have been different.

Gavriel D. Rosenfeld is Professor of History at Fairfield University.

What Ifs of Jewish History

From Abraham to Zionism

Edited by

Gavriel D. Rosenfeld

CAMBRIDGE
UNIVERSITY PRESS

University Printing House, Cambridge CB2 8BS, United Kingdom

Cambridge University Press is part of the University of Cambridge.

It furthers the University's mission by disseminating knowledge in the pursuit of education, learning and research at the highest international levels of excellence.

www.cambridge.org
Information on this title: www.cambridge.org/9781107037625

First published 2016

Printed in the United Kingdom by TJ International Ltd. Padstow Cornwall

A catalogue record for this publication is available from the British Library

ISBN 978-1-107-03762-5 Hardback

Cambridge University Press has no responsibility for the persistence or accuracy of URLs for external or third-party internet websites referred to in this publication, and does not guarantee that any content on such websites is, or will remain, accurate or appropriate.

CONTENTS

List of figures   *page* vii
List of figure acknowledgments   ix
List of contributors   x

Introduction: Counterfactual history and the Jewish
imagination   1
Gavriel D. Rosenfeld

1   What if the Exodus had never happened?   24
Steven Weitzman

2   What if the Temple of Jerusalem had not been destroyed by
the Romans?   43
René Bloch

3   What if King Ferdinand and Queen Isabella had not expelled
the Jews of Spain in 1492?   58
Jonathan Ray

4   What if the "ghetto" had never been constructed?   81
Bernard Dov Cooperman

5   What if Spinoza had repented?   103
Eugene R. Sheppard

6   What if Russian Jewry had never been confined to the Pale of
         Jewish Settlement?   123
         Jeffrey Veidlinger

7   What if a Christian state had been established in
         modern Palestine?   142
         Derek Jonathan Penslar

8   What if the Jewish state had been established in
         East Africa?   165
         Adam Rovner

9   What if Franz Kafka had immigrated to Palestine?   187
         Iris Bruce

10   What if the Palestinian Arab elite had chosen compromise
         instead of boycott in confronting Zionism?   215
         Kenneth W. Stein

11   What if Musa Alami and David Ben-Gurion had agreed on a
         Jewish–Arab state?   238
         David N. Myers

12   What if the Weimar Republic had survived? A chapter from
         Walther Rathenau's memoir   259
         Michael Brenner

13   What if Adolf Hitler had been assassinated in 1939?   275
         Gavriel D. Rosenfeld

14   What if the Nazis had won the battle of El Alamein?   298
         Jeffrey Herf

15   What if the Final Solution had been completed?: Nazi memory
         in a victorious Reich   311
         Dirk Rupnow

16   What if the Holocaust had been averted?   332
         Jeffrey S. Gurock

         Notes   355

         Index   402

FIGURES

Cover: Postage stamp from the country of New Judea

1   *The Crossing of the Red Sea* (1633–4), oil on canvas,
    painting by Nicolas Poussin   *page 2*
2   Woodcut of Flavius Josephus from William Whiston's
    translation of *Antiquities of the Jews* (1737)   11
3   Israelites building the cities, page from the Barcelona
    Haggadah, fourteenth century   27
4   *Moses with the Ten Commandments* (1648), oil on
    canvas, painting by Philippe de Champagne   35
5   *The Destruction of the Temple of Jerusalem* (1638),
    painting by Nicolas Poussin   44
6   *The Sacrifice of the Old Covenant* (*ca.* 1626), oil on
    panel, painting by Peter Paul Rubens   48
7   Engraving of Sultan Mehmed IV of Turkey   60
8   King Ferdinand II of Aragon and Queen Isabella
    of Castile   66
9   View of the city of Cracow, woodcut from the
    Nuremberg Chronicle (1493) by Hartmann Schedel   86
10 *The Ghetto, Rome* (1847), engraving by S.V. Hunt,
    Cassell & Company   95
11 Portrait of Benedict (Baruch) Spinoza, *ca.* 1665   104
12 Portrait of Heinrich Heine, 1838   118
13 Portrait of Tadeusz Kościuszko (1746–1817)   130

14   Portrait of Tsar Alexander I (1777–1825) (1814), oil
      on canvas, painting by Baron François Pascal Simon
      Gerard (1770–1837)   135
15   Photograph of Chaim Weizmann   146
16   Photograph of Christian Templer settlers in Wilhelma,
      Palestine   149
17   Postage stamp from New Judea   166
18   Map of New Judea   183
19   Photograph of Franz Kafka, Israel's first recipient of
      the Nobel Prize for Literature   188
20   Photograph of Franz Kafka in Prague before his
      departure to Palestine in 1924   195
21   Photograph of the Arab Higher Committee featuring
      Haj Amin Al-Husseini   220
22   Map of armistice lines in Palestine in 1947 and 1949   232
23   Photograph of David Ben-Gurion   240
24   Photograph of Musa Alami   241
25   Portrait of Walther Rathenau by Edvard Munch
      (1907)   260
26   Photograph of Albert Einstein   267
27   Photograph of Georg Elser   276
28   Postage stamp of Adolf Hitler   281
29   Photograph of Haj Amin Al-Husseini with Adolf
      Hitler (1941)   303
30   Photograph of General Erwin Rommel in North
      Africa   306
31   Photograph of mannequin of Jew holding Torah scroll
      in the Klaus synagogue   319
32   Photograph of Nazi ideologue Alfred Rosenberg   326
33   Photograph of Hjalmar Schacht and Adolf Hitler   335
34   Photograph of the ruins of the King David Hotel,
      Jerusalem   346

FIGURE ACKNOWLEDGMENTS

CONTRIBUTORS

RENÉ BLOCH is Professor for Jewish Studies at the Institute for Jewish Studies and at the Institute for Classical Philology at the University of Bern.

MICHAEL BRENNER is Professor of Jewish History and Culture at the Ludwig Maximilian University of Munich and holds the Seymour and Lillian Abensohn Chair in Israel Studies at American University in Washington.

IRIS BRUCE is Associate Professor of Linguistics and Languages at McMaster University.

BERNARD DOV COOPERMAN is Louis L. Kaplan Associate Professor of History at the University of Maryland.

JEFFREY S. GUROCK is the Libby M. Klaperman Professor of Jewish History at Yeshiva University.

JEFFREY HERF is Distinguished University Professor in the Department of History at the University of Maryland, College Park.

DAVID N. MYERS is Professor of History at the University of California, Los Angeles.

DEREK JONATHAN PENSLAR is the Stanley Lewis Professor of Israel Studies at the University of Oxford and Samuel Zacks Professor of Jewish History at the University of Toronto.

JONATHAN RAY is the Samuel Eig Associate Professor of Jewish Studies in the Theology Department at Georgetown University.

GAVRIEL D. ROSENFELD is Professor of History at Fairfield University.

ADAM ROVNER is Associate Professor of English and Jewish Literature at the University of Denver.

DIRK RUPNOW is Professor of Contemporary History at the University of Innsbruck.

EUGENE R. SHEPPARD is Associate Professor of Modern Jewish History and Thought at Brandeis University.

KENNETH W. STEIN is the William E. Schatten Professor of Contemporary Middle Eastern History and Israeli Studies at Emory University.

JEFFREY VEIDLINGER is the Joseph Brodsky Collegiate Professor of History and Judaic Studies at the University of Michigan.

STEVEN WEITZMAN is the Abraham M. Ellis Professor of Hebrew and Semitic Languages and Literatures at the University of Pennsylvania.

INTRODUCTION: COUNTERFACTUAL HISTORY AND THE JEWISH IMAGINATION

Gavriel D. Rosenfeld

Throughout history, Jews have been known to kvetch. A well-known example of Jewish petulance appears in Chapter 16 of the Book of Exodus. At this juncture in the biblical narrative, the Israelites have just begun to make their way out of Egypt following the destruction of Pharaoh's army in the Sea of Reeds (Figure 1). Having regained their freedom, they jubilantly sing a song of praise to God for delivering them from their enemies. Struggles lie ahead, however, for the Israelites have only begun their long trek to the Promised Land. Three days into their journey, they start to lose patience. The wilderness is bleak, they have no water, and they start to "grumble . . . against Moses, saying, 'What shall we drink?'" Aware of the challenge to his leadership, Moses turns to God for help and is soon guided to an oasis "where there were twelve springs of water and seventy palm trees." The Israelites proceed to drink their fill and their anger is temporarily appeased. But they soon begin to grumble once again, this time about the lack of food. Fearing imminent starvation, the "whole Israelite community" loudly laments: "If only we had died by the hand of the Lord in the land of Egypt, when we sat by the fleshpots, when we ate our fill of bread!"[1]

The exclamation is dramatic – indeed, hyperbolic – and demands interpretation. Do the Israelites really wish they had died at an earlier point in time back in Egypt? Do they really wish they had never lived to see their way to freedom? Knowing what we do about the subsequent course of events and the Israelites' triumphant arrival in the Promised Land, we may surmise that the exclamation is not intended to be taken literally. But then what does it mean? In seeking to

Figure 1. *The Crossing of the Red Sea* (1633–4), oil on canvas, painting by Nicolas Poussin. The first historical counterfactual that appears in the Hebrew Bible involves the Israelites complaining that they would have been better off had they decided to stay in Egypt instead of departing for the Promised Land.

understand the passage, we have a variety of interpretations to choose from. We may see the passage as a sign of the Jewish people's penchant for complaining, as a reflection of their strained relationship with Moses, or as proof of their difficulty in trusting God. All of these are plausible readings. But there is another way to understand the passage, and that is to recognize it as the first counterfactual historical reference in the Hebrew Bible.

Analyzing the passage by focusing on its counterfactual phrasing allows a range of insights. The first and most important involves its function. At the most basic level, the Israelites' exclamation about their precarious present contains an implicit assumption about an alternate past; it suggests that the course of history would have been better had they stayed in Egypt. It is questionable, of course, whether the Israelites really believe this to be true; indeed, their outburst is likely intended to serve the rhetorical purpose of exaggerating the magnitude of their suffering and amplifying their cry for help in the wilderness. Regardless of the sentiment that lies behind it, the Israelites' exclamation reveals an important fact about all counterfactual claims: they are "presentist" in the sense that they reflect contemporary concerns. The particular passage from Exodus illustrates how discontent with the present can prompt fantasies about improving the past. Yet, the opposite can also be true: a sense of satisfaction with the present can encourage visions of the past turning out worse. An excellent example of this alternative impulse appeared centuries after the Israelites' departure from Egypt, during the Middle Ages, with the composition of the famous song, "Dayenu." Traditionally chanted at the Passover Seder, the fourteen-verse song celebrates God for delivering the Israelites from Egyptian bondage, repeatedly affirming in hypothetical fashion that if God had been of less assistance – for example, if he had "brought us before Mount Sinai but not given us the Torah" – it "still would have been enough for us." The message is clear: in reciting the different ways in which the course of history might have turned out worse, those who sing the song express gratitude for their present-day reality.

These two examples from the Jewish religious tradition show how pivotal events in history – in this case, the Israelites' liberation from slavery – can inspire counterfactual speculation. Yet, while these observations help us understand the speculative character of the passage from Exodus, a fundamental question remains unanswered: what, indeed, would have happened if the Israelites had stayed in Egypt?

To ask this question is to open the floodgates of the imagination and delve into a vast universe of historical possibility known as counterfactual history. The question of how the Israelites would have fared had they never left Egypt is particularly evocative and allows for many different scenarios. But it is merely one of many hypothetical questions that loom large in Jewish history: What if the Israelites' descendants, the Jews of Judea, had never witnessed the destruction of the Second Temple? What if the Jews of late medieval Spain had never been expelled from their homeland in 1492? What if the Jews of Russia had never been confined to the Pale of Settlement? What if the Jews of Europe had never died in the Holocaust? What if the state of Israel had been established in Uganda instead of Palestine? How would Jewish history have been different?

In addressing these and other speculative questions, *What Ifs of Jewish History* breaks new ground in being the first study to systematically apply counterfactual reasoning to the Jewish past. Up until now, scholars in the field of Jewish Studies have shied away from the field of counterfactual history. This aversion is puzzling. As the list of questions above makes clear, the Jewish historical record hardly lacks for captivating "what if?" scenarios. One would think that Jewish historians would be eager to explore such scenarios, moreover, given the surging popularity of counterfactual history in recent years. Within the humanities and social sciences in general, and the field of history in particular, scholars have begun to set aside longstanding biases and employ "what if?" questions in their academic work. The wave of academic and popular studies that have been published in recent years clearly shows that counterfactual history has left the margins for the scholarly mainstream.[2] This being the case, one would expect that Jewish historians and other scholars would have begun to follow the example of their colleagues in other disciplines and started speculating about the Jewish past. Until now, however, they have largely refrained from doing so. The question is, why?

Historicizing counterfactual history

In order to understand the late arrival of Jewish historians to counterfactual history, it helps to historicize the field itself. Counterfactual history has been defined in different ways, but it is essentially a genre of narrative representation that offers speculative answers to "what if?" questions in specific historical settings.[3] These narratives typically come in two varieties. Some take the form of sober analytical essays and are mostly produced by historians and other scholars; others assume more dramatic expression in the form of novels, short stories, plays, and films. Both kinds of narrative can be classified as works of counterfactual history, but scholars often describe the latter as belonging to the literary subgenre of "alternate history."[4] These stylistic differences notwithstanding, there is considerable overlap between works of counterfactual and alternate history. Both strive to show how the alteration of a variable in the historical record would have changed the overall course of events.[5] This variable is typically called a "point of divergence" and includes many kinds of occurrences: the deaths of kings and politicians, the occurrence of decisive military victories or defeats, and the rise of grand cultural and religious movements.[6] In speculating about how these variables might have changed the historical record, counterfactual histories typically proceed in one of two directions: they imagine history taking either a turn for the better or a turn for the worse.[7] Counterfactual histories thus usually assume the form of fantasy and nightmare scenarios. President John F. Kennedy escaping assassination in 1963 is a familiar example of the first, while the Nazis winning World War II is the most famous example of the second.

These scenarios – and countless others like them – are undeniably provocative, but they beg a larger question: why do we ask "what if?" in the first place? Not surprisingly, counterfactual speculation is driven by many different motives. These motives vary considerably depending on who is doing the speculating. Among scholars, however, asking "what if?" serves several important analytical purposes. To begin with, scholars employ counterfactual reasoning to better understand the forces of historical causality. Although historians are often loath to admit it, "what if?" questions are indispensable for determining why events happen. Whenever we make the causal claim that "x caused y," we implicitly affirm that "y would not have occurred in the absence of x."[8] To cite one well-known event, the assertion that the United States Air Force's dropping of atomic bombs on Hiroshima and Nagasaki in 1945 enabled the country to defeat Japan in World War II is closely related to the counterfactual claim that if the bombs had not been dropped, the Allies might not have emerged victorious in the Pacific theater. Such claims help underscore the contingent nature of historical events and challenge the impulse to view them as preordained. Indeed, they reveal that counterfactual history is informed by a mindset that stands opposed to historical determinism.[9] For this reason, choice rather than inevitability stands at the center of all "what if?" scenarios.

This fact explains a second reason why scholars employ counterfactual scenarios: to make moral judgments in interpreting historical events. It is difficult to judge the morality of an action without being aware of what might have happened had it not occurred. The long-standing scholarly debate about whether the atomic bombs *should* have been dropped on Japan has long been inseparable from the question of how history might have unfolded had they not been. Would the war have dragged on longer? Would more Americans, and perhaps even more Japanese, have died as a result? Would the course of history, in short, have been better or worse? The answer to this basic question, which is one that lurks behind all counterfactual premises, helps determine how the past is judged – as morally justified, according to those who believe history would have been worse without the bombs, or as immoral, according to those who believe the opposite.

The third and perhaps primary reason why we ask "what if?" lies in the broader area of human psychology. It is in our very nature as human beings to wonder "what if?" At various junctures in our lives, we may speculate about what might have happened if certain events had or had not occurred in our past: what if we had lived in a different place, attended a different school, taken a different job, married a different spouse? When we ask such questions, we are really expressing our feelings about the present. We are either grateful that things worked out as they did, or we regret that they did not occur differently. The same concerns are involved in the realm of counterfactual history. Counterfactual history explores the past less for its own sake than to utilize it instrumentally to comment upon the state of the contemporary world. When the producers of counterfactual histories imagine how the past might have been different, they invariably express their own subjective hopes and fears.[10] Fantasy scenarios, for example, envision the alternate past as superior to the real past and thereby typically express a sense of dissatisfaction with the way things are today. Nightmare scenarios, by contrast, depict the alternate past as inferior to the real past and thus usually articulate a sense of contentment with the status quo.[11]

Counterfactual fantasies and nightmares, moreover, have different political implications. Fantasies tend to be liberal, for by imagining a better past, they implicitly indict the present and express a desire to change it. Harry Turtledove and Richard Dreyfus' 1996 novel, *The Two Georges*, is a good example of this sentiment, because in portraying how the defeat of the American Revolution in 1776 would have improved the course of American history, the text critiqued the United States' many domestic problems in the early 1990s. Nightmares, by contrast, tend to be conservative, for by portraying the alternate past in negative terms, they ratify the present as the best of all possible worlds and discourage the need for change. Noel Coward's 1947 play, *Peace in Our Time*, by imagining the brutality of a Nazi invasion and the occupation of Great Britain, vindicated the country's real historical triumph over the Third Reich as its "finest hour" and endorsed the postwar order upon which it was based. These political implications, to be sure, are not ironclad and should not be viewed deterministically. Nightmare scenarios can also be used for the liberal purpose of critique, as was true of Philip Roth's 2004 novel, *The Plot Against America*, whose portrait of

America turning to fascism under President Charles Lindbergh served as an indictment of the administration of President George W. Bush. Fantasy scenarios, meanwhile, can express conservative dissatisfaction with the present, as with Newt Gingrich's *Gettysburg* trilogy of counterfactual Civil War novels, which served to criticize "big government" after the turn of the millennium.[12] Regardless of their precise political function, counterfactual histories typically explore the past with an eye toward present-day agendas.

Given the innate appeal of wondering "what if?," it is no surprise to learn that counterfactual history has distant origins. Speculating about the past dates back to classical antiquity and the historiographical traditions of the Greco-Roman world. The first documented counterfactual assertion appears in the work of the Greek historian Herodotus (born *ca.* 484 BCE).[13] In his account of the Persian Wars, he famously speculated that "had the Athenians... quitted their country... [and] submitted to the power of Xerxes... the Lacedaemonians [the fighters of Sparta] would have... stood alone... and died nobly... or else... come to terms with King Xerxes... either... way, Greece would have been brought under Persia." This assertion functioned as a nightmare scenario for the purpose of validating history as it really happened (the Greeks won) and glorifying the Athenians as the "true saviors of Greece."[14] Later historians, by contrast, demonstrated a different perspective. A case in point is Thucydides (born *ca.* 460 BCE) who, in his famous *History of the Peloponnesian War*, made nearly two dozen counterfactual observations pertaining to the conflict's course, writing, for example, that "if Alcibiades had not restrained the fleet from sailing on Athens, the enemies of Athens surely would have occupied Ionia and the Hellespont immediately."[15] This observation (and others like it) served as a fantasy scenario reflecting the sense of regret on the part of the famed historian (who was a general on the losing side of the war) that events did not go better for the Athenians. Four centuries later, a similar impulse inspired the Roman historian Tacitus (56–117 CE) to speculate that if the legendary Roman general Germanicus had not died prematurely and instead lived to become emperor, "he would have outstripped Alexander in military fame as far as he surpassed him in gentleness, in self-command and in other noble qualities."[16] Written by a scholar who was convinced of the degeneracy of his age, Tacitus' remark about Germanicus resembled Thucydides' in wishing history's course had transpired otherwise. Surpassing all of these scholars in imaginative power, however, was the Roman historian Livy (59 BCE – 17 CE), who in his monumental study of ancient Rome, *Ab Urbe Condita*, provided a long and elaborate answer to the rhetorically powerful question, "what would have been the consequence...[for] the Romans, if they had...engaged in a war with Alexander [the Great?]," by concluding that, like "other kings and nations [before him]...Alexander...would have found the Roman empire invincible."[17] In arriving at this conclusion, Livy resembled his illustrious predecessors in being guided by presentist motives. Writing at a time when Augustus was consolidating power and transforming Rome from a republic into an empire, Livy intended his tale to serve as a cautionary lesson about the contemporary dangers of one-man rule.[18] Taken together, the observations of Livy, Herodotus, Thucydides, and Tacitus – not to mention similar hypothetical observations by Polybius and Plutarch – confirm that, from its very inception, the Greco-Roman historiographical tradition was particularly open to counterfactual speculation.[19]

Counterfactual history and the Jewish tradition

By contrast, the Jewish historiographical tradition has been less inclined to speculate about the past. The reasons for this are complex and require extensive explanation, not to mention a certain amount of qualification. To begin with, it is certainly true that Jewish religious texts contain the kind of hypothetical thinking required for counterfactual historical speculation. Even a cursory glance through the Hebrew Bible reveals the presence of "what if?" statements. Early in the Book of Genesis, for example, after Adam eats from the tree of knowledge in the Garden of Eden, God worries that the first human may soon commit further transgressions, exclaiming, "What if he should stretch out his hand and take also from the tree of life and eat?"[20] Later in Genesis, Abraham's effort to convince God not to punish the citizens of Sodom leads to a series of "what if?" questions involving the number of righteous citizens the patriarch would need to find in order to prevent the city's destruction (Abraham begins with fifty citizens and relentlessly bargains God down until finally asking, "What if ten should be found there?").[21] Later in Exodus, meanwhile, after God entrusts Moses with the task of guiding the Israelites to freedom, the reluctant leader anxiously asks God:

"What if they do not believe me and do not listen to me?"[22] On the face of it, these hypothetical statements would seem to qualify as "what ifs?" Yet, since they focus on the future instead of the past, they are not examples of counterfactual historical thinking.

The same is true of other conditional "if-then" statements that are found in the Jewish religious tradition. There are many such statements in the Hebrew Bible, a good number of which relate to God's covenant with the Jewish people, especially their obligation to uphold his divine laws. Some of these statements are phrased positively, as when God declares in Exodus 19:5: "If you will obey Me faithfully and keep my covenant, you shall be my treasured possession among all the peoples."[23] Others are expressed negatively, as in Deuteronomy 8:19, where God asserts: "If you...forget the Lord your God and follow other gods to serve them...you shall certainly perish."[24] Like the "what if?" statements mentioned above, however, these are oriented toward the future instead of the past. The same applies to "if-then" declarations that appear in the realm of Jewish legal thought. In the Bible and especially in the Talmud, there are innumerable "if-then" rulings on myriad religious, social, and economic questions. Many of them are phrased in the past tense: for example, "if a man ate and forgot to say the benediction...[then] he must return to his place and say it."[25] "If a field was reaped by gentiles or robbers...[then] it is exempt from Peah [the law of leaving gleanings]."[26] Yet these and other similar conditional statements, despite being phrased in the past tense, are meant to serve as guides to present or future behavior. Moreover, they pertain strictly to personal acts and have no counterfactual relevance for the course of historical events.

Also failing to qualify are specific historical episodes in the Bible, Talmud, and other religious texts that have hypothetical components. When the Babylonians are besieging Jerusalem in the sixth century BCE, the Book of Jeremiah, 38:17–18, portrays God telling King Zedekiah that "If you surrender to the officers of the King of Babylon, your life will be spared and this city will not be burned down. You and your household will live. But if you do not surrender...this city will be given into the hands of the Chaldeans who will burn it down."[27] This statement introduces the factor of contingency to historical events, but it does so mostly as a future-oriented prophecy of what will happen pending a given decision. This is also true of the Talmudic story that God offered King Hezekiah the chance to become the Messiah after his victory over the Assyrian King Sennacherib, in the year 701 BCE, but because Hezekiah failed to sing God's praises, he lost his opportunity.[28] The rabbis, however, did not go on to explore the consequences of this "road not taken" in a historical sense and instead devoted their attention to determining the theological reasons for (and implications of) Hezekiah's failure to sing for God.[29] Similarly, in Isaiah 48:18, following the Temple's destruction by the Babylonians, God admonishes the Israelites by saying, "If only you would heed My commands! Then your prosperity would be like a river, your triumph like waves of the sea."[30] This statement comes closer to expressing a counterfactual mindset, but it ultimately fails to qualify, as it does not so much depict a specific historical outcome as a general moral–religious lesson. The same can even be said about the famous Passover song, "Dayenu," which never fully explores what actually might have happened if God had not acted as he did.[31]

To be sure, some counterfactual statements about the Jewish past do appear here and there in the Jewish religious and intellectual tradition. Beyond the famous episode from Exodus, in which the starving Israelites fantasize about being back in Egypt, there is a nearly identical one in the Book of Numbers, where the Israelites say the same thing almost verbatim when told about Moses' plan to invade Canaan.[32] Fears about looming military defeat also inform a lament that appears in Joshua 7:7, when the Israelites, having been told of a looming battle with the Amorites, exclaim, "If only we had been content to remain on the other side of the Jordan!"[33] In each of these instances, apprehension about the present prompts the Israelites to fantasize about a preferable historical outcome. A different sentiment is expressed in Psalm 124, which asserts: "Were it not for the Lord, who was on our side when men assailed us, they would have swallowed us alive in their burning rage against us."[34] This nightmare scenario – reputedly written by King David following his victory over the Philistines – is a psalm of thanksgiving, an expression of gratitude for history turning out as it did. These statements are more legitimate expressions of hypothetical historical thinking, but they only make up a tiny fraction of the Tanach. Moreover, they all focus on a religious theme – the Israelites' relationship with God – and do not pertain to the realm of secular historical causality like the aforementioned instances from Greek and Roman historiography.

The exception that proves the rule is found in the work of the Jewish historian, Flavius Josephus (Figure 2). In his famous book,

Figure 2. Woodcut of Flavius Josephus from William Whiston's translation of *Antiquities of the Jews* (1737). The Jewish historian Josephus (*ca.* 37–100 CE) was the exception to the rule in the Jewish historiographical tradition, as he was willing to speculate counterfactually about the Jewish past.

The Jewish War, Josephus discusses the case of the Jewish high priest, Ananus, who was opposed to the rule of the Zealots in Jerusalem during the Revolt of 66–70 CE and tried – correctly, in Josephus' pro-Roman estimation – to surrender the city peacefully to the Roman imperial

army. Ananus was murdered by the Idumeans, who were let into the city
by the Zealots to purge those they regarded as collaborators. Viewing
this decision as tragic and avoidable, Josephus concluded, "had Ananus
survived... an accommodation [with the Romans] would have been
effected... [If] he had been spared... the Jews... would have greatly
retarded the triumph of the Romans."[35] Josephus' statement was in the
same counterfactual style as the assertions of Herodotus and Thucydides. But it was exceptional. As a scholar who was influenced by Greek
historiography and emphasized secular causality, Josephus stood outside the normative Jewish historiographical tradition. His speculative
comment was thus unrepresentative of the Jewish historical mindset,
which remained rooted in its biblical paradigm.[36]

If we accept the premise that the Jewish tradition was generally averse to counterfactual speculation, the question that needs to
be answered is "why?" Many scholars have written about the nature
of Jewish historical consciousness and the forces that have shaped it.
Their work suggests that the absence of counterfactual speculation is
rooted in the deterministic and teleological character of Jewish historiography and historical consciousness. Beginning in antiquity, the Jewish
people began to perceive their history as an expression of divine will, a
reflection of a divine plan. They interpreted their experiences – whether
successes or failures – as rewards and punishments for their behavior.
History's course was a barometer of God's commitment to the Jewish people, which varied according to their own level of commitment to
the divine covenant. The civil war between Israel and Judah, the defeats
by the Assyrians and Babylonians, the destruction of the first Temple,
the exile and eventual return to Jerusalem – all of these events were
interpreted by the prophets, especially Jeremiah and Isaiah, as reflections of Jewish moral failings and ensuing repentance. This perspective
helped solidify a Jewish view of history that was teleological, proceeding toward a specific (religious) goal: the end of days and the coming of
the Messiah.[37] For obvious reasons, this historical sensibility discouraged counterfactual speculation. The notion that history's course had to
unfold according to a specific plan minimized the role of contingency
in historical events. It discouraged reflection on how, but for a different
variable here or there, everything might have turned out differently.

The Jewish sense that history was divinely ordered and deterministic differed sharply from the contemporaneous Greek view of
history and explains why the former was less prone to counterfactual

speculation than the latter. History, in the Greek tradition, lacked the linear quality of Jewish historical consciousness; unlike the Jews, the Greeks did not see history proceeding toward a larger goal.[38] This difference reflected the polytheistic nature of the Greek religion, which imagined the Gods continually fighting without any clear direction or predictable outcome.[39] However, the Greeks did not just differ from the Jews in seeing history as the expression of chaos instead of a divine plan. As Greek historiography transitioned from the work of Herodotus to that of Thucydides, it also became more secularized. It began to deemphasize the role of the Gods in human affairs and instead sought answers for history's course in the "mechanisms of human society."[40] This secularization of historical consciousness was crucial, as it enabled the Greeks to appreciate the role of chance in history and opened up the possibility of imagining alternate outcomes to it. In short, the case of Greek historiography shows how the emergence of secular forms of historical consciousness was a necessary – though not sufficient – precondition for counterfactual speculation.

The deterministic character of Jewish historical consciousness was further consolidated with the onset of the diaspora. With this development, Jews lost what had traditionally been the subject of most historical writing in the Near East – political power. In Egypt, Mesopotamia, and Persia, historiography had traditionally assumed the form of chronicles and annals focusing on lists of royal succession and military victories (defeats were left undocumented). As long as the Jews enjoyed political authority in the unified monarchy (and even after the split), they too recorded such history.[41] But after the destruction of the Second Temple, profane history ceased to matter. Without political power, the Jews became the objects of history instead of active subjects in it.[42] The rabbis did not write history, which goes without mention in the tannaitic or amoritic literature in the years 50–500 CE.[43] They felt that the Bible contained all the historical lessons that the Jewish people needed and thus preserved the biblical tradition of seeing "obedience and rebellion as determinative of Israel's [historical] fate."[44] They continued to see historical events as a response to Jewish virtue and sin. Indeed, the very meaning of history was determined by Jewish suffering and how it proved God's power.[45] Talmudic interpretations of the Second Temple's destruction, for example, perceived the event as the predictable result of "idolatry, immorality, and bloodshed."[46] The rabbis, believing that God had distanced himself from his people, turned away from interpreting contemporary political events and toward reinterpreting Biblical history, producing volumes of Midrashic readings that reflect a nostalgic yearning for an era when Israel still enjoyed divine favor and political autonomy. The rabbinic dedication to halakha symbolized the Jewish preference for the law over history.[47]

This pattern changed little prior to the onset of modernity. During the Middle Ages, Jews continued to show little interest in historical research and writing. It was emblematic that the era's most famous Jewish philosopher, Moses Maimonides, contended that history was a "sheer waste of time."[48] To be sure, certain dramatic historical events, such as the Crusades, stimulated attention to contemporary history (and produced new methods of documentation, like *Memorbücher*, or memorial books). Yet these events were still interpreted from a religious perspective. Suffering was still seen as punishment for sin. Indeed, as Yosef Hayim Yerushalmi famously argued in *Zakhor*, medieval Jews developed a typological method of using biblical archetypes to make sense of present-day events, viewing "the latest oppressor [as]...Haman," perceiving "Christendom [as]...'Edom,'" and affixing "geographical names...from the Bible...to places the Bible never knew...so [that] Spain is 'Sefarad'...[and] Germany is 'Ashkenaz.'"[49] There were few exceptions to this pattern. During the Renaissance, there was a brief upsurge in Jewish historiography, epitomized by Azariah de Rossi's *Meor Enayim*, which exhibited something of a modern rationalist attention to the use of evidence and the pursuit of historical truth. But the total number of histories produced by Jews in this period was small, especially compared with Christian scholarship.[50] Indeed, while Christian scholars were prompted by the humanist movement to depart from the medieval tradition of "ecclesiastical historiography" and inaugurate "the rebirth of political and military historiography," Jewish scholars found this topic "irrelevant," given their impotent political status, and remained mired in premodern patterns for several more centuries.[51]

Only with the dawn of the nineteenth century did Jews finally return to writing history. Even then, however, they did not entirely distance themselves from prior traditions. The rise of modern "scientific" historiography profoundly changed Jewish historical writing by leading Jewish historians to foreground secular causality instead of divine will in crafting their historical narratives. Yet, in important ways, Jewish historiography preserved a teleological orientation. Jewish historians, despite pledging allegiance to standards of scientific objectivity, imposed totalizing narratives upon the Jewish past in the attempt to lend it a sense of unity.[52] This holistic (and often ideological) impulse led Jewish historians to portray the past as evolving in a linear direction toward one telos or another. The pioneering historians associated with the early nineteenth-century Wissenschaft des Judentums movement, such as Isaak Markus Jost and Leopold Zunz, for example, focused on historicizing the evolution of Judaism as a spiritual idea, believing that doing so would promote the goals of religious reform and civil emancipation. Later historians, such as Heinrich Graetz and Simon Dubnow, took a more nationalistic turn and focused on the development of the Jews as an independent people, believing that asserting Jewish nationhood would bring political benefits to Jews in Central and Eastern Europe. This trend paved the way for later Zionist historians, such as Yitzhak Baer, to represent Jewish history as a long struggle between *Galut* and nationhood, between the defeatist forces of assimilation and the heroic ones of national persistence. Even "acculturationist" historians, such as Salo Baron, saw a directionality to Jewish history, viewing it as focused on the struggle to preserve the Jewish people's distinctiveness while interacting with the larger gentile world.[53] These historians' work was not deterministic in the strict sense of the term, and they should hardly be seen as secular versions of the biblical view that Jewish existence was divinely guided. Yet their ideological tendencies may have made them less open to the play of chance and contingency.

Perhaps for this reason, Jewish historians generally offered few counterfactual observations in their work. This is not to say that such observations were entirely absent. Indeed, in the process of embracing modern historiographical methodologies and practices, nineteenth-century Jewish historians, like their Christian colleagues, gradually began to make counterfactual remarks in their historical writing. Isaak Markus Jost, for example, hypothesized that the Bar Kochba rebellion "might have erupted already in the years 122–3 [CE] had the emperor [Hadrian] not traveled to the east."[54] He later observed that the eleventh-century Spanish Jewish thinker, Solomon ibn Gabirol, "doubtless would have achieved more had he been granted a longer life."[55] Heinrich Graetz also offered counterfactual musings in his work. He speculated that Babylonian King Nebuchadnezzar's successor, Amel-Marduk, "might have been persuaded to let the [Jewish] exiles return home, with Jehoiachin as king, had his own death not intervened."[56] He also hypothesized that had the Jews "awaited a more favorable moment" to rebel against Rome, "success might have been [theirs]."[57] Other scholars were prone to making occasional counterfactual speculations as well. In the early twentieth century, Simon Dubnow wrote that the "terrible upheavals [of the years 1903–6] might have proved fatal to Russian Israel had it not, during the preceding period, worked out for itself a definite nationalistic attitude towards the non-Jewish world...[and] demanded their rights in full...as an autonomous nation among other nations with a culture of its own."[58] Salo Baron, meanwhile, later declared in his *Social and Religious History of the Jews* that "one may doubt whether [the Jewish]...religion would have been born...without the towering mentality of Moses."[59]

These counterfactual observations were notable for their novelty, but their significance is uncertain. On the one hand, they testified to the increasingly modern character of Jewish historiography. They confirmed that the secularization of historical consciousness was a precondition for counterfactual speculation and showed that Jewish historians were coming to resemble their Christian colleagues. During this period, counterfactual observations were increasingly finding expression in Western historical and sociological scholarship, as was shown by their appearance in the work of Edward Gibbon, Thomas Babington Macaulay, Jacob Burckhardt, G. M. Trevelyan, Heinrich von Treitschke, Arnold Toynbee, John Stuart Mill, and Max Weber.[60] Jewish historians were thus in good company in making their own speculative assertions. Yet, in an important respect, their willingness to speculate remained limited. While Jewish historians were prepared to make fleeting counterfactual observations about the past, they never went on to fully explore their possible consequences by producing more extended works of counterfactual history.

This absence was underscored by the increasing willingness of non-Jews to do so. At the very same time that the modern historical profession was coming into its own during the nineteenth century, counterfactual history was beginning to emerge as an independent genre of narrative representation. Ironically, the first examples of the genre were produced by figures from outside the historical profession, mostly novelists and other fiction writers. Unlike historians, whose positivist commitment to scientific objectivity made them loath to produce extended narratives founded on subjective speculation, fiction writers eagerly gave free rein to their imaginations and produced numerous literary examples of alternate history.[61] The first major narratives were novel-length texts from France: Louis-Napoleon Geoffroy-Château's 1836 narrative, *Napoleon et la conquête du monde 1812–1832*, Joseph Méry's 1854 novella, *Histoire de ce qui n'est pas arrivé*, and Charles Renouvier's 1857 novel, *Uchronie*.[62] These texts, which mostly focused on the reign of Napoleon Bonaparte (or which critiqued the rule of his nephew, Napoleon III), confirmed the tendency of counterfactual speculation to thrive in nations that stand at the center of pivotal historical events. This supposition was further confirmed by the fact that most other alternate histories that appeared before the year 1900 were published in Great Britain and the United States. Significantly, they were produced nearly entirely by Christian authors. This pattern continued in the next half-century leading up to the start of World War II. Although the number of counterfactual and alternate histories increased substantially during this period, hardly any were written by Jews.[63]

The absence of Jewish voices from this literary output was due to several factors. To a degree, the small size of alternate history as a fledgling genre in this early period made it statistically unlikely that many texts would be authored by Jews. But Jewish literary tendencies were also involved. Although Jews were increasingly prominent as fiction writers in this period, they were concentrated in more traditional literary genres. They were accomplished in realist fiction (I. J. Singer), folk literature (Sholom Aleichem), and modernism (Franz Kafka). But they were less represented in the larger literary genre to which alternate history belonged: speculative literature. This genre, which includes fantasy, horror, and science fiction, did not entirely lack Jewish representatives; but where they appeared, Jewish authors focused less on the past than the future. They shied away from the backward-looking genre of fantasy, for example, in favor of the forward-looking genre of science fiction.[64] This emphasis dovetailed with the penchant of many Jews in the late nineteenth and early twentieth centuries to embrace utopian thinking. Seen in the growing support among Jews for Zionism and Socialism, this thinking was highly teleological and less concerned with changing the course of bygone events than shaping those still to come. This impulse was epitomized by Theodor Herzl's utopian novel, *Altneuland* (1902), which expressed the Zionist goal of dialectically transcending the Jewish past in the pursuit of a future ideal.[65] All of these trends inhibited Jews from making a major contribution to the emerging genre of counterfactual history.

Only once counterfactual history began to enter the cultural mainstream after 1945 did Jewish contributions slowly start to appear. The early postwar years were marked by the publication of major alternate history novels. Among the most famous in the 1950s and 1960s were Ward Moore's *Bring the Jubilee* (1954), Philip K. Dick's *The Man in the High Castle* (1962), and Keith Roberts' *Pavane* (1968). They were joined in subsequent decades by other well-regarded texts, such as Kingsley Amis's *The Alteration* (1976), Len Deighton's *SS-GB* (1978), and Terry Bisson's *Fire on the Mountain* (1988). By the 1990s and after the turn of the millennium, the appearance of other novels, such as Robert Harris's *Fatherland* (1992), brought alternate history increasing media attention and heightened prominence. The growing interest in "what if?" questions reflected the political and cultural climate of the *fin de siècle*. It reflected the rise of postmodernism, which questioned the belief in metanarratives and objective truth; the end of the Cold War, which discredited deterministic modes of thinking; and the information revolution, which created a new receptivity for "virtual" modes of existence separated from reality.[66] Against the backdrop of these trends, Jewish writers became increasingly active in producing alternate histories. Although their contribution to the genre was initially modest – few novels or short stories were penned by Jewish writers prior to the 1970s – they produced important works thereafter. Indeed, two of the most prominent, in terms of critical and popular success, were Philip Roth's *The Plot Against America* (2004) and Michael Chabon's *The Yiddish Policemen's Union* (2007), both of which helped lend alternate history greater legitimacy. Moreover, the most prominent figure associated with the genre today is the Jewish writer, Harry Turtledove, the author of nearly one hundred alternate history novels and short stories, including the influential *Guns of the South* (1992).[67] All of these developments confirmed the capacity of Jews to engage in counterfactual speculation.

Unlike Jewish fiction writers, however, Jewish historians did not participate much in the new engagement with counterfactual history. Their avoidance stood in stark contrast to the trend within the general historical profession, which displayed an increasing openness to counterfactual speculation. Thanks in part to the rise of postmodernism, which helped undermine the longstanding belief in historical objectivity and truth, historians began to overcome their traditional aversion to asking "what if?" questions and increasingly tried their hand at crafting counterfactual narratives about the past. Starting in the mid 1990s, growing numbers of historians began to publish essays in high-profile collections, including Niall Ferguson's edited anthology, *Virtual History* (1997); Robert Cowley's edited volumes, *What If? Military Historians Imagine What Might Have Been* (1999), *More What If?: Eminent Historians Imagine What Might Have Been* (2001), and *What Ifs? of American History* (2003); and similar volumes by Andrew Roberts, Jeremy Black, and Philip E. Tetlock, Richard Ned Lebow, and Geoffrey Parker.[68] These important studies featured little work by scholars of Jewish history, however. More recently, individual academic monographs have begun to employ counterfactual reasoning prominently in their analyses, including Henry Turner's *Hitler's Thirty Days to Power* (2003), Frank Harvey's *Explaining the Iraq War: Counterfactual Theory, Logic, and Evidence* (2012), and Peter Bowler's *Darwin Deleted: Imagining a World Without Darwin* (2013).[69] Thus far, however, Jewish historians have not embraced this trend either.[70] To be sure, Jewish scholars and journalists have occasionally published short speculative essays in the popular press. Especially in Israel, figures like Uri Avneri, Yehoshafat Harkabi, Amnon Rubinstein, Yaacov Shavit, and Benny Morris have written scattered Hebrew-language essays about pivotal turning points in the Jewish state's modern history, such as the 1967 war and the assassination of Yitzhak Rabin.[71] But these works have been exceptional. For the most part, Jewish historians have yet to tap the potential of counterfactual history.

This lack of interest arguably reflects a longstanding disciplinary conservatism within the field of Jewish history. Jewish historians have never been methodological pioneers. Ever since the rise of Wissenschaft des Judentums, according to David Myers, they have largely adhered to a kind of "hyper-scientism." Indeed, they have adhered to the ideals of objectivity for far longer than their non-Jewish colleagues in the historical profession.[72] Although they have consistently embraced new methodological developments – going along with the shift to social, intellectual, and cultural history in recent decades – they have tended to be late, rather than early, adopters. This methodological conservatism has kept Jewish historians from pursuing work within the field of counterfactual history with the same enthusiasm and in the same numbers as scholars in other fields of historical specialization.

There is reason to believe, however, that this reluctance may be coming to an end. In recent years, Jewish historians have begun to embrace some of the same intellectual trends that have nurtured the rise of counterfactual history, especially postmodernism. As is shown by a spate of recent studies, Jewish historians have wrestled seriously with the implications of postmodern theory for their profession.[73] Certainly since the publication of Yerushalmi's study, *Zakhor*, Jewish historians have taken an "introspective turn" and become more self-reflexive about their field, admitting to their subjective authorial positions and embracing new postmodern methodologies. As Michael Brenner has written, they have embraced the postmodern hostility toward metanarratives and abandoned "any attempt to write a comprehensive Jewish history," preferring instead to write "a multitude of 'small narratives' constituting a kind of counterhistory in relation to traditional historiographical narratives."[74] Given these trends, Jewish historians are in a perfect position – both methodologically and temperamentally – to make their own long overdue contributions to the field of counterfactual history. What better way is there to challenge the reigning metanarratives about the Jewish past than to explore alternative scenarios that never happened? Indeed, if we are to realize Moshe Rosman's call to create a genuinely "postmodern Jewish historiography," Jewish historians will have to take up the challenge of counterfactual history and confront the fundamental question, "what if?"[75]

"What ifs?" of Jewish history

This volume seeks to advance this process by inviting a distinguished group of Jewish Studies scholars – from the fields of history, religious studies, and literature – to explore a series of provocative counterfactual questions. These questions span the ancient, medieval, and modern periods of Jewish history and address a variety of pivotal topics in Europe, the Middle East, and the United States. The book's early chapters deal with the formation of the Jewish people in antiquity, the centrality of the Temple, the onset of medieval persecutions, and the gradual appearance of the *Haskalah*, or Jewish Enlightenment. Later chapters then proceed to concentrate on the nineteenth and twentieth centuries and address the rise of antisemitism, the emergence of Zionism, the eruption of the First and Second World Wars, the occurrence of the Holocaust, and the creation of the state of Israel. In approaching these topics, the volume's authors draw upon their own unique disciplinary expertise to imagine how key events in the Jewish past might have unfolded differently. They pursue this task by adopting a wide range of narrative approaches. Some employ a straightforward analytical style and present readers with provocative claims about history transpiring otherwise; others adopt a more experimental, literary approach that invites readers to infer the meandering course of historical events. In so doing, the contributors advance varied conclusions. Many propose robust changes to the Jewish historical record; others submit more modest claims; some even question the entire speculative enterprise and insist that history more or less had to turn out as it did. Taken together, the chapters' varied content and eclectic form combine to produce a highly stimulating journey through Jewish history as it never was.

Steven Weitzman, a scholar of the Hebrew Bible and early Judaism, begins the volume by examining how Jewish history would have unfolded if the Exodus from Egypt had never occurred, asserting that nearly every feature of Jewish history would have been different – if indeed the Jews would have survived at all. The classicist and Jewish Studies scholar, René Bloch, then examines what might have happened had the Romans never destroyed the Second Temple in Jerusalem, proposing that rabbinic Judaism and early Christianity would have developed very differently, while Jewish life in the diaspora would have proceeded largely unchanged. Historian Jonathan Ray addresses how the history of Sephardic Jewry would have developed without the expulsion from Spain, contrasting the success of the Spanish Jewish community with the comparative suffering of Maghrebi and Polish-Lithuanian Jews. Historian Bernard Cooperman inquires how early modern Jewish history would have developed without the creation of ghettos, concluding that they were an inevitable response to late medieval needs and should be seen as a less onerous feature of Jewish life than has traditionally been believed. Historian Eugene Sheppard tackles the provocative question of how Jewish intellectual history would have evolved had the eminent philosopher Baruch Spinoza repented for his heretical beliefs, showing how a range of European Jewish thinkers would have wrestled with the philosopher's "return" to Judaism. Rounding out this section of the book, historian Jeffrey Veidlinger examines how the history of Eastern European Jewry would have unfolded if Empress Catherine the Great had never established the Pale of Settlement in Russia, presenting two different visions of how they would have been affected by the granting of greater communal autonomy or the imposition of forced integration.

The next section of the book addresses the history of Zionism and the founding of the state of Israel. Historian Derek Penslar proposes that a German victory in World War I might have led to the creation of a Protestant, instead of a Jewish, state in Palestine, provocatively suggesting that it would have engendered an equally hostile reaction from its Arab neighbors. Literature scholar Adam Rovner provides a grand tour of the history and contemporary sights of the Jewish state of New Judea, located in the former British colony of Uganda. Literature scholar Iris Bruce explores how Franz Kafka's emigration to Palestine in the early 1920s would have shaped the famed writer's fiction and subsequent literary reputation. Political scientist Kenneth Stein takes a very different viewpoint and argues that if Arab political leaders in Palestine had agreed to any number of British and American plans for limited self-governance from the early 1920s onwards, they might have been able to establish a Palestinian state by the end of the 1930s and possibly even hindered the creation of a Jewish state. Finally, historian David Myers imagines what would have happened if Palestinian Arab leader Musa Alami and Zionist leader David Ben-Gurion had been able to forge a power-sharing arrangement for Jews and Arabs under broad British Mandatory control, proposing that it might have given rise to a binational state.

The book's final cluster of chapters deals with the history of German Jewry, the Second World War, and the Holocaust. Historian Michael Brenner takes up the question of how German Jewish history would have evolved if Foreign Minister Walther Rathenau had escaped assassination in 1922, proposing that the Weimar Republic would have survived and German Jews would have thrived in the subsequent decades. Historian Gavriel Rosenfeld explores how Adolf Hitler's assassination by Georg Elser in November of 1939 would have limited, but not prevented, the mass murder of German and Polish Jews. Historian Jeffrey Herf underscores the pivotal importance of the battle of El Alamein for preventing the Nazis from invading Palestine and extending the Final Solution of the Jewish Question to the Jews of the Yishuv. Historian Dirk Rupnow explores how the Jewish people would have been remembered in a world in which the Nazis won the Second World War and completed the Final Solution. Finally, historian Jeffrey Gurock examines how an earlier start to World War II in 1938 and the prevention of the Holocaust would have had unexpectedly negative consequences for American Jews.

In answering their counterfactual questions, the volume's contributors imagine Jewish history unfolding in many different ways. Some envision it turning out better; others portray it turning out worse; still others imagine it remaining more or less the same. They also illuminate different aspects of Jewish history. Some address issues of historical causality; others reflect on the conundrums of historical judgment; and still others reflect on the workings of historical memory. The diverse approaches and diverging conclusions of the chapters – indeed, the existence of explicit contradictions between some of them – is one of the volume's distinguishing hallmarks. Unlike many historical anthologies, it does not operate within a single historiographical paradigm or seek to advance a particular scholarly consensus. Indeed, the volume lays no special claim to truth. Although its contributors possess tremendous expertise in their respective disciplines, their chapters are works of speculation and thus unavoidably subjective. They are defined as much by the personal as the empirical, by the forces of the imagination as the imperatives of documentation. This subjectivity is visible in the presentist character of many of the chapters. The ways in which they imagine Jewish history turning out better or worse subtly express a range of fantasies and fears. Discerning readers will be able to detect how present-day concerns about the legacy of the Holocaust and the future of the state of Israel, for example, color many of the chapters' counterfactual claims. Some readers may object that the chapters' subjectivity limits their plausibility; they may contend that their conclusions are needlessly pessimistic or naïvely optimistic. But they should bear in mind that they seek to be suggestive rather than authoritative. They aim to raise as many questions as they answer.

In the end, *What Ifs of Jewish History* may be just as likely to provoke as convince. But this, too, is an important part of its mission. The volume seeks to challenge conventional views about Jewish history by proposing new perspectives about how it might have been. Readers will ultimately decide for themselves whether or not they find these perspectives to be compelling. But by prompting questions, discussion, and debate, wondering "what if?" may allow new insights into the Jewish past. It may even help us understand how it might unfold in the future.

1 WHAT IF THE EXODUS HAD NEVER HAPPENED?

Steven Weitzman

How would history have been different if the Israelites had never left Egypt? We are not the first to pose this question, and for some who have sought an answer, the consequences of an Exodus that never happens are profound, affecting not just the Jews, but all of humanity. In 2003, the science fiction writer Robert Silverberg published a book called *Roma Eterna* that speculates about what would have happened if Moses had not succeeded in leading the Israelites from bondage.[1] Without an Exodus, there would have been no Israelite settlement of the land of Canaan. Without the Jews' presence there, Jesus is never born and Christianity never emerges. There is also no Islam. Although Muhammad exists in Silverberg's alternate universe, the Romans assassinate him before he can have any impact. Without any kind of monotheism arising in opposition to it, a pagan Roman Empire never falls, expanding to most of the world in the absence of any moral constraint on its power. The Hebrews still persist, and Silverberg raises the possibility that continued Roman rule merely postpones the Exodus rather than cancelling it out altogether: in the late twentieth century Hebrews in Egypt develop a space program in the hope of mounting a "Great Exodus" to the stars, but that Exodus does not happen within the confines of the novel: their rocket explodes after takeoff, and it remains to be seen whether the Hebrews will get another opportunity to escape their oppressors. In this alternate universe, the Exodus is always only a hope, a counter-reality, that never comes within reach.

That is one way to imagine history without the Exodus, but it makes assumptions about what really happened that historians should question. Silverberg's alternate history presupposes that, in our reality, the Exodus really happens – that there was a Moses, that the Israelites really did escape from Egypt. But that does not fit historical reality as some biblical scholars now reconstruct it. There is no corroboration of the Exodus in ancient Egyptian sources, no reference to Moses or the ten plagues or the destruction of the Egyptian army in the Red Sea, and some elements of the biblical account in the Book of Exodus are extremely far-fetched and call to mind the legends and myths of other ancient peoples. On this basis, many biblical scholars now doubt that the Exodus ever happened. Even those who want to salvage some history in the biblical account concede that, at best, it probably preserves a greatly exaggerated memory of the escape of a small group of slaves or a garbled recollection of the much earlier expulsion of a pre-Israelite people known as the Hyksos, but nothing like the momentous events the Bible describes.[2] If we are basing ourselves on recent biblical scholarship, we might conclude that Israelite history without an Exodus is not an alternate reality but rather a genuine reality. Indeed, we might conclude that the Bible's account of history represents the counterfactual.

Even if we accept this view, however, there is another question we might reasonably ask. The Exodus may not constitute a historical event in the conventional scholarly understanding of history, but *the story* of the Exodus is certainly a historical reality. It has been central to Jewish collective memory for as long as the Bible itself has been a part of that memory. It has an importance in Jewish experience that transcends the issue of whether or not it registers real historical experience. In a book that derives its title from the Exodus story, *Zakhor* ("Remember" in Hebrew), Yosef Yerushalmi argued that history – that is, history in the sense of a narrative of the past as reconstructed through reasoned analysis of the evidence – has never been the principal medium through which Jews have remembered their past.[3] History in this sense arose from Greek culture, and it did not take root in Jewish culture until the modern era. In the preceding 2,000 years, Jews knew about their past not by sifting through archaeological evidence and ancient Near Eastern sources but by reading the Bible and commemorating events like the Exodus during Passover and other holidays. They did not think to ask whether the Exodus really happened or not; its occurrence was the starting point from which Jews understood all subsequent historical experience. From this perspective, it does not matter whether the

Exodus qualifies as "history" in a scholarly sense; it has been part of the Jewish past as far back as we can document.

Thus, to continue with this thought experiment, we need to reformulate the question. What would have happened if, from the perspective of how Jews remembered and recounted their history, the Exodus had never taken place? It so happens that Jews engage in something like this thought experiment on a regular basis – in fact, precisely during the holiday that commemorates the Exodus, the festival of Passover. It is traditional during this holiday to read from a text known as the Haggadah, a kind of scripted retelling of the Exodus (Figure 3). There, as the telling of the story begins, one reads "If God had not led our ancestors out of Egypt, we and our children and our children's children would still be Pharaoh's slaves in Egypt." If there had not been an Exodus, the Haggadah suggests, Jews would still be toiling under the whip of their masters, still waiting for God to answer their cries. This could not be literally true, of course – slavery was legally abolished in Egypt in the nineteenth century – but the Haggadah has a point: without the Exodus, the Israelites of the Bible would still presumably be in Egypt, assuming they were able to survive the harsh decrees imposed on them by Pharaoh in an effort to stifle their population growth. Some Israelites might have been able to escape into the wilderness – Egyptian sources themselves note that some slaves tried to run away to Egypt's frontiers – while others might have been emancipated by their masters as Joseph is lifted from a life of servitude. But those were options for individual Israelites, not for the people as a whole. Aside from the Exodus itself, there is no clear evidence of massive slave revolts in ancient Egypt and, in any case, the fate of slave rebellions in later periods suggest the chances of success for a mass liberation movement were very slim. This is why it takes nothing short of divine intervention to liberate the Israelites and keep them alive during their flight; for whoever it was who produced the biblical account, there was no plausible way for the Israelites to liberate themselves; freedom in such a world required a miracle.

But it is hard to accept this alternate reality. It is not that the idea of hopeless servitude is implausible – that was the fate of most slaves in the ancient world who lived and died without any prospect of liberation. What is difficult to imagine is how such an enslaved community could have generated any kind of alternate history that we could recount here. It was the fate of the vast majority of slaves in the ancient world to die without leaving any kind of legacy behind – they did not

Figure 3. Israelites building the cities, page from the Barcelona Haggadah, fourteenth century. The Haggadah provides a clear counterfactual lesson on the holiday of Passover in reminding Jews that "If God had not led our ancestors out of Egypt, we and our children and our children's children would still be Pharaoh's slaves in Egypt."

write their own historical accounts or produce much of any kind of literary or archaeological record, leaving us with no real way to trace their history. If it were not for the Exodus – or at least the state of freedom supposedly generated by the Exodus – the Israelites would not have been in a position to produce the kind of historical record from which we know the biblical age: they would have persisted as slaves in Egypt but their suffering would be unknown to us.

Since this scenario would have aborted Jewish history before it even began – and left us with nothing to write about in this chapter – we need to refine our question yet again. Let us imagine not that the Israelites failed to be liberated from Egypt but that there was no need to liberate them. There would have been no Exodus if the Israelites had never been enslaved to begin with, and it is easy to imagine such a scenario within the range of historical options presented by the Book of Genesis. The Israelites traced their ancestry back to the family of Jacob, and things would have been very different if the members of this family had treated each other a little better. Had Jacob been a more conscientious parent, he might have decided it was a bad idea to give his son Joseph the coat that made his brothers so jealous. Things might have been different as well if they had treated each other even more cruelly: Joseph's brothers could have decided to kill Joseph rather than sell him into slavery, ending his story before he had the chance to go down to Egypt. At this early period in Israel's prehistory, a different outcome to a single family squabble could have preempted the sequence of events that led to the Exodus well before Jacob's descendants found themselves enslaved by the Egyptians.

What would have happened instead? If the Book of Genesis is any indication, Jacob's family would have simply remained in Canaan, putting down roots there – tending to their sheep and goats, welcoming the occasional guest, digging the occasional well, getting into a fight now and then with their neighbors, but eventually settling into place once they and their neighbors got used to each other. And all the while, Jacob's descendants would be having children. This was what God had promised them, and they were good at it. Jacob's twelve sons each produced many children, all of whom produced children of their own. Within a few generations, these Israelites, as they probably would have called themselves, would have been populous enough to form tribes, an extended, interconnected community of thousands of people, and these would probably have lived in the same territory, claiming the same ancestry, and worshipping the same God as the Israel of our reality. The only difference is that this other Israel never would have gone down to Egypt and, as a result, never would have experienced the Exodus.

If we approach things in this way, it is possible to ask what would have become of the Israelites if they had never experienced slavery or the Exodus, provided that we understand that "Israelite" in this context refers not to the historical people but to the imagined people depicted in biblical narrative, the Israel of Jewish collective memory and narrative tradition. What would this Israel have been like without the experience of the Exodus? And what impact would this difference have had on later Jewish history?

As it happens, we do not have to speculate about this alternate history. An anonymous author from some 2,500 years ago actually imagined such a scenario himself, developing an alternative account of Israelite history that has been hiding in plain sight for the entirety of Jewish history, preserved in the Bible itself in the narrative known in English as 1–2 Chronicles. Composed sometime between 500 and 350 BCE, this work is known in Hebrew as *Divre Hayyamim*. Our name for it, "Chronicles," approximates the meaning of that phrase fairly well. But it has a different title in the Greek, *Paraleipomena* – "the things that have been passed over," which better captures its relationship to the other historical narratives that we have preserved in the Hebrew Bible. Chronicles tells more or less the same story that appears in 1–2 Samuel and 1–2 Kings, often quoting them verbatim, but it inserts a lot of additional material that does not appear in those alternative accounts, revising and supplementing what it has taken from Samuel and Kings in ways that reflect its post-exilic author's distinctive view of Israel's history. The Chronicler also left out a lot of material, cutting out what he disliked, and it is one of these excisions that is relevant here. If you have the patience to read the Books of Chronicles, you will find that its narrative omits the Exodus. The Chronicler, however, did not merely refrain from telling its story, he actively tried to dislodge it from the sources he was drawing on. The great Israeli biblical scholar Sara Japhet has shown how the Chronicler removed or rewrote almost every reference to the Exodus story found in Samuel, Kings, and the other biblical texts he drew on, as if trying to purge its memory from the historical record.[4]

Since Jews have long become accustomed to reading Chronicles within a biblical canon that includes the Five Books of Moses, this deletion will not seem obvious at first; it is hard not to read Chronicles in light of the books that now surround it in the biblical canon if one ever has the occasion to read it all. By comparing its narrative with its source material in earlier biblical books, however, one can see the following points:

- In the Chronicler's version of Israel's history, the patriarchs Abraham, Isaac, Jacob, and Jacob's sons never seem to leave for Egypt. The Books of 1–2 Chronicles do not tell the story of the patriarchs in the way that Genesis does, but instead alludes to that period in ways that imply a radically different understanding of what happened in the period before the Exodus. According to Genesis, the sons of Joseph – Ephraim and Manasseh – were born in Egypt to an Egyptian woman named Aseneth, and they remain in Egypt their entire lives. According to 1 Chronicles 7:20–9, by contrast, Ephraim seems to spend his days in the land of Canaan, as if he had never gone to Egypt or was somehow able to return long before the Exodus, telling of how some of his sons were killed by people of Gath during a raid on their cattle, and of how Ephraim's other descendants settled the areas on the southern and northern extremes of the territory that belonged to Joseph. These descendants include Joshua the son of Nun who, according to the Chronicler's account, must have been born and raised in the land of Canaan. We know of Joshua from other biblical sources but there, of course, he is Moses' successor, among the Israelites who leave Egypt and their leader as they conquer the land of Canaan. In Chronicles' alternative account, Joshua never could have done any of this because, like his ancestor Ephraim, he was born not in Egypt but in the land of Canaan. In other words, Chronicles presupposes a history of uninterrupted existence in Canaan from the time of the patriarchs to the Babylonian exile. It is a history without Jacob's and Joseph's descent into Egypt, without the enslavement of their descendants, without the Exodus that liberated them, and without Joshua's conquest of the land that his ancestors never left.
- Because the patriarchs never leave Canaan, because the Exodus never happens, there is nothing of it for later Israelites to remember or retell: the Exodus seems to disappear from Israel's religious life, from its calendar, even from its Passover observance. We can see from the Book of Exodus how it is that the memory of the Exodus was preserved. Even before the Israelites leave Egypt, God establishes rituals to keep

the memory of the Exodus alive over the generations. "This day shall be a day of remembrance for you," God says of the day that the Israelites leave Egypt. From now on, Moses instructs the Israelites, they will observe a festival of unleavened bread – the seven-day festival later known as Passover – to help them remember how God liberated their ancestors from slavery. In Chronicles, too, remembering the past is important – "Remember the wonderful work that he has done," sing the Levites in the Temple as the Chronicler describes its rituals, "Remember his covenant forever" – but the Exodus seems to have been erased from it. What the Levites in this episode are singing, for example, is a song drawn almost word for word from Psalm 105, a song that recounts the history of Israel from the time of Abraham down to the Exodus. In Chronicles' selective citation of the psalm, however, the story stops in the time of Jacob, before he and his sons go to Egypt, ending its citation of Psalm 105 at verse 15. Joseph's imprisonment, the ten plagues, the gift of the manna – all details recounted in Psalm 105 – are left out of Chronicles' account.

• The Exodus has been erased from Israel's memory in other ways as well. Another example is how it dates the building of Solomon's Temple, one of the most important events in Israel's history. Its account of the Temple's construction is based on an earlier narrative in 1 Kings 6, which begins by dating things in relation to the Exodus: "*In the four hundred eightieth year after the Israelites came out of the land of Egypt*, in the fourth year of Solomon's reign over Israel, in the month of Ziv which is the second month, he began to build the house of the Lord." The Chronicler drew on Kings as a source, but in his revision the reference to the Exodus has, once again, been removed, the text quoting only the final clause: "He began to build on the second day of the second month of the fourth year of his reign" (2 Chronicles 3:2). In history as described elsewhere in the Bible, the Exodus is the defining event in Israel's experience. In Chronicles, the Exodus literally seems to have fallen off the calendar.

Remarkably, this is true even of the Chronicler's account of Passover, the day on which Israel is supposed to commemorate the Exodus. Chronicles reports that the most righteous kings of Israel, Hezekiah and Josiah, held large public celebrations of Passover (2 Chronicles 30 and 35). One might reasonably assume that its celebration must presuppose the Exodus. How can one eat unleavened bread or slaughter the Passover lamb without thinking of what happened in

Egypt? And yet, oddly enough, the Chronicler's description of these holidays never mentions the Exodus story or describes Passover as a time to remember it. It is possible that the connection to the Exodus is implicit in these descriptions, but they also allow for a different understanding of the festival. For example, its celebration might have been intended as a commemoration of events described in the Book of Genesis, before the Exodus. When Josiah refers to God, for example, he does not describe him as the God who led Israel out of Egypt, as one might expect in the midst of a Passover celebration, but rather as the God of Abraham, Isaac, and Jacob. Is it possible that the Chronicler's version of the Passover commemorates some event from the life of Abraham such as the Akedah, the sacrifice of Isaac? Some ancient Jewish sources claim or imply that Passover was observed already in the days of the patriarchs, discerning a connection between the ram sacrificed in place of Isaac and the Passover lamb, and there are elements within Genesis itself that can be seen as the inspiration for the various rituals of the Passover.[5] In any case, Passover was precisely the time when the Israelites were supposed to retell the story of the Exodus, and yet in the Chronicler's depiction of the festival, there is not one reference to God having rescued the Israelites from slavery, the ten plagues or the parting of the Red Sea, omissions which are consistent with its other efforts to erase the story from history.

The claim of some recent biblical scholars that the Exodus never occurred has received a lot of attention from the larger public because it seems to threaten Jewish and Christian religious belief by undercutting the historical premises on which it is based. It turns out that such a deletion mirrors something that happened around 2,500 years ago, an attempt by an ancient author to rewrite the history of the Israelites without an Exodus.

Why would the Chronicler have wanted to delete the Exodus from memory? We have no way of knowing, but we can make an educated guess. A few decades after the Babylonian conquest of Judah in 586 BCE, Babylonia itself was defeated by the Persian King Cyrus who allowed the exiles to return home to Judah in 539 BCE. The returnees almost certainly saw themselves as repeating the Exodus, forced into servitude in a strange land but now miraculously able to reclaim the land that had been promised them. This, at least, is the impression one gets from biblical texts written in this period, such as the source known as Second Isaiah (Isaiah, chapters 40–55), which draws out the parallel between the return from Babylonia and Israel's joyous departure from Egypt. But not everyone may have seen the return from exile as a welcome event. We know from hints in the literary and archaeological record that some of the people of Judah remained in the land all along, continuing with their lives there throughout the period of Babylonian rule; from their perspective, the return of the exiles may have been a threatening development, an incursion by haughty outsiders who looked down on the locals and were quick to take things over in a newly restored Jerusalem. It is conceivable that the Chronicler, writing sometime after the return from exile, was one of these never-exiled Israelites, and felt the need to suppress the memory of the Exodus because, for him, it was not a story of redemption but an unfortunate precedent for his marginalization, legitimizing the claims of the returnees at the expense of those who had never left.

However we explain the Chronicler's erasure of the Exodus, it suggests another way to frame the question we are trying to ask: what if we only had Chronicles' account for our knowledge of biblical history? To play by the rules of alternate history, we need to posit a scenario that is historically plausible, that could have happened given what we know about the past. By that measure, we cannot conceptualize the outcome if the Exodus had never happened since, in truth, we do not have any kind of certain knowledge of whether it did actually happen. We can, however, plausibly imagine a situation where Chronicles survived as the only Israelite account of the biblical past. If we wanted to remove every reference to the Exodus from the Hebrew Bible, we would have to cut out a lot of material – the Five Books of Moses, Joshua, and the other historical books that follow; many of the prophetic books and the Psalms – but it is not hard to conceive of a scenario in which much of this literature did not survive. The Bible itself refers to lost books that did not survive: the Book of Yashar mentioned in Joshua 10:12–13, and the *Chronicles of the Kings of Israel and Judah* cited by the author of 2 Kings. Such a fate could have easily befallen many of the books in the Hebrew Bible – most seem to have been composed in Jerusalem and could have been lost when it was destroyed by the Babylonians. Such an event would not have affected Chronicles, however, which was not composed until after the destruction of Jerusalem, emerging sometime in the Persian period. If its account had survived as the only record of Israel's origins, if it had become our only source for biblical history, the Exodus would not have been remembered even if it had actually taken place.

With this as our starting point, we can plausibly ask: how would Israelite culture – and the later Jewish culture that evolved out of it – have been different without the Exodus as its foundational story? If we use Chronicles as a guide, we can see that many things might still have turned out the same. There would still be an Israel settled in Canaan. It might still have been ruled by David and Solomon; the latter would still have built a Temple, and it would still have been destroyed when the Babylonians conquered Jerusalem. The Chronicler can imagine such events happening without making them follow as a consequence of the Exodus, and the irony is that, if we follow recent biblical scholarship, they probably did develop in a way that was unrelated to the Exodus.

Certainly there could have been an Israelite people settled in the land of Canaan without an experience of the Exodus. Our earliest reference to the people of Israel outside the Bible is in an Egyptian document from the end of the thirteenth century BCE, an inscription left behind by a pharaoh named Merneptah, the son of Ramses II (who is often identified as the pharaoh of the Exodus story). The inscription shows that the Israelites existed by this point in history, but it refers to them without showing any recognition of them as former slaves or fugitives. Even without any biblical evidence, we would know of an Israelite people settled in the land of Canaan, but we would have no reason to think that its history began with the Exodus. It also seems likely that this Israelite culture would have developed the sort of monarchical government recorded in Chronicles. Whether David and Solomon were real historical figures is another very controversial and unresolved issue in biblical studies, but we do know from inscriptional evidence that many of the societies that bordered ancient Israel – the Moabites and the Edomites, for example – were developing monarchies in this period, and there is no reason to think the Israelites could not have followed the same trajectory eventually, if not in the days of David and Solomon then through the effort of some other comparably cunning ruler.

Israel's settlement of the land of Canaan, the rise of the Davidic dynasty, even the building of the Temple – all these could have developed anyway in the alternative Exodus-less reality we are constructing. If we are willing to stretch the evidence a bit, we can even make the case

Figure 4. *Moses with the Ten Commandments* (1648), oil on canvas, painting by Philippe de Champagne. However difficult it is to imagine, Moses still might have been a major figure in Jewish history even without the Exodus.

that Moses himself would have persisted without this story (Figure 4). Readers familiar with the Haggadah may know that it is not so hard to conceive of an Exodus without a Moses – the prophet is practically never mentioned in the Haggadah and plays no role in the liberation that it describes – but the reverse scenario is harder to conceive: how can there have been a Moses without an Exodus?

To help us imagine such a figure, we can turn to a source written not long after 1–2 Chronicles, a description of Judea written by a Greek traveler named Hecateus in the late fourth century BCE. Known as the *Aegyptiaca*, most of this work is lost – such was the fate of most of what was written in antiquity – but some excerpts do survive thanks to their citation by a later historian. The following passage offers yet another account of the Exodus in which Moses plays a rather different role than he does in the Five Books of Moses:

> When in ancient times a pestilence arose in Egypt, the common people ascribed their troubles to the workings of a divine agency; for indeed with many strangers of all sorts dwelling in their midst and practicing different rites of religion and sacrifice, their own traditional observances in honor of the gods had fallen into disuse. Hence, the natives of the land surmised that unless they removed the foreigners, their troubles would never be resolved. At once, therefore, the aliens were driven from the country and the most outstanding and active of them banded together and, as some say, were cast ashore in Greece and certain other regions; their leaders were notable men, chief among them being Danaus and Cadmus. But the greater number were driven into what is now called Judea, which is not far distant from Egypt and was at that time utterly uninhabited. The colony was headed by a man named Moses, outstanding both for his wisdom and his courage. On taking possession of the land, he founded, besides other cities, one that is now the most renowned of all, called Jerusalem. In addition he established the temple that they now hold in chief veneration, instituted their forms of worship and ritual, drew up their laws and ordered their political institutions.[6]

Hecateus clearly knew some version of the Exodus story, though it is a surprising one in which the strangers driven from Egypt are not just Israelites heading for Canaan but others as well who migrate to Greece, and he connected Moses to this migration, but he does not mention any of the events for which Moses is most famous – the burning bush episode, Moses' role in bringing ten plagues against Egypt and in leading the Israelites out of Egypt, the parting of the Red Sea, or the miracles of the wilderness. What is important about Moses for Hecateus is his role as a founder of cities, especially of Jerusalem where he establishes a temple, a law system, and political institutions. This is very different from the role that Moses plays in the Five Books of Moses. There he

establishes the "forms of worship and rituals" – the subject of laws
in the Five Books of Moses – but he never makes it to Canaan, and
thus could not have played the role ascribed to him by Hecateus as the
founder of Jerusalem and the builder of its temple.

What we have in Hecateus' account is a hellenized version of
biblical history that reshapes Moses' role on the model of a Greek
colony founder. I am not suggesting that it tells us anything about the
historical Moses. What this testimony does suggest is that in the period
in which the Chronicler was writing – Hecateus of Abdera may have
lived only a century or two after Chronicles was written – Moses' role
in Israel's history did not necessarily correspond to his role in the Five
Books of Moses. He was a venerated figure known for his laws and his
leadership, but the memory of his life had not yet settled into a canonical
shape. It was possible for a story-teller unfamiliar with the Five Books of
Moses to remember him not as a slave-leader, miracle worker or wilderness guide, but rather as the founder of Jerusalem and its institutions.
If one knew nothing of Moses' role as described in the Five Books of
Moses, if one's only memory of him came from a source like Hecateus
or from the Chronicler for that matter, one might well remember him
not as he is remembered now – the heroic liberator who led Israel on
a great journey home – but as a figure closer to the legendary Solon of
Athens, a law-giver remembered for establishing the constitution and
institutions of city life.

While an ancient Israel without the Exodus story could have
been similar in many respects to the Israel of our reality, however, it
would also have been different in ways that would have profoundly
changed not just Jewish history, but global history. Robert Silverberg is
probably correct to say that there could not have been a Christianity or
an Islam without the Exodus story – their sacred stories and scriptural
canons are too closely interwoven with the Exodus story to disentangle
one from another. I am not sure that we would still be living under
Roman domination as a result – Christianity may well have done more
to revitalize Roman rule than bring it to an end – but those living under
political domination of any sort would have one less resource at their
disposal, especially in the modern era when the Exodus has emerged
as an important source of inspiration for mass movements seeking to
achieve freedom from oppression.[7] No Exodus story, and there are
no dissident pilgrims, no Martin Luther King, Jr, and no Liberation
Theology.

Focusing on the Jews in particular, it is impossible to trace all the ramifications of the development of their culture. Maybe they would have a scripture, but it would not include the Five Books of Moses. All that would have been left of the Jewish Bible, aside from Chronicles, are the few texts that do not depend on the Exodus story: a few minor prophets, Esther, Proverbs, Ecclesiastes, the Song of Songs, Lamentations. Maybe Jews would still celebrate Passover but not by reading the Haggadah or recounting the four sons or singing "Dayenu." Eventually perhaps, a modern secularized Jewish culture would have abandoned these traditions – assuming such a culture could have ever developed in the absence of an authoritative biblical tradition to define itself against – but these secularized Jews would not have the Exodus story to help them to adapt their culture to the values of a new epoch. No Exodus, and no tradition of Miriam's cup at the Passover Seder, for example; neither would there be any other feminist expansions of the Exodus story that aim to adapt Jewish tradition to an age of emancipation, gender equality and self-empowerment.[8]

Without the Exodus story, could Jews have even survived? If Jews had had to rely on Chronicles as their sacred story, there is little in this story that would have prepared them for how to weather the challenges of the historical experience awaiting them in future periods. History, as the Chronicler recounts it, does have its share of ups and downs, especially sinfulness and divine punishment, but God is always quick to correct things, to punish the sinful without delay, to return exiles without delay, and to get the course of history back on track as soon as possible, within a single lifetime. This may be one reason that the Chronicler had to delete the Exodus. In the Chronicler's account of history, God's presence in the world is easily discerned and comprehended. But that is not how God works in the Exodus story. In that narrative, Abraham's descendants find themselves forced from the land promised to them; they face extinction despite divine assurance that they will be as numerous as the stars in the sky; they do not know when or whether God will ever intervene to save them. The Exodus story creates too much cognitive dissonance to be assimilated into the Chronicler's straightforward and impatient conception of how God works: how can one trust a God who seems to punish the innocent? How can he be just if he allows his people to be enslaved for hundreds of years without any apparent reason? If he always intended to rescue the Israelites, why take so long to do so? Cutting out the Exodus story makes these problems go away, but at a cost: without such a story to model a long-term, multigenerational approach to the logic of divine intervention, there is little solace or insight to be found in Chronicles about how to cope with a prolonged deferral of redemption.

The Exodus story is the paradigmatic story of not giving up hope, and for that reason, Silverberg might be right that there is something inevitable about it: if the Jews survived long enough, sooner or later they would have had to come up with something like the Exodus story as a way to focus their hopes, to assimilate suffering and displacement without giving up on God and his promises. In fact, over the Second Temple period, Jews did develop another such narrative, a story of a messianic savior who comes at the end of time to deliver Israel from its enemies. Chronicles is not a messianic text itself – it never anticipates any kind of future savior or messianic age – but it does contain some of the key ingredients of later messianic belief, including a promise from God that David and his successors would rule forever (1 Chronicles 22:10) that seems to have fed expectation that God would one day restore the royal dynasty disrupted by Babylonian conquest. If we ignore for the moment that Jewish messianism also has roots in the Exodus story, we can suppose that some sort of messianic narrative could have developed out of Chronicles and filled the vacuum left by the absence of an Exodus story, giving Jews another way to imagine an eventual end to their woes.

Even if such a story did take shape, however, it would have been different from the Exodus story in ways that would probably have had a major impact on the course of Jewish history. One possible difference has been noted by Michael Walzer in his study of the Exodus story. The messianic narrative is a story about the future, and the change it promises involves much more than the end of slavery; it entails a radical alteration of nature itself, including the end of death. The messianic narrative can only happen in an alternate reality; it cannot happen within reality as it exists now or has existed in historical times because it depends on a fundamental restructuring of the social and natural order. This is why there is something destructive about the messianic narrative: it can only be acted on through cataclysm. By contrast, the redemption brought about by the Exodus is achievable in a real geographical place, in historic time, mostly through human effort. It does depend on acts of divine intervention as well, but the focus is on what the Israelites do to secure their own redemption, how they get themselves from a house of bondage to a promised land. If Judaism had only had a messianic narrative, its utopian, otherworldly tendencies might be even stronger than they are now. The Exodus allows for a less radical but more successful approach to redemption that has made it possible for readers to strive for a better future within the constraints of present-day reality.

For all these reasons, I have reached the conclusion that, despite what one might conclude from recent biblical scholarship, there is no meaningful way to imagine Jewish history without the Exodus story. In a way, all of Jewish history can be understood as one long attempt to untell this story. In Christian tradition, the Exodus became another story altogether, a coded form of a narrative about Jesus, while the story that Jews told on Passover became, in some medieval communities, a pretext for persecuting them (the blood libel accused Jews of using the blood of Christian children in the making of matzah). Modernity undermined the texts that told the Exodus story, relegating them to the same status as forgotten myths of Mesopotamia, and raising doubts about whether any of its events really happened. The Holocaust went even further in making the story untellable: for some, the experience of massive, unredeemed suffering shattered the theological premises of the Exodus story and its notion of a God who intervenes to save his people from destruction.[9] History has provided Jews with many reasons *not* to tell the Exodus story, not to find it relevant, and yet, for some reason, they continue to do so: the Haggadah remains the most widely circulated Jewish text outside of the Bible itself; according to a survey of American Jews conducted in 1990, 86 percent of Jewish households attended a seder; and even theologically traumatic experiences like the Holocaust have done nothing to deter the retelling of the Exodus story as the central part of this ritual.[10] To the contrary, as documented by Liora Gubkin, the memory of the Holocaust has itself become a ritualized part of how many Jews remember the Exodus, altering how it is commemorated but also being absorbed into its narrative.[11] There may never have been a story in all history so resistant to being erased.

If the truth be told, even if we go back to the very beginnings of Jewish culture, not even the Chronicler could completely succeed in expunging the Exodus. He tried, but he was working with sources where the story was already central, and now and then he let something slip through, as in 2 Chronicles 5:10, a passage lifted from 1 Kings 8–9, which retains a fleeting reference to the Exodus. The Chronicler lived before many of the developments that made the Exodus so central to Jewish culture – more than a thousand years before the earliest known Passover Haggadah from the ninth century CE – and yet even at this early period, the Exodus was so interwoven into Israel's history that it could not be completely excised. It has become possible for recent biblical scholars, like the Chronicler, to conceive of a history of the ancient Israelites that does not include the Exodus, but their findings can have no impact on the role of the story of the Exodus in Jewish history. To speculate about what Jews would have been like without that story would be like trying to imagine a Christianity without the Gospels or an Islam without the Quran; the exercise is bound to fail because Judaism, Christianity, and Islam only exist by virtue of their engagement with their respective foundational stories.

But if we cannot delete the Exodus from Jewish history, is it not at least possible to imagine a future Judaism without an Exodus? If the process of assimilation and declining Jewish literacy continue, is it not conceivable that the descendants of today's Jews will, at some point, cease to remember the story or lose the motivation to pass it on? Losing the Exodus story may have been a possibility in the days of the Chronicler, but it has become so interwoven into Jewish identity that it seems like an impossibility now. A more plausible scenario, I would submit, is that the Jews themselves will come to an end before the Exodus story does – not a claim I can or want to prove, of course, but one for which I have support from recent writers who have registered in various ways the story's strange capacity to outlive its tellers. In the semi-fictional *People of the Book*, Geraldine Brooks tracks the history of the Sarajevo Haggadah through various perils that left the Jewish communities of Spain and Bosnia devastated – the expulsion from Spain, the Holocaust, the Bosnian War.[12] The people who read from this Haggadah mostly do not survive – there are less than a thousand Jews in Sarajevo today – but the Sarajevo Haggadah itself manages to escape again and again. In a recent novel by Joshua Cohen entitled *Witz*, the Jews are completely undone by a catastrophe suspiciously similar to the Exodus, slain by a plague with the exception of their first-born, who mostly die off too by the next Passover with the exception of a single Jew named Benjamin.[13] Even in this post-Jewish world, however, the Exodus story lives on, embraced by non-Jews now obsessed with the Jews in the wake of their demise. We have reached a point in history when, for a convergence of reasons, it has become possible to imagine a world without the Jews, but even that kind of scenario, it turns out, is just another occasion for retelling the Exodus.

2 WHAT IF THE TEMPLE OF JERUSALEM HAD NOT BEEN DESTROYED BY THE ROMANS?

René Bloch

In the summer of the year 70 CE, in the midst of the turmoil of the Jewish-Roman War, the Roman commander Titus summoned his advisors for a military council. After persistent and heavy resistance by the Jewish rebels, the city of Jerusalem was finally about to be captured by the Roman soldiers. Jews and Romans were fighting in the immediate vicinity of the Jewish Temple, which was still standing (Figure 5). The Roman victory was only a matter of time. But what should be done with the Temple of the Jews? Together with his advisors in Jerusalem, Titus "deliberated," in the words of the late antique Christian historian, Sulpicius Severus (fourth/fifth century CE),

> whether he should destroy such a mighty temple. For some thought that a consecrated shrine, which was famous beyond all other works of men, ought not to be razed, arguing that its preservation would bear witness to the moderation of Rome, while its destruction would for ever brand her cruelty.[1]

The solution was not an obvious one. For the Romans to destroy a temple was in opposition to their concept of piety (*pietas*), a venerable ideal that had gained renewed importance in the age of Augustus (who

I would like to thank the following for their helpful and critical remarks: Sara Bloch, Leonhard Burckhardt, Ulrich Luz, Gavriel Rosenfeld, and Seth Schwartz (naturally some reaching conclusions different from mine). An earlier version of this chapter was presented as the Emil Fackenheim Lecture in the fall of 2013 in Berlin.

Figure 5. *The Destruction of the Temple of Jerusalem* (1638), painting by Nicolas Poussin. According to ancient sources, Titus actually hesitated before ordering the Temple's destruction, raising many hypothetical questions about how Jewish history would have been affected had he decided to spare the holy edifice.

had built and restored a great number of temples), but was certainly older. When Roman leaders who had dared to plunder or even destroy temples were defeated in battle, this could be understood as divine punishment.[2] In the case of Titus and the young Flavian dynasty, there was good reason to be cautious with regard to the destruction of temples. Approximately half a year earlier, the Capitol, the great Temple of Jupiter in Rome, had burned down when Vespasian attacked the city. The Roman historian Tacitus speaks of the "saddest and most shameful crime that the Roman state had ever suffered since its foundation."[3] After taking office, Vespasian made sure to rebuild the Capitol.

Titus was not the first Roman who had the opportunity to destroy the Temple of Jerusalem. When Pompey captured the city in the year 63 BCE (having been practically invited to do so by the belligerent Hasmonean brothers, Aristobulus and Hyrcanus), he famously entered the Temple, but "out of piety" did not "touch" anything.[4] A decade later, Marcus Licinius Crassus, who was in charge of the province of

Syria, showed less deference when he ordered the plundering of the Temple. For Crassus, the treasures of the Jewish Temple were a welcome means of financing his campaign against the Parthians. According to Josephus, he "took away all the gold of the temple" and stole its treasure.[5] But the Temple did not fall.

So which decision did Titus take toward the end of the Jewish-Roman war? We do not know for sure. According to Sulpicius Severus, he did not follow the arguments of those who pleaded for moderation. Titus and others argued that the destruction of the Temple was

> a prime necessity in order to wipe out more completely the
> religion of the Jews and the Christians; for they urged that these
> religions, although hostile to each other, nevertheless sprang from
> the same sources; the Christians had grown out of the Jews: if the
> root were destroyed, the stock would easily perish.[6]

In fact, it is unlikely that Christianity played into Titus' decision about what to do with the Temple of Jerusalem. Severus probably revised his source, most likely Tacitus, and gave it a Christian reading.[7] One can assume that Severus' source only said that Titus decided to destroy the Temple and bring the war to an end.[8] A very different story, by contrast, was offered by the Jewish-Roman historian Josephus, who in his *Jewish War* insisted that Titus did everything in his power to spare the Temple. In Josephus' version of the military council, the accusation of impiety, which the destruction of a temple would have provoked, is also discussed. But here, in the end, Titus

> declared that, even were the Jews to mount it [the Temple] and
> fight therefrom, he would not wreak vengeance on inanimate
> objects instead of men, nor under any circumstances burn down
> so magnificent a work; for the loss would affect the Romans,
> inasmuch as it would be an ornament to the empire if it stood.[9]

According to Josephus, the destruction of the Temple was an accident, precipitated by a Roman soldier "awaiting no orders." Indeed, when Titus heard about the fire, he "ran to the Temple to arrest the conflagration."[10]

So are we to believe Josephus or Sulpicius Severus? Both versions of the story have found their adherents.[11] It seems clear to me, however, that Josephus' report was heavily influenced by his pro-Flavian bias. As someone who relied on imperial patronage, Josephus sought to whitewash Titus and the Flavian dynasty of any responsibility for the Temple's destruction. In reality, Titus probably decided to plunder and destroy the Jewish Temple. After all, the edifice was the "symbol and strength of Jewish resistance."[12]

However, and this is important for the following argument, Titus *could* have decided differently, as is evident from the differing views in ancient sources, but also their interpretation in modern scholarship. The counterfactual question "What if Titus had not given the order to destroy the Temple of Jerusalem?" is thus a legitimate one. Exploring this provocative counterfactual question allows us to better understand the origins and consequences of what is generally considered one of the most pivotal events in Jewish history.

Roman financial policy

We do not have to doubt that the Romans would have brought the rebellion to an end, even if they had not destroyed the Temple. Maybe Titus would have merely plundered it, which would certainly have been a less sacrilegious act than its destruction. He had good reason to seize the wealth of the Jewish Temple. The young Flavian dynasty needed money. Since the great fire of 64 CE, which destroyed large parts of the city of Rome, the acquisition of money was a high priority. And with the civil war of 68–9 CE the situation certainly did not improve.[13] There is little doubt, then, that if Titus had spared the Temple of Jerusalem, he would have made sure to profit financially from the Roman victory over the Jews. Either he would have plundered the Temple or imposed heavy taxes on the Jews – and he may have done both. After the Temple's destruction, Jews, "wherever they were," had to pay a new tax called the *fiscus Iudaicus* to the Roman Capitol.[14] It replaced the former Temple tax that Jews had sent to Jerusalem for generations. If the Temple had not been destroyed, there would not have been such a humiliating redirection of this tax. But in one way or another, the Jews would have suffered financially. The suppression of the rebellion and the capture of Jerusalem were unusually difficult and expensive for the Romans; indeed, it took "roughly one-seventh of the whole Imperial army ... to complete the capture of the city."[15] Moreover, the Roman army would have remained stationed in Judea, as it did after the destruction of the Temple, when Titus left the tenth legion together with some troops of cavalry and infantry in Jerusalem.[16]

The victorious Flavian emperors, who were newcomers on the Roman political stage, made sure to profit from their victory as ostentatiously as possible.[17] The spoils of the Temple of Jerusalem were displayed in a large triumph in the year 71 CE.[18] Most famously, the spoils were later shown (and continue to be visible today) on the Arch of Titus, which was completed on the Via Sacra in 81 CE. The vessels of gold from the Temple were displayed in the newly erected Temple of Peace (*Templum Pacis*).[19] Similarly, the great new amphitheater, opened in the year 80 CE and later known as the Colosseum, was financed "from the spoils of war," as is stated in an inscription found at the site. This inscription could only refer to the Jewish-Roman War, which means that the Colosseum was built with the gold and other valuables from the Jewish Temple in Jerusalem.[20] If the Temple had not been destroyed (or at least plundered), the Flavians would have had to find other financial sources for the amphitheater, which would have been no easy task. Moreover, the Arch of Titus, if it had been built at all, would not have been able to flaunt its famed relief portraying the triumphal procession of the year 71 CE with the booty seized from the Temple.

The end of sacrifice

The Jewish-Roman War did not end with the fall of the Jewish Temple. After destroying the Temple, the Romans laid waste to almost the entire city of Jerusalem.[21] The number of Jews killed or enslaved by the Romans during the war was very high, even if Josephus' numbers are certainly exaggerated.[22] If we assume that the Temple was not destroyed, the Temple cult could only have persisted if Jerusalem had remained habitable and if enough of its inhabitants had been able to stay in the city. But Jews would have continued sacrificing, if at all possible. In the case of Crassus' plundering of the Temple in 54 BCE, we do not hear of any long-term consequences for the ritual practice.

But for how long? For how long would Jews have offered sacrifices to their god? It may be a surprising question and, at first glance, sound like pure speculation to suggest that the Jews might have stopped performing sacrificial rites even if the Temple had not been destroyed

Figure 6. *The Sacrifice of the Old Covenant* (*ca.* 1626), oil on panel, painting by Peter Paul Rubens. If the Temple had not been destroyed, would the Jews have stopped performing sacrificial rites?

(Figure 6). To be sure, one needs to be aware of apologetic pitfalls.[23] In the Middle Ages, Maimonides argued in his *Guide for the Perplexed* that the fact that God restricted the sacrificial cult to one place and to one family – the Temple and the *Kohanim* – while prayers are open to all Jews, proved the inferiority of the former to the latter.[24] What was difficult for the medieval philosopher to accept is even more problematic in modern Western society. Few people today would consider the idea of cultic sacrifices persuasive. Jews, it has even been said, should be grateful to Titus for having released them from sacrificial rituals "before any other society."[25] The idea that Jews would have stopped sacrificing even without help from the outside, without the destruction by Titus, may be particularly attractive. It is impossible to know with any certainty what would have happened to the sacrificial cult had the Temple itself survived, but there is indeed good reason to believe that Jews would have abandoned it anyway. The Jews lost their Temple at a time when sacrificial rituals were being called into question. Critiques of sacrifice had been common already in ancient Israel. The prophets contrasted the superficiality of sacrificial offerings with the ideals of justice and righteousness. In the words of the prophet Isaiah:

> What to me is the multitude of your sacrifices? Says the LORD; I
> have had enough of burnt offerings of rams and the fat of fed
> beasts; I do not delight in the blood of bulls, or of lambs, or of
> goats . . . learn to do good; seek justice, rescue the oppressed,
> defend the orphan, plead for the widow.[26]

To be sure, we should not assume that within Judaism sacrifices were consistently questioned. On the contrary, so long as no outside force prohibited it – as at the time of the Seleucid King Antiochus IV – the sacrificial service in the Temple of Jerusalem was always upheld. Sacrifices were offered even during the dire conditions of the Jewish-Roman War.[27] But the old critiques of the prophets continued to linger. They can be tracked in the writings of Qumran and the New Testament. Matthew, for example, takes up an early, probably pre-70 CE, critique of sacrifice in the Jesus movement, citing Hosea 6.6: "I desire mercy, not sacrifice (the knowledge of God, rather than burnt offerings)."[28] Early Christian critiques of sacrifice continued, and further expanded an inner-Jewish dialogue.[29]

In his now classic book, *Map Is Not Territory*, Jonathan Z. Smith – in a brief afterword to his article "Earth and Gods" – offered a skeptical counterfactual claim about the survival of the Temple cult. As he put it:

> Indeed, I should want to go so far as to argue that if the Temple
> had not been destroyed, it would have had to be neglected. For it
> represented a locative type of religious activity no longer perceived
> effective in a new, utopian religious situation with a concomitant
> shift from a cosmological to an anthropological view-point.[30]

Beginning in the Hellenistic period and then accelerating in late antiquity, according to Smith, a groundbreaking transition took place from sacred space as a fixed center to a "relatively unfixed form" of rituals. "Rather than celebration, purification and pilgrimage," he wrote, "the new rituals will be those of conversion, of initiation into the secret society or identification with the divine man."[31] In making this argument,

Smith followed Peter Brown who, writing about late antique society, declared:

> Ancient religion had revolved round great temples ... their ceremonies assumed a life in which community, the city, dwarfed the individual. In the fourth and fifth centuries [CE], however, the individual, as a "man of power," came to dwarf the traditional communities ... *the emergence of the holy man at the expense of the temple marks the end of the classical world.*[32]

In late antiquity, the practice of religion withdrew more and more to the private sphere. Temples disappeared, as did animal sacrifices.[33] Sacrifice remained an important religious paradigm, but it was filled with new, symbolic meaning. Christians saw in Jesus Christ the eternal sacrifice to God, while Jews replaced the sacrifice with the study of the Torah, including the study of the sacrificial laws.[34]

Greek and Roman philosophers had also questioned the utility of sacrifice early on. Theophrastus, a student of Aristotle, criticized the killing of animals and interpreted sacrifice as a substitution for cannibalism, and Varro (first century BCE) employed the same language as the biblical prophets in denying any divine demand for sacrifices, declaring: "Real gods do not wish or ask for them."[35] In late antiquity, with the rise of Christianity, this critique was phrased in much more rigid form. An antipagan law under the Emperor Constantius II from the year 341 states "that the folly of sacrifices be abolished" (*sacrificiorum aboleatur insania*).[36]

Given these trends, it is indeed reasonable to assume that Judaism – never isolated, but part of larger cultural contexts – would have abandoned its sacrificial cult over the long run. Even if the Temple of Jerusalem had not been destroyed, the decline of pagan sacrificial rituals and the diminished importance of temples throughout the region make it unlikely that the Jewish sacrificial system would have survived late antiquity, a time period when more individual and less centralized forms of religious services prevailed. Over time Jews, too, would have distanced themselves from sacrificial rituals.

The Jewish diaspora

While the Temple had always played an important role in Jewish theological thinking, it was not the only religious center for Jews in the ancient world. On the contrary: when the Temple fell in the year 70 CE, the majority of the Jews had been living outside Palestine, in the Jewish diaspora, for a long time.[37] There is evidence of synagogues being present in Egypt as early as the third century BCE. Jews from all over the ancient world sent their Temple tax to Jerusalem, but their religious geography was widespread and, to employ J. Z. Smith's nomenclature, not "locative." In Judea, too, the synagogue was not only a post-Temple phenomenon, but existed previously, even in Jerusalem.[38] In the diaspora, Judaism had remarkably always been "a religion without animal sacrifice."[39] The vast majority of Jews in antiquity never personally saw the Temple of Jerusalem. It is true that other Jewish temples had existed at various junctures; in the sixth and fifth century BCE, Jews on the island of Elephantine in Upper Egypt had their own temple. And in the second century BCE, the Jewish high priest Onias built a temple in the Egyptian city of Leontopolis. But these were temporary exceptions.[40]

This is not to say that the Temple was not important to diaspora Jews. To Philo of Alexandria, the great Jewish-Hellenistic philosopher of the first century CE, it was unimaginable that the Temple one day would no longer be there. In the context of the annual contribution of a half-shekel that diaspora Jews sent to Jerusalem, Philo writes:

> the revenues of the Temple are derived not only from landed estates but also from other and far greater sources which time will never destroy. For as long as the human race endures, and it will endure forever, the revenues of the Temple also will remain secure coeternal with the whole universe.[41]

Philo also mentions Jewish pilgrimage to Jerusalem, observing that:

> countless multitudes from countless cities come, some over land, others over sea, from east and west and north and south at every feast. They take the Temple for their port as a general haven and safe refuge from the bustle and great turmoil of life, and there they seek to find calm weather.[42]

Jewish pilgrimage certainly constituted an important bond between the diaspora and Jerusalem. Yet Philo exaggerates its significance. Most pilgrims came from Judea, not from the diaspora.[43] Philo himself apparently visited Jerusalem only once. He mentions his visit to Jerusalem and the Temple merely in a side remark in his tractate on Providence, showing more interest in the birds that he saw on his journey than in the sacrifice: "While I was there [in Ashkelon] at a time when I was on my way to our ancestral temple to offer up prayers and sacrifices I observed a large number of pigeons at the cross roads and in each house."[44] The Temple was important to Philo.[45] But his interest in its rituals was also very much of a philosophical and theoretical nature.[46] Philo refers to a number of synagogues in Alexandria. This is where people went to pray and, as Philo would say, to study philosophy.[47]

Even the Jewish-Roman historian Josephus, who differed from Philo in that he spent half of his life in Jerusalem and half in the diaspora, rather quickly, or so it seems, found ways to adjust to nonsacrificial diaspora Judaism. Josephus showed genuine emotion in mourning the Jews' defeat at the hands of the Romans and the loss of the Temple.[48] Having grown up in a priestly family in Jerusalem, the historian viewed the Temple as an intrinsic part of Judaism. In his apologetic treatise *Against Apion*, written toward the end of his life and about thirty years after the Jewish-Roman War, Josephus spoke of the unity of Temple and God: Judaism has one god, one Temple, and one scripture.[49] But this slogan is also part of Josephus' polemic against inconsistent paganism, with its countless temples, changing gods, and myriad books.[50] Although it is difficult to prove, Josephus probably adjusted sooner rather than later to the religious conditions of diaspora Judaism.[51] If the sacrificial rites in the Temple had gradually been abandoned, Jews in the diaspora would have taken note, but their daily religious practice would not have been substantially affected. When the Temple fell in the year 70 CE, the event was certainly a massive shock for Jews throughout the world. But Judaism was well prepared for such a shift, especially in the diaspora.[52]

Bar Kokhba and Julian

Sixty years after their defeat in the Jewish-Roman War, the Jews launched another rebellion in the form of the Bar Kokhba revolt (132–5 CE). What immediately triggered the revolt is still a matter of dispute. But the fact that coins produced by the Bar Kokhba rebels depicted both the Temple of Jerusalem and the ark of the covenant indicates that the rebels wanted to restore the Temple – or, at the very least, employ it as an evocative rallying symbol.[53] The Romans' eventual suppression of the Bar Kokhba revolt had far-reaching consequences for the Jews. The province of Judea was renamed Syria Palaestina; Jews were entirely banned from Jerusalem; and on its site a Roman colony, named Aelia Capitolina, was established. However, if the Temple had not been destroyed in the year 70, if there had not been such a rupture and Temple services had continued, there probably would not have been a Bar Kokhba revolt.[54]

What if the Roman emperor Julian had made good on his plan in the fourth century CE to rebuild the Temple of Jerusalem? In the short period that he ruled (from 361 to 363 CE), Julian promoted the revival of pagan cults, polytheism, and sacrifice.[55] Julian embraced common anti-Jewish stereotypes, but he admired ancient Judaism's sacrificial system. He believed it was similar to pagan rituals and, even more importantly, stood in stark contrast to Christianity.[56] The sources on Julian's intention to rebuild the Temple are not free of polemics, to say the least, and are difficult to evaluate. The emperor's main targets were the Christians who, for their part, reacted nervously to the prospect of a new Jewish Temple, whose ruins were understood as proof of the sins of the Jews. If we are to believe contemporary Christian authors, Jews answered Julian's unexpected endeavor with enthusiasm.[57] On the other hand, rabbinic responses are marked by "an almost complete silence in both Talmuds concerning Julian and his plan."[58]

In the end, Julian's plan to rebuild the Jewish Temple in Jerusalem came to naught, as did his efforts to bring back traditional cults. The endeavor to rebuild the Temple of Jerusalem was abandoned at an early stage and Julian died during his campaign against the Persians in 363, after having reigned for less than two years.[59] Time could not be turned back. If Julian had been able to restore the Temple, this would have raised further provocative questions for Jewish history. In the words of Michael Avi-Yonah: "Would the conflict between Rome and Israel be resolved peacefully in the fourth century, as it was not in the first? . . . Would there be a revival of the Jewish aspirations to complete political independence? Would there be a repetition of the tragedy of the year 70 and a third destruction?"[60] Needless to say, none of these questions would have had any relevance if the Temple of Jerusalem had not been destroyed by the Romans in the first place. Had the Temple survived, had Jewish sacrifice faded out around the same time, Julian would have taken an entirely different approach to dealing with the

Jewish cult and would have had no occasion to resort to such a revolutionary and polemical project in the first place.

Christianity and rabbinic culture

The survival of the Temple would have also had major consequences for early Christianity and rabbinic Judaism. According to early Christian accounts, the Temple's destruction signified the end of God's affection for Israel. It became an important argument – indeed, it was seen as concrete proof – that God had decided to choose a new Israel and punish the Jews for their denial of Jesus Christ. The Gospels refer in parabolic language to Jerusalem's destruction as confirmation of God's reorientation. In Matthew, Jesus says: "The king was enraged. He sent his troops, destroyed those murderers, and burned their city. Then he said to his slaves, 'The wedding is ready, but those invited were not worthy.'"[61] And in Mark: "What then will the owner of the vineyard do? He will come and destroy the tenants and give the vineyards to others."[62] As noted above, critiques of the Temple were already common before 70 CE. But with the edifice's destruction, such critiques became an anchor of early Christian thinking and an anti-Jewish argument for centuries to come.

   If the Temple of Jerusalem had not been destroyed, the metaphorical insistence on Jesus as the final and eternal sacrifice, replacing actual animal offerings, would have been difficult to sustain.[63] Against the backdrop of ongoing Temple sacrifices, interpreting the crucifixion as the sacrifice to end all sacrifice would have been less convincing. Both theological tenets – the destruction of the Temple as a sign of divine punishment and Jesus as the consummation of all sacrifices – were important elements of early Christian thought. While it is true that "the Jerusalem Temple plays no significant role in either Paul's pre-70 CE letters or in the epistolary literature following him," it does in the Gospels and other early Christian texts, such as the *Letter of Barnabas* and the work of Justin Martyr.[64] For Christian authors, such as Origen, Eusebius, and Hegesippus, Josephus' report on the fall of the Temple in the *Jewish War* served as a prooftext for the divine punishment of the Jews.[65] Had the Temple not been destroyed, the early Christian community could not have distanced itself theologically from the Jewish religion so easily. It is probably safe to say that the development of Christianity as a world religion would not have taken flight as it did.[66]

What about rabbinic Judaism? In Jewish mythology, the destruction of the Temple was a disaster of cosmic proportions. The destruction (*khurban*) marked the beginning of the exile – including the exile of God from Zion – and the introduction of chaos into the world. It signaled the removal of the people of Israel from the source of its blessing and the abandonment of its direct access to God. This view of the destruction as a cataclysmic event was most poignantly phrased by Samuel Yosef Agnon in his acceptance speech upon receiving the Nobel Prize for Literature in 1966 when he said: "As a result of the historic catastrophe in which Titus of Rome destroyed Jerusalem[,] and Israel was exiled from its land, I was born in one of the cities of the Exile. But always I regarded myself as one who was born in Jerusalem."[67] Historically speaking, the significance of this rupture was greatly exaggerated in rabbinic Judaism. And Agnon was not simply born in Galicia because of Titus. The Jewish diaspora was not the result of the Second Temple's destruction, but was much older, extending back to the destruction of the first Temple in the sixth century BCE.

One thing that rabbinic Judaism shared with early Christianity was the fact that they both "remained sacrificial religions, but very special sacrificial religions because they functioned without blood sacrifice."[68] In rabbinic literature, the Temple discourse was quite distinct from the early Christian interpretations. Whereas Christianity revolved around salvation through the final sacrifice of Jesus, the rabbis kept the sacrificial world alive by continuing to study and explain it. The Mishna, written down around 200 CE, is acutely aware that the Second Temple was gone, destroyed on the same day as its predecessor about 650 years earlier: "On the ninth of Ab . . . the Temple was destroyed the first and the second time, and Beth-Tor was captured and the City was ploughed up."[69] The fall of the Temple was thus turned into a mythic history of catastrophe and entered the liturgical calendar. At the same time, however, the rabbis of the Mishna were unwilling to accept the Temple's fate. Ingeniously combining denial with the messianic hope for the Temple's future restoration, the rabbis discussed sacrificial rites as if the holy edifice were still standing. The fifth order of the Mishna, *kodashim*, comprises eleven tractates on issues related to the Temple and sacrificial rites, thus upholding the status of sacrifice in Judaism, albeit in an intellectualized and imaginary form.[70]

If the Temple had not been destroyed by the Romans, rabbinic Judaism probably would not have developed in the way it did. Commentary, scriptural arguments, and interpretations, as we know them from the Mishna and the Talmud, surely had precursors long before the Temple's destruction. Literary and historical evidence for the earliest rabbis (the five "pairs" and the first generation of the Tannaim) is scanty, but one can also refer to Qumran, Philo of Alexandria, and also the Septuagint for pre-70 interpretive narratives.[71] The idea of engaging scripture as a form of religious service existed before the Temple fell. The rabbis had predecessors and did not simply arise in the vacuum left by the sudden cessation of sacrifice. But the Mishna's development stands in direct relation to the Temple's destruction; its detailed descriptions of the Temple service preserve the memory of the Second Temple period and simultaneously serve as a "blueprint for the messianic era."[72] Had the Temple survived, there would have been no Mishna – certainly not in the form in which we know it. The same would be true for the Gemara, which commented on the Mishna, and thus for the Talmud.

The rabbis later imagined a smooth transition from the destruction of the Temple to the constitution of the first rabbinical school in Yavne – from Temple to text, so to speak. We now know that things were more complicated and that the rabbinic movement established itself in an authoritative form only later.[73] Is the success story of the rabbinic movement imaginable without the destruction of the Temple? Hardly. It was the Temple's disappearance that largely triggered the paradigm change that accompanied rabbinic culture. Moreover, the Temple's destruction, together with the fall of Jerusalem, played an important role in rabbinic theology as the primary rupture. The Temple's fall was understood as a divine punishment for (and a warning against) moral flaws among the Jews.[74] Titus became the emblematic archenemy and paganism was convincingly presented as an anticulture to be avoided.[75] If we prefer to think that there would have been a Talmud with the Temple still standing, it would have looked quite different. If rabbinic Judaism had not emerged or had manifested itself in a much less consequential form, Judaism's long-term development would have been profoundly affected.

A watershed in Jewish history?

The extent to which the Romans' destruction of the Temple of Jerusalem marks a watershed in Jewish history continues to be a matter of scholarly disagreement.[76] As our counterfactual discussion has shown, there is no simple way to assess the event's significance. But there is good reason to interpret the Temple's destruction as having profoundly affected the history of both Judaism and Christianity. The sudden loss of the cultic center of Judaism was formative not only for rabbinic culture, but became a crucial point of orientation for all subsequent periods of Judaism. In orthodox Jewish liturgy, the restoration of the Temple continues to be a theme of great importance. The classic interior architecture of the synagogue – most notably, the Torah Ark (*aron hakodesh*) and the "eternal light" (*ner tamid*) – are concrete physical reminders of the Temple. Without that formative event, Jewish history and Jewish myth would have looked entirely different.

In other respects, however, the events of the year 70 CE were less decisive for Judaism's subsequent development. Even if the Temple had not been destroyed, Jewish sacrificial rituals would have slowly faded out of their own accord during late antiquity. Similarly, neither the Jewish diaspora nor the first synagogues were brought about by the Temple's destruction. Diaspora Judaism had always been nonsacrificial (a few exceptions notwithstanding) and was certainly less affected by the Temple's fall than Judaism in the land of Israel. In the end, counterfactually speculating about the Temple's survival, while admittedly hypothetical, helps us understand the deeper forces that profoundly shaped Judaism in the ancient world.

3 WHAT IF KING FERDINAND AND QUEEN ISABELLA HAD NOT EXPELLED THE JEWS OF SPAIN IN 1492?*

Jonathan Ray

The University of Madrid Press (Servicio Publicaciones – Universidad de Madrid) is proud to announce the publication of a new collection of primary source documents, *The Sephardic Jewish History Reader*. Co-edited by Professor María Elena Delgado Fernández of the University of Madrid and Rabbi Yosef Toledano of the Madrid-based National Rabbinical Institute (Institúto Rabínico Nacional), the volume offers scholars, graduate students, and advanced undergraduates a rich trove of primary-source documents dealing with the rich history of Sephardic Jewry.

To give potential buyers a preview of the book's content, we have reproduced two representative documents from Section II of the volume, "The Jews of Early Modern Spain: 1391–1700." The documents are introduced by a short editorial description that outlines their historical context and significance; they are accompanied by footnotes providing additional historical explanation; the documents conclude with a set of study questions meant to facilitate classroom discussion.

Please visit our website to learn more about the volume and other online resources offered by the University of Madrid Press.

The letters of Joseph Benveniste, Rabbi Mayor of the Jews of Spain

The following are two letters written in the 1670s by Joseph Benveniste y Abravanel, the Chief Rabbi (Rabbi Mayor) of Spain and courtier to

* This chapter is a work of fiction.

King Carlos II (1661–1700). As the leading Jewish authority of imperial Spain, Benveniste took it upon himself to write these letters in an attempt to resolve the two great Jewish refugee problems of the seventeenth century: that of North African Jews fleeing the harsh policies of the Moroccan sultans in the early 1670s, and the flight of Jews from Poland-Lithuania following the Chmielnicki pogroms of 1648.

The first letter was sent by Benveniste to Sultan Mehmed IV (1648–87) as part of the Spanish Jewish community's response to the repressive policies of the Sultans of Morocco, Moulay Rashid and Moulay Ismail, toward Maghrebi Jews in the late seventeenth century (Figure 7). As is well known, the Sultan responded favorably to Benveniste's petition to allow Maghrebi Jews to settle in the Ottoman Empire, reversing hundreds of years of indifference and abuse of the Jews at the hands of the Turkish sultans. However, this change was short-lived. The Maghrebi Jews never successfully integrated into Ottoman society, often clashing with Armenian and Greek Christians and the native Romaniote (Greek) Jews. By the early eighteenth century, most had drifted eastward to the Iberian colonies of eastern India and the Philippines, where they established the vibrant Jewish communities that exist there today.

The second letter was sent by Benveniste to the rabbis of Poland and Lithuania offering counsel to the stricken Ashkenazi community. Unfortunately, Benveniste's efforts to find safe haven for the Ashkenazi Jews were less successful. Most either remained in Eastern or Central Europe, practicing a highly mystical form of Judaism and establishing communities that refused to recognize the primacy of the Spanish Rabbi Mayor. Today, the Jews of Spain are the only Jews to retain the medieval practice of the Chief Rabbi, a position of great authority that is often called the "Pope of the Jews," and which remains the single most powerful figure in the Jewish world.

DOCUMENT 1
A letter of petition to Mehmed IV (*ca.* 1672)

To his Highness Mehmed, Sultan and Grand Señor of the Ottoman Turks. The Humble Addresses of Don Joseph ben Jacob Abravanel y Benveniste, Rabbi Mayor and Royal Physician to His Majesty Don Carlos, King of Spain, on behalf of the children of Israel.

MAHUMET QUARTUS,
MAGNUS TURCARUM IMPERATOR,

Figure 7. Engraving of Sultan Mehmed IV of Turkey. Since the Jews of Spain were one of the few European communities to be spared the great wave of expulsions during the Middle Ages, they were able to save their Maghrebi co-religionists from persecution.

Give me leave to speak to Your Highness on behalf of the children of Israel, which is to say the Jews, about our present condition, and to defend a holy people who have been unfairly maligned and condemned. Today, in the ancient cities of the Maghreb, the seas rage against the remnant of Israel, and they are left as sheep without a shepherd. For this reason, we, the exiles of Jerusalem that are in Spain, must intercede on behalf of our brethren, due to the antiquity and nobility of our lineage and the esteem with which we are held by our lord king, the King of Spain, by the lord pope, the head of all the true Christians. We humbly follow the path laid out for us by our ancestors, the noble Chief Rabbis of Spain, who rescued for the Jews the great learning of the academies of the East when those venerable institutions faltered, and created in Spain a citadel of peace and learning. We write in the name of Hasdai ibn Shaprut and Samuel ibn Naghrela, the Nagid, of blessed memory, who served the Ishmaelite kings of Spain, and also in the name of Don Isaac Abravanel, my own ancestor, who served their Catholic Majesties, King Ferdinand and Queen Isabella, and convinced them not to expel the Jews from their realms. And so we have lived and prospered and gone from strength to strength down to this day. For this reason the pious and holy sages who are among the Jews of the Maghreb, together with their men of wealth and distinction, have turned to me for help, seeing the great respect in which the Holy Office of the Rabbi Mayor is held by the rulers of our land, and seeing also the many honors that we are granted when we are in their lands to carry out the business of our Lord and king, the King of Spain.

On the tribulations of the Jews of the Maghreb

And so it is with trembling hand that I take up pen and write to you, and set out my case before you on the matter of the Jews of the kingdoms of Marrakesh and Fez and the surrounding lands. The Jews of these lands are of a great and noble lineage; that is the lineage of the Jews of Spain. Many can trace their families back to the days of the Jews of Seville, Lucena, Cordoba, and Granada, when those cities formed part of the same kingdom as the cities of the Maghreb. Others are from families who remained in these cities as they passed to the Christian lords of Spain, but then left in the days of the great *shemad*, a time of persecution and catastrophe unequaled in our history. I refer to the

murders and forced conversions of the Jews that took place throughout the towns and cities of Spain, which was in the year 5151 in our
calendar, which corresponds to 793 in the Ishmaelite calendar.[1] They
found there in the Maghreb a good home and kings to shield and protect
them, and they lived in peace, every man under his vine and under his
fig tree.

But today there has arisen a new king over the land of the
Maghreb who knows not the noble and loyal courtiers who have served
his predecessors. He has embittered the lives of those who would serve
him, and cast them out, men of peace and piety, nobles of the highest lineage, who had dwelt there untroubled for over a thousand years.
And due to the wars between princes in that land, the Jews have been
caught in a snare, and there came a day of darkness and lamentation
when the faithful servants of the king were put to death though they
were innocent.[2] The great political upheaval in these lands has also
emboldened the wicked and allowed for the rise of pirate-lords who
prey upon the ships at sea. These men do not follow any laws nor do
they honor the traditions of their fathers, whose good customs it has
always been to keep and protect all the children of Abraham. Instead,
they look upon all ships and travelers and their possessions as plunder
to be sold. Many of these men who sail on the sea and capture other
vessels do so against the wishes of their own leaders, paying no heed to
authority or to laws. Indeed, throughout the kingdoms of Marrakesh
and Fez, madness and chaos now rule in the place of law and tradition.
The whole of this region has become fertile ground for preachers who
do not respect authority and seek to incite the ignorant masses to serve
their own ambitions. They whisper in the ears of the usurpers who call
themselves kings,[3] and convince them to pour out their wrath upon the
Jews.

All this overturns the traditions of justice and loyalty that has
long been the bond between the Jews and their lords. For many years,
the children of Israel lived and traded in the lands of the Maghreb, and
they excelled in all manner of trade and skilled crafts, and served their

[1] The reference here is the riots and conversions (*shemad*) of the Jews in Spain in 1391.
[2] When Moulay Rashid conquered Marrakesh in 1670, he publicly burned the Jewish
courtiers who had served the former king.
[3] This is most likely a reference to the Alaouite dynasty, which came to power in
Morocco in 1659 by overthrowing the Saadian dynasty.

lords, the kings of the Maghreb, as is proper. In Fez, the king gave to the Jews their own *autónoma*, which is called *mellah* in Arabic.[4] And soon the King of Marrakesh grew jealous and wanted loyal Jews to serve him as well, and so he built for them a *mellah* in that city, so that the Jews would come and live there in autonomy and under his protection, and this they did. But today, these ancient bonds of friendship and trust have been broken. Indeed, the Jews there have been subject to repeated forced conversions and humiliations at the hands of zealous preachers and weak-willed rulers who sought to curry favor with the vulgar masses. Even the lords of those Christian lands from which the Jews have been exiled look across the sea with horror and confusion at such destruction. For why should there be compulsion in matters of faith? Does not your own Law forbid this?

On the autonomy of the Jews and the protection of righteous kings

Here in Spain, many years ago, there was also rioting, and many Jews were forced to accept the faith of the Christians against their will.[5] This calamity came about when foreigners and missionaries conspired to attack the innocent. But the lords of the land, the kings of Spain, shielded my people, and this evil deed was never repeated. Indeed, the One and True God, God of heaven and earth and of all peoples, has not forgotten his covenant with his people. He is a Shield and a Support for His children, and rewards just and righteous kings. Those were dark times, when evil and angry men stalked the house of Judah and ravaged her gardens. But the Holy One, our Rock and our Redeemer, stood by His people, and through divine compassion we have survived and indeed flourished. For He sent to the Jews a series of protectors, the great kings of Castile and Aragon, who crushed zealotry and lawlessness, and protected their people. And it cannot be other than that we were saved and protected from so great a calamity in order to be of service to the great kings and lords of the world until such time as the Holy One, blessed be He, sees fit to redeem His people Israel.

---

[4] The *autónomas* were independent Jewish neighborhoods or towns that greatly expanded the small Jewish quarters of the Middle Ages. In several countries they endured well into the twentieth century as symbols of Jewish cultural and political independence.
[5] This is a reference to the riots and mass conversions of 1391.

The great success of the house of the kings of Spain is divine recompense for their just rule. Behold! Look and see the success of the kings of Spain who exceed all the kings of Edom in lands and riches, and whose armies stretch across the seas. Meanwhile, those wicked kings who exiled their Jews unjustly and treated them like criminals and did evil to them, they have inherited only sorrow. Their kingdoms, the kingdoms of England, France, Provence, and Germany, are beset by wars and unrest and bloodshed over which is the true sect of their faith.[6]

Our great and enlightened lords, the kings of Spain, have always treated us honorably and with affection, as a father who has compassion for his children, here and in all lands over which they hold sway. They intervened on our behalf in Rome and in the Italian cities, when wicked and jealous men sought to remove our ancestral rights and restrict our movement. Today, as a result of this, the Jews there live in peace and security in their own *autónomas*, following the dictates of their own Law, and trafficking in all manner of goods and in this way do they enrich the realms of their lords. And furthermore, all the princes of Italy follow the custom of the nobles of Spain and Portugal, so that in every city and town all have Jews, who assist them as physicians and diplomats and in the management of their revenues. Indeed, there is no duke, prince, or governor in these lands who does not have a Jew to aid him in administering his lands and managing his affairs.

The kings of Spain have been guided by righteousness, and so too the great kings of the Turks, your ancestors, may they be blessed. For well you know that when the armies of the kings of the Turks swept across the East, they brought justice and peace to the peoples of these lands. The members of your royal house did not exile the Jews that lived under the rule of the Greeks, but saw fit to bring them to Constantinople, to the capital city, and settled them in the shade of the royal palace. There they honored the leaders and great men of the Greek Jews, and protected them. And when they extended their hand over the holy city of Jerusalem and also over Egypt, they brought peace to that land, and to the most ancient and holy sites, that all of the children of Abraham might reach these sites in peace and tranquility and fulfill the divine mandate of holy pilgrimage, each according to his Law.

[6] This is an apparent reference to the wars of religion that raged throughout Europe in the sixteenth and seventeenth centuries.

On Spanish Jews not oppressing Muslims

Let me now speak to you in defense of the children of Israel and about their character and their treatment of the children of Ishmael. For we have heard from the mouths of those who speak falsehoods about us and condemn us, accusing us of speaking blasphemies against the Muslims and attacking their Law, and that this is the reason for our many troubles in the Maghreb and other lands. To these harsh words I will now respond, with the strength and guidance of Heaven, saying that these are naught but lies that have been spread by wandering preachers seeking to foment dissent in their lands, and stir up the populace against royal authority. True scholars of every faith know that Jews have a long history of peace and loyalty in the lands of Ishmael.

And regarding the Jews and Muslims here in Spain, I fear that Your Highness may have heard terrible rumors that Jews sought to do harm to the Moors who once lived here in great numbers. But well you must know that such rumors hold no truth. The enemies of Israel say that when the Moorish kingdom of Granada fell to the armies of the King of Spain in the year 5252, which is 897 by your counting,[7] the Christians committed many abuses there, and the Jews of this kingdom rejoiced. But this is utter falsehood. For after the Christians seized the city of Granada together with its entire kingdom the storm subsided and peace returned to the land. In truth, there were, in those days, wicked men who whispered to the King and Queen of Spain[8] great lies and falsehoods about the Jews as well as the Moors, saying that they would seek their revenge against the Christians and that both should be exiled to foreign lands (Figure 8). But God in His divine mercy placed at the royal court great and noble advisors from the house of Judah.[9] And they silenced the tongues of these stammerers, and spoke words of peace and truth that the Jews and Moors of Spain were naught but loyal servants. And this just and pious king heeded their pleas.

And those Moors who wished to go and live in the land of the Maghreb were allowed to leave, and indeed many did so, and they live there happily and securely even to this day. Others, though, could not

---

[7] That is, 1492.

[8] Ferdinand II of Aragon and Isabella I of Castile, who reigned jointly from 1475 to 1504.

[9] Don Isaac Abravanel, a Jewish courtier and ancestor of Benveniste, is generally credited with interceding on behalf of the Jews at this time.

Don fernando y doña y sabel
Reyes de castilla y de aragon.

Figure 8. King Ferdinand II of Aragon and Queen Isabella of Castile. Although the king and queen were urged to expel the Jews of Spain, they refused to do so.

bear to leave their homes and their fields, for the love of this rich and pleasant land, or for reasons of poverty and fear and dread of such a great journey to a land not their own. And so these Moors remained in their homes and in their fields, much like the Jews and also like the

Christians. So acts a righteous king, as well you know, for so acted your ancestors when they conquered the lands of the Greeks and the other Christians of the East and took under their protection Jew and Christian alike, letting each man pursue his trades and worship God as he saw fit.

On the Jewish refugees from the Maghreb

And so I come now to the heart of my petition, and that is to entreat Your Highness to intervene in this matter on behalf of our brethren. First, we humbly beseech you to intercede in this matter with the King of Marrakesh and with the other princes of the lands of the Maghreb, and with the preachers and holy men there, and to remind them of the ancient pact between the children of your Law and of ours. And I have faith that the rulers of the Maghreb will heed your good counsel, for all of the kings and princes in the lands of Ishmael know of your greatness and hold you in awe. And if Your Highness will honor this petition from your humble servant, I pledge to send my own son, Isaac, and the sons of other noble houses of the Jews of Spain, to help establish and build up new Jewish communities in the Maghreb, and to continue to act as diplomats between the King of Marrakesh and our lord king, the King of Spain.

Second, I implore you to accept some of the refugees into your lands and under your protection, since we here in Spain can only take so many. The Jews of the land of the Maghreb speak many languages and boast many skills. They wait to serve Your Highness at your court as they serve all great kings. Also they seek to trade, if only given the opportunity and the honor of your protection and privileges, and in this way they will enrich you as they have the kings and princes in all lands where they have received protection. Indeed, not only here in Spain, but also in the lands of the Eastern Franks, the Jews are accustomed to learn many languages and possess great knowledge of all the customs and usages of monies, weights, and measures. In the kingdoms of Poland and Lithuania as well as in the lands of Rome and Venice, the Jewish exiles from France and Germany have risen to prominence and demonstrated their worth to their new lords.

Now, I have heard that there are, in the great city of Constantinople, Jews who have sent petitions and representatives to you so that you will not accept these Jews into your realm, saying that the Maghrebi Jews are paupers and will be a burden to Your Highness, and

also cause strife among other Jews. Yet, if it is true that many of the
refugees are poor, there are among them great scholars to lead them
in the ways of obedience and piety that are befitting to the children of
Israel. Our holy Torah teaches us humility, morality, fairness in trade,
respect for authority and care for the poor. Indeed, it is their respect
for the Law of God and for the men who are learned in its ways and
noble in their lineage that give the Jewish communities their strength,
their orderliness, and their moral guidance. Many of these refugees have
already come to settle in the holy cities of our ancient homeland, the
land of Israel, that you watch over as master and protector. Look and
see that they live in peace with all men! Moreover, the Holy Office of
the Rabbi Mayor of Spain is also willing to send monies with them in
order to help them settle in your lands, so that they will not be a burden
to Your Highness.

On why the Maghrebi Jews will prefer the lands of the Turks to the territories of the King of Spain

In the lands of Maghreb, and also in the kingdoms of Poland and
Lithuania, the recent wars and upheavals in these places have dislodged
many Jews from their homes, causing them to wander as sheep without
a shepherd. And although our lord king, the King of Spain, has sheltered
many of these in his domains both here and in his lands in Italy, and
protected them, yet there is a limit as to how many of the dispossessed
he can shield. Even the lands of the King of Spain that lie beyond the
sea,[10] these are not an adequate refuge for the Jews, for although they
are vast they possess few synagogues or houses of study, and the Jews
who go there occupy themselves with buying and selling and abandon
all piety and the study of our Law. The word of God is like a closed
book to them. Their mouths are filled with profanity, and they eat the
bread of the Gentiles and there is nothing left of them that is holy and
pure save the name "Jew." At hearing such stories my heart is filled with
sorrow and mourning. And knowing this to be their lot, how can I send
more sons of Israel to suffer such a fate?[11] Rather, we beseech you to

[10] This reference is to the colonies in the Americas.
[11] Compare this passage with Benveniste's description of Jewish life in the Iberian
colonies in the letter to the rabbis of Poland-Lithuania. It is not clear why he presented such different views of Jewish life in Asia and the Americas, but many scholars

open the gates of your cities to the Maghrebi Jews, for your empire is also vast, and it encompasses the lands of the Arabs whose language and customs are already familiar to them.

On the Jews as loyal subjects

To those who might speak out against the settlement of the Maghrebi Jews in your lands we respond in the following manner. As you are no doubt well aware, the Jews are an ancient and holy people. All peoples know and recognize that in our synagogues and study houses as in our homes and at our tables, the Jews are a people who praise the name of the One and True God. In this way, we have long lived among both Christians and Moors in peace and harmony, seeking only to serve God through the observance of the Law as He has charged us, and to serve earthly lords as they command. It is for this reason that all princes, kings, and emperors have always allowed the Jews to dwell in their lands, and have protected them, their rights, and their possessions. This law has been law among Jews, Christians, and Muslims throughout Spain, and in the lands of His Majesty the King of Spain where the children of Abraham have come to bring the great and holy Name of God to those peoples who previously lived without divine guidance.[12]

The children of Israel have always been good and faithful servants to their lords. Indeed, it is only through jealousy that lesser lords and lowborn preachers have conspired to turn the hearts of the kings against us. They incite the rabble, causing all manner of destruction to property, both Jewish and Gentile, showing contempt for order and without fear of royal justice. But you, great king, are of the lineage of good and pious lords. And thus I beg and petition you that your gates shall always be open to your servants, day and night, and never be shut against those who would serve Your Highness with their skills and increase the revenues in your domains. For as it is known, in those lands where the Jews are supported by just kings, we flourish and repay our lords through services, loyalty, taxes, and trade.

---

have surmised that he thought it unlikely that the Maghrebi Jews who came to Spain could be convinced to leave it for the colonial territories.

[12] Here Benveniste refers to the Christian missionaries in Asia and the Americas.

On the Jews and the Messiah

Moreover, we have heard rumors that some people in your lands believe that we Jews pray daily for the coming of the messiah, and await the time when we might regain power over all the world, and that it is for this reason that we seek to settle in the cities of the Holy Land so that our prayers will be better received by God. Yet these are naught but distortions and lies told by ignorant or malicious men. Verily, we dismiss such talk as baseless calumny by those who wish us ill, and madness by those of our own ranks who speak when they should listen. It is a great falsehood that no doubt arises from the confusion of the ignorant masses. Those Jews who settle in the land of Israel seek only to honor God, not to ask for vengeance. For in our days we pray only for a return of God's presence among us; that is, the fomenting of peace among all peoples through the establishment of divine justice, so that the world below may truly come to reflect the world above in harmony, balance, order, and peace. Likewise, our preachers preach decorum and respect for authority. They are paid through the generosity of their holy congregations and its wealthiest members, who delight in hearing discourses on the words of God.

On the Jews of Constantinople

We have heard that, in your own royal city of Constantinople, the Jews there are sometimes subject to the hatred and excesses of the mob, and it grieves us to hear of it. But this must not be seen as a result of their adherence to our holy faith. Rather, if their character be less than noble, it is only due to the fact that, at present, they lack the great sages that we have here in Spain. For the academies of Toledo, Salamanca, and Seville have no equal. They are the heirs to the academies of Babylonia and Yavneh, Cordoba and Lucena, and all questions that were formerly sent to the scholars of other lands are now directed to the sages of Spain. Notwithstanding there are some fine people among the Jews of Constantinople, but they are like sheep without a shepherd. And so it is that when they return home from their businesses, or on the Sabbath, and at other times when a man should turn to study and prayer, they engage instead in frivolous activities and diversions, for they have no teachers to guide them, and the great traditions of our holy sages are all but lost among them. In this matter, the acceptance within your realms and under your protection of the Jews of the Maghreb will be of great assistance, for at the heads of these communities stand men of great wisdom, piety, and refinement who, if only allowed to do so, would devote their fullest energies to your services and to the guidance of the Jews of your realm.

Is it not the place of just kings to order the good and prohibit the bad, to make laws and confer justice? As well you must know, it has been the tradition of all the princes in all the lands of the Jewish exile to safeguard the Jews as their royal treasure. Your own fathers, the great lords of the Turks, collected to the city of Constantinople all of the Jews of Greece[13] so that they might live there under direct royal protection. It is for these reasons that I most humbly supplicate Your Highness, and appeal to your great compassion and mercy to accept as settlers the refugees who wish to flee there that they may live and travel and trade safely and securely within your vast realms. If, in times past, there was a great Jewish multitude in the lands of Ishmael, so too can there be once again.

May the One True God strengthen you and prolong your days. I remain your humble servant, Don Joseph ben Jacob Abravanel y Benveniste, Rabbi Mayor and Royal Physician to His Majesty Don Carlos, King of Spain.

DOCUMENT 2
A letter of consolation and instruction to the rabbis of Poland and Lithuania (*ca.* 1673)

To the Illustrious Sages of the Holy Congregations of Poland and Lithuania, from Don Joseph ben Jacob Benveniste y Abravanel, Rabbi Mayor of all the Jews of Spain, I bid you abundant peace.

Consolation for the tribulations of the Jews of Poland

From the letter that you wrote to us, in which you poured out your grief over the destruction in your homeland and the many troubles that consume and scatter you, you wondered if God had almost hidden His

---

[13] These are the Romaniote (Greek) Jews, many of whom were forcibly relocated to Constantinople in the fifteenth century.

countenance from His people.[14] Yet you must know that our people still flourish in many lands. Here in the kingdom of Spain but also in the kingdom of Portugal, look and you will see how the light of Torah still shines! And also in the lands of the kings of Spain and Portugal that are across the sea, to the East and to the West,[15] there live a great number of Jews. And although many Jews who dwell in these distant lands are of the humblest origins and have no education in either medicine or philosophy or the science of grammar, and only the most rudimentary learning in our holy Torah, nonetheless they have risen to positions of great honor and wealth through their involvement in trade.

The Jews there trade in all manner of goods, such as diamonds, indigo, pepper, coffee, and tea. With their profits they buy the lands on which many of the goods that they trade are grown or mined, and this is something that is still denied to us in the lands owned by our lord and king the King of Spain. Those Jews who live and trade in lands of the East have also come to own the ships that are used in trade, so that they fill them with whatever merchandise is available, and from this merchandise earn profits.

The Jews who have come to dwell in India have learned the languages and also the customs of the many princes there, some who are sons of Ishmael and follow their religion, and some who are worshippers of stars and pray before idols. But the Jews there do not debate over matters of religion. Rather, they advise only in matters of trade, in the different values of the coins that are used by different peoples, in which they have become most expert, and also in the science of navigation and in map making. It is said that all the Christians from Spain and Portugal as well as those from England, France, and Holland who go to these lands to trade cannot buy or sell anything without the aid of the Jews. Thus, although in their homelands their priests speak against the Jews, whispering in the ears of their kings and governors and telling them all manner of lies about the Jews because of their hatred for us, and although because of these evil men our people have been expelled from many lands here in Edom, there in the lands of the East every man says: "Where can we find Jews to help us? For they know the languages

---

[14] A reference to the Chmielnicki pogroms of 1648.
[15] The Spanish and Portuguese colonies in India, the Philippines, and South America had already become home to a sizable population of Jewish merchants and plantation owners.

and the customs here, and we are naught but strangers, and we cannot buy and sell here without them."[16]

On the problem of the refugees

Now it is customary to allow the poorest members of your congregations to wander and to become refugees, like sheep without a shepherd. But when these unfortunate ones arrive in new lands they are a burden to the Jews there, and can offer no service to their lords, and in this way bring shame upon all Israel so that the princes and lords wish to shut their doors to even the wealthiest and noblest among us. For this reason you should take care to stop this practice, and instead to send with these refugees men of distinction, that is to say men of wisdom and understanding, learned in Torah, who know many languages for buying and selling and are familiar with the governments of the Gentiles and so that they may intercede on behalf of other Jews. These men must see that the poor do not become a burden upon the Gentiles and that they are taught morality and respect for authority from books of our sages of blessed memory.

Take great care in your dealings with the Gentiles, and do not enter into disputes with them. Be ethical in matters of business and in your personal conduct, and give no reason for them to rage against you, lest they say that our Torah does not teach proper morals. In this way will you find favor in their eyes.

On the Holy Office of the Rabbi Mayor and the rights of the Jews

Indeed, you must be well aware of the great services that I and my father, of blessed memory, have performed on behalf of the Jews of Italy when first he, then I, served as ambassadors of our lord, the King of Spain, in the great city of Rome. The influx of poor Jews from the lands of Ashkenaz and Poland to Rome, Venice, and the other cities of Italy had begun to incite anger and hatred among the Christian merchants and bankers there. There were those among the Christians who sought

---

[16] Economic necessity pushed the English, French, and Dutch trading companies to employ Jews in their colonial possessions, a practice that contrasted sharply with the anti-Jewish policies that prevailed in their homelands.

to restrict the settlement of the Jews, turning these already poor neighborhoods into prisons. Some even threatened to take from the Jews the keys to the gates to the Jewish quarters, robbing Israel of its sacred autonomy. They wished to close the Jews in at night, and open the gates again in the morning, and to control all day the number of Jews who could come and go. May such a thing never be allowed to happen! But my father, of blessed memory, interceded on behalf of the Jews and stopped this evil decree by virtue of the awe and respect that the lord pope and all the princes of Italy had for him and for his master the lord King of Spain. And in this way, the Holy Office of the Rabbi Mayor of Spain helped to build and to expand the Jewish *autónomas* in that land so that the Jews might come to live and trade in peace and independence to this day.

And surely you must know that it was the great rabbis of the Holy Office,[17] men of piety and vigor, who succeeded in stamping out the *marrano* heresy here in Spain, just as earlier generations of courtiers had done with the Karaite sectarians. Those who went out from the house of Judah and abandoned the heritage of their fathers were called *marranos*, which in the Spanish language means "swine," for that is what they most truly were. Many among them became enemies of Israel, revealing their sinfulness and that they had never been faithful Jews but instead had waited for the opportunity to throw off the yoke of heaven, and indulge in all manner of forbidden activities. They changed their faith and pursued sinfulness with uncommon zeal, so as to prove their value to their Christian brethren. I speak here not of those who converted against their will, for even many Christians viewed these conversions as invalid. Rather, I speak of those forced converts who, when given the chance to flee their cities and to seek shelter in other lands where they could openly take up the yoke of the Law, chose not to do so. These wicked ones accepted their plight as a liberation from the divine yoke, and an opportunity to pursue every vice. And these wicked ones dissembled so in matters of faith, and caused such enmity among the Christians, that the king and queen sought to punish apostate and Jew alike and to exile their faithful servants from our homeland.

---

[17] In Spain, the Holy Office of the Rabbi Mayor greatly outlived the Catholic Holy Office of the Inquisition, upon which it was modeled. The crown dissolved the latter in the late sixteenth century, but continued to use the institution of the Rabbi Mayor for centuries as an effective way of governing the Jewish population of its far-flung empire.

But Don Isaac Abravanel, may his memory be a blessing, stopped the destruction of his people. He acted zealously for the Law of God, and in order to preserve the good and honest life of the remnant of Israel that is in Spain he enforced the separation of the faithful Jews from the apostates, ordering that no Jew should communicate with the wicked, nor accord them any favor, nor stay with them under the same roof. And in this way he nullified the evil decree of the Christians, and the wealthiest men of our community also gave the king and queen many gifts and canceled the debts that they had incurred with the men of our community.

On the Jews of the Maghreb and Ottoman Empire

On the matter of our brethren from your lands who seek refuge here in Spain, we must advise against this. It is true that the lands of the kings of Spain and Portugal are rich and that their Jews are honored and protected, but as you must know, we have already begun to take in the refugees from the recent destruction and tribulations in the lands of the Maghreb.[18] Many have already come here to Spain, although truly we have little room for them. By order of our lord king, the Jews who come here must settle among us, crowding our neighborhoods until we can no longer move. And still more come every day. And though they live among us they remain apart, refusing to join our holy congregations or bow to the authority of our councilors and sages. I recount these things with sorrow and dread. And I say that indeed there are many among these refugees who are charlatans and who pass themselves off as physicians, although they know no real science. Indeed, they are no more than wonder workers and vendors of magic spells. Furthermore, many make promises to the Christian lords that they have connections to great wealth in Africa, with royal concessions to mine gold and transport all manners of goods, but these are lies, for they are no more than petty merchants.

    The Maghrebi Jews that come here to Spain do not wish to join our communities, but stand aloof from us. But when they fall into debt,

---

[18] The reference is to the exodus of Jews from Morocco that was sparked by the repressive policies of Moulay Rashid and Moulay Ismail, from 1670 to 1672. See also Benveniste's letter to Mehmed IV, published here.

their synagogues and public buildings are taken from them – which is a disgrace to all Jews – and the light of Torah is extinguished in their communities, and it is left to us to support them. Their rabbis and wise men, together with the heads of the richest and most noble families, claim lineage from the Jews of Spain who left this land many generations ago as *anusim*,[19] who fled the lands of Spain in order to return to the faith of our fathers there in the lands of Ishmael.[20] These have indeed kept the good customs of our land, speaking our language, learning Torah and science, and loving justice. Still, many others claim this noble lineage falsely.

For this reason, we have sent a letter to Sultan Mehmed, King of the Turks, in Constantinople, beseeching him to open his gates to the Jews of the Maghreb. And if you wish, we will write a letter to him on behalf of the Jews of your lands as well. Be not afraid of the King of the Turks, for if your people go and settle in his lands surely the Lord will be with you. You have heard of the tribulations of the Greek Jews, whom the Turks expelled from their ancient lands, taking them to the royal city of Constantinople.[21] But this dispersion is not the same as the many expulsions from the lands of the Christians. Whereas the latter expelled Jews contrary to their own laws and customs, or to blot out the name of Israel, the Turks removed them not as a punishment but as a means of concentrating them in the capital city, which is the greatest of the East, and to make them a people more useful to the king. This is his right, and the Jews there happily serve him, for it is our nature since ancient days to serve just kings.

Perhaps you have begun to repair the breach between the Jews and the lords of Poland and Lithuania, and this would be a very good thing. For it is true that in our days the children of Israel are most welcomed and their lives safeguarded in the lands in which the Catholic Church predominates. This is because the Catholic Church is the most ancient and honored of all the churches in the lands of Edom. Their chief, the lord pope, commands them to respect the Jews as guardians

---

[19] That is, "forced" converts, and thus still considered to be Jews in Jewish law.
[20] Some of the Moroccan refugees had left Spain following the riots of 1391, and had preserved much of their Spanish heritage.
[21] A reference to the forced migration, or *sürgün*, of Romaniote Jews to Constantinople in the fifteenth century. Fear of the Ottomans' harsh treatment of the Jews discouraged the refugees from Poland-Lithuania from seeking settlement there.

of the Law of God. But the sectarians[22] have no regard for the Jews, nor do they respect the traditions of their own faith.

On sacred texts, printing, and the study of the *Kabbalah*

I will now speak to you about one of the fundamental matters of our faith, namely what is permitted and what is forbidden with regard to the study of our sacred Torah. We urge you to guard against the dangerous doctrines of secret knowledge, of the books of the *Kabbalah* and of the *Sefirot*.[23] You should be more active in guarding against the spread of these books, as has been the practice here in Spain. In truth, our sages of blessed memory wrote "the more books the more knowledge." But, due to our many sins, ours is not a generation of understanding and discernment, and the dissemination of knowledge without control brings only confusion and strife. For this reason, my great-grandfather, the Rabbi Mayor Don Samuel Benveniste, saw fit to control and regulate the printing of books in Spain. Here, while any man may print books of stories and popular accounts of travels or histories in any language he chooses, books on sacred subjects written in Hebrew or Aramaic and meant for the study and understanding of our holy Law may only be published by the Holy Office of the Rabbi Mayor, and bearing our seal. In this way, we have succeeded in enlightening the wise and protecting the simple. Look and see how different it is among the Jews of other lands! For we have seen with our own eyes that the Jews who live and dwell in Italy see fit to print the greatest and most sacred secrets, confusing the minds of the simple and distorting knowledge. We instruct you to intervene in this matter, and to take care to prevent such practices and the many problems and blasphemies that they cause.

In every age, our great men and sages have warned against the controlling knowledge of our holy Torah, since its secrets should only pass from the trembling lips of a master to the ears of a discerning student. But in our days, so many speak before they have finished studying,

---

[22] A reference to Protestant churches, perhaps most likely the Lutherans and the Church of England, which maintained virulent anti-Jewish policies throughout the early modern period. The exclusion of Jews in Protestant lands stood in contrast to their presence in Catholic countries such as Spain, Portugal, and Poland-Lithuania.

[23] Literally, "emanations." The doctrine of the *Sefirot* was central to medieval Jewish mystical tradition (*Kabbalah*) that had become popular among the Jews of Poland-Lithuania.

and print books before they have finished learning, because they care only to see others read their books. These men seek only honor and fame, but what honor is there in deforming the tradition of our ancestors, and in seeking praise from the vulgar? It would be better that they were silent, and produced no books but faithful copies of the works of the greatest men of our tradition.

In Italy, books are printed without regard to the nature of their contents, but only as a means to gain profit. Some take a few scrolls here and a portion there and think, mistakenly, that they have collected the whole of this sacred tradition and print it, so that the eyes of any man might gaze upon these words. And so men read these books without proper preparation, and without a teacher to guide them, and they understand nothing of their true meaning, for they are like a locked chest that does not reveal its secrets. It is for this reason that, here in Spain, we have taken great care to restrict the study of such texts to all but the most accomplished scholars. We have banned the printing of the *Zohar* and other such books, for we see that they are a danger to those without a proper grounding in the fundamentals of our faith.

The proper focus of study should be on the holy Torah, and on the laws and customs that our sages have derived from it. Those with discerning minds and willing hearts should restrict their study to philosophy, natural sciences, and especially medicine for it is well known that it is through our success in medicine that we have gained favor in the eyes of the great men and lords of the earth. But regarding the *Zohar* and other books of the *Kabbalah*, it would be better that they turn away from these books. Thus we encourage you as good and wise leaders to guard against the publication of books that reveal that which should be hidden and make popular that which should be restricted. Indeed, if it is true that a preacher should refrain from expounding in public on a complicated matter of our tradition, how much more so should we take care not to allow such generalities and distortions to be printed in books, that can travel farther and live longer than any preacher.

And on the matter of *halakha*,[24] the great bulwark of our faith, I am told that there are those among you who wish to establish even more printing presses, both in your lands and in the Italian cities, and to print the great and holy works of our master, Rabbi Moses ben Maimon of blessed memory, and to translate them into *lashon*

---

[24] Jewish law.

Ashkenaz.[25] Those who speak thus say that we must make accommodations for those who sin because they cannot read and study the *lashon ha-kodesh.*[26] They wish to combine the traditions of the Ashkenazim with those of the sages of Sepharad, weaving together the *sefer mitzvot gadol,* the *arba'ah turim,* and the *mishneh torah.*[27] This, too, I must oppose. While it is good and proper for all Jews to study works of *halakha,* I would argue that such translations would only result in lowering our holy Torah. For if a man cannot be bothered to read Hebrew, or to study with a learned teacher, then what good are translations? Better he should follow the dictates of those who are able to do so. For this reason, here in Spain, we have contented ourselves with the wisdom of our teachers and have avoided translations or the composition of new codes of law. Indeed, this is what we have counseled our brothers, the sages of the Jews living in the Holy Land and throughout the lands of the Ishmaelites. And they have seen fit to follow our advice, and they are filled with humility and awe for the scholars of the past, saying: who am I to add to this great tradition? It will be enough if we can learn and teach the words of our teacher Rabbi Moses ben Maimon, of blessed memory, and of the other great sages of the past. There, too, the wise labor against the spread of superstitions and the belief in amulets and other abominations that have become popular among the ignorant. The works of *Kabbalah* are not to be found in their study houses, as in your lands and the lands of Italy, where they are studied by the Gentiles, of all people!

Also, regarding what you wrote about the faith of the children of Israel in your lands, that they no longer follow the authority of your wise men and judges, may God protect them, let me respond that it is natural that they behave in this way in times of tragedy such as those that you have recently suffered. This is all the more reason why you must work day and night to give them guidance, shoring up breaches and demanding obedience to the Law.

Discussion questions

1. Compare and contrast Benveniste's characterization of the Maghrebi Jews in each letter. How do you account for these differences?

---

[25] That is, Yiddish. [26] That is, Hebrew.
[27] The great medieval legal codes of Ashkenazi and Sephardi Jews.

2. What role did the Chief Rabbis of Spain play in the promotion of Jewish rights in other lands?
3. Why did Ferdinand and Isabella threaten to expel the Jews of Spain, and how did the Jews avoid this fate?
4. Describe Benveniste's attitude toward Jewish mysticism.
5. According to Benveniste, what qualities did the Jews possess that made them ideal subjects?
6. What might the Jewish world look like today if the Jews had actually been expelled from Spain?

4 WHAT IF THE "GHETTO" HAD NEVER BEEN CONSTRUCTED?

Bernard Dov Cooperman

What if Jews had never been required to live in ghettos in so many cities of late medieval and early modern Europe? The question may seem to be little more than a light-hearted amusement for bored historians. But, as is true of many counterfactual scenarios, it opens up a Pandora's Box of revision that forces us to reconsider basic questions about the Jewish past. Why did ghettos emerge? What was their function? What living arrangements did ghettos replace? If not in ghettos, where would Jews have lived? And under what conditions? We can find sources that describe life in the ghettos; but how shall we describe what never happened? Imagining an alternative path of historical development is especially difficult, moreover, because the European ghetto was constructed not only of stone walls and iron gates. It was also "constructed" in the minds of historians and in the collective Jewish consciousness. Before we can imagine how Jewish life might have evolved without the ghetto, therefore, we must explore the construction of its very meaning.

Let us begin with the word itself. Despite clever attempts to argue otherwise, there is little doubt that the term "ghetto" originated in the early sixteenth century. In 1516, Venetian authorities allowed Jewish settlement in an abandoned industrial zone called the *ghetto nuovo* (new foundry) on the outskirts of their city. Later, in 1541, the Jews' residential area was extended to the contiguous *ghetto vecchio* (old foundry) zone. Over time, the prosaic origins of the word "ghetto" faded from memory and the term came to denote a restricted Jewish residential quarter. When Venice extended the Jewish zone yet again in 1633, the appended area was therefore called a *ghetto nuovissimo* (newest ghetto), even though there had never been a foundry there previously. Similarly, in Rome, the closed zone marked off in 1555 as a "Jewish quarter" or *serraglio* was commonly referred to as a ghetto by its inhabitants at least from 1589. By the end of the sixteenth century, the term had become universalized and was applied elsewhere in Italy and abroad.[1] The gates of the Venetian ghetto were dramatically forced open by Napoleonic forces in 1797. The gates of Rome's ghetto, the last in Europe, were finally removed in 1870.

I emphasize the early modern Italian history of the word "ghetto" not just for the sake of lexical accuracy. By focusing attention on sixteenth-century Venice, I wish to exclude more modern usages of the word that would hopelessly confuse our inquiry. Today, the word "ghetto" brings to mind the brutalities of the Nazi era – overcrowded urban prison camps in Eastern Europe, where Jews were starved and enslaved until they were shipped to their deaths.[2] In the United States, meanwhile, the word evokes inner-city neighborhoods with high concentrations of ethnic minorities, poverty, crime, and social pathology.[3] These modern uses of the term have clouded the original meaning of the early modern Jewish ghetto, which was substantially different in origin and function.

The significance of the original Jewish ghetto has also been obscured by historians who have "constructed" it as a key narrative element in the grand tale of Jewish history.[4] Jewish historians have long used the term "ghetto" loosely as a keyword to refer to almost *any* Jewish residential zone.[5] In so doing, they have universalized a concrete site of local topography into an abstract concept. As a result, the "Ghetto" – now capitalized – has become a stock metonym for the premodern Jewish historical experience. Indeed, it has come to epitomize the total denial of the Jews' right to participate in civil society.

One of the best-known scholars to popularize this meaning of the word was the Jewish historian, Salo Baron, who in a famous 1928 article described "Ghetto and Emancipation" as polar opposites.[6] The "generally accepted view," he argued, imagines the premodern Jew as a "prisoner in the Ghetto." There, the Jew lived "in a state of extreme wretchedness under medieval conditions subject to incessant persecution and violence" until the French Revolution and the Enlightenment "opened up the gates." Almost half a century later, and in a very different Jewish world, Jacob Katz continued this line of argumentation. His 1973 book, *Out of the Ghetto*, described Jewish modernization as "the process through which the Jews, isolated in ghettos on the fringe of society...made their first steps toward integrating into the mainstream." For these and many other writers, "ghetto" was not just a spatial term: it epitomized the essence of an era. For Katz and other scholars, the premodern period was simply "Ghetto Times."[7]

From works of high-level academic scholarship, the dark and metaphoric ghetto moved on to become a stock concept in textbooks and popular histories. Generations of American college students were introduced to *The Course of Modern Jewish History* by Howard Sachar, who led his readers past the "majestic silhouette of spires and battlements...of Frankfurt" to "a dwarfed, walled-off collection of alleys and creaking ancient buildings, its ugliness and loneliness...a prison community...This little encincture – a hideous anomaly in one of Europe's most dynamic market communities – was the *Judengasse*, the ghetto of the Jews."[8]

In popular histories, "ghetto" became a term of opprobrium for all that was to be remembered only with a shudder. In Michael Goldfarb's enthusiastic and triumphalist *Emancipation*, to take one recent example, Jewish modernity (equated with "Revolution and Renaissance") is rooted in "liberating Jews from the Ghetto." Jumbling the many diverse patterns of Jewish settlement indiscriminately together, Goldfarb informed his readers that European Jews had been "sequestered in rural hamlets or locked away at night in restricted areas of towns and cities."[9] Recent Israeli writers have put their own spin on the terminology, equating those who reject the mature freedom and responsibilities associated with life in the Jewish nation-state with people choosing to live in a ghetto.[10]

In a parallel progression, we can find the term "ghetto" deployed adjectivally and nostalgically in popular Jewish discourse to describe an authentic place that was lost in the passage to modernity. While the "ghetto Jew" might still be a caricature, in this approach he or she also became a font of Jewish wisdom, the very model of the piety, domesticity, and morality that assimilated generations wished to find in the past. *Ghettoliteratur* was the generic term for this style of writing.[11] In the English-speaking world, the usage is associated especially with Israel Zangwill, who described his book, *Children of the Ghetto*, as "a study through typical figures of a race whose persistence is the most remarkable fact in the history of the world, the faith and morals of which it has so largely molded."[12]

The word ghetto has thus become an essential element in the Jewish vocabulary, a key feature of that "socially constructed" imaginary through which chaotic change was constantly reshaped into continuous Jewish identity.[13] For popular writers and for academic historians alike, ghetto walls defined not just the topography, but the very essence of the premodern Jewish everyday. Intent themselves on escaping what the ghetto *must have been*, modern Jewish historians missed what the ghetto really was. Paradoxically, I suggest that a counterfactual approach to examining what might have been may give us a better understanding of the ghetto's actual significance.

Kazimierz: Cracow's "Jewish city"

To understand the early modern ghetto, we begin our investigation not in Venice, as lexical purity would require, but almost five hundred miles to the northeast in the Polish city of Cracow. When the medieval fortress town was chartered in 1257 and given a measure of urban autonomy under so-called "Magdeburg Law," the steady stream of new settlers from the Germanic west included a significant number of Jews. During the ensuing century and a half of urban development, a growing urban patriciate – heavily Germanic in origin and mercantile in occupation – organized to seek group privileges, autonomous jurisdiction, and control over market space.[14] Population growth within the enclosed urban area inevitably reinforced both the stratification of the populace and the functional specialization of space. Competition over real estate in the city was increased by the spatial demands of the Akademia Krakowska (the forerunner of Jagiellonian University). Revived in 1400 under royal sponsorship, that institution made constant demands on its neighbors in the "Jews' Street" (*Judengasse*; later St. Anne's Street). In 1469, Jews ceded their older communal buildings to the Akademia in exchange for new space. At the same time, the town's organized Christian merchants waged an ongoing battle against what they saw as illegitimate Jewish competition. In 1485, the city's Jews collectively promised to encroach no further on Christian trading space in the town market, but this promise was often honored only in the breach, as Jews found ways to circumvent the ban and eventually had it repealed. More than once, tensions exploded into open rioting when a devastating fire, a military invasion, or the incendiary words of a wandering preacher like Juan de Capistrano (1453–4) exacerbated local social and economic divisions.[15] Finally, in 1495, Cracow's Jews were once again relocated – this time across a branch of the Vistula to Kazimierz, a separate urban jurisdiction established in 1335 where there already was a nuclear Jewish community (Figure 9).

Should we label the developments in Cracow as ghettoization? Certainly Majer Bałaban, the author of the foundational history of the city's Jewry, thought so. He writes of "the expulsion of the Jews from Cracow" and often replaces the contemporary term for Kazimierz's "Jewish city" (vicus judaicus) with the anachronistic term, "ghetto," emphasizing the gates that separated that area from the Christian part of town.[16] He similarly dismisses the official language of the 1469 legal document by which Jews "voluntarily, out of good will and considered opinion," exchanged their current real estate holdings for other land. For him, the surviving cession text is "the only witness to a tragic agreement . . . to the sighs of past time, and to the tears spilt by the leaders of the community and the simple folk of the ancient Jewish community of Cracow."[17] Bałaban also disregards the terminology of the 1485 document in which the Jewish elders, in the name of the entire community, ceded their trading rights in Cracow "of our own will and without being forced in any way." Bałaban writes:

> How much bitter irony is contained within these words? How many sacrifices were made and how many tears spilt? What threats and terror were presumably applied by the burghers before the heads of the community went to the town hall to publicly forego their human rights – to forego their right to make an honest living?[18]

Thus, Jewish Kazimierz is portrayed as an imposed and restrictive enclosure, an inherently unfair source of constant suffering inspired by religious hatred – in short, a classic ghetto.

More recent Polish historians have challenged Bałaban's interpretation and pointed to evidence of a limited but ongoing Jewish residence in Cracow proper. They have insisted that Jews remained intimately involved in the economic life of the city, which lay just across a short bridge from their assigned neighborhood.[19] Even in

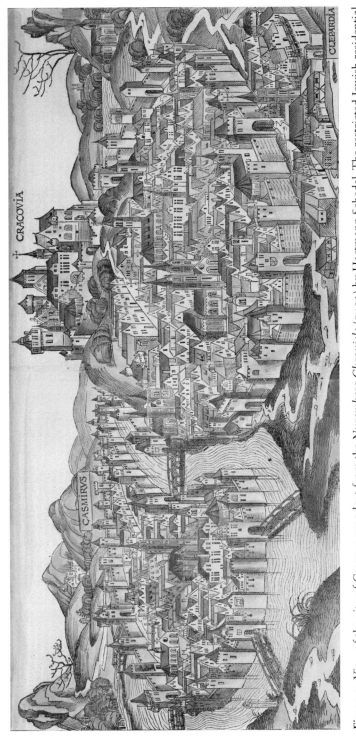

Figure 9. View of the city of Cracow, woodcut from the *Nuremberg Chronicle* (1493) by Hartmann Schedel. The restricted Jewish residential zone of Kazimierz (left) actually protected the Jewish community. It provided them with their own licensed zone of settlement in the city.

Kazimierz, the zone assigned to the Jews was not at first a fixed, walled environment. For decades the Jews were engaged in constant residential rivalry with Christians. Jews continuously bought up properties owned by Christians in the so-called *vicus judaicus*, although Christians continued to live in the area at least until 1564. (In that year, the Jews successfully petitioned King Sigismund Augustus to forbid Christian settlement in the Jewish quarter – thereby effectively receiving the right *de non tolerandis Christianis*!) This Jewish zone continued to expand de facto and even de jure; at least until 1608, the royal government was willing to accommodate the growing Jewish population with more space, despite the objections of the town's Christian population. The boundary between the Jewish and Christian neighborhoods was converted from a fence of some sort (*parkan*) to a more formal "wall" in 1627 with three gates. Closed at night, these gates were manned by Jewish guards. Even after that, individual Jews continued to buy property and to reside outside the Jewish zone.[20]

Whether or not the Jewish residential zone in Cracow should be described as a ghetto, the realities on the ground in Kazimierz reveal the range of factors that were involved in the formulation, mechanics, and variability of imposed spatial segregation in the late medieval and early modern eras. They help us recognize that the ghetto was an urban quarter *defined by law, both in a positive and a negative sense.* On the one hand, charters and grants delineated the zone where Jews were given the right to settle; on the other hand, laws and regulations often (but not always) precluded their dwelling or even trading in specific other zones within a city. Specifics varied not only from place to place but even in a single location over time. Ghetto walls might be more symbolic than physical, and in any case were never impermeable, if only because gates were open all or much of the time. Commercial and personal contacts continued across these often labile boundaries, and even residential segregation was not necessarily absolute. Above all, ghettos were urban real estate and were inevitably shaped by the same forces that affect cities everywhere: physical location, migration patterns, housing prices, and political influence.[21]

None of this is to ignore the invidiousness of the ghetto. Gaining control over a specific area implied losing access to another. Guaranteed settlement rights in a restricted zone inevitably attracted further settlers, leading to overcrowding and concomitant problems of social welfare and control. Jews of the era were rarely, if ever, in a position to dictate their place in urban society unilaterally, and any success they achieved would necessarily be partial. Still, the early modern ghetto was a negotiated space reflecting a compromise between the Jews' needs and demands, on the one hand, and those of a legally recognized, municipal leadership, on the other. The ghetto was part of the contingent municipal and social reality familiar to anyone who has ever bought or sold real estate.

What then would have happened if Cracow's "Jewish city" had never been constructed? Christian burghers would have continued to lobby for the Jews' expulsion or at least their economic restriction. The Jews who migrated to Cracow, for example those expelled from Czech lands at the beginning of the sixteenth century, would have had to turn further east or south, to the less developed zones of the Lithuanian Grand Duchy, Moldavia, Hungary, or the Ottoman lands. Is it perhaps an overly macabre exercise in historical imagination to remember that many of the descendants of those Jews who settled in the eastern Ukrainian provinces fell victim a century later to the Khmel'nitz'kyi uprising?[22] If we see the ghetto as a solution, or at least a partial resolution, to economic and social tensions, we realize that the alternative could have been far worse. At least we can say this: the *vicus judaicus* expressed, in the terminologies of municipal jurisdiction and zoning, the negotiated and shifting balance between real-world commercial and demographic forces. To imagine its nonexistence is to imagine a world in which these forces did not exist – that is, to imagine a Cracow that was still a fortress surrounded by farms and not yet a growing center of trade and population. Insofar as the "Jewish city" successfully balanced these pressures, to imagine that it did not exist is to imagine a world in which the large *kahal kadosh* (Holy Community) of Cracow and its brilliant cultural and religious legacy never arose at all.

Economics, demographics, and the ghetto of Venice

I have suggested that Kazimierz's "ghetto" was established not by any arbitrary act of hostility, but by the broader demographic and structural forces that shaped early modern Polish and Jewish urban history. Can we say the same about the walled enclosure for Jews in Venice – by definition the original and "true" ghetto? Historians have usually portrayed Venice's ghetto not in terms of zoning policy but as an expression of Christian anti-Jewish hostility. The famed historian, Heinrich Graetz, for example, labeled Venetian policy as the first instance of an Italian state opting to imitate Germanic hatreds toward Jews.[23] This view reached its apogee in the writing of the sociologist Richard Sennett, for whom Venice's ghetto was an "urban condom," a "prophylactic space" intended to protect Venetians from touching the "impure" Jews whom they needed for financial services, but upon whom they projected their own self-loathing. Spatial segregation, Sennett writes, "increased the Jew's daily Otherness" and "raised the stakes of contact with the outside world" if a Jew were so bold as to venture outside the walls. The ghetto itself created hatred and paranoid fear of the Jew, thus making life far more dangerous for "People of the Word" who "for over three thousand years [!] . . . had survived in small cells mixed among their oppressors, a people sustained in their faith no matter where they lived."[24] In other words, the ghetto created, or at least enhanced, the very social pathologies that made the Jews need walls for self-protection and identity maintenance.

Scholars are often tempted to read proofs of their pet theories into the most unlikely places, and this may explain why Sennett's rhetoric about the Venetian ghetto is so hyperbolic, though it does not justify his outright errors of fact. He approaches the Venetian ghetto as part of his ongoing exploration of the interrelation between urban architecture, on the one hand, and the degree to which personal identity (interiority) was censored or expressed in public space, on the other. To make his broader point, Sennett quotes selectively from the contemporary memoir of Rabbi Leon Modena to prove that Venetian Christians projected all kinds of crimes on the Jews behind the ghetto walls, "such as the imprisonment of Christian children in the Ghetto, and an orgy of circumcision." Sennett writes that, in 1636, "fantasies surrounding concealment came to a head" when the ghettoized "Jews suffered one of the worst pogroms they had ever known in Europe." It is not clear where Sennett got the impression that there was a terrible pogrom in Venice in that (or any other) year, but in the cited passage Rabbi Modena was not discussing a fantasy, but a *real* accusation that Jews in the ghetto had been fencing stolen property! Modena's own son-in-law had been among those found guilty. Not content with such real-world crime, however, Sennett turns it into a somewhat garbled allusion to the blood libel and then throws an imagined pogrom into the mix for good measure. Far from describing fantastic hatred, Modena in fact stressed that the ghettoized Jews had been universally loved by Christians until this scandal ruined their reputation and labeled them "a band of thieves."[25]

Of course, we should take Modena's assertion of universal Christian love for Jews prior to 1636 with a considerable quantity of salt. But even so, it raises a crucial question: how could a Jew locked each night behind ghetto walls imagine relations with the outside world as positive? The answer, I would suggest, is that Venetian Jews of the day had a realistic understanding of the ghetto's historical significance. Previously, with brief exceptions, Jews had simply not been allowed to live in Venice at all. Jewish moneylenders and petty traders (mostly vendors of second-hand goods) could come to the city in search of customers only during fairs or with special fifteen-day passes; afterwards they would have to return across the lagoon to Mestre and wait for various lengths of time until they might apply for another pass. When it came to the most lucrative areas of Venetian commerce and the Levant trade, the Jews (like other foreigners) had been blocked altogether by the rigidly protectionist policies of the merchant-governed state. What was astonishing, therefore, was that when Jews flooded into the city in 1509 as refugees fleeing the forces of the League of Cambrai during the early sixteenth-century Italian Wars, Venetian authorities decided to let them stay and, a few years later, allocated them the zone known as the ghetto for their exclusive residential use. Reports speak of five hundred Jews in the city in 1509, and of far more by 1516. While the terms of the arrangement had to be renegotiated regularly and expulsion sometimes seemed to threaten, the invitation held good and Jews continued to live legally in Venice under its provisions for centuries to come – indeed until the very end of the republican era in 1797 when the matter became moot.[26]

It is unclear why the Venetians changed their longstanding policy toward Jews, but we can point to the important role in the local economy played by Jewish moneylenders, such as Anselmo del Banco (Asher Meshullam), who provided relatively low-cost credit to the populace as well as significant tax revenues to the state. Venice had long licensed such pawnbanks in Mestre on the mainland, and in 1503 extended a ten-year settlement privilege in the city proper to three Jewish bankers. Seen from the perspective of policy elsewhere in central Italy, this was not a radical decision: time-limited residence licenses to Jewish pawnbankers were regularly issued in many cities, including those on the Venetian terraferma. The new residency privileges were also related to the fact that the moneylending business was part of a broader commercial sector that included trade in second-hand goods, the rental of occasional clothing and furniture, and the retailing of low-end cloths.[27] In the late fifteenth century, Venetian legislators were still trying to restrict this trade. No doubt because of complaints from Christian shopowners who resented the competition, councilors forbade renting storage facilities in Venice to the Jews and insisted that Jewish merchants come into the city only at the time of fairs.[28] But the underground economy had its own logic, and by 1515 Venetian authorities had agreed to license ten such shops that were soon set up in the city's main business district, the Rialto.[29] Finally, Venetian authorities may have admitted more Jews to the city as a way to increase their control over a very "gray" credit market and force down the cost of credit to consumers. Locating the shops in Venice closed off certain practices that were known often to lead to abuse.[30] Over the years, the government repeatedly succeeded in reducing the maximum legal interest rate, and eventually the Jews were required to maintain three *banchi dei poveri* where interest was held to an unprofitable 5 percent.[31] The Venetians had effectively turned the Jews' private banks into regulated *Monti di Pietà* – charitable lending institutions that required support subsidies from the larger Jewish community, whose members were now essentially paying a fee for the privilege of living in Venice.[32]

These facts provide no more than a partial explanation for the Jewish community licensed in Venice in 1515, however. Ultimately, the decision to admit the Jews was based, as in Cracow, upon demographic and economic imperatives. To begin with, the Jewish population of the Venetian region had swelled as a result of migration from German- and French-speaking areas. Over the course of the sixteenth century additional Jewish refugees made their way to Venice from elsewhere in Italy and from the Iberian Peninsula. Economic forces were also transforming Venice: the once powerful Queen of the Adriatic had little choice but to open her market to the increased presence of these small-scale merchants, just as she would have to admit Levantine and Ponentine merchants later in the century.[33] But whatever the reasons, the second decade of the sixteenth century was marked by the revolutionary decision to accept a Jewish residential and commercial presence of unrestricted numbers in the city proper.

Of course, admitting so many Jews into the city created social anxiety. Old superstitions and prejudices were still very much alive even among the elites of Venice, as is made clear in the Senate debates recorded by Marin Sanudo when the charter came up for renewal a few years later.[34] And even if the fulminations of old-timers in the Senate could be dismissed, there were also more substantive reasons to protest the admission of the Jews. Their shops competed with Christian shops for space and custom. Their homes and institutions put direct pressures on the real estate market. In Venice, as in any city, the influx of a large immigrant population created pressures on the existing pattern of social and physical realities. The answer to this demographic and economic challenge was to confine the Jewish residences and shops to a ghetto, which was finally established in 1516.[35]

Seen from this economic and urban perspective, the origins of the Venetian ghetto were not dissimilar from those of the "Jewish city" in Cracow. Driven by broader patterns of migration and urban growth, Jews were attracted to settle in Venice and ended up competing with established commercial groups, who were unable to block the newcomers outright. Municipal zoning rules were invoked to define and limit the Jews' residential and commercial space. Paradoxically, the very stability of the assigned space allowed for, and continued to attract, Jewish immigration and expanded Jewish trade. In 1541 a contiguous block of buildings, the so-called *ghetto vecchio*, was incorporated into the Jewish zone to accommodate Levantine Jewish merchants chartered to develop trade between Venice and the Ottoman Empire. In 1589, the ghetto was expanded yet again when a *ghetto nuovissimo* (newest ghetto) was enclosed for the use of Portuguese merchants who received their own charter. Even with these two extensions, however, the ghetto could not easily accommodate the Jews who sought to come. Architectural evidence shows that apartments were subdivided and buildings given extra stories to provide more residential units. The ghetto buildings became the tallest residences in Venice.[36] If the ghetto had been intended to limit the number of Jews in Venice, it proved ill-suited for that purpose. The ghetto is what allowed early modern Venice to conceive, confront, and accommodate a substantial Jewish community for the first time in its history.

And so we can ask: what would have happened had Venice not constructed the ghetto and admitted Jews? First, one of the largest Jewish collectives in Western Europe, a community of some 2,500, never would have arisen. The much smaller community on the mainland would not have expanded for lack of direct and continuous access to the

Rialto market. Second, the ghetto in Venice was part and parcel of an economic license. Without the ghetto, Jews in Venice could not have participated in the Levant trade or later in the vast Iberian trade networks. In the centuries before the internet, when merchants required physical access to markets, segregated residential arrangements opened the crucial Venetian markets to Jews. And, finally, it is hard to imagine the explosion of Hebrew printing for which sixteenth-century Venice is so justly famous without the large Jewish presence in Venice. Admittedly, the two most important men in the story of Venetian Hebrew printing did not live in the ghetto – Daniel Bomberg, because he was a Christian who hailed from Antwerp, and his main assistant, Cornelius Adelkind, because he converted to Christianity. But the Bomberg workshop, which defined and designed almost all the central Jewish canonical texts from the rabbinic Bible to the Talmud, would have been inconceivable without its scholarly Jewish editors, proofreaders, and – most importantly – local Jewish clientele, all of whom were residents in the ghetto. Without the ghetto, in short, some of early modern Jewish history's most precious cultural treasures would never have been created.

The ghetto as religious discrimination: the case of Rome

To discuss the ghetto merely in terms of zoning policy and competition over real estate may seem somewhat ingenuous. After all, the ghetto was an expression of religious and ethnic discrimination, if not outright hatred. Surely religious difference was more than an available set of rhetorical categories that early modern Europeans used to articulate their economic interests? The medieval Catholic Church had regularly sought to limit contact between Jews and the faithful, restricting the presence of Jews in public spaces on holy days, forcing them to wear badges in public, and prohibiting Christian domestics from living in Jewish homes. Are these medieval regulations not directly connected to the demands for separate Jewish urban quarters?[37] An often cited proof text is the 1267 conciliar decree issued at Breslau (Wroclaw) insisting that Jews in cities and villages reside next to each other and that their homes be separated from those of the rest of the population by a fence, wall, or trench.[38] We do not know whether or not this demand was ever enforced, but it was clearly not a regular part of Church policy. Note that it had to be justified by the claim that Christianity was new in Poland and therefore unusually fragile and vulnerable. The clerics realized they needed special justification for these unusual measures to restrict opportunities for social contact with Jews, "lest the Christian population here . . . succumb to the influence of the counterfeit faith and evil habits of the Jews living in their midst."[39]

Of course, overly free social contact between Christians and Jews evoked religious anxiety, but it is therefore especially noteworthy that medieval popes did not pursue a policy of spatial segregation in their own territories – particularly in the city of Rome – until a relatively late date.[40] It was only in 1555 that Pope Paul IV famously ordered the creation of a ghetto in Rome (and papal Ancona) with the bull *Cum nimis absurdum* (Figure 10). Historians have long interpreted the policy as an expression of the Catholic Reformation – that is, of the puritanical rigidity exemplified in the rulings of the Council of Trent and of the doctrinaire reaction to the rise of European Protestantism. Further, the bull has been linked to the personality and piety of Pope Paul IV, a man so rigidly austere that his reign was resented and his death celebrated by the entire population of Rome. As the Inquisitor General, he had ordered the burning of the Talmud in the Campo dei Fiori in 1553; after donning the papal tiara, he reversed years of tolerance toward former *conversos* in Ancona by ordering several dozen burned at the stake in that same Roman piazza. Was it any surprise that less than two months after he was elected pope, he forced Rome's Jews to sell any real estate they held and concentrate their community in a narrow walled enclosure?[41]

The most recent scholar to take up this approach to ghettoization was Kenneth Stow who, in a hallmark 1977 study, described *Cum nimis absurdum* as marking a tactical change in the Church's longstanding campaign to bring the Jews to Christian truth. Motivated by intense eschatological expectations, Paul IV abandoned the earlier program of positive inducement and began instead to apply relentless negative pressure on the Jews. The overcrowded ghetto was part of a program to make Jews painfully aware that their rejection of Christ had condemned them to a life of servility and isolation.[42] Stow's conversionist reading of the papal decree has been widely cited. The problem is that there is little evidence for it in the language of the bull itself. As one reviewer pointed out, Stow's interpretation of the Latin text is forced and led him to misunderstand the sentences upon which he bases his entire argument.[43] The bull was clearly concerned with, and is best understood against the

Figure 10. *The Ghetto, Rome* (1847), engraving by S. V. Hunt, Cassell & Company. Had Pope Paul IV not established the ghetto in 1555, Rome's Jewish community could have become as wealthy and culturally prolific as the communities of Venice and Livorno.

backdrop of, the very same issues of urban competition that we have already identified elsewhere.

If we examine Roman ghettoization within its civic context, it becomes clear that one of the most important issues was the intensification of housing pressure created by demographic growth. Except for the substantial but temporary setback caused by the sack of 1527, Rome's population (both Gentile and Jewish) doubled over the sixteenth century, placing both supply- and demand-side pressures on the available housing stock.[44] Up through the early sixteenth century, Jews had been granted relatively liberal residential privileges by successive popes and began expanding beyond their traditional neighborhood, the *rione* Sant'Angelo.[45] These Jews presumably included wealthy loan-bankers licensed since 1521, who were seeking nicer homes.[46] Before long, however, a backlash set in. Already during the reign of the "liberal" Pope Paul III, several decrees prohibited Jewish "expansion" outside of the Jewish quarter near the Piazza and Via Giudea.[47] *Cum nimis absurdum* took on the festering issue directly, demanding the spatial segregation of Jews in a single contiguous residential area "separated completely from the dwellings of Christians." The bull clearly explained the reason for this demand: Jews were "insolently" building homes in elegant neighborhoods, thereby raising social anxieties by threatening the established patterns of demarcation that defined Roman society.

Over time, of course, the Roman ghetto took on a special symbolic and religious significance beyond its immediate urban context. Its overcrowding and insalubrious location made it especially appalling to observers. Moreover, the Church seemed relentless in extending the policy, creating ghettos in any new urban areas incorporated into the Papal States. In Rome itself, the ghetto was stubbornly maintained until 1870, when the city was incorporated into the Italian state and the popes were finally stripped of their territorial powers. By then, the ghetto had become the quintessence of everything the new state wished to uproot. As Ettore Natali put it a few years after the ghetto was razed: "Rome, the capital of a free Italy, had to completely demolish the ghetto because it was its most shameful and infected quarter. It stood not just as a disgraceful dwelling place for Semites, but as a violation of modern law, unworthy for a civilized people."[48]

What then would have happened if Rome's ghetto had never been constructed? Would the Jews have been expelled altogether? This seems unlikely, given the Roman Church's long history of tolerating

Jews as witnesses to Christian truth. But could the city's growing Jewish community have continued to expand into new neighborhoods? This also seems unlikely given the increasing rigidity of Counter-Reformation popes. From the start, Rome's ghetto was a compromise between existing realities and theological doctrine, and as with many compromises, it did little more than to allow an uncomfortable situation to continue unresolved. And so the ghetto remained as an integral expression of an increasingly anachronistic theocracy, whose clerical bureaucracy lacked the flexibility and competence needed for changing times. In this sense, the physical ghetto walls reified the virtual walls that were gradually encircling the Papal State itself. They represented a delicate equilibrium that was never so intolerable as to force the Jews out, but never so embarrassing as to force the Church to change its policies.

This is not to say that the Roman ghetto made no difference. Ghettoization certainly limited the demographic and economic growth of Roman Jewry. The ghetto decree specifically restricted Jewish engagement in certain spheres of the economy. Although the exact significance of these restrictions remains to be clarified, they certainly indicate an intentional restriction of the Jewish economy. The second half of the sixteenth century was a period of tremendous urban expansion in Rome: Jews were now precluded from participating in that growth. Had Paul IV not imposed the ghetto, there is every reason to believe that Rome's Jewish community could have become as wealthy and as institutionally and culturally prolific as Venice and Livorno. Toward the end of the century, individual popes were aware of this possibility, expanded ghetto space, and provided for a greater mercantile role for Jews. But ultimately this was to no avail. As is often the case with protective legislation, Rome's ghetto policy stymied economic growth.

The ghettos of Tuscany

Perhaps the most puzzling set of ghettoization policies in sixteenth-century Italy were adopted by the Medici dukes of Tuscany. Historians have long credited the dynasty with an enlightened and consistently favorable policy toward Jews. While Florence's republican governments had regularly sought to ban Jewish usury and expel Jewish bankers from the city, the Medici consistently allowed the Jews to return and to reopen their banks. Equally importantly, in 1551, Duke Cosimo, in an effort to stimulate trade, had chartered the settlement of Levantine merchants. The privilege, negotiated by a certain Servadio (Obadiah), a Greek Jew from Damascus, specifically included Jews; indeed, Jews were its primary beneficiaries. Umberto Cassuto, whose brilliant Italian study of the Jews in Florence during the Renaissance remains the standard work on the subject a century and more after its publication, was unabashed in his praise of the Medici, arguing that their pro-Jewish policies derived from a combination of personal tolerance and administrative sagaciousness.[49] Cassuto tells us that Cosimo was willing, "out of his sense of obligation as a Catholic ruler as well as from considerations of political expediency," to follow papal orders in purely religious matters – for example, when it came to confiscating and burning copies of the Talmud in 1553. However, Cosimo was also jealous of his jurisdictional independence, and so when it came to secular matters, he maintained his positive approach to the Jews. Thus, in 1557, when Jews from Città del Castello fled the new rigors of papal policy and moved a few miles to the east into Tuscan Arezzo, the Aretines complained about the invasion of immigrants who were renting houses and bringing their "stuff" (*arnesi*). The Duke's Council, however, could see no reason to block the immigrants coming

> to Arezzo or any other territory of . . . the state. From the point of view of religion, the Church tolerates and receives [Jews]. And from the point of view of the ducal treasury, the [Jews] cannot but be of benefit. The Aretines will similarly [benefit] when they rent them homes and sell them food.[50]

Cosimo followed his councilors' advice and welcomed the Jews, insisting, however, that they not be allowed to engage in moneylending, since Jacob Abravanel was already licensed to do so in that region.

All of this was suddenly reversed in 1570, when Florence canceled the licenses of Jewish moneylenders in Tuscany and required all Jews in the ducal dominions to leave their homes and move into a newly created ghetto in Florence.[51] Cassuto interpreted this harsh decree as a grudging concession to papal pressure: in order to gain Rome's support for a more elevated dynastic title, Cosimo had to toe the harsh papal line about the Jews. More recently, Stefanie Siegmund has argued that ghettoization was integral to Cosimo's efforts to create a modern state. Florence's ghetto, she writes, reflects a "specifically Italian [type] of early modern confessionalization – and of the state building so intimately linked to it." Rather than presenting the ghetto as merely one more "moment in the continuing history of the persecution of the Jews," she understands it as a deliberate act of an early modern state, an innovation in the use of spatial control to express state power.[52]

However plausible they may be, neither of these explanations addresses the self-contradictory nature of Medici policy vis-à-vis spatial segregation of the Jews. Though it was not mentioned in the 1557 ruling concerning Arezzo, the idea of spatial segregation was in fact already in the Florence air even before 1570. The obviously "liberal" 1551 invitation to Levantines that included trade and settlement rights "in our city or other place in the ducal dominion" was careful to add

> that you will be granted and assigned houses for your residence in places *separate from the houses and residences of Christians*, with the right to exercise not only trade but also the right to create mosques and synagogues as you see fit (with the requirement that you first obtain a license from Pope Julius III).[53]

Two decades later the confusion seems to grow. Now, Jews were to be expelled from Tuscany's small towns and allowed to live only in a ghetto in Florence, but the very same decree makes it clear that Jews were actually welcome in Florence and even encouraged to settle there.[54] Perhaps most confusingly of all, beginning in 1591, Cosimo's son, Grand Duke Ferdinando, invited Jews (as well as all other foreigners) to settle and trade in Pisa and to take advantage of the newly built port facilities and free-trade privileges in nearby Livorno. The privileges associated with the *Livornina* (as the invitation, reformulated in 1593, came to be called) were among the most liberal granted in early modern Europe, and for centuries served as the legal basis for what was arguably the largest and wealthiest Jewish community in Italy. What is most striking is that the invitations included no reference to spatial segregation of any sort. Jews occupied some of the new homes built on Livorno's finest street, the Via Ferdinanda. Though Jews were eventually required to move a few blocks away, the grand dukes firmly rejected every effort to establish any form of walled segregation in the port.

The apparent inconsistency of Medici policy actually confirms what we have seen in place after place in early modern Europe. The creation of a ghetto often served as a legislative mechanism to legitimize a new or expanding Jewish physical presence and economic role within cities. By identifying a special space for Jews to live, governments addressed religious, social, and, above all, economic objections to their very presence. Residential segregation was the alternative to expulsion or nonadmission. While the ghetto expressed and reified religious and ethnic hostilities, it was paradoxically a form of tolerance. The policy defined in the *Livornina* was perfectly consistent with this approach: there was no need for a ghetto in Livorno because the area was already jurisdictionally cordoned off. As a free port with an elaborate set of privileges for all settlers, Livorno was already exempt from the competitive forces of Florence's guilds and established economic interest groups. Any further spatial restriction was superfluous and undesirable insofar as it might have threatened the economic powerhouse that had been the intention of the policy in the first place. Defining Livorno as a customs-free zone allowed the port to develop as a lynchpin in a worldwide trading network – a network of Jews and non-Jews that could not have otherwise existed.[55] Furthermore, the same legislative definition of an almost extra-territorial precinct famously made the city a safe haven for Portuguese New Christians seeking to join an open Jewish community. Tuscan religious tolerance is a product of this legal separation of space. Ironically, without ghettoization, "liberalism" could not have developed. Again, had this virtual "ghetto" not been defined, one of the largest and wealthiest Jewish communities in early modern Europe never would have arisen.

Conclusion

Ghettoization, as I have described it, was a zoning policy aimed at legally marking out a space for a substantial Jewish presence within an urban area. Although it could assume significantly different forms, the ghetto was everywhere a response to the pressure that the Jewish community placed on the stock of urban real estate. At the same time, ghettoization was also a response to an expanding Jewish economic role, a shift from simple moneylending to wider forms of commercial activity. Ghettos addressed the demands of the Jews' competitors by reifying limits in spatial terms, and ghettos almost always involved certain trade restrictions as well. Ghettos were justified in religious terms, but they belong primarily to the legal and commercial realm. Although often surrounded by physical walls, ghettos were defined primarily by the imaginary boundaries of municipal jurisdiction and customs rules. Though they restricted where Jews could live, ghettos formalized and legitimized a Jewish urban presence and thus paradoxically tended to attract new Jewish settlers and new forms of Jewish economic activity, whether through formal license or less formal "gray markets." Finally, to the extent that ghettoization created a Jewish quarter to be maintained and administered by Jews, it also had the effect of strengthening the tendency within the Jewish community to more elaborate institutions of self-government.

The later Middle Ages were marked by a wave of outright expulsions or forced conversions that ended centuries-old Jewish communities in large areas of Western Europe. The reasons for these expulsions were complex, but we must recall that they were the real alternative to the construction of the ghetto. Where ghettos were not successfully established, even age-old communities were in danger. Ghettos emerged specifically in areas where political and economic circumstances made expulsion undesirable or unfeasible – or, to put it another way, where a Jewish presence was desirable and encouraged. Even where urban Christian merchant groups were able to block a Jewish presence (the right *de non tolerandis Judaeis*), this often meant relegating Jewish residence to an area just beyond municipal jurisdiction – in effect another form of ghettoization. The Jews continued to enter the city for visits of shorter or longer periods. In this sense, there was little practical difference between the Jewish town in Kazimierz, the ghettos of Venice and Rome, and the unwalled free port in Livorno.[56] All of these residential arrangements permitted Jews to pursue their livelihoods and spared them the far less desirable alternative of expulsion.

In light of this fact, we can return to the second part of the question with which we began: could Jewish historians have constructed the image of the ghetto otherwise than they did? It is easy to understand why nineteenth-century historians portrayed the ghetto so bleakly. Their "construction" was of the ghetto in decline, the crowded, dusty, and smelly place filled with strange sounds and frightening people that Goethe remembered from his boyhood in Frankfurt.[57] More importantly, these historians despised the ghetto walls that kept Jews from participating in freedoms that were the very hallmark of the new civility – the right to live in the public space and participate in its discourse. Attacking the ghetto was part of the struggle for Jewish political emancipation that defined them as Jews. They despised the Jewish identity that they believed had been created by ghetto walls – an inward-turned Jewishness that rejected the new values learned in broader civil society. While they might look back with some measure of nostalgia to the "authenticity" of past ghetto Jewishness, they did so with a conscious sense of distance. Each was, as Alfred Kazin would declare with a considerable measure of ambivalence, "a walker in the city," who had escaped from the old Jewish neighborhood and now returned "with dread and some unexpected tenderness."[58]

Granted their own time and place, Jewish historians had little choice but to imagine the ghetto as the product of religious intolerance and pathological xenophobia. They were not able to understand the ghetto as a physical sign of changing urban realities, an alternative to exclusion and, paradoxically, a step on the complex and slow path toward defining a place for the individual Jew in the modern state. But had they been able to contextualize the ghetto differently, they might have been able to give their readers a more accurate, and certainly a more positive, picture of Jewish agency in the early modern era. They might have realized that the deteriorating conditions toward the end of the ghetto period were proof of that institution's very success. For had ghettos not existed, neither would any of the large communities they made possible – the communities that in the eighteenth century would burst their bounds and demand a place in general society.

5 WHAT IF SPINOZA HAD REPENTED?*

Eugene R. Sheppard

The following text is an English translation of an unpublished encyclopedia entry entitled "Baruch de Spinoza" (Figure 11). The author of the entry was the controversial Jewish philosopher and publisher, Jakob Klatzkin (1882–1948). He wrote the draft sometime after 1933, three hundred years after Spinoza's birth, for the German language edition of the *Encyclopedia Judaica*. Klatzkin co-edited the encyclopedia with the Jewish historian Ismar Elbogen for the Eshkol Publishing Society in Berlin. Between 1928 and 1934, the first ten volumes appeared, spanning the entries "Aach" to "Lyra." An additional five volumes were planned. The volume in which the entry for Spinoza would have appeared was never published, due to the crushing political and financial strains upon Jewish publishing houses in Nazi Germany.

Born in Bereza Kartuskaya, Russia, Klatzkin was the son of a respected orthodox rabbi. At age eighteen he traveled to the university town of Marburg, Germany, to study philosophy with the famed German Jewish neo-Kantian philosopher, Hermann Cohen. Klatzkin went on to receive his doctorate at the University of Berne in 1912. During the Second World War, Klatzkin took refuge first in Switzerland before fleeing to the United States, where he lectured at the College of Jewish Studies in Chicago. In 1947, after a brief period in New York,

---

* This chapter is a work of fiction. It is dedicated to the memory of Richard Popkin. His ceaseless skepticism regarding the state of historical knowledge about early modern scientific skepticism inspired and informed some central assertions attributed to Spinoza in what follows.

Figure 11. Portrait of Benedict (Baruch) Spinoza, Dutch philosopher, *ca.* 1665. His act of atonement in 1672 exerted a subtle but powerful impact upon generations of Jewish thinkers.

he returned to Switzerland where he died in 1948. Throughout his career, Klatzkin was an ardent Zionist who polemicized against Jewish assimilation and promoted a militantly *vitalist* vision for a Jewish state. Vitalism for Klatzkin meant that a biological national *will* determined all standards for Jewish existence. In his worldview, Zionism entailed the thoroughgoing recovery and secular transformation of concepts deriving from the Jewish people, the Hebrew language, and the land of Israel. All of Jewish history and thought – indeed, the entire history of the world – needed to be reconceived within a cosmological drama centering on the exertion of the Jewish national will. For Klatzkin, Zionism gathered its strength as it freed itself from the reliance on foreign culture and the political conditions of powerlessness. Klatzkin's political philosophy further represented a Jewish version of Nietzschean *Lebensphilosophie*. He sought to transform the unhealthy foreign influence of the classical legacy of Greece and Rome upon the Jews by translating that legacy into Hebrew. This effort was part of a larger nationalist campaign to once more root the Jewish people – like Judaism itself – in their primordial land and language.

Readers may wonder what relevance, if any, Klatzkin's philosophy had for his views on Spinoza. After all, Spinoza's intellectual persona was profoundly shaped by a fierce independence from – and, indeed, an attack on – Jewish sources and philosophical traditions. Moreover, Spinoza became the hated or celebrated forerunner of the modern assimilated Jew who sought to live in a world and think in terms beyond the confines of Judaism and Christianity. Klatzkin was incensed by the way in which Spinoza's punishment for transgressing Judaism's proscribed boundaries became the source of non-Jewish *Schadenfreude*. In the eyes of many observers, the Amsterdam Jewish community's notorious ban against the philosopher became the marker of Jewish narrow-minded and cruel dogmatism. And, yet, Klatzkin surprisingly affirmed Spinoza and his legacy. In the early 1920s, Klatzkin wrote a Hebrew book on Spinoza's "life, works, and system of thought" and translated Spinoza's *Ethics* into Hebrew (*Torat hamidot me-et Baruch Spinoza*). Based on nationalist criteria as well as his own hubris, Klatzkin viewed his translation as a more original achievement than Spinoza's original Latin text. Klatzkin sought to overcome the double distortion of Spinoza's text: its Latin composition as well as the philosophical reliance on geometric method. In his view, both elements mangled Spinoza's authentic Jewish voice, which could only be recovered by returning to the Hebrew of his original thinking. Klatzkin's translation generated a philosophical vocabulary that helped shape such a lexicon during a formative moment in the development of modern Hebrew. He was determined to capture and return Spinoza to the national fold, an effort that, for him, marked a natural continuation of Spinoza's own belated atonement and return to Judaism. Spinoza's philosophy marked a systematic rebellion against the classical rabbinic and medieval Jewish philosophical traditions of a personal transcendent God and the acceptance of rabbinic dogma. For Klatzkin, however, these factors provided all the more reason to elevate Spinoza into a modern nationalist hero. At the center of Spinoza's revolt lay the status of a transcendent God, a paradox confirmed in Spinoza's pivotal – if private – legalistic return to the Jewish fold in the year 1672.

Philosophical "Spinozism" and Spinoza's critique of revelation remained anathema to Klatzkin's teacher, Hermann Cohen. But even this liberal founder of neo-Kantian idealism eventually conceded that Spinoza's malicious motives for his critique of Judaism were mitigated by his willingness to officially atone for unspecified actions and opinions that were contrary to the true teaching of the Torah; this was especially true given the fact that his atonement was intended to protect the Jews of Amsterdam who were vulnerable to persecution following the French seizure of the city in 1672. For Cohen's Zionist opponents, Spinoza's repentance was especially important. Several Zionist thinkers, religious and secular, looked to Spinoza's politically motivated return to Judaism as a crucial turning point in Jewish history. They believed that he acted as he did in order to secure the safety of Amsterdam Jewry, thereby solidifying his place in the national memory as a precursor to the type of political consciousness approaching modern Zionism. In his *Ethics*, Spinoza argued that the incorporation of mathematics into philosophy allowed the latter to finally be released from scholastic theological presuppositions. A concomitant reliance on mundane political causation allowed him to forge a new political project: helping the Jews return to their ancestral homeland without the aid of messianic intervention.

Spinoza was already living outside Amsterdam's Portuguese Jewish community and circulating openly among Quakers and free-thinking Christians when the *herem* (or religious ban) was issued against him in the year 1656. According to Klatzkin, Spinoza simply wanted to live out of the reach of what he believed was the falsely pious, financially minded lay leadership (*parnasim*) of the Amsterdam Jewish community, who could use their financial leverage at any time to crack down against the presence of a confession-free man in their midst. The official document of excommunication, like the document that formally accepted his repentance and return to the community, lay unnoticed in the back of a closet of the Etz Chaim library for almost two centuries. Up until that point, Pierre Bayle's famous account of the events in the French *Encyclopedia* offered the consensus view of what had happened: the Amsterdam Sephardic Jewish community tried to prevent Spinoza from being too disruptive and keep him within the communal fold. Spinoza tried to be one of the first individuals to live without any religious affiliation, but found that he could not escape his past and was pestered constantly about the Jewish view of things by his philosemitic millenarian friends.

At this juncture, he finally came to breaking point and called in a few favors. The intervention of his friend, Rabbi Benjamin Musafia of Copenhagen, together with pressure from the Venetian authorities and Menash ben Israel, convinced the Amsterdam Sephardic mercantile leadership to perform a second, semi-private ceremony, this time to re-admit Spinoza into the community. Just as he was most likely absent when he was officially banned, he was probably absent for his re-admission. And, yet, one can imagine that there was a dramatic scene similar to the one experienced by the famed apostate, Uriel da Costa, who underwent a painful and humiliating penance in Amsterdam in 1640. Indeed, it may have resembled the scene depicted in Berthold Auerbach's famed biographical novel, *Spinoza* (1840), in which the writer embellished da Costa's own account of lying underneath the front door of the synagogue so as to facilitate his own public trampling. On a formal note, the banishment was neither rescinded nor annulled. Instead, the banned individual confessed guilt for his transgressions, begged forgiveness, and pledged to follow the authority of the Torah. There is an element that appeared in the case of da Costa that was curiously absent in the case of Spinoza: in the latter, the banned individual was not required to affirm the authority of either the communal leadership or the congregation. Even though he may have never seen the document, Rabbi Musafia probably knew that the absence of any promise to obey communal authority was too incredible to pass muster with other rabbinic authorities if it ever became public.

Once the discovery of Spinoza's repentance document secured him official re-admission into the Amsterdam Jewish community, the philosopher's legacy began to exert a subtle but powerful impact upon generations of Jewish thinkers. His heretical views remained essentially untouched by his statement. Nevertheless, figures ranging from Moses Hess to Rav Abraham Isaac Kook proceeded to lionize Spinoza for his momentous and spiritually questionable act of atonement. Non-Jewish critics of rabbinic and Jewish communal authority, meanwhile, were no longer able to gloat that ghetto-bound Jews retained punitive powers in matters of dogmatic belief.

Klatzkin's encyclopedia entry reveals a particularly Jewish nationalist and Zionist ambivalence regarding earlier renegades such as Spinoza. For even if Spinoza's atonement was illegitimate in spirit, even if Spinoza had never made any such gesture, Klatzkin's reception history would not change all that much when it came to Zionist engagements with this seminal Jewish heretic and hero.

Eugene R. Sheppard, Director
Center for Exilic Studies
1665 Spinoza Street
Jerusalem
Isarel

Baruch de Spinoza (*Encyclopedia Judaica* entry, unpublished)

Baruch/Benedictus de Spinoza was born on November 24, 1630 to Portuguese Jewish parents in Amsterdam. He was excommunicated by the Amsterdam Sephardic community in 1656. While learned in medieval and classical thought (Jewish, Greek, and Roman), he boldly carried a vision of philosophy and science beyond the medieval world into the modern era. He became one of the most famous and controversial thinkers by the late eighteenth century for attempting to construct a philosophical system – from root to branch – without any theological assumptions. He was just as controversial politically. His *Theologico-Political Treatise*, initially published anonymously in 1670, presented a republican form of government free from the pernicious effects of ecclesiastical hypocrisy and intolerance. He demanded that philosophy not be forced to play the maidservant to theology. This political vision was connected to a critical historical approach to the Bible, one that restored the words of a putatively sacred text to the natural world of humanity. Along the way, Spinoza launched a sustained assault upon rabbinic Judaism. To name but a few examples, he denied the Mosaic authorship and origin of the Pentateuch, arguing that the texts were written, compiled and redacted over several generations. As for the legitimacy of any Jewish claims to being elect among the nations, Spinoza argued that divine election of the Hebrews was conditioned upon sovereignty. Now that there was no longer a Hebrew commonwealth, Jews had no claim to chosenness. One further implication of this political reading of Judaism was that rabbinic authority had no juridical authority on post-exilic Jewry. The validity of the Torah as a legal constitution was also purely dependent on sovereignty. Once Jewish sovereignty ceased to exist, so did any legal obligations and authority based upon it.

Spinoza's legacy raises difficult questions for scholars. Was he a "God intoxicated philosopher," as claimed by the German romantics? Or was he a skeptical atheist, who ultimately broke with his nascent community and never looked back? There is little doubt that Spinoza must be considered one of the first modern Jews: a Jew who crossed the threshold beyond rabbinic authority and nevertheless ultimately remained faithful to the nation of his ancestors. Perhaps he did appoint himself as the founder of a new church, one that insisted upon commitment to the dictates of reason; yet, he recognized that in order to secure the possibility of individual and collective felicity, creative accommodation to certain beliefs and even covenants was required. He had the political impudence to transform Amsterdam Jewry according to the dictates of his *Theologico-Political Treatise*, wherein wisdom would no longer be held captive to the medieval ghetto authority of an unenlightened clergy. Spinoza never had the chance to implement his grand political scheme, but he made the ultimate intellectual sacrifice to do so. In the midst of intrigue and foreign occupation, he found a way to officially repent and return to the then-recognized authoritative structure of Judaism without fully compromising his radical materialism and rationalism.

The paradoxes of Spinoza's life and thought explain the dynamic reassessment, appropriation, and rejection of his legacy in the centuries that followed. As an elitist who weighed the power and felicity of a polity's constituents as the decisive force in determining the value of any state; as a Jew who sought to cast off the shackles of Jewish rabbinic and communal authority, but who only stepped into the political arena in the hope of salvaging a people whose official opinion of him was one of indifference or contempt, Spinoza has remained problematic for most individuals in positions of Jewish religious and communal leadership. Given his desire to live beyond the constraints of normative Judaism and his transgression of the boundaries of received prejudice, how could Spinoza have acquiesced to religious authority and affirmed his loyalty to Judaism and the Jewish people?

Although initially confounding, his actions become more comprehensible once we understand how the philosopher viewed the terms of his testament. Despite the outward appearance of his apology – indeed, despite his affirmation of a biblical and rabbinic tradition of revealed legal authority – Spinoza remained true to his own free intellectual spirit. He successfully returned to Judaism and the Jewish community without undergoing the kinds of physical and spiritual humiliations experienced by Uriel da Costa. Spinoza's peculiar confession of atonement explicitly affirmed Jewish religious authority while subverting the very pillars of received belief that would crumble over the coming centuries. In the end, Spinoza's act must be seen as a nationalistic one, wherein Judaism's theological bases were translated and recast in political nationalist terms.

Familial and *marrano* background

Although Spinoza was born in Amsterdam, his parents originally hailed from Portugal, where they had lived as official Christians (*conversos*) before inquisitorial authorities had them arrested for Christian heretical practices and beliefs. They both confessed to being Judaizers and then left Portugal for the Netherlands, where they lived under the auspices of the Sephardic Jewish authorities in Amsterdam. The Sephardic community of Amsterdam had officially established itself in 1638 by unifying three synagogues into "The Holy Congregation Talmud Torah." This young community was self-conscious about its status in the eyes of surrounding Jewish and even Christian authorities, given the unorthodox ways in which returning *marranos* observed rituals and read canonical texts. While living as official Christians under the threat of the Inquisition, secret Jews would perform Jewish rituals in a covert or inverted way so as to avoid detection: sweeping dirt into the house on the Sabbath; lighting candles for favorite Christian saints on Friday; observing Christian fast days around the time of Yom Kippur (the Day of Atonement). But similar strategies became common when reading sacred texts as well. After all, crypto-Jews could not be caught with Hebrew books, much less post-biblical rabbinic works. They obtained knowledge about Judaism through an over-reliance on the Hebrew Bible. They also read Christian texts, such as the Gospels and even Christian polemics, in order to glean information about dietary laws and rites of mourning. The same held true about such topics as Jewish election, the nature of the afterlife, the Messiah, and Jesus. These reading habits instilled an interpretative approach to the Hebrew Bible that was unhinged

from traditional conventions of commentary and often produced skepticism regarding beliefs and positions prescribed by normative orthodox Judaism. While no longer Christian, several prominent returnees
to Judaism came to scrutinize and subvert rabbinic glosses on biblical texts. Thus, Isaac Orobio da Castro and Uriel da Costa could not
simply abandon the type of intellectual independence they had exercised
when confronting authoritative meanings, be they Jewish or Christian.
There seems to have been a remarkable proclivity of many intellectu-
ally prominent *marranos* to veer toward innovative, but highly heretical,
forms of skepticism.

Many scholars have speculated that Spinoza, being the son of
marranos, absorbed some of his community's religious syncretism and
tendency to subvert orthodoxy. Like other Iberian refugees who later
returned to a normative Jewish practice, Spinoza's paternal grandfather was circumcised only after his death in 1619. The religious practices of the offspring of former *marranos* were regularly questioned in
returnee communities established in places such as Amsterdam during
the sixteenth and seventeenth centuries, as the fate of former apostates
remained a highly sensitive issue for rabbinical authorities struggling to
re-absorb new Christians. They officially atoned for their sin of apostasy
and made *teshuvah*, or repentance. Spinoza never converted to Christianity, but scholars have often projected his famed heretical skepticism
back into his youth and claimed that it led to eventual banishment from
the Amsterdam Jewish community.

The excommunication

Spinoza's life and thought, like his reputation and legacy, are defined
by sharp paradoxes. Tumult and tranquility, impiety and piety, virtue
and wickedness permeate the scholarly literature on this Jewish heretic,
who was expelled from the official Amsterdam Portuguese Jewish community in 1656. While the writ of excommunication (*herem*) offers
the most extreme language of curse and banishment that was available at the time, the document does not disclose the nature of his
actions that put the budding thinker beyond the pale of acceptable
behavior. Although representative of an extreme form of excommunication, the document was still *pro forma*. The lay leadership of
the Spanish-Portuguese community (the Senhores of the Mahamad)
proclaimed that their repeated attempts to get the young Spinoza to

recognize the wrongness of his opinions and actions had proved futile. His "horrible heresies, which he practiced and taught," as well as his "monstrous actions," necessitated a harsh punishment of excommunication, whereby all interaction with the banned be forbidden. The document pronounces the ban as follows:

> After the judgment of the Angels, and with that of the Saints, we excommunicate, expel and curse and damn Baruch d'Espinoza with the consent of God, Blessed be He, and with the consent of this holy community in front of the holy scriptures with its 613 commandments, with the anathema with which Joshua banned Jericho, and with the curse with which Elisha cursed the youths, and with all the curses which are written in the Law. Cursed be he by day, and cursed be he by night; cursed be he when he lies down, and cursed be he when he rises up; cursed be he when he goes out, and cursed be he when he comes in. The Lord will not pardon him; the anger and wrath of the Lord will rage against this man, and bring him all the curses which are written in the Book of the Law, and the Lord will destroy his name from under the Heavens, and the Lord will separate him to his injury from all the tribes of Israel with all the curses of the firmament, which are written in the Book of the Law.

While the rhetorical explosions contained in the writ of the ban received considerable attention upon its discovery in 1841, several Europeans in the seventeenth century still joyously pointed to the simple fact of Spinoza's excommunication as symbolizing an intolerant ghetto Jewish mentality. Yet after the discovery of Spinoza's testament of repentance, few Europeans have recognized that it implicitly permitted the banished individual to return to Judaism and the Jewish people. It was this possibility of return that proved so influential for subsequent Jewish historians and intellectuals of Jewish descent from the late eighteenth to the nineteenth century in Germany, whether the leader of the Berlin Jewish Enlightenment, Moses Mendelssohn, the founders of the academic study of Judaism (Wissenschaft des Judentums), the Jewish writers associated with Young Germany (Heinrich Heine, Ludwig Börne, and Berthold Auerbach) and the Young Hegelians (Moses Hess). Moreover, Spinoza's legacy takes on a new importance within the Hebrew-based participants in Italian Jewish thought (Samuel David Luzzatto, Shadal) and the Eastern European Jewish Enlightenment and historical study of Judaism (*Hochmat Yisrael*) (Salomon Rubin and Meir Halevi Letteris). The contested legacy of Spinoza takes on a different trajectory among twentieth-century Jewish philosophers and other academic thinkers (Hermann Cohen, Franz Rosenzweig, and Joseph Klausner). Moreover, Jewish nationalists – in particular, Zionists – seized upon Spinoza's return as an inspiration for deracinated modern Jews to return to Judaism in a nationalist spirit.

Political intrigue and repentance: suppressed and recovered

It is only fitting that the document marking Spinoza's nominal repentance and official return to Judaism in the year 1672 discloses precious little information about the motivations behind his about-face. The surviving document attesting to Spinoza's public act of *teshuvah* (literally meaning a return, but signaling an act of atonement or repentance) was authorized by the same body that had excommunicated him some sixteen years earlier, this time under the influence of Benjamin Musafia, the Chief Rabbi of Copenhagen, in the winter of 1672. We can only speculate that Spinoza refused to make any direct concessions to the lay communal leadership that had expelled him. Musafia was indebted to Spinoza for having intervened on behalf of his son-in-law the previous year, but he was also in the natural position of interceding on Spinoza's behalf prior to the arrival of the French armies, which invaded and occupied the Netherlands beginning in 1672. Spinoza was most likely motivated by his fears for the Dutch Jewish community's safety under the French in deciding to return to the Jewish fold. The fascination of Louis de Bourbon, Prince of Condé (1621–86), with different traditions of thought, culture, and religion, as well as his specific interest in joining an impressive network of Christian Hebraists, informed his offer to Spinoza to join his court. He wished to have a court Jew of Spinoza's intellectual stature, but he insisted that the philosopher be recognized as a full-fledged Jew in good standing with his community. In return, the prince promised to extend special consideration to the Jewish community of Amsterdam, suggesting that he would not persecute them. Thanks to the prince's efforts, Spinoza ultimately found himself officially readmitted as a Torah-believing Jew. Although his repentance document stresses his complete acceptance of the teachings of the Torah, there is no mention of his willingness to accept the authority of the board. This act, regardless of the political intrigue associated with it, shaped Spinoza's subsequent reputation as a new type of Jewish man, one who stepped outside the comfort zone of speculation and attempted to change the political fortunes of a community under duress.

In Spinoza's confession, the reader may be shocked to find the philosopher invoke Psalm 55:23: "Cast your burden on the Lord, and He will bear you; He shall never allow a righteous man to falter." But upon closer study of Spinoza's philosophical writings, one can see that his recommendations for how to approach the intellectual love of God parallel more traditional ones. The last part of the *Ethics* can therefore be seen as a modernization of the Psalms, as Harry A. Wolfson has recently suggested. Consolation requires that all of one's affections and images of things be put in relation to the idea of God (*The Ethics*, Prop. xv). Spinoza could honestly invoke Psalm 55 in his confession that "God is the great provider, the great comforter, the rock of our salvation, the only reliable refuge when confronted by evil." Spinoza's confession and *Ethics* both mirror traditional expressions found in Spanish rabbi and philosopher Bahya ibn Paquda's eleventh-century *Duties of the Heart*, which speaks to the heart's tranquility as it rests from worldly cares and enjoys relief from the fluctuations of the mind. Turning to a contemplative stance toward God and acceptance of his providence was the best way to find comfort amidst the mind's anxiety over its disappointments and bodily desires. The troubled soul could only turn to God for true consolation. The only question was whether the God in question was one of transcendent revelation or immanent substance.

Had Spinoza's document been successfully suppressed – whether by his well-meaning Christian supporters or by the more ambivalent Amsterdam Jewish communal leadership – we might be entitled to ask whether the philosopher's fidelity to humanity precluded him from linking his own affiliations with the fate of his fellow Amsterdam Jews. But, as we know, the document did eventually come to light. It did not appear for some time, however, and in the absence of accurate information, rumors swirled around the circumstances of Spinoza's actions.

Early reports and reception

Pierre Bayle, for one, painted an unflattering portrait of Spinoza's behavior, stating that the philosopher had actually wanted to be given an academic chair at the University of Heidelberg, but that the offer was withdrawn during negotiations when he expressed hesitation at a genuine conversion and teaching dogmatics. Bayle also reported that Spinoza met with the Prince of Condé along with the infamous Egyptian physician and libertine, Dr. Henri Morelli. Bayle described how Spinoza turned down the offer due to a fear of Catholic persecution. What Bayle did not know was that this was part and parcel of the prince's plan to include a Jew in his court upon the occupation of the Dutch center of Amsterdam. In the wake of his excommunication, Spinoza circulated amongst free-thinking Christians as well as libertines. He even translated two Quaker tracts into Hebrew in 1657 and 1658.

Spinoza's earliest biographer Jean M. Lucas offered a report, based on interviews with Spinoza's landlords, about some of the notable visitors that Spinoza entertained. The Egyptian physician, Morelli, came to the Hague to care for several aristocrats who were suffering from illness. He was accompanied by the Sephardic Jewish merchant Gabriel Milan (1631–89), who was conducting shady business transactions in the name of the Danish crown. Milan was the son-in-law of the Chief Rabbi of Copenhagen, Rabbi Benjamin Musafia, who ultimately played such a crucial role in Spinoza's repentance. Spinoza appears in official records as a witness for Milan. We now know that Spinoza called upon Rabbi Musafia to orchestrate his own official act of Jewish repentance or "return" to Judaism. For his part, Milan had converted to Lutheranism in order to curry favor with the Danes and in 1684 rose to power as the Danish governor of the Virgin Islands. Only a few years later, however, he was arrested, tried, and executed for fraud and treason. It appears that Milan prevailed upon his father-in-law to accept Spinoza's act of *teshuva*. Milan returned to the Hague at the time of the Prince of Condé's invasion and instructed Rabbi Musafia to tell the leadership of the Amsterdam Sephardic-Portuguese synagogue that they were to accept Spinoza's statement of atonement and authorize his readmission into the community. The Prince of Condé made it clear to Spinoza that his former community could only be protected if he had a Jew in good standing serving at his court to represent its interests. Otherwise, Condé suggested, Amsterdam Jewry would face the prospect of expulsion along with a modicum of public violence in order to win over non-Jewish support for the occupiers. At a time when Dutch Jewry faced overwhelming uncertainty and potential catastrophe, Spinoza proved himself to be a virtuous Jewish disciple of the Machiavellian school of *Machtpolitik*. In the end, it was the political goal of protecting

Amsterdam Jewry from persecution by an occupying force that legitimated Spinoza's questionable "return" to the Sephardic Jewish community. Spinoza continued to live outside of Jewish Amsterdam even after his putative return.

Reception in the nineteenth century

The impact of Spinoza's return to the Jewish fold can be registered in the nineteenth century. The Italian Jewish scholar Samuel David Luzzatto (Hebrew acronym, Shadal, 1800–65) wrote several different works that expressed his ambivalent attitude toward Spinoza. Luzzatto consistently rejected Spinoza's method of biblical criticism and his rationalist critique of emotions. His early Hebrew polemic, *Against Spinoza* (*Neged Spinoza*), left no doubt as to what he thought of Spinoza's effect on Jewish philosophical ethics. Spinoza's misplaced confidence in reason and nature rather than faith in a providential and transcendent God had to be rejected entirely. Like many other interpreters, Luzzatto turned to Spinoza's biography for confirmation of his theoretical criticism. He vehemently rejected the portrait of Spinoza as a truly pious Jew circulated by the Galician enlightener Meir Halevi Letteris (1800–71) in the mid 1840s, following the discovery of Spinoza's apparent act of atonement and return to the community. Letteris was among the first interpreters to recognize the Hebrew, and therefore essentially Jewish, foundation of Spinoza's writings and life story. For Letteris, Spinoza only stayed away from the synagogue and Jewish community out of fear for his life. By contrast, Luzzatto saw Spinoza's separation from Jewish communal life as an outward manifestation of a deeper rejection of Jewish norms, such as belief in providence and ethical reliance on compassion above doctrines determined solely by intellect. Spinoza's intellectual arrogance allowed him to cut himself off from any ethical impulse to sympathize or empathize with other human beings. Luzzatto recoiled when he quoted Spinoza's revealing credo: "I have striven not to laugh at human actions, not to weep at them, nor to hate them, but to understand them" (*Political Treatise* I.4). Such dispassion was nothing short of inhuman for Luzzatto.

Luzzatto repeatedly returned to the rather grim, if not "pathetic," last chapter of Spinoza's life: living his last years outside the geographical boundaries of the Amsterdam Jewish community, ultimately dying alone, without a wife or children. Moreover, Luzzatto called attention to the fact that the physician who treated Spinoza in his final moments absconded with what little money the philosopher had managed to save.

After Luzzatto learned of Spinoza's *teshuvah* document, however, he came to regard the philosopher as having made an about-face by disowning his earlier impertinent notions. This later interpretation viewed Spinoza as a genuine penitent who was determined to secure not only his blessedness in this world, but in the world to come. In other words, Spinoza's action mitigated and even canceled out the harm associated with his previous impious actions and dangerous philosophy. The key, for Luzzatto, was Spinoza's newfound ability to feel compassion for his fellow Jew and place his fate in the hands of a providential God.

German thinkers were also eager to reassess Spinoza. The famed writer and poet Heinrich Heine was drawn to Spinoza's universalism, but from the heretical vantage point of apostasy rather than excommunication (Figure 12). Heine had participated in the early founding of the circle of Jewish university-educated intellectuals that launched the Scientific Study of Judaism a half decade or so before he converted to Christianity in 1825. Heine incessantly projected his own wishful character onto his protagonists and seized on Spinoza's excommunication from the Jewish community as demonstrating his Christ-like character and significance. "It is a fact that Spinoza's life was beyond reproach and pure and spotless as the life of his divine cousin, Jesus Christ. Like Him, he too suffered for his teachings; like Him he wore the crown of thorns. Wherever a great mind expresses its thought, there is Golgotha."

Spinoza's ordeal of excommunication not only verified his purity of soul, but condemned his Jewish persecutors as executioners of sadistic pomp. Heine narrated the solemn rite of excommunication of Spinoza, culminating in the terrible shriek of the ram's horn (the shofar) rendering the banned Spinoza stripped of any claim to Jewishness. "His Christian enemies," Heine wryly noted, "were magnanimous enough" to still view him as a Jew. By contrast, the Jews, "the Swiss guard of deism," remained vehement in denying Spinoza's place as a Jew with dignity, even after he attempted to rejoin the community. Heine recognized Spinoza's act of atonement as a foolhardy exercise in futility. He subjected himself to the most miserable indignities: being trampled by the community under the front doors of the Portuguese synagogue in Amsterdam, the very site where "they once tried to stab Spinoza with their long daggers."

Figure 12. Portrait of Heinrich Heine, 1838. The famed Jewish poet regarded Spinoza's act of atonement as a foolhardy exercise in futility.

Heine's critic Berthold Auerbach systematically engaged Spinoza and his legacy. In the historical novel *Spinoza* (Mainz, 1837), Auerbach reflected how German Jews viewed their own commitment to culture, science, and ethics as embodying the most universal agents of progress in the first half of the nineteenth century. Auerbach's historical novel celebrated the independent man of reason who transgressed the boundaries of all normative religious convention and authority – even the most free-thinking Dutch representatives of the Jewish, Catholic, and Protestant faiths. While his skepticism moved him beyond the limits of Judaism in his time, Spinoza embodied a new type of individual whose reflected experience as a Jew detached from particular dogma essentially shaped his independent ethos of concrete universalism. While Spinoza paid a heavy price for his principles, the novel ends with Spinoza paving the way for a type of secularized redemption that can be realized by future generations of those very Sephardic Jews who exiled him and held him in such contempt.

Of course, following the discovery of Spinoza's repentance documents in 1842, Auerbach needed to modify his portrait of the philosopher. Auerbach had translated Spinoza's complete works into German in 1841. But in his revised scholarly biographical portrait written in 1843, Auerbach emphatically denied that Spinoza was a universal individual before his time. Instead he saw him as representing a new kind of complicated heretic with a conscience. When the moment came, Spinoza sought to prevent pointless martyrdom of his people. His practical statement of atonement did not have to be seen as hypocritical, but rather as a heroic act of historical necessity. Spinoza had heard about several acts of martyrdom under the Inquisition, not only of Jews and *marranos* but also Christian scientists, such as Giordano Bruno. He certainly would not undergo the horrifying humiliation that he saw Uriel da Costa suffer. Auerbach's novel opened with a young Spinoza empathizing with the repentant sinner, whose trampling and whipping eventually drove him to suicide. The novel closes with a broken-hearted Spinoza remaining true to his universalist principles outside the contours of the Judaism of his day, but embodying the most essential realization of Judaism's universal commitments to science and ethical behavior. Spinoza's world and his Jewish community did not exhibit these attributes, but this is all the more reason why he inspired nineteenth-century German Jews, who were striving to realize Spinoza's great efforts. When Auerbach published Spinoza's writings and translated them into German a year later, he took note of the atonement, which had been brushed aside in the novel as an unsubstantiated rumor. Rather than seeing Spinoza as a tragic and ultimately isolated hero, Auerbach's introduction framed Spinoza's life between his excommunication and his return. Auerbach saw the act of return as the mark of a new type of Jew and

Judaism – a Jew who stayed loyal to his ancestral people and essential religious principles, but who nevertheless still remained incapable of accepting dogmatic belief and authority.

Knowledge of Spinoza's return to the Jewish community was subject to wild speculation for almost one hundred and fifty years after his death. Some of the best-known images of Spinoza are captured in Ernst Altkirch's book, *Spinoza im Porträt* (Jena, 1913). In addition to icons of the philosopher as a dangerous source of malicious atheism and as a somewhat secularized Christian ascetic, readers will not be surprised to find Spinoza as a more traditionally observant Jew. Friedrich Roth-Scholtz's 1725 copper-plated engraving (*Kupferstich*) features Spinoza wearing rather conventional dress from the 1670s, but upon closer inspection one sees the barely visible presence of a tallit, a Jewish prayer shawl, under his overcoat.

While Moses Hess is largely known for his notable participation in Young Hegelian philosophico-political disputes, less well known was his rather consistent claim to be a disciple of Spinoza from his early works in the 1830s to the 1860s when he penned his socialist Zionist work *Rome and Jerusalem* (1862). In his earlier book, *The Holy History of Mankind* (1837), Hess described himself as a disciple of Spinoza but portrayed his significance in Hegelian dialectical terms. Christ's triumph over Judaism was a necessary precondition for Spinoza to eventually resuscitate the "kernel" of Judaism within a form recognizable to Christian conceptions of theologico-politics. "The old law whose body had been buried with Christ has been clarified and resurrected in Spinoza." Spinoza, the Master, offered a clarification of Jewish universalism that was based not on abstract notions but provide a conception of salvation tied to reason in a concrete, material world. In his writing after 1841, Hess perceived not only world historical significance in Spinoza's excommunication, but in his documented atonement as well. The latter was seen in philosophical terms as a sublation and overcoming of that alienation from his ancestral religion in which Spinoza sacrificed his own seemingly universalist principles for the good of a particular people. This form of overcoming marked not only the reconciliation of the universal and particular, but provided the hypostatic model of modern Jewish liberation more generally. The fact that Spinoza still remained aloof from official Jewish authority and synagogue life demonstrated that he never abandoned his fierce individuality and yet found a way to reconcile it with the collective good. Spinoza recognized that freedom was enhanced and not diminished when the individual sees himself as a particular part of a greater totality and labors with others to perfect that collectivity. For Hess, Spinoza's dive back into the ghetto waters marked an anointment rather than a Jewish baptism. Hess described Spinoza's return to Judaism not in legalistic but rather conventional poetic terms: "there were tears in the evening and joy in the morning."

Hermann Cohen, the founder and leader of the Marburg school of neo-Kantian philosophy, would have none of the posthumous white-washing of Spinoza's legacy. In the midst of World War I, Cohen offered a strong condemnation of Spinoza, repentant or not. Cohen would later attempt to systematically present Judaism in neo-Kantian terms in *The Religion of Reason out of its Sources in Judaism*. For Cohen, the root manifestation of Spinoza's deeper enmity with Judaism lay in the foundations of his philosophy of immanence and historical attack upon the prophetic basis of the Hebrew Bible. Spinoza's God-or-Nature formula collapsed the fundamental distinction between "is" and "ought" so crucial to ethical monotheism and neo-Kantian ethics. Spinoza's world did not allow for any divine transcendence nor its ensuing prophetic voice pointing toward a messianic world of the ought. Cohen mobilized a list of offenses that Spinoza had committed against Judaism which were taken from his philosophical works, his historical bringing down to size of the prophets and their writings, and of course his biography. For Cohen, Spinoza's politically motivated decision to formally "return" to the Jewish community made no sense other than to exemplify Spinoza's own all-too-worldly orientation.

By contrast, a string of early twentieth-century Jewish nationalists and especially Zionists perceived Spinoza as a properly Jewish Jew. The first Ashkenazi Chief Rabbi of the British Mandate of Palestine, Abraham Isaac Kook (1865–1935), famously recovered Spinoza's revolutionary zeal as an inspiration for the type of radical transformation of Judaism that could only be integrated within the new confluence of heresy and piety of religious Zionism. Just as the political events of Spinoza's time prompted him to reembrace his Jewish existence, so the confluence of Zionist unfolding in Palestine would mark the return of all Zionist settlers, regardless of current belief and level of observance.

In 1927, an array of celebrations took place commemorating the 250th anniversary of Spinoza's death. One of those celebrations took place at the Hebrew University of Jerusalem. The university's newly hired Professor of Hebrew Literature, Joseph Klausner, invoked

Spinoza as a heroic model of nationalistic Judaism during the inauguration of the Hebrew University at Mount Scopus. Klausner went beyond affirming Spinoza's repentance by turning his attention to the historical wrong done to him by the Amsterdam Jewish community. He called for historical restitution in the form of a formal nullification of the original 1656 ban. He called out in liturgical solemnity "To Spinoza the Jew...from the heights of Mount Scopus," from the modern version of "the Temple" which is the Hebrew University. Klausner declared the ban to be officially nullified: "The sin of Judaism against you is removed and your offense against her atoned for twice over. Our brother are you, our brother are you, our brother are you. Baruch Spinoza, you are our brother."

Klausner's secularized priestly rite sought to rectify any hesitations regarding Spinoza's share in Jewish peoplehood. It affirmed Spinoza's Hebrew core, and reminds us all that the power of the national will cannot be expunged.

J. K.

WHAT IF RUSSIAN JEWRY HAD NEVER BEEN CONFINED TO THE PALE OF JEWISH SETTLEMENT?

6

Jeffrey Veidlinger

Between the years 1772 and 1795, the Great Powers of Russia, Prussia, and Austria partitioned Poland between them, thereby wiping from the map of Europe the state that housed the largest number of Jews in the world. During Poland's golden age in the sixteenth and seventeenth centuries, the country's distinguished Jewish leaders hailed their homeland as a place of learning and enlightenment, a place where they enjoyed unprecedented autonomy. As Nathan Hanover put it in his chronicle, *Abyss of Despair,* "throughout the dispersions of Israel there was nowhere so much learning as in the kingdom of Poland."[1] Russia's gradual takeover of Poland, however, placed this legacy in jeopardy. In annexing Polish territory, Russia – which had previously prohibited all Jews from living within its borders – suddenly acquired for itself approximately 600,000 Jews, a population that would grow to 5.2 million by 1897. At the time, Russia's tsarist government recognized no conception of equal rights and instead divided its population into a dizzying array of legal entities, known as *sosloviia,* each of which had its own distinct rights and privileges. These entities could be grouped around corporate estates, occupations, ethnicity, religion, or geography, and often included numerous overlapping subgroupings and subdivisions. The sudden addition of approximately 600,000 people who did not fit into any of the existing categories confused and irritated the tsarist government. In addressing the situation, however, Empress Catherine the Great (1729–96) simply decided to maintain the status quo and keep the Jews where they were, thereby deferring the quest for a better solution to a later date. It was with this gesture of governmental inaction that the Pale of Jewish Settlement began.

Although it was remembered otherwise in popular Jewish memory, the Pale of Jewish Settlement was not one large ghetto. For one thing, it was enormous, encompassing some 473,000 square miles, almost three times the size of California. In 1897, the region's total population was about 42 million, of whom some 4.8 million were Jews. By contrast, the current population of California – a third the size of the Pale – is about 38 million, of whom about 1.2 million are Jewish. This was hardly the type of overcrowded and cramped living space that we associate with the ghettos of early modern Europe, let alone with the more notorious ghettos established during the Holocaust. Furthermore, for all the difficulties that Jews endured in the Pale, life was not much better in the Russian interior. Russian serfs, for instance, who comprised about 34 percent of the total population, had even fewer possibilities for physical mobility: they were confined to the piece of land where they were born, a situation that only began to change with their emancipation in 1861. Living in a society in which all rights were tied to the group to which one belonged, Russian Jews were often more willing than Jews in Western and Central Europe to see the benefits of separation. It is little wonder that Russian Jewish intellectuals and politicians often favored territorial and communal autonomy over simple civic equality. There is no denying that the Pale was poverty-stricken and underdeveloped. But the rest of Russia was no better.

At first glance, therefore, it seems unlikely that the counterfactual elimination of residency restrictions for Jews in the Russian Pale at some point in the nineteenth century would have changed their lives very much. There is no reason to assume, for example, that it would have prompted a mass eastward migration of Jews to the Russian interior. The vast majority of Russian Jews would have continued to remain in their ancestral homelands. At the same time, major waves of migration still would have taken place to the Americas and, to a far lesser extent, Palestine. Certainly a sliver of the population, those with aspirations in the Russian civil service, in medicine, in law, perhaps in the arts, would have been attracted to St. Petersburg; in fact, even with the residency restrictions in place, about 180,000 Jews lived in the imperial capital by the turn of the century. It is reasonable to assume that St. Petersburg would have emerged as a destination of Jewish migration on a par with Vienna or Berlin, both of which attracted migrants from the Polish lands annexed by Austria and Prussia respectively. Jewish history on the whole, though, would probably not have been altered significantly by the removal of the residency restrictions that defined the Pale of Jewish Settlement.

Yet what if the Pale had never come into being, or never had much time to become consolidated, in the first place? It is possible to imagine two intriguing scenarios that relate to this hypothetical possibility. The first proposes that Poland was never partitioned in the late eighteenth century, thereby enabling the Jewish population to become an autonomous enclave within a reformed Polish Republic instead of being incorporated into Russia. The second accepts Poland's partition and the incorporation of its Jews into the Russia Empire, but imagines that Tsar Alexander I (1777–1825) implements a radical proposal to abolish the Pale as a means of hastening the Jews' conversion to Christianity. As we shall see, both would have dramatically altered the course of Eastern European Jewish history.

Scenario I: Jews in the Republic of Poland

The fate of Polish Jews in real history was determined by the peculiarities of the Polish state. When the French *philosophe* Jean-Jacques Rousseau proposed ideas for a new Polish constitution in 1772, he began with the observation that "it is hard to understand how a state so oddly constituted can have survived so long."[2] Rousseau declared that Poland was devoid of a cultural core, noting that the country lacked the type of "national institutions" that "give form to the genius, the character, the tastes, and the customs of a people."[3] He chastised the Polish nobility for acting like the French nobility and urged them instead to embrace their Polishness. As he noted: "see to it that your king, your senators, everyone in public life, never wear anything but distinctively Polish clothing, and that no Pole shall dare to present himself at court dressed like a Frenchman."[4] Doing so, he believed, could help offset the Polish Republic's lack of national consciousness and cohesiveness. Similarly, Edmund Burke, who would later praise the Polish constitution of 1791, wrote: "*Poland* has at present the Name of Republick, and it is one of the *Aristocratick* Form; but it is well known, that the little Finger of this Government is heavier than the Loins of arbitrary Power in most Nations. The People are not only politically, but personally Slaves, and treated with the utmost Indignity."[5] Indeed, the Republic of Nobles, as the Polish-Lithuanian Commonwealth was known, was, by its very nature, an exclusive club to which only the nobility were invited. One of the problems with Poland, these enlightened thinkers agreed, was that it granted its minorities too much autonomy. Each group lived with its own customs, laws, and culture, and the running of the state was a monopoly of the nobility.

Up until this time, there had been few attempts in Poland to integrate the Jews, who comprised about 10 percent of the country's population. This situation stood in stark contrast to the situation in Austria and France. In these countries, the Jews – either in part, as in Austria, or in full, as in France – had been offered legal equality in exchange for cultural assimilation by the nineteenth century. Many Central and Western European states, guided by Enlightenment principles, had agreed to varying degrees to emancipate the Jews if they relinquished their separate legal systems and adopted the national dress, language, and educational system of the state. In Poland, however, the Jewish population retained its distinct status and autonomy as embodied in the *kahal* system, in which individual Jewish *kehilles* (communities) collected their own taxes, administered their own affairs, and determined their own membership. This type of "state within a state," as its critics alleged, was part of what Burke, Rousseau, and other observers saw as a threat to the establishment of a true Polish nation-state.

By the late eighteenth century, however, the Polish-Lithuanian Commonwealth was in crisis. Segments of the state had already been partitioned between Austria, Russia, and Prussia in 1772, and the rest of the country was being threatened anew. The Polish parliament, or Sejm, was deadlocked and unable to issue sensible legislation. With the fate of the Commonwealth hanging in the balance, the Sejm met in 1788 for what was to be a four-year session and debated the country's fate. Reformers argued that a future Poland must tear away the nobility's monopoly on power and instead gradually enfranchise burghers and perhaps, over time, even a certain number of peasants. Polish municipal authorities welcomed the opportunity to have a greater stake in national politics, but they fiercely guarded the expansion of their rights from the Jews.

Even liberal reformers did not envision granting Jews municipal citizenship. The first draft of the law on towns, for instance, decreed that citizenship would be extended to all "who own property, irrespective of their birth, calling, trade and religion, with the exception of Jews."[6] Stanisław Staszic spoke for many of the reformers when he blamed the Jews for the corruption of the Polish peasantry, declaring: "The Jewish race impoverishes our villages and infects our cities with rot. This disgusting race, having cheated the peasant out of his last morsel of bread, steals his money, deprives him of all industry, health, and even reason."[7] Even Mateusz Butrymowicz, a Sejm representative who maintained particularly favorable views toward the Jews, advocated near total assimilation, calling for the abolition of rabbinical courts except for religious matters, a ban on Hebrew books, the abolition of Jewish dress and dietary restrictions, and a curtailment of the number of Jewish holidays. Jews, he argued, should be compelled to use the Polish language and should school their children in Polish.

The four-year session culminated in the constitution of May 3, 1791, one of the most liberal constitutions of its day, rivaling even the recently adopted American constitution. "All authority in human society originates in the will of the people," the constitution declared. Although the ideals of the French Revolution, with their notions of equality before the law were circulating in Poland, the constitution of May 3 retained the estate system, thereby ensuring that nobles, burghers, and peasants were subjected to completely different legal systems. Nevertheless, the constitution expanded the vote by tying enfranchisement to land ownership. As a result, burghers – a growing and important segment of the population – were given the vote, whereas the petty nobility, who owed their status solely to heredity and who were widely blamed for forestalling meaningful political and economic reform, were deprived of it. Although the constitution retained the institution of serfdom, it set in motion the process of its eventual elimination. The constitution made no mention of Jews, however. The separation of the Jewish population was too complete for all but the most liberal reformers to imagine its integration into Polish society. Even reformers who supported Jewish assimilation, such as Staszic, did so as much out of spite as pity, believing that it would eradicate the Jewish lifestyle they so abhorred.

As events turned out, these deficiencies ended up being moot, as the Polish constitution was stillborn. Sensing the threat that the constitution's liberal ideas posed to its own political system, Russia vowed to crush the nascent state in its infancy. Just over a year after the constitution's passage, on May 18, 1792, the Russian army invaded at the invitation of disgruntled Polish noblemen and conquered much of eastern Poland. The constitution's supporters responded by taking up arms in defense of their liberties. The uprising was led by Tadeusz Kościuszko, a Polish nobleman and defender of Enlightenment ideals, who had recently returned from fighting in the American Revolutionary War.

Among those who fought alongside Kościuszko was a Jewish agent for the bishop of Vilna, Berek Joselewicz. Like Kościuszko, Joselewicz had spent time in France and imbibed the ideals of liberty and freedom. With Kościuszko's support, Joselewicz established a brigade of Jewish volunteers, thereby becoming commander of the first official Jewish military unit since antiquity. Joselewicz attracted some five hundred Jewish volunteers to fight for Polish independence. His appeal to the Jews of Poland to take up arms for Poland, issued in Yiddish, was full of Judaic allusions. "Hear, o sons of the tribes of Israel," he declared, "all in whose hearts is implanted the image of the Lord Almighty, all who seek to help fight for the fatherland." Joselewicz further permitted his soldiers to preserve their traditional ways. They ate kosher food, observed the Sabbath, and wore long beards, which earned them the nickname, the "Beardlings." The participation of Polish Jews in the uprising demonstrated that they could display the same unwavering loyalty toward their government as their German and Austrian counterparts, but without integrating and assimilating. Their efforts, however, were ultimately for naught. Joselewicz's forces, like the uprising in general, met with defeat.

But what if they had triumphed? The narrative below imagines how history might have turned out differently by interweaving a hypothetical course of events (in italics) with the events of real history (in roman type).

In early November, 1794, Joselewicz's forces, including the Jewish "Beardlings," unexpectedly defeated Russian forces in the Praga suburb of Warsaw. Their victory helped Polish Republicans triumph over the Russian tsar and ensured the implementation of the constitution of May 3. Joselewicz became a symbol for how Jews could contribute to the Polish state and national mission while retaining their separate identity. He further became an inspiration for subsequent attitudes toward the Jews in Poland. *The victory also stimulated a more in-depth discussion about the future of the Jews in what was now the Polish Republic.* Some, like the Polish Jew Zalkind Hourwitz, whose essay "The Vindication of the Jews" (1789) had famously won the city of Metz's Royal Society of Arts and Sciences essay contest on how to make the Jews more useful in France, now turned his attention to his homeland. He advocated emancipating the Jews in exchange for an end to Jewish separateness. In essence, Hourwitz sought to import French models to Poland. His effort, however, met with fierce opposition from both Christian burghers and Jewish communal leaders. The famed Elijah, Gaon of Vilna, urged his followers to immerse themselves in study and to forego involvement with the gentile world. He taught that all disputes among Jews must be settled internally and that to take any matter to gentile courts would be heretical. Joshua Herszel ben Joseph, the rabbi of Chelm, similarly argued against any type of accommodation; Jews should retain their dress, their language, their holidays and customs, and, most importantly, their communal autonomy. Even those Polish Jews who had participated in the Enlightenment movement in Germany, such as Mendel Lefin, returned to Poland convinced of the need to retain Jewish communal autonomy. The system of yeshivot that eventually emerged throughout the region, in places like Volozhin and Mir, continued to foster Jewish reclusiveness and separateness. Hasidic Jews were even more resistant to the threats of assimilation, and established an array of courts across the nation, each of which was led by a tsadik, or rebbe, who held political power by oratory and example, and soon by hereditary descent.

The Jewish community of Poland continued to splinter into disparate kehilles, each of which staunchly defended its independence and autonomy in the modernizing Polish Republic. The Jewish community, though, was divided between the northern kehilles, which broadly rallied around misnagdic principles, and the southern kehilles, which embraced Hasidism. In the year 1797, following the death of the famed Gaon of Vilna, who had been a staunch opponent of the Hasidim, growing hostilities between the communities led to the eruption of the Hasidic Wars, which, following the major battle of Lubawicze (Lyubavitsh), essentially divided the communities between the north and south. The fighting in the north eventually died down, but without a common enemy, the coalition of Hasidic kehilles subsequently fell apart, and new hostilities emerged between the southern kehilles, which splintered between an array of groups, including the kehilles of Braclaw (Breslov), Skvyra, Bobowa, Karlin, Berdyczów (Berdichev), and others. While mass violence was rare, assassinations of Hasidic tsadiks and misnagdic rabbis became commonplace in the ensuing two decades. The hostilities among the kehilles discouraged the Polish government from

Figure 13. Portrait of Tadeusz Kościuszko (1746–1817). As the first President of the Polish Republic in the first imaginary scenario, Kościuszko gave regional Jewish communities considerable local autonomy.

interfering: "Poland can sit back and watch the Jews destroy them-selves," said one Polish deputy on the floor of the Sejm.

The first President of the Polish Republic, Tadeusz Kościuszko, modeled his attitudes toward the Jewish communities on his Ameri-can counterparts' treatment of the American Indians (Figure 13). He allowed the regional voivodeships to conclude separate treaties with each of the Jewish kehilles, recognizing them as legal entities but without granting their members Polish citizenship. Many of these treaties were modeled on the Privileges that medieval Jewish communities had negotiated, allowing the Jews to retain their own languages, dress, legal courts, and taxation. Over time, these kehilles came to be recognized as "domestic dependent nations," internally autonomous, but under the jurisdiction of the Polish Republic. Individual Jews were granted the legal right to leave the kehillah and settle in cities or the countryside, but in doing so, they would abrogate all rights and privileges associated with their sovereign rights as members of the Jewish nation. Few took advantage of this opportunity, preferring to remain within the community and live according to halakhic law.

The kehilles' separatism led to dramatically different patterns of economic and social development in the Polish Republic. The Polish, Ukrainian, and Belorussian regions of the Republic rapidly industrialized and advanced technologically, whereas the predominantly Jewish regions remained economically stagnant. Theater, opera, music, literature, and the values of middle-class European life were widely embraced in Polish cities, but were staunchly rejected by the kehilles, which retreated into Talmudic study, kabbalistic mysticism, and fervent prayer. The Republic flourished and rapidly expanded to the east, as Polish homesteaders sought to purchase vast tracks of land in Left Bank Ukraine and began to encroach upon historic Russian territory. By the 1830s, Polish expansion into Russia was endemic. But back in the Polish heartland and Right Bank Ukraine, the thriving Polish bourgeoisie was turning against the Jewish kehilles in their midst. Much of the anti-Jewish rhetoric of the time was focused on the accusation that Jews were spreading vice among the Poles. Historically, many Jews had served as tavern-keepers and liquor-distillers in the region, and were commonly blamed for promoting peasant drunkenness. *In the kehilles, where they were exempt from government taxation, Jews continued to sell liquor and run inns and taverns, in which they established entertainment and gambling facilities to earn profits from the Poles. This activity, however, soon caused problems. The Jews' inexperience with drinking, combined with the sudden infiltration of cheap alcohol and the lack of productive economic activity in the kehilles, encouraged the spread of alcoholism within the Jewish community. The Hasidic lands, in particular, became bastions of vice,* where some rebbes encouraged drunkenness and urged their followers to embrace a life of fervent joy.

There were even widespread accusations that the Hasidic *kehilles* were engaging in orgies and deviant sexual practices.

By the 1820s, individual voivodeships began expelling the Jews from the land by forcing them to accept unfavorable treaties. The voivodeship of Braclaw was particularly forceful in expelling and reset-tling the Jews. The appeals of the Braclav kehillah made it to the Polish supreme judiciary in 1830, resulting in the landmark case of Braclaw Kehillah v. Voivodeship of Braclaw, in which the judiciary declined to rule on the merits, but legally classified the kehilles as "domestic depen-dent nations," thereby deciding that they lacked standing to sue as a "foreign" nation. The case led to the "Jewish Removal Act" of 1830, in which many of the kehilles were forced to sign treaties exchanging their land and holdings west of the Dnieper River for lands east of the river. Each kehille was settled upon a reservation and placed under the direct jurisdiction of a local hereditary rabbi or rebbe.

The Polish Republic continued to flourish and expand to the east: in 1846 it formally annexed Left Bank Ukraine – the territories the Polish-Lithuanian Commonwealth had ceded to Muscovite Russia in the 1667 Treaty of Andrusovo. The reversal of Andrusovo subju-gated the tsarist state and signaled Poland's new role as a major Euro-pean power. Poland's steel, coal, and iron industries continued to fuel its economy, meeting the demands for industrial and railway expansion throughout Europe and Russia. Much of Poland's steel went through the Baltic port of Gdansk, which grew into one of Europe's largest and most active ports.

Polish influence extended throughout the region, but its Jew-ish population retained its historic autonomy. The Polish government hoped that Polish Jews would follow the example of German Jews across the border in assimilating into the strengthening state, but the strong tradition of Jewish autonomy in Poland persevered and the Jew-ish kehilles refused to dissolve themselves. None of the attempts suc-ceeded in breaking down the fierce independence of the Jewish kehilles, which continued to be ruled strictly by halakhic law under the super-vision of the rabbinate. Children continued to be schooled in religious heders and some went on to study in yeshivot. Few residents spoke any language other than Yiddish, and the culture of the kehilles continued to revolve around the Judaic calendar. Thus, the Jewish kehilles contin-ued to slide into poverty at the same time that the state that surrounded it increased in wealth and influence.

Today there are sixty-five federally recognized Jewish kehilles in Poland, each of which has legal autonomy, including the right to form governments, enforce laws, tax, regulate commercial and educational activities, and determine membership (including the right to excommunicate). State efforts continue to combat the endemic poverty and social problems that plague the territories, including high rates of diabetes and tuberculosis, as well as alcoholism and suicide. Unemployment is rampant, and the schools, which remain under rabbinical and Hasidic control, have adamantly refused to introduce any vocational training. Jewish children are set up to succeed only in the many yeshivot that exist throughout the territories; most kehilles do not even teach school-aged children arithmetic or the Polish language. The existence of absentee fathers, who are encouraged to leave their families for the yeshiva, combined with the staunch resistance to family planning programs, are among the reasons the Jewish territories have the highest birth rates in Europe.

Outsiders sometimes admire the resiliency of the kehilles and the ways they have managed to ardently preserve their religious lifestyle in separatist enclaves. But for the most part, the regions are most often visited by outsiders seeking cheap alcohol and gambling opportunities. Some areas have also been opened up for tourists, who enjoy wandering through the streets, listening to the sound of public prayer, and feeling as though they have stepped back in time. The kehilles are closed to all visitors during the Jewish Sabbath as well as during the myriad Jewish holidays observed in the reservations. A particularly popular time to visit is during the festival of Purim, when a rowdy holiday atmosphere permeates the region. Controversies have recently erupted over the appropriation of Jewish symbols by Poles, particularly for the names and mascots of Polish sports teams, but for the most part the only indication of a Jewish presence in modern Poland are the kitsch souvenirs that can be found in tourist shops.

Scenario 2: The resettlement and integration of the Jews in Tsarist Russia

In the first partition of Poland in 1772, Russia acquired the province of Vitebsk in Belorussia, with a population of perhaps 30,000 Jews. The Jews of Vitebsk became the first legally sanctioned Jewish community in the Russian Empire. Empress Catherine the Great provided them with incentives to convert and encouraged them to enroll in the estates of the burghers or merchantry, whose respective laws would determine the Jews' legal status. However, ambiguities remained in Russia's actual treatment of the Jews, for the tsarist state continued to differentiate between people belonging to the merchantry and "peoples of foreign belief" (*inovernye*), a category that included Jews, Muslims, Siberian peoples, and others. Thus, while in some ways the Jews were regarded as members of the merchant class, in other ways they continued to be treated as a separate estate. In 1791, for instance, Catherine explicitly decreed that Jews had no rights to register as merchants in the Russian interior, a decree that has long been viewed as having established the Pale of Jewish Settlement. Although the Russian state's policies toward the Jews were generally haphazard, they were ultimately intended to integrate the Jews into Russian society as an initial step toward their ultimate conversion to Christianity.

With Russia's subsequent acquisition of the lands partitioned from Poland in 1793 and 1795, Catherine came into the possession of territories with much larger Jewish populations. Her initial reaction was to continue the previous policies of encouraging Jews to enroll in one of the existing estates, while prohibiting them from leaving the territories in which they were already residing. The policies of the tsarist state were also influenced by the proposal put forward in 1797 by the Russian Jewish merchant, Nota Khaimovich Notkin, who proposed that Jews be encouraged to settle as agricultural workers in recently annexed Turkish lands and move into manufacturing as factory workers. The basic contours of these policies served as the blueprint for her successor Alexander I's 1804 statute on the Jews, an all-encompassing document outlining the rights and responsibilities of Jews in the Russian Empire (Figure 14). The statute began with a section on Enlightenment, urging that all Jewish children be enrolled in Russian schools, and requiring all Jews to wear German or Polish-style dress, and keep all internal bookkeeping, bonds, bills of exchange, and legal documents in the Russian, Polish, or German languages. All Jews were also required to adopt legal surnames to be used in all official documentation. In these clauses, the statute echoed similar edicts issued by Central European states, most notably Austrian Emperor Joseph II's famous Edict of Tolerance of 1781.

In order to fit the Jews into the existing structures of the Russian Empire and to increase their usefulness to the state, they were

Figure 14. Portrait of Tsar Alexander I (1777–1825) (1814), oil on canvas, painting by Baron François Pascal Simon Gerard (1770–1837). In the second imaginary scenario, the Russian government's forcible implementation of the Tsar's 1804 statute on the Jews paved the way for rapid Jewish assimilation into Russian society.

also required to enroll in one of the existing Russian estates: burghers, farmers, merchants, or manufacturers. Jews who wished to farm the land, but were unable to purchase it on their own, were permitted to relocate to one of the less-populated regions of the Crimea, where they would be given land as a government grant free of taxation for ten years. Similarly, Jews wishing to engage in manufacturing could be given government loans to establish factories and workshops. Those unable to do so could apply to receive special government grants to establish such enterprises in less-populated areas. Guilds, for their part, would be required to admit Jews.

As was often the case with Russian legal enactments, however, the new laws were unevenly enforced. Following the Napoleonic invasion of 1812, the tsarist government abandoned its previous embrace of enlightened principles in favor of more forcible and reactionary policies. The 1804 statute, which was supposed to be implemented gradually and voluntarily, *was instead implemented by force and coercion.* Russian government officials partnered with Jewish Enlightenment reformers (Maskilim) to ensure that their policies were carried out. So-called "educated Jews" were recruited from among the Maskilim to work with the government to reform Jewish society. This partnership made the Maskilim into agents of social engineering and granted them a privileged status within the Russian state. *Jewish proponents of educational and institutional reform readily accepted the coercive powers given them by the government, and worked with a vengeance to ensure the reform of the Jewish population. The main instrument of coercion available to the Maskilim was the threat of the draft.* The Russian military reforms of 1827, decreed by the new Tsar, Nicholas I, allowed for the forcible drafting of Jews for a twenty-five-year term of military service. When those selected for the draft refused to cooperate, Jewish communal authorities engaged hired henchmen to kidnap the reluctant draftees.

Maskilim, with the backing of the Russian state, were encouraged to forcibly snip off the beards of Jews who refused to present themselves as clean-shaven, and to cut the traditional Jewish frock coats if they fell below the knees. Anyone caught speaking Yiddish in public was subject to severe punishment. Most importantly, despite the original 1804 statute's tolerance of Jewish religious practice, Nicholas I embraced Orthodox Christianity as one of the defining characteristics of his empire *and interpreted the 1804 statute as prohibiting Jewish religious practice, an interpretation embraced by some of the more radical Maskilim.* Many traditional Jews even regarded the reform schools established by the enlightened German rabbi Max Lilienthal in the 1840s as a ploy to convert the Jews to Russian Orthodoxy. *The 1804 statute, with its provisions and anticipation of resettlement, provided the ideal opportunity to separate the Jews from their communities, and, at the same time, grant them all the rights and privileges of Christians if they converted.*

The initial waves of reform were vigorously opposed by more traditional segments of the Jewish community and eventually led to the Jewish uprising of November 1830. The uprising, which was led initially by a group of powerful kahal leaders, soon spread throughout the region, but was forcibly stamped out by Russian forces. The leaders of the uprising were brought to St. Petersburg and hanged. The reforms continued, dividing the Jewish population between those who embraced the economic and social opportunities offered by conversion and those who continued to defend Jewish religious belief. In January 1863, another insurrection began, this time led by Jewish yeshiva students who were being forcibly recruited into the Russian military. The defeat of this uprising prompted an even more determined tsarist reaction and led to mass arrests and property confiscation. Although pockets of resistance remained, by the turn of the century, the vast majority of former Jews had abandoned their religious heritage.

Indeed, from the beginning of the reform wave, the majority followed the laws – perhaps with resentment, but without rebellion. By the 1840s, hundreds of thousands of Jews had signed up, enticed by the promise of free land and freedom from taxation. With enrollment quotas abolished, Jewish parents eagerly enrolled their children in the Russian-language schools in the hopes they would receive the type of education necessary to succeed in the Russian civil service or in business; the mandatory religious component of the schools seemed like a worthwhile sacrifice for their children's long-term professional success. Once resettled in the cities of the Russian interior, the agrarian lands of New Russia and the mining and industrial centers of the Urals, these individuals invariably distanced themselves from their Jewish roots. Isolated from established Jewish communities, many embraced the freedoms bestowed upon them and profited from their educational advantages, eventually abandoning their Jewish faith and merging with the Christian Orthodox population. In territories with low rates of literacy, the Jews had little difficulty in obtaining high administrative positions, provided they took part in the Christian ceremonies that were such a crucial aspect of the Russian bureaucracy. Their continued social connections with other former Jews across the empire also facilitated their newfound roles as mediators between cultures, and allowed those enrolled in the merchant guilds to prosper by negotiating advantageous trade agreements. Experience in artisanal work, trade, and service industries benefited the Jews, many of whom became quite affluent in their new lives.

Other Jews enrolled as farmers, taking advantage of the land grants offered by the government in the Crimea and across newly conquered territories of Russia. A few failed in farming and fell into serfdom, but many more managed to establish vast estates with their own serfs. By the time serfdom was abolished in 1861, some of the largest serf-owners in the empire were of Jewish heritage. But the majority who went into farming managed to make do in the peasant villages, eventually adopting the peasant lifestyle and living in peasant huts complete with the ubiquitous icon corner. Visitors to villages sometimes reported that certain families lit candles in front of their icons on Friday evenings, but nobody could recall the custom's origins. The influx of well-educated farmers led to the introduction of new agricultural techniques, helping Russia achieve its reputation as a world leader in farming technology.

Still others moved to the major Russian industrial centers of the Urals and the Baltics, where they worked in factories, plants, and mines, rapidly increasing the industrial workforce and contributing to Russia's rapid industrialization.

The majority of former Jews, though, enrolled in the burgher class, where they were incorporated into Russian cities, and took up jobs as porters, coachmen, shop assistants, tavern owners, small shop owners, and vendors. A few flourished, beginning their urban lives as peddlers before saving up enough money to buy a small shop. Some eventually opened up large department stores, thereby transforming the commercial landscape of St. Petersburg's Nevsky Prospect and Moscow's Arbat. The success stories of these individuals inspired others to follow in their path. Many historians today credit former Jews with facilitating Russia's transformation into an industrial and commercial powerhouse.

Former Jews also helped develop the Russian mining and oil industries. The immense wealth created by the early exploitation of

Russia's natural resources allowed the country to lead the world in enacting progressive child labor laws and humane working conditions. It also greatly enriched the tsars and influenced their style of political rule. Successive tsars showed more interest in maintaining their opulent lifestyles and governing passively from a distance than implementing any type of progressive reform. Thanks to the generous oil revenue payouts that the state distributed to its population, popular unrest was rare. The rising living standards across the empire contributed to the absence of the types of revolutionary unrest that plagued the rest of Europe and America.

The spectacular fortunes made by several former Jews became legendary. The oil tycoon Lev Davidovich Bronstein, for instance, was born on a farm in southern Ukraine in 1879, and had become one of the world's wealthiest oil barons by the 1920s. Like many former Jews, Bronstein embraced Russian Orthodox Christianity the way only a convert could, famously changing his name to Lev Troitsky (Trinity, in Russian). Bronstein used much of his vast fortune to build "mega-cathedrals" in every city in the empire. By the 1930s, these massive religious edifices had spread throughout the entire country, boldly displaying their enormous bronze onion domes in virtually every city center. Bronstein gathered a group of followers, who took their name from the Russian word for mega-cathedral (bolshoy sobor), and came to be known as Bolsheviks. Some of Russian Orthodoxy's leading theologians can trace their roots to the Jews of the Pale. Indeed, former Jews were among the most zealous supporters of the pro-religious campaigns of the 1920s and figured prominently in virtually all branches of the Russian government by the 1930s.

Today, it is only historians and genealogists who are aware that so many of Russia's early twentieth-century oil and industry barons have Jewish backgrounds. The success of former Jews throughout Russia – in the realms of farming, industry, technology, finance, science, education, and entertainment – is truly remarkable and a testament to the success of the 1804 statutes and the subsequent mass conversion of Russia's Jews.

The two preceding scenarios are grounded in what I believe to be reasonable analogies and suppositions. The Polish Republic that the reformers envisioned was modeled on the American Revolution and was defended by a fighter in the American Revolutionary War and personal friend of Thomas Jefferson. Despite some important differences, it seems reasonable to imagine that the Polish Republic would have treated its indigenous minorities much as the American Republic did, as sovereign nations within a democratic republic. The Jewish tradition of autonomy that remained, albeit in a weakened state, in the waning days of the Polish-Lithuanian Commonwealth could easily have provided a model for communal autonomy in the Republic. If Berek Joselewicz's army, which in reality met its end in defeat at the Praga suburb, had played an important role in a victorious triumph for Kościuszko's uprising, it is reasonable to imagine that the Jews would have been rewarded with continued autonomy. In such a case, we can imagine the existence of Jewish enclaves comparable in some ways to modern-day New Square, Bnei Brak, Mea Shearim, and Monsey, and in other ways to the Indian reservations of America.

The second scenario imagines Russian Jews as a mix between early modern *conversos* and modern Russian Jewish oligarchs. The forcible conversion of Russia's Jews was a dream of many tsarist officials, and there was certainly a cohort of radical Maskilim who could have gone along with such a plan. Indeed, when Russia did engage upon a massive drive against religion under the Soviets, there were many Jews leading the assault. There are ample cultural and sociological reasons to believe that with the removal of restrictions and prejudices against them, people of Jewish heritage in Russia would have achieved enormous success in politics, business, and culture as certain individuals did in the early Soviet period and early post-Soviet era.

It is difficult to say which scenario would be better: in the first, Judaism flourishes but the Jews do not; in the second Jews flourish but Judaism does not. Perhaps the Pale, in which both Jews and Judaism struggled along, was the best scenario. Neither assimilation nor complete segregation would have benefited Jewish history. One is reminded of Rousseau's introduction to his notes on the constitution of Poland, the only time in which he referenced the Jews in the entire document:

> Determined that his people should never be absorbed by other peoples, Moses devised for them customs and practices that could not be blended into those of other nations and weighted them down with rites and peculiar ceremonies. He put countless prohibitions upon them, all calculated to keep them constantly on their toes, and to make them, with respect to the rest of mankind,

outsiders forever. Each fraternal bond that he established among
the individual members of his republic became a further barrier,
separating them from their neighbors and keeping them from
becoming one with those neighbors. That is why this odd nation –
so often subjugated, so often dispersed, so often, to all
appearances, annihilated, but always utterly faithful to its law –
has, scattered among other peoples but not absorbed by them,
nevertheless preserved itself down into our own times.[8]

For Rousseau, the barrier that Jews had erected between themselves
and those in whose midst they lived was the secret to their success:
Poland, he believed, would benefit from emulating the Jews. The Pale
was, in many ways, just another barrier separating the Jews not only
from their neighbors, among whom they lived in the Pale, but from the
imperial society beckoning them to assimilate. As Rousseau realized, the
dispersion of Jews among non-Jewish neighbors prevented them from
acquiring the type of enclave culture imagined in my first scenario, while
the barriers separating the Jews shielded them from the type of assimilation imagined by the second scenario. Without the Pale, Jews would
have been at the mercy of the twin dangers of the Reservation and the
Melting Pot.

7 WHAT IF A CHRISTIAN STATE HAD BEEN ESTABLISHED IN MODERN PALESTINE?

Derek Jonathan Penslar

The Israeli–Palestinian conflict commands greater attention than any other on the globe. Why? Other conflicts are just as enduring and far more violent. The Palestinians are not the world's only persecuted stateless minority and Israel is not the only country to oppress them. Israel is but one of many states that privilege one ethnic or religious community over another. So why, then, is Israel singled out?

Most supporters of Israel would make the following argument: Israel is the victim of a vicious double standard and is judged more harshly than other states that engage in far greater atrocities. Condemnation of Israel is a manifestation of self-righteous anger that masks unforgivable hypocrisy. Israel's detractors seek to delegitimize the Jewish state and advocate its radical reconstruction, if not its utter destruction. The reasons for this global obsession with one small country are clear: Israel is a Jewish state, and anti-Zionism is but another form of antisemitism. Supporters of Israel would buttress this argument with quotations from Arab and Muslim public figures, whose anti-Zionist rhetoric is peppered with classic antisemitic stereotypes, or from left-leaning European and American academics who flirt with antisemitic myths of vast Jewish economic and political power manifested in a monolithic "Israel lobby."

Israel's detractors, on the other hand, would point to the anomalous nature of the Israeli polity. Its establishment was approved by the United Nations despite the express will of its native majority, and it refused to allow the return of hundreds of thousands of refugees who had fled in panic or had been expelled from their homes in 1948.

Israeli law virtually guarantees citizenship to individuals of only partly Jewish origin (and their families) but practices institutionalized discrimination against indigenous Palestinians. Since 1967, Israel has steadily confiscated and colonized territory in the West Bank, applying Israeli law over its Jewish citizens while subjecting Palestinians to a harsh regime of surveillance and collective punishment. Israel's critics may admit that there are more violent conflicts in the world, but they would claim that there are no more egregious cases of expropriation and occupation. They would add that there is no equivalent case of prolonged state-sponsored oppression carried out with the tacit approval of Israel's patron, the United States.

The pro-Israel approach focuses on perception, while the anti-Israel approach focuses on essence. To be sure, Israel's defenders dismiss certain accusations made against the country as blatant lies, but for the most part their concern is how the world sees Israel, how people fail to appreciate Israel's security predicament, and how they neglect to place the country's actions in an appropriate context. For Israel's critics, the problem is what Israel allegedly does: it is said to act immorally and without justification, yet the international community sits idly by while the rights of the Palestinians are consistently trampled. The rhetoric used to defend both of these positions, emphasizing extrinsic and intrinsic factors respectively, possesses an internal logic but is based on selective evidence and limited by predetermined outcomes. Both of these positions' arguments are rooted in heartfelt convictions that are impervious to revision through rational demonstration or counter-argument.

Given the unreliability of the arguments by interested parties to the conflict, how may we determine whether antisemitism is anti-Zionism's source or its byproduct? How can we measure whether Israel's distinctiveness is a matter of perception or is inherent in the state's actions? To answer these questions, I propose a counterfactual thought experiment in which the Zionist movement failed and a European Christian state was instead established in Palestine. I will trace how this hypothetical state would have come into being, how it would have behaved toward the Arabs within and beyond its borders, and how the international community in general, and the Muslim and Arab worlds in particular, would have dealt with it.

To be sure, some critics may dismiss the results of such a thought experiment as overly speculative. Many historians today remain skeptical about counterfactual reasoning. If they support it at all, they prefer to deal with "what if?" scenarios that have a high degree of plausibility. This preference seems reasonable. Yet how do we distinguish a plausible from an implausible counterfactual scenario? Niall Ferguson has proposed that for a counterfactual scenario to enjoy plausibility, it ought to have been conceivable to the historical figures that determined events at the time they occurred. According to this standard, a good counterfactual should not invoke supernatural authority, indulge in anachronistic projection (for example, placing computers in the Renaissance), or impose upon historical actors affective states or levels of knowledge or agency that they could not possibly have possessed. In short, a good counterfactual should not be unrealistic.

That said, even unrealistic counterfactuals can still have value, for as Richard Ned Lebow has argued, they can "help us work through moral and scholarly problems."[1] The counterfactual scenarios advanced in this chapter blend the realistic with the whimsical. As we shall see, it is quite easy to imagine the Zionist project failing in Palestine. By contrast, it is far more fanciful to imagine a European Christian state arising in its place. Yet, while these two scenarios may not enjoy the same degree of plausibility, exploring their respective ramifications can help us untangle conceptual and ethical knots about the nature of the state of Israel and the Israel–Palestine conflict.[2]

The failure of Zionism

Any number of historical factors could have led to Zionism's failure. The early Zionist movement depended upon a handful of great leaders to forge a small and inchoate mass of activists into an organized political project. It is hard to imagine Zionism having ever achieved global standing without the achievements of Theodor Herzl and Chaim Weizmann. Yet the factors that led Herzl to Zionism and that gave Weizmann access to world leaders were serendipitous.

Let us assume that the basic structures of late nineteenth-century European history remained unchanged – that is, there were still pogroms in Russia, political antisemitism in the Dual Monarchy and Germany, and the Dreyfus Affair in France. Even so, Herzl was driven to Zionism not only by the crisis of the Jews but also by his own tortured psyche. His greatest love was the theater, but he was a mediocre playwright. Herzl had a fragile ego that had been scarred by his dominating mother and was further damaged by a disastrously unhappy marriage. Bedeviled by the "Jewish problem" in European society as well as by his career and personal frustrations, Herzl searched for a cause that would put both antisemitism and his inner demons to rest. After a few false starts (e.g. socialism, mass conversion of the Jews to Christianity), Herzl fell upon Zionism, to which he devoted the final nine years of his tragically brief life.

Herzl was raised in a thoroughly assimilated home and had no natural affinity with Judaism or Jewish culture. Weizmann's embrace of Zionism, on the other hand, was organic, as his upbringing in Minsk had been steeped in Jewish ethnicity, Yiddish, and Hebraism (Figure 15). Of course, Weizmann's embrace of Zionism was not fore-ordained; many Jews in his life-situation became Bundists or Communists, while others embraced a nonnationalistic orthodoxy. What matters here is not that Weizmann became a Zionist, but rather that he became a great Zionist leader, a position he attained only through relationships with the British governing elite that resulted from his successful chemical research in munitions production during the First World War. Had he been a mediocre chemist, Weizmann would have remained a bench scientist who whiled away his leisure hours as a provincial Zionist activist.

Zionism lends itself well to counterfactual analysis because the entire enterprise was so utterly improbable, so unlikely to succeed. When Herzl founded the Zionist Organization in 1897, scarcely 15,000 Jews in all of Europe belonged to Zionist associations. By the time of Herzl's death in 1904, some 100,000 Jews belonged to the ZO. But impressive as this number may sound in comparison with earlier periods, it still amounted to only 6 percent of world Jewry. On the eve of World War I, Palestine was home to no more than 65,000 Jews, less than one-tenth of the territory's total population. This minuscule foothold could not have developed into a state had it not been for a series of geopolitical events over which Zionists had no influence.

During the war, Weizmann's persuasive power was only one of many factors behind Britain's decision to issue the Balfour Declaration in support of a Jewish national home in Palestine. (Among other reasons, Britain was looking for a pliant postwar client in the Middle East, and British leaders held greatly exaggerated views of Jewish political influence in the United States, which Britain wanted to enter the war on its side, and in Russia, which Britain hoped would keep on fighting after

Figure 15. Chaim Weizmann (1874–1952) played an important role in Great Britain's decision in 1917 to issue the Balfour Declaration in support of a Jewish national home in Palestine. But what if Great Britain had lost World War I to Germany?

the tsarist regime fell in March 1917.) For Zionism to have any chance of succeeding, Britain needed to win the war and to adhere afterwards to the terms of the Balfour Declaration despite the obvious damage it did to British relations with the Arab world. The League of Nations had to be willing to accept the terms of the Balfour Declaration in its award of the Mandate for Palestine to the United Kingdom. Britain had to allow large-scale Jewish immigration and grant the Zionists extensive autonomy. The toil, devotion, and courage of the Zionist community in Palestine, the Yishuv, were also necessary preconditions for Israel's creation, but they were hardly sufficient.

In hindsight, Germany clearly entered the First World War at a disadvantage compared with the Entente, but the Entente's victory was not predetermined. It is certainly possible that the Triple Alliance could have won the First World War, especially if the United States had remained neutral. A victorious Germany in World War I would have helped sustain its longtime ally, the Ottoman Empire, whose government and populace vociferously opposed Zionism. As in Britain, Germany's wartime rulers saw Jews as possessing vast economic power and believed they would be useful clients in the Middle East. But the ties with the Ottoman Empire were too strong and the German elites' dislike of Jews too entrenched for the forging of an alloy of *raison d'état* and romantic biblical philosemitism.

Even a victorious Triple Alliance could not have indefinitely preserved the Ottoman Empire or its Christian multinational ally, the Dual Monarchy. Nationality conflicts and economic weakness would have eventually led to the Ottomans' collapse, yet a hegemonic Germany would have prevented the British conquest of Palestine, without which the Balfour Declaration would have had no value. A vast *Mitteleuropa* under German hegemony, a region extending deep into Ukraine and down into the Balkans, would have been supportive of Jews as counterweights to restive, stateless eastern European nationalities. Jewish nationalism might well have developed throughout the globe – indeed, given the ubiquity of nationalist movements during the interwar era, it is hard to imagine it not doing so. But without having been galvanized by the likes of Herzl and Weizmann, and without a foothold in Palestine strengthened by a friendly European colonial power, Jewish nationalism may well have remained focused on the diaspora rather than on the land of Israel.

The nationalities within Germany's *Mitteleuropa* would, in time, have revolted against their masters, and there may well have been a Second World War in which Germany and Britain fought for supremacy in the eastern Mediterranean, with France most likely supporting Britain given their neatly divided interests in the Maghreb and France's historic animosity toward its neighbor to the northeast. Yet the Germany in this counterfactual universe, however expansionist and chauvinist it may have been, would never have fallen into the desperate straits that made possible the rise of Nazism. During our counterfactual Second World War, Jews may well have been harshly persecuted, but there would have been no Holocaust. Zionism would have been deprived of its chief reservoir of sympathy from within the post-1945 international community. Millions more Jews would have survived the war and sought to flee the turmoil of Europe, but they would have been mere refugees, like the rest of Europe's victimized peoples, not victims of industrial genocide whom the world singled out for pity.

A Christian state in Palestine?

In contrast to the highly plausible scenario of the Zionist movement failing to establish a Jewish state in Palestine, the possibility of a Christian state being created in its stead is more far-fetched. Nevertheless, it remains highly instructive for understanding and assessing Israel's contested status in contemporary world opinion.

In this scenario, Germany is an ally of the Ottomans but also a Great Power looking to enhance its own prestige by protecting its citizens abroad. It looks after and fosters the ongoing settlement in Palestine of Swabian Templers, a Protestant sect that established several colonies in pre-1914 Palestine (Figure 16). Let us imagine that in time the Templer movement, bolstered by persecuted ethnic German Protestants in the Soviet Union and a congeries of economic refugees from many lands, obtains a critical mass. Under cover of the chaos of the counterfactual Second World War, this new Christian community overthrows its Ottoman and German masters and after the war declares the independence of a Protestant state, which it calls New Israel in commemoration of the ancient biblical kingdom and the Templers' own sense of identity with the ancient Hebrews. Attracting educated, technologically sophisticated evangelical Christians from the Western

Figure 16. Christian Templer settlers in Wilhelma, Palestine, not far from Jaffa. What if this German Christian community had succeeded in overthrowing its Ottoman and German masters and had declared an independent Protestant state in Palestine after World War I?

world, in time it attracts persecuted Christians of sundry denominations from throughout the Middle East, where newly independent states increasingly conflate Arab with Muslim identity. New Israel soon outgrows its agricultural roots to become a powerhouse industrial and service-based economy, akin to that built up at around the same time by Mormons in the American southwest. Yet New Israel also becomes a pariah state, in constant conflict with its Arab neighbors, and dependent upon a Great Power for political and military support.

In our counterfactual world – as in the real one – postwar Europe is an economic shambles and is unable to maintain its empire. One major difference is that decades of German colonial occupation of the territory from the Baltic to the Black Sea have reduced the political heft of the Soviet Union, so that there is only one superpower, the United States, a Protestant country whose populace feels a deep spiritual connection with the ingathering of Protestant exiles in the state of New Israel. New Israel receives the steadfast support of America's evangelical Christian political bloc, while a belatedly emergent Soviet Union seeks allies amongst the Arab states.

Against the backdrop of these hypothetical events, how would the new country have behaved? How would the world have perceived it? Answering these questions helps us determine whether hostility to Israel stems from the state's Jewish character or from other factors. As a European colonial entity, New Israel's treatment of the indigenous Palestinian Arabs would have spanned a range of policies typical of settler-colonial states, including disenfranchisement (Algeria), institutionalized segregation (South Africa), and even mass murder (German Southwest Africa). New Israel would be an exogenous implant, even if its native sons quickly indigenized and felt themselves to be no less Palestinian than those Arabs who remained among them. The question is whether the behavior of this counterfactual New Israel can be seen as similar to that of the real state of Israel. As we shall see, there are – or would have been – enough similarities between the two states to make clear that present-day criticism of the latter is an expression of anticolonialism as well as antisemitism.

Israel and settler-colonial states: similarities and differences

Israel's detractors routinely describe the state as "colonial." They see it as a component of Western conquest and control of the Middle East dating back to Napoleon Bonaparte's invasion of Egypt in 1798 and continuing into our own day. (This view was enshrined in the infamous United Nations resolution of 1975 that equated Zionism with racism and colonialism.) This shrill and tendentious rhetoric has elicited equally propagandistic claims from Israel's defenders that Zionism and Israel bear no resemblance to modern colonialism. In this view, the Zionist project entailed the return of an exiled people to its native land, not conquest and dispossession. Colonial projects sought to extract wealth from conquered lands for the benefit of a mother country, but Zionists were determined to pour labor, capital, and technology into Palestine for the benefit of Jewish immigrants and resident Arabs alike.

To some extent, Israel's champions are right. Zionism differed from extractive or exploitative forms of colonialism. Zionists were unique in thinking of mass immigration to a distant land under foreign rule and inhabited by an indigenous people as an act of homecoming. I would add that the term "settler state" or even "settler-colonial state" is not necessarily pejorative in that some of the world's most democratic and prosperous countries (e.g. the United States, Canada, and Australia) are settler states and products of the era of colonialism. And, like them, the Zionist project was a product of that era and bore that era's common features, e.g. the dual sense of compassion and condescension toward the natives, of a *mission civilisatrice*, and a compulsion to separate from them; faith in Western technology to revive a once fertile but now desertified land; and the marshaling of international investment capital for plantation societies and other potentially profitable projects. Even the Zionists' most hallowed moral scruple that the land should be worked by Jews rather than hired Arab labor was analogous to North American pioneer settlers' belief in the divine commandment to husband the land by the sweat of one's brow.

In many ways, the intentions and actions of Zionist settlers paralleled those of European immigrants to colonial North America, South Africa and Algeria. Each place had unique features, but all were sites of settler colonialism. The state of Israel, like New Israel and settler states throughout the world, faced a fundamental problem regarding the indigenous population of the lands they claimed. For example, in seventeenth-century New England, Puritan settlers feared that they would not succeed in creating a replica of England, tranquil and civilized, in their new environment but would succumb to the savagery of New England's harsh environment. Nature, rough and savage, was to be conquered, subdued, and exploited. Early Zionist settlers, too, often dreaded the land of their ancestral yearnings, invoking the biblical "land that devours its inhabitants," this time through disease, heat, and arid, unforgiving soil.

For the Puritans, as for the Zionists, native peoples were both human and objects of nature. While some Europeans fantasized about the Indian as "noble savage," Puritans were more likely to see the Red Man as sempiternally cursed – a latter-day Canaanite, even the seed of Amalek, whose destruction was to be celebrated rather than mourned. John Winthrop, having witnessed the "miracle" of Native Americans dying en masse because of disease, said: "If God were not pleased with our inheriting these parts, why did He drive out the natives before us?"[3]

In Israel, the mass flight of Palestinians in 1948 was seen as equally miraculous, unexpected but welcome – so much so, that the refugees were not allowed to return, even though the vast majority had not taken up arms against Israel.

Perhaps the most interesting parallel between the colonial North American and Zionist experiences lay in the New World Englishman's simultaneous anxiety about and celebration of a loss of refinement as a result of distance from the European homeland. In the late seventeenth century, the fiery preacher Cotton Mather described his son Increase as "a *tame* Indian, for so the Europeans are pleased sometimes to denominate the children that are born in these regions."[4] In a sermon delivered in 1686 at the age of twenty-six, Mather fretted lest the English fall into a state of "creolian degeneracy," a fate that could be avoided only by willfully and consciously performing an English identity. Mather simultaneously lamented the roughness of his and his peers' manner and celebrated the directness and simplicity of their speech and character. The "Americans," as the colonists increasingly came to be called, were obliged to assert their Englishness through dress, furnishings, and high culture while maintaining the moral integrity of the plainspoken provincial. Like the sabra who remained deeply attached to European culture while being a child of the land, who prided himself on knowledge of Arab ways while strictly limiting contact with the natives, Cotton Mather spoke a seventeenth-century form of Israeli blunt speech known as *dugri* while embracing Anglophilia as a prophylactic against "creoline degeneracy."

Zionists did not think of themselves as journeying to a foreign land but returning home. There is a fine line, however, between the Zionist conception of homecoming to the land of the Bible and the common settler-colonial view that a New Jerusalem would be established upon virgin soil. Puritans in North America and Dutch Reformed Afrikaners in the Cape Colony did not merely compare themselves to the ancient Israelites, they believed themselves to be the Hebrews' successors, fulfilling divine promises made to the children of Israel millennia ago. The Zionist idea of the Jews' return to history by moving en masse to the land of Israel is itself an adaptation of a Protestant reworking of an ancient biblical ideal. It is no coincidence that Christian schemes to restore Palestine to the Jews preceded the beginnings of Zionism by several decades. In our counterfactual universe, that state happens to have taken on flesh and blood, but the connections between the two states, Jewish and Christian, real and imagined, are inextricable.

Even in cases where settler colonialism did not justify itself via the Old Testament there was a similar need to root the colonial project in antiquity. In the early 1900s, French administrators interpreted Algeria through Latin classical literature on the Maghreb, which they read in the same intimate way that Zionists read the Bible. Just as Zionists venerated biblical history, French military strategy in Algeria harked back to ancient Roman practices, and French scholars zealously pursued archaeological excavations of Roman ruins so as to cement the link between the ancient and modern Latin rulers of the land. The motley immigrants from the northern Mediterranean who became the pied-noirs were called the "Latins of Africa," said to comprise a new race, fair of form, committed to hard labor and to reviving the land from neglect at the hands of ostensibly indolent and fanatical Arabs and Berbers.

By the late 1800s, Mediterranean settlers in Algeria were calling themselves "Algerians," or "the Algerian people," and expressed this identity via a distinct, earthy French dialect. This new collective identity, like that of the new Hebrew nation arising in Eretz Israel, was created with astonishing speed, only a few decades after the onset of mass colonization. There are obvious parallels between all these phenomena and Zionist aspirations for a global ingathering of Jewish immigrants, simultaneously inventing and restoring an ancient nation and culture, as well as Zionist views of Palestinians as the land's long-time residents but neither its stewards nor its owners.

Most of the natives in North America were killed or died out long before the post-1945 era of decolonization. They were too few and weak to present a serious threat to the United States or Canadian governments or to constitute an anticolonial liberation movement like the Algerian Front de Libération Nationale, the Palestine Liberation Organization, or the African National Congress. (The American Indian Movement, founded in 1968, made modest gains for native peoples, but its accomplishments cannot be compared with those of the FLN, PLO, or ANC.)

The founding of our counterfactual New Israel, like the real state of Israel, would occur in the midst of the era of decolonization, and its expropriation of the native population would be witnessed and decried by the international community. In both the Christian and

Jewish Israels, the Palestinian Arabs would win the sympathy of the developing world (also known as the "global South") and of leftist intellectuals and activists throughout the West.

This is especially likely to have happened given the fact that, in real history, there was a European colonial state that had a strong Christian identity and became a pariah within the international community for having persecuted the indigenous population – South Africa. Comparisons between Israel and South Africa are ubiquitous in anti-Zionist rhetoric, so I hasten to draw a distinction between the use of the term "apartheid" as a deliberately provocative and manipulative tactic and the sober comparative study of Israel and South Africa, which has been undertaken by respectable scholars.[5] Adopting the latter approach reveals important points of similarity between Afrikaner society and Israel.

Unlike North America, South Africa did not witness the decimation of the native population. White settlers in southern Africa were always vastly outnumbered by the natives and faced a demographic threat that in the early twentieth century was termed "swamping." The need to limit native access to land claimed by whites and restrict Africans to particular places led to the Native Lands Act of 1913, which institutionalized many longstanding practices of segregation and can be considered a legislative precedent for apartheid. Ironically, the rhetoric of demographic threat intensified even during the period of High Apartheid, with the acceleration of white out-migration during the 1970s. The terror of being swamped led to a panicky rejection of *gelykstelling*, the equalization of white and black – or what in the Israel–Palestinian conflict is known as the one-state solution.

White fear led to the construction of a number of psychological defenses. Classic Afrikaner historiography defensively refers to southern Africa as having been thinly populated at the time of the white invasion and of the Bantus as immigrants who arrived in substantive numbers only after the whites had established themselves. The natives were therefore not really natives but newcomers, as opposed to the old-stock Afrikaners. Unfortunately for white South African nationalists, the black population's allegedly tardy arrival did not prevent them from constituting a constant danger, one that was not swept away as in North America by disease and decisive warfare that reduced the native population to a few remnants bottled up on reserves. The apparently insoluble white–black conflict inhibited the production of favorable views of natives as noble savages – an image propagated in North America precisely when the native no longer presented a threat. During the twentieth century South African white youth did not have a tradition of playing Vortrekkers and Zulus after the manner of Euro-Americans playing Cowboys and Red Indians. Israeli Jewish youth are similarly unlikely to enjoy a spirited game of Zionists and Arabs, at least not one where the two sides fight on equal terms and with some degree of moral equivalency. There are additional parallels between Afrikaner and Zionist sensibilities, such as the notion of "demographic threat" and claims that Palestine prior to the arrival of the Zionists was a mostly empty land.

Zionism has long defined itself as the national liberation movement of the Jewish people. Decades before the Zionist movement attained critical mass, Afrikaners were calling themselves a colonized people and characterized their wars against the British as anticolonial rebellions. The Zionist labor movement, which dominated the politics of the pre-1948 Yishuv and the state of Israel until 1977, placed the national interests of the Jews above socialist solidarity with impoverished Palestinian Arabs. During the interwar period, Labor Zionists mounted strikes against Jewish businessmen who employed Arab laborers, while in South Africa white workers went on strike against mineowners who preferred cheap black labor. Labor Zionism's mantra of "Hebrew labor" reflects the sentiments voiced by the white mineworkers of the 1920s who declaimed "Workers of the World Unite, and Fight for a White South Africa."

There are indeed many differences between South Africa and Israel, and I will discuss them below. Here I want to highlight similarities, which in recent decades have manifested themselves in Israel's systematic expropriation of Palestinian land and restrictions of Palestinian freedom of movement within the Occupied Territories. Israel's policies are not identical to apartheid – indeed, they could not be, as apartheid was the name given to one particular legislative system in one particular country. The fact remains that in the West Bank there are two sets of laws: one for the Israeli colonizer and one for the Palestinian colonized. The former enjoys Israeli government services, including the provision of abundant electricity and piped water, while the latter does not. The Palestinian Authority, unlike the South African homelands, has been recognized by the United Nations' General Assembly as the government of a state, and it receives massive amounts of international aid, but it is a Potemkin government that survives on Israeli sufferance.

If Israel were a Christian state and acted similarly, there is no reason, given the international community's treatment of apartheid-era South Africa, to assume that it would be treated more gently. If anything, New Israel would be even more universally excoriated as it would lack the state of Israel's claim to having restored the rights, dignity, and hope of the Jewish people in the wake of the Holocaust.

The comparison between South Africa and Israel throws light on another important issue. Israel has long prided itself on being the only democracy in the Middle East. Its democratic spirit may derive less, however, from the intentions of its founders or deep-seated Judaic values than from Israel's status as a settler state that like the United States, Canada, Australia, and South Africa has developed as a frontier democracy. Frontier societies are based on an inextricable mixture of inclusion and exclusion – inclusion of all whites and exclusion of natives and slaves. These are new societies, free of the heritage of graduated privilege and social hierarchy that continued to weigh heavily in the Old World. Within the bubble of the enfranchised community, freedom of expression is protected, even cherished, and the state operates according to the rule of law.

The contradictions between settler democracy and racial or ethnic oppression grow stronger over time. The United States never retreated from its policy of marginalizing natives. But divisions over slavery pushed the country into a civil war that led to the abolition of slavery and, eventually, to a vibrant and increasingly inclusive democracy. In the South Africa of the 1970s and 1980s, violent resistance against apartheid at home and global condemnation of the regime led some of the country's most powerful leaders to admit that apartheid must be reformed or eliminated. Yet during the mid 1980s the regime retreated from democracy as it imposed a state of emergency, and the long-reigning National Party, which had implemented apartheid in the first place but was suspected by some Afrikaners of indecision and even treachery, was threatened by a new, far-right Conservative Party. Similarly, in 2003 Israeli Prime Minister Ariel Sharon called Israel's presence in the Palestinian territories an "occupation" that cannot continue forever, and six years later Prime Minister Benjamin Netanyahu reluctantly endorsed a two-state solution to the Israel–Palestine conflict. These signs of moderation fomented challenges from both within and outside of Netanyahu's Likud Party, and Netanyahu has refused to implement a two-state scenario in the foreseeable future.

Different variables, different outcomes

The comparison between Israel and other settler states shows that changing one variable – exchanging Israel's Jewish character for a Christian one – would not change many aspects of the state's behavior. But in other ways a Christian Israel would be quite different from the Jewish one.

As noted above, settler societies in their early years are often beset by fears of the aboriginals. This fear leads them to separate themselves from the natives – to dominate, marginalize, or even eradicate them – while at the same time extolling the settlers' indigeneity. Israeli identity is particularly fraught because even after several generations of existence, the state's future appears to many Jews not to be assured. What is more, the Jews' long historical memory of the Holy Land has caused Israeli identity to be mediated, reflective, and overwrought. Long before Jews moved to the land of Israel in sizable numbers, the land was an idealized image in the Jews' imagination.

For Israelis and diaspora Jews alike, the centrality and sacrality of Israel is intensified by existential fear. Israel's supporters tend to attribute the Israeli government's ongoing expansion of West Bank settlements, which undermine the establishment of a Palestinian state, to the threat that such a state would pose to Israel's security. Regardless of whether or not this assumption is correct, Israel has resisted international pressure far more successfully than did France over Algeria or South Africa over apartheid. During the 1970s and 1980s, globalization and neo-liberalization of the South African economy weakened apartheid as many white South Africans traveled abroad, became increasingly cosmopolitan, and came to feel that their state was hopelessly out of sync with the rest of the world. Since the 1990s, Israel has experienced rapid economic growth and has become a pillar of global high technology, yet expropriation of Palestinian lands and the expansion of settlements in the West Bank has accelerated. Organized religion is another force that can weaken settler regimes, as in South Africa, where in 1982 the World Alliance of Reformed Churches suspended the

South African Dutch Reformed Church because of its support for the apartheid. No pressure on such a scale has come from Jewish religious organizations in the diaspora.

Perhaps because of the rigidity of borders between Jews and Arabs in Ottoman and Mandate Palestine, and later the state of Israel, even extreme right-wing Zionism did not develop a conceptual framework of theoretical apartheid. What is more, Arabs within the state of Israel are citizens; indeed, the country's declaration of independence proclaims the "social and political equality" of all the country's inhabitants regardless of "race, creed or sex." Despite institutionalized discrimination, the political position of Israel's Arab citizens has improved over time. This situation differs sharply from the Cape Colony, which began in the late 1800s to whittle away its longstanding policy of nonracial citizenship, and, after union with the Afrikaner republics in 1908, made no attempt to extend citizenship to blacks throughout the country.

Unlike South Africa, in post-1948 Israel, the Arab minority has not constituted an essential component of the workforce. The same is true even for the Arabs of the West Bank and Gaza, who provided an abundant supply of cheap labor after Israel conquered the territories in 1967. During the 1970s and 1980s Arabs from the territories were omnipresent as menial laborers and appeared to be pillars of the construction sector, but the Palestinian intifada of 1987 – a movement intended to "shake off" Israeli rule – demonstrated how easily Israel could shake off Arab labor, replacing it with guest workers from Thailand, the Philippines, and Romania.

In the early twentieth century, Arabs outnumbered Jews in Palestine by a factor of ten to one, about the same ratio as that between blacks and whites in South Africa at the time. But the radical Zionist youth of the Second Aliyah did not want to profit from the Arab's body or to be a master of any sort of slave. The Zionist youth desired that the land desire them; they were suffused with a heartfelt, artless sense of homecoming. European colonists elsewhere did not experience a personal psychic transformation; they conquered and loved the land but were not infatuated with it; they did not aspire to melt into its landscape. For the Zionists, Arabs were not merely indolent, they lacked a vital life-force and were too organically linked with the soil to be its faithful husband; instead, they were undifferentiated extensions of its flora and fauna.

The Zionist project called upon two great world-historic forces: colonialism, on the one hand, and, on the other, the revolutionary reshaping of humanity that was undertaken throughout the twentieth-century Western world. The transformative torque of each force was vast; it has taken the combination of the two to put Israel on the map and keep it there. Israel, as it took form in 1948, was minuscule, but the amount of political energy required to create this statelet was akin to the energy required to fuse hydrogen atoms into helium.

Zionism was the only manifestation of colonialism that was structured by a movement with a coherent ideological structure. Zionism was a powerful form of Jewish nationalism. And like other nationalisms, it cherished language as the repository of the folk-soul. Zionism transformed Hebrew from a stiff language reserved for religious and legal topics into an earthy spoken vernacular and a supple literary medium capable of expressing the whole range of human sensibility. By contrast, the Afrikaans language for many years lived in the shadow of Dutch, only replacing its European parent in 1925 as an official language of state. The first Afrikaans novel was published only in 1913; the Afrikaans Bible appeared twenty years later. In the Maghreb, the transformation of motley Mediterranean communities into French Algerians was quick yet unchoreographed, and the pied-noirs' dialect, although featured in colloquial speech in novels, was not a literary medium in and of itself.

Not all Jewish immigrants to the land of Israel have been nationalists. It was impossible, however, to live in the Yishuv of the late Ottoman and Mandate period, not to mention the Israeli state, without being profoundly shaped by a top-down structured collective identity. Israeli nation-building was as rapid as the growth of the pied-noir community in Algeria, but the former was far more directed and purposeful, its linguistic base vastly richer, and its culture more enduringly adhesive.

Many of these Jewish features of modern Israel would have been lacking in a Christian New Israel. This hypothetical country would have been a settler state, but not a project of national revival and salvation. New Israel would not have been fueled by the Jewish people's collective memory of the land of its forefathers and its yearning to return there. Its Christian population would have been spared the crucible of the Holocaust in the face of which a Jewish state was seen by Jews the world over as a desperate necessity. A Christian Israel might have been less resilient, less determined to survive, and hence more likely to succumb to a native revolt or to surrender political hegemony peace-fully. (These two scenarios played out in Algeria and South Africa respectively.) Jews, traumatized by millennia of persecution and a lack of sovereignty, created a state whose military was sacrosanct. Although Israel is a parliamentary democracy governed by civilians, its politics are dominated by security concerns, and the country's most successful politicians are often former generals or members of elite commando units. A Christian Israel, like apartheid-era South Africa, would have a powerful army and live in a state of constant military preparedness. But Israel's military ethos is as much a product of Jewish history as it is of the troubled environment in which the country exists.

Conclusion

Our counterfactual thought experiment suggests that anticolonialism and anti-Westernism are powerful sources of hostility to Israel in the contemporary Middle East. Antisemitism is certainly present, and it often takes the form of an ideological superstructure supported by a geopolitical base. This claim may appear to be belied by the antisemitic fulminations of the leaders of Hamas and Hezbollah and the former Ira-nian President Mahmud Ahmadinejad and former Egyptian President Mohamed Morsi. But these figures would not be taking a more mod-erate line if the state of Israel were Christian in character. They would simply substitute anti-Christian for anti-Jewish texts from the Koran, and they would make even more analogies between Israel and the Cru-sader kingdoms of the Middle Ages.

Surprisingly, our counterfactual experiment reveals a stronger link between antisemitism and anti-Zionism in the West than in the Middle East. In our alternate universe, Western intellectuals would no doubt condemn the Christian state of New Israel as a noisome legacy of colonialism, but this state would be unlikely to generate the same angry rhetoric that can be found amongst the Western world's intel-ligentsia today. The reason has to do with the West's bad conscience with respect to the "Jewish Question." Europe bears a vast burden of guilt for having perpetrated, abetted, or stood by passively during the Holocaust; it is equally guilty of having colonized and dominated much of the world, including the Middle East. The West's difficulty in cop-ing with its responsibility for these misdeeds has manifested itself in an obsessive fixation on Israel's actions and an aggressive attitude toward the original victim of guilt-inducing behavior.

Let us conclude with a final counterfactual: what if no European state had ever implanted itself in historic Palestine? Would newly independent Egypt and Syria have devoured a Palestinian state before it could even be born? Israel has historically been strong enough to maintain itself militarily against its neighbors, but a Palestinian state would have been far weaker. Moreover, the second weakest state in the region, Jordan, owes its very existence to Israel, which saved it from a Syrian-backed Palestinian coup attempt in 1970. Without Israel, there would very likely still have been a "Palestine problem" and the Palestinians' plight may have been similar to that of the Kurds, who are for the most part denied citizenship in Syria and basic cultural freedoms in Turkey. There would not, however, be a "Palestinian problem," that is, the loss by some 750,000 Palestinian Arabs of their homeland in 1948 and the creation of a vast collective exile. There would be a Palestinian diaspora typical of most nationalities in the developing world, whose members go wherever economic opportunity or political tranquility are to be found. But it would be a diaspora, not an exile. And this difference is vast.

Still, the exceptionality of Israel cannot be reduced merely to the state's actions. As I noted at the outset, one must look as well to perceptions of those actions. Antisemitism plays its role, but no less important is a biblically informed philosemitism. Consider the enormous interest that the idea of the restoration of Jews to Palestine has played in the modern Western world. (What are we to make of the fact that George Eliot, arguably the most intelligent, perceptive, psychologically astute writer in the English language in the nineteenth century, devoted her last novel, *Daniel Deronda*, to a philosemitic fantasy about a young English gentleman who discovers his Jewish origins, marries a Jewess, and sails off for the Holy Land to do great things for "his people"?) Although in recent years the liberal Protestant churches have become highly critical of Israel, the fundamentalist and evangelical ones have retained a close identification with the ancient Hebrews and modern Zionism.

Israel cannot help but be visible to the Christian civilization that is both dependent upon and set against the Jews; that views modern Israel through the ancient lens of the Holy Land. Just as obvious are the deep connections to the Holy Land among Muslims, whose claims to have superseded both Judaism and Christianity are embodied in the

Dome of the Rock and the Al-Aqsa Mosque on the ancient Jewish Temple Mount. It is no surprise that Israel is the cynosure of attention from over half of humanity, dwelling in Christendom and dar al-Islam alike. Any state whose borders include the Holy Land would attract global attention; a Jewish one all the more so.

The international community typically focuses on international conflict more than violence within a state's borders. Great Powers like Russia and China have been loath to support armed intervention in Syria not only because of geopolitical interests but also because humanitarian intervention in one blood-soaked state sets a precedent for intervention in others. Whether the violence crosses borders or stays within them, most people go about their business and care little about what seems far away and of little consequence. Casual indifference to human suffering is universal; acute awareness of Israel's conflict with the Palestinians is exceptional. The complex sources of this hyperactive consciousness cannot be dismissed as mere antisemitism. A Christian state in Palestine would also be a lightning rod for international condemnation. To be sure, there is a special valence to debate about Israel that derives specifically from the country's Jewish character. There are good reasons why. Slightly more than a tenth of the victims of World War II were Jews, yet the Holocaust has become paradigmatic for the savagery of that great conflict; indeed, it has become the most potent symbol of man's inhumanity to man. Is it any surprise that the Jews, never far from the center of either Christianity or Islam, victims of the most zealous program of mass murder in human history, would remain central to human consciousness once gathered into a sovereign Jewish state?

Israel is a state of exception. As the philosopher Carl Schmitt famously wrote, sovereignty is defined by the ability to suspend the rule of law and govern by emergency decree. The sovereign is not beholden to any power, not even that of the law. Israel has been run under one form or another of military law since its creation. The newly created state invoked the temporary British emergency measures proclaimed in 1945 in order to justify military rule over the country's Arab citizens, a practice that lasted until 1966. Palestinians in the West Bank, even those who live within areas controlled by the Palestinian Authority, are still subject to Israeli military regulations. The state of Israel has no constitution and no borders. Such a state in modern Palestine, whether Christian or Jewish, would still be exceptional.

Some exceptional states are more exceptional than others. Following Schmitt, Israel's geopolitical fuzziness is the ultimate testament to the country's strength. It is held together by the collective will of its Jewish citizens and the governing elite's access to their human capital as well as financial support from world Jewry. Exerting a power and influence far greater than its size, Israel is the exact opposite of the disempowered diaspora Jewish "ghost people" decried by the early Zionist thinker Leo Pinsker. But it is just as uncanny. It is feared for its power, yet in fact it is not powerful enough to utterly marginalize its native population as the major settler-colonial states successfully did. This is the hidden side of strident critiques of Israel – the understanding that Israel's reach exceeds its grasp, that it projects vast might but is in fact small and amenable to pressure.

A Christian Israel that subjected Palestinian Arabs to military occupation would be condemned, feared, and hated in much of the world. It would likely be the object of an international boycott, divestment, and sanctions campaign. Yet there is a startlingly unique as well as profoundly disturbing aspect of critical rhetoric about Israel: the challenge to its "right to exist." The phrase has shown up here and there in the history of national movements to justify their claims to autonomy or statehood. But its persistent and ubiquitous application to Israel is without parallel, as is its frequently negative valence, that is, that Israel does not have a right to exist. In contrast, only a minuscule and fanatical fringe denies the right of the Anglo-Saxon settler states (the United States, Canada, Australia, New Zealand) to exist. Even in the face of the worst excesses of the old South Africa, the international community called for the end of an apartheid regime, not the destruction of a state. Israel's most radical critics at times call for the "destruction of the Zionist regime," but this language effectively denies Israel a right to exist, as it does not recognize Jewish as well as Arab collective rights in Palestine or call for peaceful and mutually respectful relations between the two nations.

States are products of historical development and positive law, not of abstract right. Those who frame the question of Israel/Palestine as one of the right to exist rather than the right to life, self-determination, security, and dignity transform the struggle for the collective good into a total war in which there can be no victor. Such language evokes the venerable Christian claim to have superseded Judaism, particularly in its late medieval form, wherein Jews were allowed to live amongst

Christians only by sufferance and not by right. Since World War II, Christian supersessionism has faded, but it maintains a secularized afterlife in the debate about Israel's existential legitimacy, just as Christian messianism lives on in fantastical notions that peace between Israelis and Palestinians would single-handedly stabilize the entire Middle East and even the world as a whole.

A Christian Israel would be a pariah, perhaps even more so than the Jewish state. Its partition or transformation into a binational state would be seen as redress for the tragedy of the Palestinian people and restoration of dignity to the Arab and Muslim worlds. But few would expect miraculous results. In that sense, our counterfactual universe is, ironically, more realistic than the one in which we live.

8 WHAT IF THE JEWISH STATE HAD BEEN ESTABLISHED IN EAST AFRICA?*

Adam Rovner

THE TOUGH PLANET GUIDE TO NEW JUDEA

Introducing New Judea

For the men and women who pioneered the country's settlement in the early twentieth century, the land of New Judea gave birth to a new species of Jew. The archetypal Judean is hardy, stands firm in his opinions, and boasts a thick skin. New Judeans often alarm first-time visitors with their combination of verve, hospitality, and, at times, acidic treatment of others. But once you get to know Judeans, you will find them to be sweet and tender. For this reason, they are colloquially called "passions," after the ubiquitous passion-fruit grown, consumed, and loved by all. And passion describes the Judeans' attachment to their African Zion as well.

New Judea at a glance

Capital: Zikhron Herzl
Government: Parliamentary Democracy ("Knesset")
Flag: Two horizontal blue bands with a blue six-pointed star in the center (Figure 17).
Founded: April 22, 1919

* This chapter is a work of fiction.

Figure 17. Postage stamp from New Judea.

Neighboring countries: East African Republic of Kenya, Ethiopia, Uganda

Size: 20,650 km²

Population: 12 million

Life expectancy: 80.4 years

Demonym: New Judeans or Judeans

Economy: Advanced free market with sizable sectors including high technology research and development; cut diamonds; agricultural exports (tea, grain, produce); tourism. Oil from New Judea's Jabal-Sudan Territory has been a major source of revenue since the 1950s.

Climate: The high plateau of the capital and the surrounding agricultural region is temperate, though rain may fall year round. Lakeside Tel Aviv sees high rainfall and humidity, particularly March through May. Northern regions around Beit Zangwill and Lake Chamberlain are semi-arid to barren.

Language: Hebrew is the only official language, though English is widely used. Swahili and Yiddish are also commonly spoken. Tribal languages are preserved by the elderly.

> **Religion:** Eighty-six percent identify as Jewish, though an estimated
> 4–8 percent of this total are converted indigenous peoples
> who practice syncretic rituals. There are sizable minorities
> of Goan Catholics (6 percent) and Protestants (5 percent), as
> well as a small Hindu community and tribes that maintain
> animist beliefs.
> **Currency:** New Judean Shekel (NJS)
> **Motto:** "To Be a Free People, In Our Land – The Land of Africa,
> New Judea"

In the late nineteenth century, Jews began to work for the reestablishment of a homeland in Palestine. The perpetual internecine violence
in that region today between loyalists to Transjordan and mercenaries
funded by Iraq's King Faisal IV, and among the heavily armed Christian, Shia, and Sunni warlords, means that Westerners see Palestine as
little more than a blood-soaked sandscape flickering to life (and more
often, death) on network news. But for twenty-five years, from 1880
to 1905, Palestine was the focus of a heroic, if misguided, effort to
recreate a Jewish nation in the heart of the Arab Middle East. The story
of abortive settlement in Palestine had been mostly forgotten until
the publication of American author Leon Chaim Bach's best-selling
alternate history, *The Arabic Policemen's Union*. The novel takes as its
point of departure the idea that a binational Arab–Jewish state arose in
Palestine. The popularity of the novel, its recent film adaptation, and the
highly publicized death threats against Bach mean that even holiday-
makers may be more than just a little curious about how the Hebrew
State of New Judea came to be founded in East Africa in the first
place.

> Leon Chaim Bach's darkly comic novel, *The Arabic Policemen's
> Union*, envisions a secular, binational state arising in Palestine
> soon after a Nazi genocide in Europe claimed 4 million Jewish
> lives. Rabbi Avigdor Geyer, leader of a New Judean extremist sect,
> charged Bach with blasphemy because he dared imagine a return
> to Jerusalem led by secularists. Such a return, Geyer insisted, could
> only be brought about by the messiah. Bach's subsequent mockery
> of Geyer in a *New York Times* op-ed enraged the rabbi and his

followers, who held a public ceremony invoking kabalistic curses against the author. New Judea's homegrown talent, Avner Yoavi, published his own counterfactual novel, *The Jew in the High Castle*, last year. The heroes of his book escape a war-torn theocratic Jewish Palestine to travel to – of all places – a pristine East Africa in search of sanctuary. Yoavi too has provoked Geyer's curses.

British colonial influence and white settlement were largely confined to the tropical coastal regions of what was then called the East African Protectorate until Nairobi was established as the administrative capital in 1899. Soon, British interests expanded westward along the route traced by the Uganda Railway, today operated by the Kenya-Yehuda co-op. His Majesty's Government poured millions of pounds into the completion of the railway from Mombasa to the shores of Lake Victoria, where today Tel Aviv's spires soar upwards and its exurbs sprawl outwards. Fierce bands of Maasai warriors united to battle the creeping British presence, but the introduction of rinderpest and smallpox devastated their herds and their way of life. The Maasai were quickly forced to cede their heartland to the "iron snake" that swallowed up their grazing pastures.

A handful of Jews arrived in the region in the early 1900s. Most journeyed from South Africa during the Boer War in search of economic opportunity. Farmer Abraham Lock, later the founder of Nordau-Nakuru's grandiose Asylum Resort, is credited as the first Jew to have established a permanent home within the borders of present day New Judea. Lock and other early Jewish settlers formed an alliance with the displaced Maasai, whom they believed to be one of the lost Israelite tribes. In recent years, leftist Judean academics – the so-called New Historians – have documented how the colonial Judeans and their Maasai accomplices dispossessed the more numerous Kikuyu and divvied up their land.

Defenders of such colonization practices stress that Jews had no land of their own for more than 1,800 years until New Judea declared its independence in 1919. Nearly a quarter-century earlier, Austro-Hungarian author and political visionary, Dr. Theodor Herzl, convened an international Zionist Congress dedicated to solving the so-called Jewish Question. The Zionist Organization (ZO) he helmed can best be understood by casual readers as a national liberation movement that aimed to provide a territorial solution to Jewish homelessness and persecution. But by the time the Sixth Zionist Congress met in 1903, the ZO had only attracted a small number of adherents, both fervent and bemused. However, the support of European intellectuals and authors gave the underfunded ZO a level of prestige that exceeded the numerical roll of its membership. And it was Herzl's friendship with Anglo-Jewish author Israel Zangwill that granted the charismatic leader entrée into Whitehall's drawing rooms of power.

Getting there and around

To/From Zangwill International Airport: New Judea's main international airport is located northeast of Tel Aviv. Flag carrier Kanfei Nesharim ("KeN") flies daily from major European cities. Express trains run every twelve minutes to central Tel Aviv's Pinsker Railway Terminal. The journey takes about thirty minutes.

To/From Herzl International Airport: Travelers transiting from African nations generally arrive in Zikhron Herzl's airport. Flights from Addis Ababa, Kampala, and Nairobi are frequent. Tourists on an extended stay should note that KeN offers weekend getaway specials to other African capitals.

Train: New Judea's rail network is one of the best in the world. Travelers can purchase a one-, two-, or four-week pass before their arrival, or upon arrival for an additional fee.

Car: The iconic white-gloved female traffic police are long gone from Tel Aviv's major intersections, but traffic signals have not diminished New Judea's famed roadway courtesy. While hiring a car is hassle-free, visitors from the US are reminded that Judeans drive on the left.

Soon, Herzl and his British adherents had concluded an agreement with influential Colonial Secretary Joseph Chamberlain for an autonomous Jewish settlement within the confines of the East African Protectorate. The nascent Jewish colony would arise along the northern border of the newly completed Ugandan Railway. A draft charter for the Judean Colony was hammered out by Great Britain's future Prime Minister, solicitor and MP David Lloyd George. Visitors to Zikhron Herzl can view the original charter in the austere National Library and Archives, which stands in the shadow of the imposing Jabotinsky Opera House, built after the Italian fascist style by Guido Ferrazzo. Inside the Opera House, New Judea's first Prime Minister and self-styled Judge, Ze'ev Jabotinsky, famously convened a Senatus Populusque Judaeorum ("Senate of the Jewish People") to deal with the growing crisis of European Jewry in 1936.

For the adventurous

1. **Walk the treetops in Ben-Yehuda Forest:** Walkways suspended 75 feet in the air near the village of Kook Amega offer an unforgettable way to see colobus monkeys up close and personal.
2. **Simba Judea Preserve:** You're sure to spot lions at this research center on the outskirts of Zikhron Herzl. The man-eating lions of Tsavo that gobbled up dozens of railway workers are taxidermied in the on-site museum. Hebrew–Swahili cult film favorite *Bwana Dybbuk* is based on the story.
3. **Camel-riding on the shores of Lake Chamberlain:** For those who've packed outdoor gear with their business suits, there's no better way to see the "Jade Sea" than atop these gawky beasts.
4. **Kayak Lake Victoria:** Hippos and crocs once terrorized pioneers, but now you can paddle at your ease with the stunning Tel Aviv skyline as your backdrop.
5. **Cherangani Winds:** Mountain-bike through the wind farms on the Cherangani Hills that harvest power from the skies to supply much of New Judea's energy needs.
6. **Hike the "Road of Ages":** This network of trails skirts the western rim of the great Rift Valley from New Judea's southern to northern border – over 100 miles!

Travelers familiar with the New Judean cult of unity during the country's early years are often surprised to learn about the fractious past of Jewish national politics. In fact, what has come to be called the

Chamberlain Declaration almost derailed plans for a Hebrew state in 1903. Surprisingly, nearly 40 percent of delegates attending the Sixth Zionist Congress voted *against* pursuing Great Britain's pledge of land in East Africa – a proposal originally and mistakenly referred to as the "Uganda Plan." Jabotinsky himself, then a young journalist, raised his voice against the plan, making him perhaps the only leader of a nation-state to have, at least initially, opposed the state's very existence. The substantial nay-saying minority was led by a mostly forgotten Russian Zionist, Menahem Ussishkin. A long-time antagonist of Herzl, the combative Ussishkin did not attend the Congress, preferring instead to organize a counter-congress in what was then Ottoman Palestine (today Transjordan). After the motion to explore the British land grant in East Africa was approved, Ussishkin claimed that the vote sabotaged the fundamental aspirations of the Jewish people and he denounced Herzl as a traitor.

First steps

By 1903, approximately 100,000 Jews were living in Palestine, as compared to at least 500,000 Arabs. Estimates indicate that more than two-thirds of the Jewish population opposed resettlement in Africa, even though Eliezer Ben-Yehuda, the man credited with reviving the Hebrew language, propagandized on behalf of the Chamberlain Declaration. The "Palestinomaniacs," as they were termed, proved intransigent until the assassination of Herzl's lieutenant, Max Nordau, in the early morning hours of December 20, 1903.

The story is familiar to every Judean school child. A young man approached Nordau while the elder statesman attended a gala in Paris. The stranger handed Nordau a calling card bearing his name in Hebrew characters: Chaim Selig Louban. Nordau took the card, bowed politely, and then excused himself to speak with a friend on the edge of the crowded room. Louban followed at their heels, drew a small-caliber revolver, and shouted in French: "Death to Nordau the East African!" He fired, sending a bullet into Nordau's temple. The wounded author somehow managed to raise a hand against his assailant, but Louban squeezed off another round into his chest. Gunpowder filled the air and panicked guests stampeded to escape. In the chaos, the murderer fell to the ground and was subdued. The twenty-three-year-old declared himself a "son of Palestine" who had been selected by lot to kill Nordau by adversaries of the Chamberlain Declaration. Police searched Louban for incriminating documents but found just a single 10 centime coin among his threadbare clothes. A search of his residence revealed a letter indicating that Louban came from a town near Ekatarinoslav, where Ussishkin made his home. Louban hanged himself in his cell within hours of his incarceration, and his co-conspirators – if there were any – remain a matter of conjecture to this day.

Widespread anger, circumstantial evidence, and the verdict of gossip meant that in the days following Nordau's assassination, guilt was placed on Ussishkin's head. It did not help that the engineer disappeared after the murder and only resurfaced several months later in Palestine under an assumed name. There he was shot and killed by Arab marauders while trying to defend a homestead, a fate which garnered him some small amount of posthumous sympathy. Ben-Yehuda, meanwhile, whipped up a frenzy against the remaining foes of the Chamberlain Declaration. In part to redeem his reputation, a chastened Jabotinsky volunteered to travel with the Zionist Commission sent to explore the land set aside by Great Britain for a Jewish home.

The Commission, funded by donations from around the world, consisted of Otto Warburg, a prominent German Jewish leader and expert in tropical agriculture, and two non-Jewish members: English geologist John Walter Gregory, and Great Britain's former Uganda Protectorate administrator and veteran African explorer, Sir Harry Johnston. Gregory, who coined the term "Rift Valley," was quick to note that the fault extended north to the biblical land of Israel, and hence was connected to the ancient site of Judean sovereignty. The Commission concluded that the region Chamberlain had proposed was indeed suitable for immediate Jewish colonization. Jabotinsky's colorful dispatches from along the route played an important part in popularizing the plan, especially among his skeptical fellow Russian Jews. One of his reports noted that the same Hebrew letters (*aleph-fay-reysh*) appearing in the word "Africa" also featured in sequence in the word "Ophir" – the mythical source of King Solomon's wealth. Religious Zionists from the sizable Mizrachi faction lent credibility to Jabotinsky's speculative claims. The Mizrachi leadership advocated orthodox Jewish immigration to Africa in part to deflect theological criticism of settlement in the holy land prior to the messianic age.

Itinerary: The best of New Judea

Safe modern cities, an efficient bureaucracy, and a high-speed rail network lead many visitors to joke that the Hebrew state is "Belgium with Lions." But there are numerous reasons to travel to the small East African nation – the stark beauty of the north, the Nordau-Nakuru game park, and the colorful religious culture preserved in many small villages. H. N. Tur-Yona, consultant to *Tough Planet*, offers the following highlights: "If you only have a week, spend your first two days on Lake Victoria in the cultural capital of **Tel Aviv**, or as locals call it, "**Telly**." Be sure to wander through the historic Bauhaus district, and don't miss the chic window-shopping along Matthew Nathan Boulevard. A dinner cruise is a great way to see the skyline, especially at night. Catch a bullet train east to **Nordau-Nakuru** for an overnight (or two if your budget allows) at the renovated Asylum Resort. There you can see zebras and flamingos – or if you're lucky, a leopard. Pack your walking shoes when you head north for two days to visit the capital city, **Zikhron Herzl**. There tour the Knesset, the Jabotinsky Opera House, and the National Archives. Though you may be reluctant to visit while on holiday, the Scrolls of Fire monument to Jewish victims of Nazism is a moving experience that is sure to make your travels more meaningful. The world-famous Simba Judea Preserve is nearby. On your return, stop at Ben-Yehuda Forest for a tree-top view of the countryside near **Kook Amega**, a former goldrush town. A farewell dinner at **Telly**'s legendary wild game restaurant, Bassar, is a must. Founded in 1920 by beloved Judean children's author Franz 'Tzvi' Kafka (a former vegetarian!), a meal here is a carnivore's dream. Be sure to order the guinea fowl noodle soup with matzo balls, which Kafka's wife credited with curing her husband of his tuberculosis."

As for Ben-Yehuda, he captained a flotilla of ardent followers that sailed from Jaffa to Mombasa via Trieste in April 1904. He hailed the abandonment of Palestine for Africa as "the greatest event in the annals of the nation of Israel." The linguist's departure signaled the demise of Palestinocentric Zionism and the advent of a new era of Jewish nation-building. Zangwill and Herzl joined Ben-Yehuda for part of the journey aboard the steamer *Africa*, now restored and preserved

174 / Adam Rovner

in historic Tel Aviv Harbor. While docked in Trieste, they and dozens of supporters announced the formation of a "New Hebrew Organization" (NHO) to succeed the ZO. The iconic photograph of Herzl standing at the *Africa*'s helm, his hand on the ship's wheel, is found in public buildings throughout New Judea. It was to be the final public image of the beloved leader. Herzl's health deteriorated in the following months and he suffered a fatal heart attack in July 1904. News of the great man's death reached Ben-Yehuda and his band of like-minded settlers while they were still in Nairobi fitting themselves out for colonization. Before the year was out, Ben-Yehuda's initial vanguard founded the first Jewish city in modern times in East Africa's fertile red soil: Zikhron Herzl.

The Judean colony

Due in large part to Ben-Yehuda's example, a slow but steady stream of Jews abandoned their hard-scrabble agricultural settlements in Palestine for East Africa beginning in 1904. Only about 50,000 Jews remained in Palestine by the outbreak of World War I. This first decade (1904–14) of African colonization remains a mythologized period. Pogroms throughout Russia, as well as the failed 1905 revolution and the consequent economic and political insecurity, led to a massive wave of Jewish emigration from Czarist lands. At the same time, the Aliens Act limited the number of Jewish immigrants arriving on British shores. However, Chamberlain and a coalition of politicians and humanitarians persuaded lawmakers to allow Jewish refugees to enter Great Britain on strictly controlled transit visas. The NHO set up a network of information offices in the Pale of Settlement that encouraged Jews to leave for Britain, and from there to travel onward to Mombasa. Some members of the British public resented colonial land grants to foreigners, but Chamberlain deflected their anger. The "Hebrew unfortunates," he said, would bring "great fortune to crown and country." Indeed, the influx allowed Great Britain to consolidate its hold on the region and enriched its coffers. More than 625,000 immigrants found their way to East Africa during the first decade of the Judean colony's existence. Immigration swelled after Jabotinsky testified before the American Senate in favor of the Dillingham–Lodge National Origins Act (1912), which stipulated a strict quota system.

This era also saw the rise of several elements of Judean society and culture that still leave their imprint on the state and its people: the centralization of power, a technocratic civil administration, the establishment of the first compulsory Jewish military organization (Shomrim), the creation of a network of rural cooperatives planned by Franz Gefen, the draining of the Saiwa swamp and other efforts to eradicate malaria, and the courting of indigenous tribes and their subsequent conversion to Judaism. The archetypal New Judean character also emerged during this period to indicate one who is obedient to authority, disciplined, and physically tough, secular, aloof, passionately nationalistic, and politely dismissive. Some say that only the British and the New Judeans are capable of being both well-mannered and rude in the same breath.

Gefen (1864–1943), born Franz Oppenheimer, was a German physician, sociologist, and economist. He fell under the sway of a fellow Jew, the Austro-Hungarian economist and social theorist T. Hertzka, in the late nineteenth century. It was Hertzka, a colleague of Herzl's, who had first suggested the colonization of East Africa. At the invitation of Herzl, Gefen addressed the Sixth Zionist Congress on the subject of planned mass colonization. He later helped establish the first successful agricultural settlement in the colony, Chofshi, south of Zikhron Herzl.

Much of the character of the Judean state developed as a result of the close relationship between the Jewish Matthew Nathan, the colony's first governor (1904–11), and Zangwill, who emigrated to the colony with his pregnant wife in 1906. A year earlier, Nathan, Zangwill, and the two British members of the Zionist Commission had successfully petitioned H. M. Government to expand the territory of the fledgling Judean Colony westward to the shores of Lake Victoria (encompassing the east bank of the Pishon [Nzoia] and Gikhon [Turkwel] Rivers), and north to Lake Chamberlain and Ethiopia. Zangwill and Nathan also used their connections with wealthy diaspora Jews, including American banker Jacob Schiff, British financier Leopold de Rothschild, and German industrialist James Simon, to underwrite the rapid industrial development of the colony. Another of their notable achievements was to end the wholesale slaughter of animals for the fur trade, then dominated by Russian trappers and furriers. The creation of Nordau-Nakuru Park in 1907 meant that some of the savannah's majestic beasts would survive in their native habitat.

The militarist aspect of the state developed from a similar bond of friendship between Protestant philosemite J. H. Patterson, the colony's second governor (1911–19), and Jabotinsky. Patterson, a lieutenant-colonel who rose to fame as the hunter who shot the man-eaters of Tsavo, worked with Zangwill and Jabotinsky to turn the ragtag Shomrim militia into an all-Jewish battalion: the First Judeans of the King's African Rifles. Under the joint command of Patterson and the one-armed veteran of the Russo-Japanese War, Josef Trumpeldor, the First Judeans distinguished themselves at the battle for Lake Tanganyika (1915–16). Their decisive victory (with the Royal Navy) over the Kaiser's forces was to have far-reaching consequences. Jabotinsky, who had received a commission, fought on the front lines with Trumpeldor and was wounded in his left leg. Zangwill later sniped that their respective injuries, both on their left side, were responsible for the colony's tilt toward rightwing policies. The battle meant that Great Britain was now free to extend its influence in Africa nearly uncontested from Cape to Cairo. Prime Minister Lloyd George, who had first drafted the plan for the Judean colony, rewarded Zangwill and Jabotinsky with a promise of full independence. At the conclusion of the Passover holiday in 1919, Patterson handed over interim rule to Zangwill, who promptly declared the independence of the Hebrew state of New Judea. A majority of the Jews who had not fled Ottoman Palestine during the war years, or following the locust plague and ensuing famine of 1915, now flocked to the newly established state. Approximately 15,000 stubborn "Palestinomaniacs" remained behind. Ironically, only the prosperity and generosity of New Judea kept this far-flung spiritual center from complete starvation.

Years of independence

Zangwill's chronic bouts of malaria meant that he was sidelined by Jabotinsky almost immediately. By the time Zangwill departed to receive treatment in London in 1921, the last original architect of New Judea had been removed from the state's governance. When the author tried to return, Jabotinsky insisted he remain in London as ambassador, a position Zangwill held until his death in 1924. It was to be a familiar pattern: Jabotinsky co-opted his tractable opponents, shipped uneasy allies off to diplomatic exile, and actively suppressed his most deter-mined foes throughout his career. Jabotinsky was elected Prime Min-ister in 1922 and installed Trumpeldor as his Minister of Armaments and Defense. In that role, Trumpeldor instituted mandatory conscrip-tion for all men and women regardless of ethnicity, tribal affiliation, or religion. He and a cadre of veterans of the First Judeans formed the core of the sophisticated and well-trained Judean Defense Forces (JDF), even though the state was, as a well-worn slogan had it, "a small coun-try surrounded by allies."

Another of Jabotinsky's early acts, surprising in light of his later penchant for autocracy, was to draft a progressive constitution lauded by the League of Nations. The Knesset ratified the constitution's provi-sions, which did not discriminate between Jewish and non-Jewish citi-zens. Nonetheless, Hillel Kook, a prominent NHO activist, recruited a network of loyalists to lead single-sex scouting brigades comprised of Jewish and tribal youth. The not-so-hidden agenda of the youth group known as BeN – an acronym of Brit Nordau ("Nordau's Covenant"), but also meaning "son" – was to convert and Westernize the younger generation of Luhya, Luo, and Maasai. Kook was remarkably success-ful in converting the Maasai, most of whom took the surname "Ben-Israel," though the more populous Luhya and Luo resisted. Jabotinsky himself was convinced that the Maasai were one of the lost tribes and published a book on the topic, *By Your Blood You Shall Live*. Though discredited time and again, the Maasai and a majority of New Judeans continue to maintain this convenient fiction.

New Judea enjoyed a robust economy during much of the interwar period, despite the malaise in Europe and America. Jabotin-sky's promotion of an "initial phase of authoritarian capitalism" contained elements of corporatism, autarchy, and social democratic reform. Scholars suggest that the vague nature, indeed incoherence, of Jabotinsky's economic policies enabled him to maneuver on both the political right and left. Agricultural exports of grain and tea from the Gefen settlements enriched the state and provided much needed revenue to the British administration of the Protectorate to the east, whose railways were required for export. Karen Blickstein's *Into Africa*, a memoir of her time managing a tea plantation, is perhaps the most famous depiction of this halcyon era. This period also saw the establishment of a diamond exchange in Tel Aviv, which channeled South Africa's mineral wealth through the Hebrew state. And, in the early 1930s, the discovery of gold in the forests around the renamed Kook Amega turned the sleepy village into a boomtown. But Jabotinsky faced criticism at home and abroad for his hostility to unions and his suppression of communist parties. Moderate socialist groups continued to function, but were compromised by agents of Jabotinsky's growing security apparatus. Still, prosperity held serious opposition in check until New Judea gave tacit support to Italy's annexation of Ethiopia in 1936 in exchange for the construction of a never-completed northern railway route from Tel Aviv to the Red Sea port of Assab.

Jabotinsky earmarked financial surpluses to establish the Hebrew University of Zikhron Herzl and the Technical University of Tel Aviv. This move helped boost his popularity among a restless younger generation. Both institutions expanded after Hitler came to power and drove academics, researchers, and students to the African safe haven. Yet the arrival of these refugee scholars also helped radicalize disaffected young Judeans who viewed the founding generation's militarism as a home-grown manifestation of the fascism that had overtaken Europe. By mid 1936, shortly after Jabotinsky assumed his fourth term as Prime Minister, domestic unrest – protests, strikes, and incidents of industrial sabotage – forced him to suspend the constitution and dissolve the Knesset. For the first time, the unity that had defined New Judean politics fractured.

Years of war

Turmoil in New Judea coincided with a rise in antisemitic agitation in Europe and Germany's rearmament. Jabotinsky shrewdly used these crises to reunify his fragmented country. After dismissing the Knesset, he called for new parliamentary elections for the representative body, but its democratic character was curtailed. Military matters, internal security, and foreign policy would no longer be subject to Knesset oversight. All cabinet and ministerial positions were to be appointed by Jabotinsky without Knesset review. He also adopted the biblical title of "Judge" and handed over sole control of the armed forces and the security services to Trumpeldor. The trusted war veteran single-handedly – literally – mobilized the citizenry for the coming war.

Once he had quelled the rumblings of domestic discontent, New Judea's Judge traveled to Poland in 1937 to negotiate with its regime of colonels, whose antisemitic rhetoric and legislation had sparked anxiety, violence, and a new wave of emigration. Jabotinsky worked out a closed-door agreement with the Poles to ship 1.5 million Jews to New Judea on the basis of League of Nations provisions for population transfer as a means to solve ethnic conflict. He also struck deals with the Nazi Reich and the dictatorial rulers of Hungary and Romania for the transport of a further 750,000 Jews to New Judea. Historian Benjamin Odinga-Morris first revealed in *New Judea's Secret Wars* how Jabotinsky clandestinely funneled foreign currency, agricultural products, raw materials, and even arms to these regimes in exchange for the lives of Jews. In parallel, Jabotinsky secured the assistance of international organizations, both Jewish and non-Jewish, to aid in the forced evacuation of European Jewry to New Judea, a plan known as Operation Nordau. Jabotinsky's scheme channeled an estimated 200 million dollars in loans and grants toward the construction of settlements, the expansion of infrastructure, and the establishment of light industrial projects in New Judea. NHO operative and future Prime Minister, Menachem Begin, directed the mission in Europe.

Only twelve years old at the time of her forced transport, Anne Frank's *Diary of a Young Exile* reports on the life of evacuees with sensitivity and clarity. The precocious author and her family arrived in the development town of El-Dorot in autumn 1941. Her record of the three weeks she spent at sea aboard a badly listing ship is especially vivid. After her death from malaria in 1948, Anne's father published her diary. Following its translation into English, the *Diary* became a modern classic and remains the best-known account of Operation Nordau and of life in a deprived New Judean development town.

The Judge's conspicuous success with dictators made many American and Jewish leaders wary of what they considered the "fascist countenance" of Jabotinsky's policies. Rabbi Stephen Wise, co-founder of the World New Judean Organization (WNJO), used his influence with President Roosevelt to try to scuttle support for Operation Nordau. But the President and his cabinet recognized that Americans would be unwilling to accept millions of Jewish refugees, and so they cooperated – for a time – with Jabotinsky's government. By the outbreak of war in September 1939, approximately 2.4 million European Jews, mostly young men and women, had been transferred to New Judea, often by force. They remonstrated against their "kidnapper," Begin, and the "pirate policies" of the New Judean state. Some whose property had been liquidated to cover the expenses of transport committed suicide or jumped ship when their vessels stopped en route in Alexandria or Aden. Many of those who suffered forced evacuation during Operation Nordau were fully assimilated Jews, ardent Yiddishist intellectuals, social revolutionaries, orthodox Jews, unreconstructed Palestinocentric holdouts, or other opponents of the NHO and its nation-building program. They railed against the "penal colony" to which they had been sent against their will and resisted their absorption in Judean society. Some refused to live in the development towns to which they had been assigned or work in the factories built to employ them. Others simply lamented the cultural backwardness of the Hebrew state.

An uneasy coalition of secular Yiddishists and orthodox Jews organized an opposition settlement program financed by donations from political radicals and religious institutions in the diaspora, especially America. In northern and northwestern New Judea, these mutually antagonistic factions worked together to establish illegal out-posts. Trumpeldor's military police initially imprisoned and harassed those who fled from state control, but later the security services ignored them. Virtually all of the Yiddishists have since sought accommodation with the state, but towns inhabited by traditionalist Jews still lack sewage, electricity, proper schools, and access to medical care. The warrens of their tumble-down villages and subsistence farms are a close approximation of the *shtetls* destroyed by the Nazis and their collaborators.

Menachem Begin continued to direct Operation Nordau as World War II raged across the continent. After the occupation of Poland, Begin operated from Lithuania, and later in the Soviet Union, the Balkans, southern Italy, and British Palestine. There he arranged for the deportation of most of the ancient homeland's small Jewish commu-nity, who feared a threatened Nazi invasion. A furious Stalin informed

Roosevelt that Begin was trading African gold and diamonds to the Soviets for petroleum, which then found its way to a supply-starved Wehrmacht. In order to placate Stalin and stop what his Secretary for War called the "Jews-for-Gas" plan, Roosevelt ordered a risky bombing campaign in late 1942 of rail networks that brought Jews to Axis-held ports for evacuation. The destruction of Operation Nordau's population pipelines resulted in the improvised internment and, later, organized mass murder, of the remaining Jews of Europe. In all, the evacuation program succeeded in rescuing over 4 million Jews from the Nazis. Some historians believe that Hitler might have succeeded in murdering hundreds of thousands, if not millions, more Jews had Operation Nordau not been implemented in time. Others suggest that Jabotinsky's open alliance with the British in North Africa prevented more Jews from being saved. However, all agree that the death toll reached well over a million by the time Germany was defeated in June 1944. Both the Soviets and the Americans blamed New Judea for supplying the Nazis with fuel that had allowed the war to drag on as long as it had. Tensions with successive US administrations and with organized American Jewry dogged New Judea into the 1950s.

When Mussolini declared war on Britain, New Judea covertly sided with exiled Ethiopian Emperor Haile Selassie I against his country's Italian occupiers. Jabotinsky placed units of the JDF at the disposal of British Army officer Orde Wingate, a Judean sympathizer who had been ordered to harass Axis Italy's forces in East Africa. Even domestic opponents hailed Jabotinsky's "calm obstinacy" in pursuing Operation Nordau while he quietly mobilized against Mussolini. They also welcomed his dispatch of a "steel column" of JDF soldiers to fight in North Africa, despite his much-touted Transfer Agreement with the Nazis. For a time, the trade in Jewish lives continued unaffected by Jabotinsky's brazenness. But the epic journey of armored units and infantry north to Cairo in support of British forces allowed for the defeat of Field Marshal Rommel's Panzerarmee at El Alamein in 1942. After his surrender, the Nazi pact with Jabotinsky finally unraveled. Some Axis puppet regimes maintained shipments of Jews in exchange for bribes of cash and goods, but African-bound transport ships were afterwards often torpedoed by U-boats.

Postwar era

Jabotinsky grew increasingly paranoid in the late 1940s and retreated to his ostrich ranch near Zikhron Herzl. There, the limping Judge surrounded himself with a phalanx of female Maasai bodyguards and only emerged for the annual Independence Day Parade. Trumpeldor died in 1948, Jabotinsky in 1950. Their passing left a political vacuum that was filled by Begin, who was loathed and admired in equal parts. New Judea's second elected Prime Minister, Begin proved himself a capable administrator and a canny politician. He appointed the first Maasai chief-of-staff, Olaldapash Ben-Israel. And while America remained ambivalent about the Hebrew state, the British recognized the strategic importance of the country for maintaining their own colonial possessions. Great Britain had struggled to assert its hold on the neigboring East African Protectorate for years. Kikuyu tribes sought autonomy from their colonial masters and resented their relocation from New Judea by early Jewish settlers and their Maasai allies. With anticolonial movements growing around the world, Kikuyu intellectuals who had been schooled in Marxism revolted against both the British and the Judeans in 1952. A series of grisly murders spawned retaliatory raids by British and New Judean military forces, often led by Maasai officers. But the Kikuyu "Mau Mau" forest armies proved difficult to defeat. Prime Minister Begin launched aerial bombardments on supposed guerrilla camps in Jabal-Sudan and ordered an invasion of its oil-rich region by marines based on Lake Chamberlain (Figure 18). The capture of Jabal-Sudan was largely a pretext to control its lucrative oil concessions, but was nonetheless welcomed by tribal peoples who had long been persecuted by Muslims from the north and overrun by Kikuyu guerrillas from the south. Many in Jabal-Sudan had preserved the memory of the Jewish-born Emin Pasha's abolition of slavery and thus warmed to their Judean rulers.

Jewish-born physician Isaak Schnitzer left his native Germany in the 1860s as a result of discrimination. He entered Ottoman service and after a period of wandering found his way to British Equatoria, roughly comprising the Territory of Jabal-Sudan. At some point he adopted the name Emin Pasha, and later served under Charles George Gordon until the general was killed during the

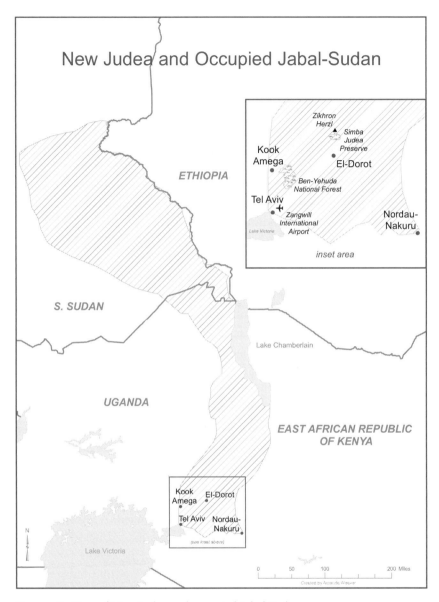

Figure 18. Map of New Judea and occupied Jabal-Sudan.

Mahdist revolution. Emin Pasha outlawed slavery in the region and was himself murdered by vindictive Arab slavers in 1885, but his memory has been perpetuated throughout Jabal-Sudan by Jewish traders and tribal elders since the first days of Jewish settlement in East Africa. Today, New Judea's military protects the territory's resources from hostile Islamists to the north and west. Following the occupation, Arab nations in North Africa and the Middle East expelled their Jewish citizens in solidarity with Khartoum. The last remaining holdouts of the Zionist community in Palestine were dispersed during this period. In the 1970s, the New Mahdi Army failed to drive Judean forces from Jabal-Sudan's oil fields. A majority of Jabal-Sudanese have since voted to maintain the status of their land as a New Judean territory in a series of referenda.

New Judea's decision to back the British against the Kikuyu-dominated Mau Mau found broad domestic support but ended in disaster. Begin's counter-offensives lost their appeal when casualties and evidence of human rights abuses mounted. Independence movements across Africa put Begin's stubborn policies on the wrong side of history. One after another, former colonies achieved independence in the 1960s: Burundi, the East African Republic of Kenya, Malawi, Uganda, Tanzania, Rwanda, Zambia. Each in turn targeted New Judea as an alien entity in the heart of Africa and cut off diplomatic and economic ties. Some provided moral and material support to groups like the New Mahdi Army (NMA), which attacked Judean targets in occupied Jabal-Sudan. When the East African Republic of Kenya's founding Prime Minister, Jomo Kenyatta, closed the rail lines and forbade the entry of ships with cargo bound for New Judea, the Hebrew state found itself isolated and economically battered.

Anger at Begin's policies increased the popularity of previously marginalized left-leaning political parties. They agitated for the reintroduction of the constitution Jabotinsky had suspended. A violent crackdown on opposition protests in 1967 further damaged Begin's reputation and that of his Maasai head of internal security, Leboo Ben-Israel. Begin called for new elections, which brought long-time Labor Party opposition leader and retired general Yigal Allon to power in a coalition with Yiddish autonomists. The dovish Allon reinstated the constitution, reduced the power of the military, dismissed the unpopular Leboo Ben-Israel, and opened direct negotiations with Kenyatta's government. His emissary to Kenyatta was Fernando Da Gamma-Rosen, a New Judean-born lawyer of mixed Goan Catholic and Jewish parentage. Da Gamma-Rosen, who had extensive family and business connections in Nairobi, was accepted as an honest broker by both sides. Today his portrait adorns the newly minted 20 shekel coin. Allon and Kenyatta formalized a peace treaty and free trade agreement in 1969. Normalization with other states soon followed. By 1973, New Judea had been accepted as a full member of the Organization of African Unity (OAU).

Recent decades

Tourists are often impressed by New Judea's support for humanitarian causes in the region. Lucrative oil profits from Jabal-Sudan have allowed successive Labor governments to fund development work in neighboring states. Such high-profile efforts have helped repair relations with African leaders. Prime Minister Shimon Peres' vocal criticism of South Africa's apartheid system, and the Judean military's support of the African National Congress in the 1980s, threatened to drag the country back into regional conflict. But public opinion recalled the misguided support for colonial regimes and ultimately backed Peres. With the dismantling of state-sponsored racism in South Africa, New Judea's principled stance gained the country many admirers. The export of advanced agricultural and water management technologies to Jabal-Sudan and Ethiopia also helped improve the country's international standing in the 1980s and 1990s. Some observers suggest that Judean engineering and hydrological research have prevented drought and stabilized democracy in the region. But public policy and cutting-edge science have so far failed to reduce the scourge of AIDS in East Africa. Of all its neighbors, only New Judea, with an infection rate of 8 percent, has had success in combating the spread of the disease. Travelers who indulge in Telly's red light district are cautioned to patronize only registered establishments.

Yaya Brenner became Prime Minister in 2000. Judeans know him as the grandson and namesake of Hebrew literature's only Nobel Prize-winning author, Yosef Haim Brenner. The elder Brenner arrived in New Judea in 1909 and went on to become the voice of the early settlers and a symbol of the emerging nation's historical burden. Brenner's masterpiece, *Yesteryear*, presented the fictionalized memoir of his talented protégé, the writer S. Y. Agnon, who was murdered in Berlin during a pogrom in 1923. *Yesteryear* is well worth the read for travelers looking to understand the country's turbulent past. Yaya traded on his famous grandfather's name, garnering support from European politicos and diaspora intelligentsia early in his career. His vision of a post-ethnic Hebrew state benefited from his appointment of Ehud Barak Obama, a bi-racial Luo convert to Judaism, as Foreign Minister – the first Luo to hold a cabinet position. Unfortunately, the move has resulted in tensions with the less numerous but politically potent Maasai, who have long been part of the governmental and military elite.

In 1994, Defense Minister Y. H. "Yaya" Brenner unilaterally committed troops to prevent massacres between rival Tutsi and Hutu populations in both Burundi and Rwanda. He was censured for this action by the OAU and the United Nations. Political opponents, led by Begin's son, capitalized on the unpopular move and nearly succeeded in replacing Brenner's government with a coalition led by the Ze'ev ("Wolf") Party. But their isolationist stance no longer proved viable. Since Allon's Labor Party took the reins of power, New Judea has become an important strategic ally of the United States and has tied its economic future to American trade. Joint exercises with the American military and intelligence-sharing have allowed the two nations to limit the spread of Wahhabism and other Islamist ideologies in the Horn of Africa. American tourists should beware, however, that NMA terror cells have targeted US citizens in isolated areas of Jabal-Sudan.

Diaspora Jews continue to flock to New Judea as tourists and have embraced the country as the Jewish homeland. Since the turn of the twenty-first century, more than 250,000 young Jews from around the world have traveled to New Judea as part of the "Birthplace Judea" program. The fully funded ten-day trip is aimed at forging a greater connection between the diaspora and the mercurial Hebrew state. The country's wealth and stability promise to endure, but the perils of sustainable development in a volatile part of the world will challenge its leaders as New Judea's centenary approaches.

9 WHAT IF FRANZ KAFKA HAD IMMIGRATED TO PALESTINE?*

Iris Bruce

The following essay, "Franz Kafka in Israel: 'It Was No Dream,'" is reprinted here with the permission of the Viennese publishing house, Paul Zsolnay. Written by Tel Aviv University literature professor, Hugo Immerwahr, for the edited anthology, *Jewish Nobel Prize Laureates in Literature: 1910–2005* (Vienna, 2010), the essay discusses the life and career of the famed Israeli novelist and 1966 Nobel Prize-winner, Franz Kafka. In addition to his fellow prize recipients, Harold Pinter (2005), Imre Kertesz (2002), Nadine Gordimer (1991), Joseph Brodsky (1987), Elias Canetti (1981), Isaac Bashevis Singer (1978), Saul Bellow (1976), Boris L. Pasternak (1958), Henri Bergson (1927), Paul Heyse (1910), and Elie Wiesel (who won the Nobel Peace Prize in 1986), Kafka was one of the twentieth century's literary giants. In this probing essay, Immerwahr, one of the world's leading Kafka authorities, explores the former Prague lawyer's metamorphosis into a *chaluz*, a school teacher at Ben Shemen, a member of the underground resistance, and, finally, a celebrated Israeli cultural figure (Figure 19). Readers will be fascinated by how Kafka immersed himself in the culture of his adopted homeland and eventually returned to his writing in the midst and the wake of the Jewish catastrophe in World War II.

Professor Lucian Himmelsturm
Editor, *Jewish Nobel Prize Laureates in Literature:*
1910–2005

* This chapter is a work of fiction. I would like to thank Gavriel Rosenfeld for his excellent suggestions, pushing me further and further into alternative realities. Many thanks also to Dr. L. Gross for his inspiring insightful ideas.

Figure 19. Franz Kafka, Israel's first recipient of the Nobel Prize for Literature.

Franz Kafka in Israel: "It Was No Dream"
Hugo Immerwahr

"It was no dream," comments the narrator in Kafka's famous novella, *The Metamorphosis*, after the protagonist, Gregor Samsa, wakes up one morning to find himself transformed into a "monstrous vermin." The rest of the narrative shows how Gregor is wounded, expelled from his family, and dies. Without pushing the comparison between this fictional novella from 1912 and more recent contemporary history too far, the assassination of Israeli Prime Minister Yitzhak Rabin in November

1995 was, in my view, also "no dream." Recognized for his peace negotiations with the Palestinians worldwide and the signing of the Oslo
Accord (1993), Rabin (along with Shimon Peres and Yasir Arafat) was
awarded the Nobel Peace Prize in 1994. Ironically, a year later, Rabin
was gunned down by a fanatically religious, right-wing terrorist. There
is a Kafkaesque link between the fates of Gregor Samsa and Yitzhak
Rabin: the brutal irony of being condemned and killed by someone in
the family, on whose behalf the individual has worked tirelessly. To be
sure, the history of Zionism in Israel, with its turn to the political right,
is a complex chapter in and of itself. My modest attempt in this essay is
to revisit Kafka's involvement with Zionist ideas and depict their impact
on his fiction. By examining how Kafka chronicled events in Palestine
and Israel from his emigration there in 1924 until his death in 1968,
we will learn about a writer who rebelled against restrictive ideologies,
transcended national boundaries, and won international recognition for
his literary realism, powerful symbolism, courageous satire, and independence of thought.

   Franz Kafka saw Zionism as "positively the only path...that
can lead to spiritual liberation."[1] His friend Max Brod (1884–1968)
testified to the fact that Kafka often talked "about his intention to emigrate to Erez-Israel. He wanted to live there as a simple craftsman. He
thought like a *chaluz*, a pioneer."[2] From 1910 on, several of Kafka's
friends and acquaintances began to travel to Palestine. On September
12, 1912 he invited three of these *Palästinafahrer* to his home: Dr. Hugo
Löw, Dr. Viktor Kellner (1887–1970), and Dr. Hugo Bergmann (1883–
1975). They were traveling to Palestine during the Second Aliya (1903–
14), when approximately 40,000 Jews emigrated there. Kafka's high
school friend Hugo Bergmann had visited the country in 1910; Viktor
Kellner, a leading member of the Zionist Bar Kochba club in Prague,
emigrated in 1911 and was teaching at the first Hebrew high school in
Jaffa; Hugo Löw, the editor of the *Prager Tagblatt*, was in the process
of emigrating and planned on working in the Palestine Office in Jaffa.
Reflecting on their veneration for Palestine, Kafka placed this evening
in an ironic light:

> Another traveler to Palestine [*Palästinafahrer*]. Is taking his bar
> examination a year before the end of his clerkship and is leaving
> (in two weeks) for Palestine with 1,200 K [crowns]. Will try to get
> a position with the Palestine Office. All these travelers to Palestine

(Dr. B[ergmann], Dr. K[ellner]) have downcast eyes, feel blinded by their listeners, fumble around on the table with the tips of their extended fingers, their voices quiver, they smile weakly and prop up these smiles with a little irony.

Everyone listened with great interest to Viktor Kellner's first-hand experience with the students, whom he called "chauvinists, [who] have the Maccabees forever in their mouths and want to take after them."[3] Kellner reported that the school had grown considerably since it started out in 1910 with nineteen students and three teachers.[4] A substantial donation by a British donor – justice of the peace Jacob Moser, Lord Manor of Bradford – had enabled them to erect a new building (the biggest yet in Palestine) and hire more teachers, including Kellner himself. Moser had also requested that the school be renamed after Herzl: the Herzlia Gymnasium. By September 1911, there were 254 students from all over the world (Russia, Romania, Portugal, Australia, South Africa, and Canada), and about 60 more students arrived in 1912. The school would eventually expand in size and accommodate some five hundred students.[5]

Many Prague Zionists were interested in this kind of humanistic, practical Zionism. Although they were influenced by the leading cultural Zionist, Ahad Ha'am (1856–1927), the circle of friends around Kafka felt especially close to Micha Josef Berdyczewski (1865–1921), who "emphasize[d] more consistently than Ahad Ha'am that the national foundation of Zionism exist[ed] independent of any ideology." More importantly, Berdyczewski identified all Judaism with humanity: "We are Jews only because we are human beings that are part of the Jewish people and our humanity is our Judaism."[6] Bergmann described their ideological position to Martin Buber (1878–1965) in 1915 as follows:

I long for the simple way in which people of other nations grow up and become themselves by the very fact of serving their nation – I long for that, not only because I feel (and Kellner said much the same thing to me recently in reference to his work at the Gymnasium) that we can serve our Jewishness by our humanity and that Jewish work that interferes with our development as human beings cannot be fruitful; I feel also, above all, that such a life has no reality.[7]

Two important projects of this nature became especially significant for Kafka: the Jewish *Volksheim* (People's Home) in Berlin, which was established during World War I (1916) for the Jewish refugee children from Eastern Europe; and the practical community work he and others engaged in at the Jewish Elementary School in Prague in 1923.[8]

Like many of his contemporaries, Jews and non-Jews, Zionists and non-Zionists, Kafka participated in the *Körperkultur* (popular body culture) movement at the turn of the century. He supported the call of Max Nordau (1849–1923) for physical exercise to create a new "muscle Jew": he went swimming, rowing, and hiking, and in July 1912 he spent three weeks at a nudist colony, the Jungborn sanatorium (under the guidance of Christian naturopath and occultist Adolf Just).[9] Furthermore, Kafka's passion for gardening derived from the cultural Zionism he was exposed to in Prague, as well as at the Eleventh Zionist Congress in Vienna, which he attended in 1913. By this point, a shift toward cultural Zionism had taken place, and the Congress was presided over by Dr. Otto Warburg (1859–1938), a botanist from Berlin. At the Congress, Kafka met his friend Viktor Kellner again, as well as Davis Trietsch (1870–1935), an expert on Palestine and the Orient, whose recent lecture in Prague on "Palestine as Land of Colonialization" he had attended and greatly enjoyed.[10]

Kafka never felt that the achievements of Western culture made Western Jews superior or meant that they should be role models for Eastern Jews or the new Jews in Palestine. He was extremely self-critical and saw himself only as a

> typical example of the Western Jew; as far as I know I'm the most Western-Jewish of them all. In other words, to exaggerate, not one second of calm has been granted me; nothing has been granted me, everything must be earned, not only the present and future, but the past as well – something which is, perhaps, given every human being – this too must be earned, and this probably entails the hardest work of all.[11]

Thus, in 1916, he did not think that Western Jews had much to teach the Eastern Jewish refugees in the Berlin *Volksheim* and criticized the teachers' attempts to "raise them to the standard of the contemporary, educated, West European Jew, Berlin version, which admittedly may be the best type of its kind. With that, not much would be achieved."[12] For

Kafka, "Zionism and sweeping enthusiasm [were] not enough," and it was the Western Jew who ironically needed help.[13] The only real alternative Kafka saw was to go back to the sources – to learn Hebrew and read the traditional texts – which was "the hardest work of all." Kafka's friend, Hugo Bergmann, was acutely aware of this dilemma when he wrote, "I cannot imagine that our generation's artificially acquired relationship to biblical and to hasidic Judaism, etc., will ever become so natural to us as our relationship to ... Fichte or to that man of European culture who showed us the way to humanism [Goethe]."[14]

In May 1917, Kafka began to teach himself modern Hebrew. During this period, the Balfour negotiations were causing a stir in the Middle East, and Kafka and Brod were following the events. "What things are going on in Palestine!" Kafka remarked to Brod, referring to Field Marshal Allenby's "campaign against the Turks in Palestine, which was to end Turkish rule in that region in November 1918."[15] As for the Balfour negotiations, Kafka remained skeptical. His short tale, "Jackals and Arabs," written a month before the Balfour Declaration was proclaimed, depicted the impotence and naïvety of a Northerner (a likely allusion to Max Nordau) – that is, a Western acculturated (Jewish) traveler to Palestine – who is unable to mediate between the Arabs and Jews, let alone solve any racial problems on a political level, because of his inability to understand the Middle Eastern mindset.[16]

In August of that same year, Kafka suffered his first hemorrhage and was eventually diagnosed with tuberculosis. The doctors remained optimistic, however, because they believed that the disease was treatable and even curable in this early stage. Indeed, Kafka biographer Reiner Stach claims that Kafka was cured when he was convalescing in the country on his sister's farm. By October 1918, Kafka was said to have "recovered from TB, and the Spanish flu represented the real threat."[17] More than 20 million people died in the influenza epidemic, and Kafka was lucky that he was not infected. There was no further indication of TB.

Kafka continued to take an intense interest in all aspects of life in Palestine. After the Balfour Declaration, he and his friends were troubled by the territory's escalating racial and political problems. In 1919, Brod mentioned a "dream in which I was tormented by Jewish and Zionist catastrophes. The situation in Palestine was critical at the time." Kafka himself was so preoccupied with the racial conflicts that in 1920 he complained to his friend Felix Weltsch (1884–1964), editor of the Zionist newspaper *Selbstwehr*, that he had not received the paper: "And just at this moment, when Palestine, according to a newspaper story, has been overrun by Bedouins and perhaps the little bookbinder's workbench in the corner has been smashed." At this point in his life, Kafka was toying with the idea of becoming a "bookbinder in Palestine."[18] The racial turbulence continued, however: in 1921, in Jaffa, forty-seven Jews were killed during an Arab attack, including the writer Y. H. Brenner (1881–1921). All the newspapers that Kafka read, such as *Selbstwehr, Der Jude, Das jüdische Echo,* and *Die Welt,* provided readers with continual reports about the situation in Palestine: agricultural disasters, racial clashes, the spread of diseases, the condition of the hospitals, the availability of jobs, and the like. Kafka and Brod shared this information with one another and discussed it all intensely.

Meanwhile, on the home front, growing antisemitism encouraged more of Kafka's friends to leave for Palestine. Hugo Bergmann emigrated to Jerusalem in May 1920, and Irma [Miriam] Singer (1898–1989), with whom Kafka had studied Hebrew, moved to the first kibbutz, Degania Alef, founded in 1909. Kafka was deeply disturbed by the antisemitic November riots in Prague in 1920: "The other day I heard someone call the Jews a 'mangy race.' Isn't it natural to leave a place where one is so hated? (Zionism or national feeling isn't needed for this at all.) The heroism of staying on is nonetheless merely the heroism of cockroaches which cannot be exterminated, even from the bathroom." He knew that departing was the only "way out" when he wrote to his gentile lover, Milena Jesenska (1896–1944), that he agreed with the antisemitic Czech newspaper: "The *Venkov* is very correct. Emigrate, Milena, emigrate!" This is why he found it "odd," in January 1921, that his friend Max Brod "hesitat[ed] to throw all [his] professional energies... into Zionism."[19]

When Bergmann returned from Palestine in 1923 for a visit, the Prague Zionists organized a series of lectures for him at the Zionist club, Keren Hayesod, on "The Situation in Palestine."[20] After one of these lectures, Kafka approached him and said, "You gave this talk only for me."[21] In his Hebrew notebook of this time, Kafka wrote down the words for "bookbinder" and "waiter" (his imaginary professions in Palestine).[22] He proceeded to throw himself into his Hebrew studies, taking lessons with two friends, Friedrich Thieberger (1888–1958) and Jiři Langer (1894–1943), as well as with the native speaker Puah ben Tovim (1903–91).[23] He also began making his own connections for a possible move to Palestine, starting with Aharon D. Gordon (1856–1922), one of the leaders of the Zionist Labor movement, and other Palestinian Jews, who were present at a meeting of the socialist Zionist Party Hapoel Hatzair and its youth organization Zeire Zion.[24] While vacationing with his sister's family in Müritz (outside Berlin) in July 1923, Kafka was excited to receive his first letter in Hebrew from Hugo Bergmann and replied that this holiday was to test his fitness for travel to Palestine. Bergmann's wife Else happened to be in Prague and encouraged Kafka to accompany her on her return to Jerusalem. Unfortunately, all the tickets were sold out.[25]

Instead, Kafka moved to Berlin with his new love, Dora Dymant (1898–1952), who, like himself, dreamed of going to Palestine. They imagined opening a restaurant in Tel Aviv, where Kafka would work as a waiter and Dora as a cook. In Berlin, Kafka read "only Hebrew," in particular "thirty-two pages of a novel by Brenner, a page every day. The book is entitled *Shekhol ve-Kishalon* ['Breakdown and Bereavement']."[26] Dora shared his love of Hebrew and both attended classes at the Rabbinic Institute in Berlin for a few months. In February 1924, they finally made their momentous decision: through a travel agency in Vienna, they bought tickets not for the cheaper mail-boat, but for the more expensive express steamer to Jaffa. Kafka and Dora were on their way to Palestine (Figure 20).

At the old Jaffa port, Miriam Singer and her husband Jakob Berkowski were waiting to take them to Degania Alef. Following in the footsteps of A. D. Gordon, they first paid a visit to the early settlements Petah Tikvah (1878) and Rishon LeZion (1882), recovering with friends from their exhausting journey before heading to the Sea of Galilee. A few days later, on their way north to Degania Alef, they understood how harsh life was for the *chaluzim* (pioneers): they saw the hard physical labor that was required for building roads; individuals were hammering away at blocks of rock in the heat for days on end. Kafka had seen such pictures in *Schiwath Zion*[27] ("Return to Zion"), a 1921 silent film by Ya'akov Ben Dov that depicted the lives of the *chaluzim* after coming to Palestine. Kafka and Dora were lucky that they had been allowed to proceed to Degania Alef to do agricultural work. Normally, all new arrivals were sent to build roads, drain swamps, or help with the construction of buildings for six months, a year, or sometimes even longer.[28] When Kafka met Gordon in Prague in 1920, the latter had just moved to Degania Alef. Now Kafka and Dora themselves were arriving there

Figure 20. Franz Kafka in Prague before his departure to Palestine in 1924.

two years after his death and living the life of the poor, in touch with the land and the people. Kafka had long envisioned pursuing this kind of frugal existence in an early kibbutz. Sometimes there were days when he literally lived on bread, water, and dates. However, Kafka soon became the intellectual leader of this small group of pioneers. He drew up a plan, "Workers Without Possessions," to create a new structure for an alternative existence, outlining the workers' "duties" and "rights" in an environment that had no need for money or material possessions. Individuals should only own a simple gown, as well as some books and food. They should have no possessions; all should be shared with the poor. Everyone should earn his or her living through work alone, and a supervisor might delegate work to the workers. Other duties involved the workers' relationship to the employer. Kafka was adamant that he wanted no lawyers there: no legal courts should ever be involved, and one should only have personal relationships based on trust. His famous statement from this period is that "the average set of lawyers...must first be ground to dust before they may reach Palestine. Palestine needs earth but it does not need lawyers." As for workers' "rights," Kafka suggested a maximum of six hours of labor and, in the case of heavy physical labor, four to five hours of work a day. He also envisioned building hospitals and old-age homes to provide for the sick and old.[29]

In their daily lives, Kafka and Dora worked as agricultural laborers. Kafka had long ago tried to prepare himself and others to be pioneers in Palestine. As early as 1913, he had worked in vegetable gardens and at the Pomological Institute for Viniculture and Gardening in Troya, close to Prague. He also spent much time in the garden and fields at his sister Ottla's farm house in Zürau in 1917–18 and fed the animals: a horse, a pig, goats, and geese. Afterwards, he went again to the Pomological Institute, and when he was vacationing in Turnau (September 1918) he did gardening "in the largest nursery in Bohemia (Maschek, Turnau)." He encouraged Ottla to do "an apprenticeship in an agricultural winter school in Friedland [in the Iser mountains]." He also pushed to get her into the Hachschara, an agricultural school near Cologne, and promised to donate a thousand crowns to the Jewish National Fund if Ottla were to be successful, but the place was full. This was in 1920, when Hugo Bergmann's family and Miriam Singer emigrated, as well as several of Ottla's other friends from the Club of Jewish Women and Girls; but Ottla married Josef David, a non-Jew, in July 1920 and stayed in Prague. Kafka continued to recommend agricultural schools to young Jews who were searching for a focus in their lives, such as the Israelitische Gartenbauschule (Israelite Agricultural School) in Ahlem. Even when he was living in Berlin, just before his emigration, it did not take him long to find a "famous gardening school at Dahlem."[30]

When he immigrated, Kafka brought along the "renowned study on land reform: Adolf Damaschke's *Die Bodenreform*" (1902), which was "declared the basis of the policy of the future state" at the Zionist Congress in 1903.[31] Apart from a mass of practical, everyday expressions, his Hebrew notebook from this period contained much agricultural vocabulary such as "pitchfork," "pumpkin," "harvest," and "grains." A Department of Agriculture had been established a few years earlier, and Kafka took a keen interest in plant diseases and insect pests. Several veterinary hospitals existed as well, and a field staff of veterinary surgeons had recently come to deal with a contagious livestock disease.[32] Kafka's Hebrew notebook mentions the introduction of the Karakul sheep to Palestine and "cattle breeding," and he wrote down the Hebrew names for various animal diseases that he learned about from the Degania veterinarian Ilan Gross – another recent immigrant and relative of Kafka's friend, the late Viennese psychoanalyst Otto Gross (1877–1920), a famous anarchist who was well known for his bohemian life style.

During the late summer of 1924, Kafka's Viennese friend, the writer and journalist Felix Salten (1869–1945), came to Palestine, and Kafka traveled to Tel Aviv to meet him. He had known Salten since the latter's first lecture in Prague (together with Martin Buber) in 1909. Salten's recent novel *Bambi* (1922/3) had been widely discussed not only in Europe, but also among European intellectuals in Palestine. In Zionist circles, *Bambi* was hailed as a new type of Zionist children's literature. The old King of the Forest was easily recognizable as Theodor Herzl (1860–1904), and the dangers of assimilation were obvious in poor Gobo's fate, who was shot by a hunter. Kafka remarked that he saw *Bambi* as a "novel of abandonment," since it was written so many years after Herzl's death, with no new charismatic leader in sight.[33] The two writers discussed the impact of Zionism on their creative work. Kafka insisted he had always been critical of dogmatic Zionist discourse and would never write "*the* Jewish novel," with a Jewish hero, which many Zionists called for. Salten, too, replied that he had consciously cast *Bambi* in a universal light. Kafka acknowledged that even though he had indeed presented an obvious, devastating critique of the assimilated Jew in "Report to an Academy" (1917), this was a commonplace theme by now in Zionist literature, and he had moved beyond it. He also drew attention to his satires of Zionism and colonialism: his parody of the excessive, arrogant nationalism of young Western Zionists in Blumfeld's bouncy blue and white balls (1915), his critique of religious fanaticism in Palestine in "Jackals and Arabs" (1917), and his satire of practical Zionism in "Investigations of a Dog" (1922). Had Zionism not intervened, Kafka joked, his literary work "might easily have developed into a new secret doctrine, a Kabbalah."[34] In fact, Kafka remarked, he had been very impressed with the "national poet" Chaim Bialik for having achieved a balance between nationalism and humanism and was hoping that Salten might meet Bialik later on in Tel Aviv.

Felix Salten had traveled in the Middle East before, but this trip was different. He had come to tour Palestine, to observe life in the colonies, and to write a book about it afterwards. Salten had a car and a driver, and he now invited Kafka to come along, beginning with Mikve Israel, the first agricultural settlement with its famous agricultural school (1870), established and maintained by Karl Netter (1826–82). Here they made the acquaintance of Shlomo Zemach (1886–1974), whose book, *Jewish Peasants*, Kafka had read in 1919.[35] Zemach was a close childhood friend of David Ben-Gurion and had already immigrated in 1904. They learned that he had worked as an agricultural laborer and as "director of the extension service of the WZO's Agricultural Experiment Station" at the *moshav* (cooperative farming settlement) Ben Shemen (1905), southeast of Tel Aviv, where he "offered instruction in irrigation and established experimental irrigated fields in some of the Galilean settlements."[36] Then, again, for several years he had returned to Europe, obtained a degree as an agricultural engineer in France, and continued his literary pursuits. When Zemach came back to Palestine in 1921, he chose to work at the Mikve Israel agricultural school as a teacher. A blonde German Jewish guide proudly showed Kafka and Salten around: he had escaped the antisemitism in Germany, was only eighteen years old, and considered himself "a child of a new time." At the end they asked to see the grave of the founder Karl Netter. Their next stop was Rishon LeZion (1882), a larger *moshava* (private farming) with 1,500 inhabitants and known for its famous winery. The problem they encountered here was that the second generation was leaving the *moshava*: they returned to Europe or moved on to America or Australia. The main reason for this was the failing wine business caused by the Prohibition laws in the United States and Russia. Since there was no longer a market for wine, *moshava* farmers were now focusing on tobacco.[37]

Kafka and Salten continued driving north to the Galilee. Along the way, Kafka pointed out the Hashomer watchmen (Jewish defense organization) on horses with their mustaches, keffiyehs, rifles, and bullet belts across their chests. These men were of all ages, some of them even in their fifties or sixties, who had often lost their families in pogroms in Europe. Salten observed that they could not overcome their pain and therefore decided to take on this difficult job, putting their lives in constant danger. Arriving at Kafka's home in Degania Alef, the two friends spent several days with Dora. Then they moved on to see three small colonies in the Jezreel Valley: Ein Harod (1921), Tel Josef (1921), and Beit Alfa (1922). The view of the Gilboa Mountains was stunning. Many young people, students from Europe, had come to these new *kibbutzim*. Though surrounded by swamps that needed to be drained (a breeding ground for malaria), Ein Harod had trees and fresh water, because it was located near the Harod Spring. The students here still lived in tents. Kafka and Salten had a heated argument there with an opinionated Zionist. Salten insisted that it was unnatural to separate children from their mothers and thought the Zionist was quite a fanatic, but Kafka countered that he had always agreed with Jonathan Swift, who said that children should be brought up away from their families, and not by their parents. Salten was also adamant that individuals must keep their property, whereas Kafka was happy to give it all up. For the *kibbutznik*, Salten's views represented typical bourgeois thinking, which had to be wiped out.[38]

The next colony, Tel Josef, was close by, named after Joseph Trumpeldor (1880–1920), the famous Hashomer commander who had fought valiantly to defend the farming village Tel Hai in the Galilee in 1920, when he was killed by Arabs. There they met an interesting Arab writer, Asis Domet (1890–1943), who had made a name for himself especially in Europe as a Christian Arab who had fought for the Zionist side and had written a play about the national hero Trumpeldor's heroic death. Salten had met Asis Domet once before, in Vienna, but for Kafka, this was a new and fascinating encounter. The youngest little kibbutz, Beit Alfa, was located further east from Ein Harod and Tel Josef, in the shadow of Mount Gilboa. Here Kafka and Salten encountered young people from Austria and Bohemia; again, there were very few houses and people lived mostly in tents. Yet there were also a few older settlers who already spoke Hebrew and had lived in the area for a while. Kafka and Salten had come especially to see an old friend who had been a lawyer in Europe. He had arrived not long before Kafka and Dora, but he had been made to perform all sorts of odd jobs when he arrived: stone-breaker, road-builder, handyman, locksmith, blacksmith, carpenter, and house painter.[39]

Finally, traveling further south toward Jerusalem, Salten and Kafka stayed with Hugo Bergmann's family for a few days and admired the splendid sights of Jerusalem, before ending their tour in Tel Aviv with its over thirty thousand inhabitants. They were especially curious to see Ruttenberg's new Jaffa Electrical Company, which had just been established in 1923. The composer Mordechai Zeira (1905–68) was working here as an electrician. Kafka had made his acquaintance already: Zeira had also immigrated in 1924, and for a little while had lived not far from Degania Alef, on the land of the later kibbutz Afikim. Kafka admired Zeira because he refused to be only an artist: he wanted to be useful to the community. Zeira stressed the greater importance of technology, which related to the Arab–Jewish conflict. He told them that for quite some time Jaffa had wanted nothing to do with this electrical plant, but now the Arabs no longer resisted, and at this very moment the electricians at the plant were working on a connection to provide Jaffa with light and electricity for streetcars. The advancement of technology, according to Zeira (and Salten agreed), was the key to peaceful Arab–Jewish coexistence.[40] Zeira was also an accomplished musician, and had worked with the well-known composer Joel Engel (1868–1927), now living in Tel Aviv.[41] Engel had been a friend of the late S. Ansky (1863–1920) and had been part of his famous expedition in 1912, traveling with a group of artists through Ukraine to collect Jewish folk art and music. Kafka knew about Ansky's expedition and was fascinated by the group's collection of Jewish folklore. Engel also wrote the musical score for Ansky's 1914 play *The Dybbuk*. Kafka and Salten spent a very pleasant evening with Engel and Zeira, listening to some of Zeira's popular settler songs.

Their very last evening was reserved for Israel's national poet Chaim Nahman Bialik (1873–1934), who had just emigrated from Berlin to Tel Aviv. Bialik frequently invited guests to his beautiful home in Bialik Street (named after him before he even arrived): Kafka and Salten admired the architecture and inside decoration, the zodiac and folklore motifs on the pillars in his living room, and the magnificent garden. Bialik and Kafka had lived in Berlin at the same time, but their paths had not crossed, though Kafka and Dora had studied at the Rabbinic Institute in Berlin, and Bialik had contacts there as well. Now Kafka told him how much he had admired his powerful condemnation of the Kishinev pogrom (1903) in his poem, "In Schhite Stot" ("In the City of Slaughter"), when he first heard it recited in Yiddish in 1911. Also present that evening was Bialik's close friend Ahad Ha'am, whose cultural Zionism had inspired not only the Prague Zionists but Felix Salten in Vienna as well. It was an experience to meet Ahad Ha'am in person. They were later joined by another close friend, the painter Reuven Rubin (1893–1974), some of whose gentle, visionary paintings of Palestine decorated Bialik's living room. Kafka's and Salten's earlier discussion about nationalism and humanism, and the meaning of humanist Zionism for their art, resurfaced that evening, with Ahad Ha'am present, and all agreed with Bialik that a great artist can combine the national and universal in him or herself, because the universal element is always present in any national consciousness. At the end of the evening they were invited up to the roof terrace with its view of the sea, where Bialik pointed out the lights of the growing city around them.

After Salten left Palestine, Kafka returned to Degania Alef and resumed his agricultural activities in the community. Gordon remained an inspiration to both Kafka and Dora throughout this whole period. They identified with the pacifist, socialist, Zionist Hapoel Hatzair (The Young Worker), which Gordon had founded, and which attracted intellectuals of all kinds: agricultural workers, writers, and teachers. Dora participated in the feminist activities of Hapoel Hatzair, together with Ada Fishman-Maimon and Yael Gordon, the late A. D. Gordon's daughter. Gordon had strongly believed in an equal education for boys and girls; his daughter was the product of her father's educational projects in Eastern Europe (which reminded Kafka of his own involvement with the Jewish elementary school in Prague) and she became a Hebrew teacher and advocate for women's rights. Kafka was hoping that at some point there might be a possibility for him and Dora to become teachers as well. In his last letter to Kafka, Martin Buber had confided in him that it was his dream to

> establish a school of adult education (a *Volkshochschule*) as an
> instrument for the education of the people. Not in Germany,
> where such a school would stand in the shadow of the university,

but in Palestine, where no university had yet been created. There
lay the chance to make a reality of [his] concept: "An institution
for real popular education, not for certain classes who enjoy the
privilege of education, but, as the name *Volkshochschule* implies,
for the whole nation that is coming into being."⁴²

Ironically, two years later in 1926, when Buber had a chance to realize this dream, he did not want to leave Europe: he had been asked to
become chancellor of the new Hebrew University after it opened on
Mount Scopus in Jerusalem (1925).⁴³

    At Degania Alef, Kafka and Dora briefly made the acquain-
tance of the poet Rachel Bluwstein (1890–1931), who inspired Kafka
to return to his fictional writing. However, finding a new literary style
was very difficult for him. He had read Zemach's realist fiction in
Jewish Peasants (1919) about the hardships of daily survival, conflicts with the Arabs, and the increasing hatred on the Jewish side.
Kafka, too, had by now participated in defending farms from external attacks, and for this reason appreciated some of Zemach's realism. At the same time, he loved Brenner's Hebrew fiction, though he
found him too bleak and wished for a rebirth of Jewish literature in
Palestine. Nonetheless, the novel *Shekhol ve-Kishalon* ("Breakdown
and Bereavement") was a great work of art, far more so than the
melodrama that Zemach produced. In Zemach's story, "Brachfeld"
("Barren Field"), a Jewish man, was left badly injured after an Arab
attack: in his "frozen look there was irreconcilable hatred," and "the
spilled blood . . . cried out from the depths for retaliation and the cut-off
finger lying in the mud called out: Revenge, Revenge!" Kafka fundamentally disliked the heavy-handedness of this kind of expressionistic writing about Palestine, which had already filled the Zionist newspapers in
the old country. He had criticized the militant Berlin Zionist, physician,
and writer Hans Bloch's "Legende von Theodor Herzl" ("Legend of
Theodor Herzl") for the "Geschrei" (the "scream") of his expressionistic style, his "effusiveness with mere words": "('life in me began to
rebel and let out a piercing cry like that of a mortally wounded beast,'
etc. – no, that's no good, or rather it's childish and might mean anything). Undoubtedly, he will write better things, or has already."⁴⁴ It
was not only the melodrama that Kafka criticized but also the nationalist and frequently racial discourse in this type of Zionist literature and
politics.

In Jerusalem in the late 1920s, Kafka tried to contact S. Y. Agnon (1887–1970) who was a close friend of Martin Buber during the years Agnon lived in Germany. Agnon had already immigrated to Palestine in 1909, but moved to Germany in 1913, and had only returned to Tel Aviv the same year that Kafka and Dora immigrated. He was considered *the* literary icon in Palestine now. Yet Agnon showed little interest in Kafka and claimed that he barely knew the titles of Kafka's few short stories that had been published in Europe. Neither did Agnon appreciate it when readers approached him and asked if he knew Kafka's writings, since some of his stories seemed similar to Kafka's. He insisted he had never read Kafka. Kafka himself admired Agnon for his literary work, as well as for his knowledge of Jewish tradition. He knew that he would never be able to write in Hebrew like Agnon, who was instrumental in developing the Hebrew language through his art. As Gershom Scholem rightly said, Agnon "stood at the 'crossroads of Hebrew'; his Hebrew exemplified the development of the language of religious tradition into the revived spoken language."[45] There were rumors that Agnon was planning to write a monumental novel about the second Aliya, a magnum opus capturing his time – his later 700-page epic, *Tmol Shilshom* ("Only Yesterday," 1945), which Kafka considered a masterpiece when it came out. Kafka did not aspire to such heights; he still felt very much like the Western Jew who had to acquire everything. There was also a fundamental ideological difference between Agnon and himself; Kafka was not interested in preserving the Jewish religious tradition. Not only did he lack a basic knowledge of the original texts, but he was a satirist at heart, who loved to pun and make fun of the religious heritage. Though his Hebrew was good and he was able to communicate, he could not play on words in Hebrew in the same way that he could in German. For a satirically inclined writer like himself, it was virtually impossible to write in the new language.

Kafka therefore decided to rewrite and finish his three unfinished novels in German and have them translated into Hebrew later. *Amerika*, the land of immigration in his first novel, had now been replaced by Palestine. The immigrant Karl Rossman, "The Man Who Disappeared" in the Promised Land of America, would not disappear in Palestine but begin a new life. *The Trial* had been inspired by the 1913 Beilis ritual murder trial and the Dreyfus affair.[46] But all of this seemed like history now. There were new possibilities for Joseph K., who Kafka decided must not die. Finally, in *The Castle*, bureaucracy prevented the land-surveyor from finding a home: there might be a new home for him here as well. For the moment, however, Kafka was so busy at Degania and with his Haganah (literally, "Defense"; Jewish paramilitary organization) activities that he felt no urgency to write.

During these four years on Degania Alef, Kafka remained close to a group of friends including Arthur Ruppin (1876–1943), Hugo Bergmann, Martin Buber, Gershom Scholem (1897–1982), Hans Kohn (1891–1971), and Ernst Simon (1899–1988). All firmly believed in their vision of a cultural, humanistic Zionism, which found expression in "Brit Shalom" (A Peace Treaty), a peace group they founded in 1925. Supported by Judah L. Magnes (1877–1948), Buber, Walter Benjamin (1892–1940), and Albert Einstein (1879–1955), Brit Shalom advocated peaceful coexistence between Jews and Arabs, and Buber especially stressed that "the altogether desirable immigration of steadily increasing numbers of Jews into Palestine should take place without any violation of the rights of the country's Arab inhabitants."[47] Magnes, who shared Buber's pacifism, spoke up for many, saying: "The Jewish national homeland must not be established by force of arms – 'not in the way of Joshua' – as he expressed it in his opening speech at Hebrew University in 1929, the year of the Arab riots."[48] Kafka shared these sentiments. Yet self-defense was paramount for him at Degania during this period and was part of daily life. Like most, he was working in the Haganah to help protect the farms and *kibbutzim*. This did not alienate him from his intellectual friends, nor did it mean that Kafka did not support their humanistic form of Zionism.

Kafka and Dora stayed in Degania Alef until 1928. The situation in Europe had become increasingly desperate, and they decided to move to the youth village, Ben Shemen, which was established outside Tel Aviv in 1927 by their old acquaintance from Berlin, Siegfried Lehmann (1892–1958), who had arrived in Palestine that same year. Kafka had always supported Lehmann's work for the Jewish *Volksheim* during World War I, which provided boarding and an education for Jewish refugee children from the East. He had encouraged his fiancée Felice Bauer to be one of the helpers at the *Volksheim*. Kafka and Brod had also been engaged in similar activities helping Jewish refugees in Prague. These convictions explain why he and Dora wanted to help Lehmann bring children from Jewish orphanages in Berlin and elsewhere to Palestine. At the same time, Kafka and Dora finally saw an opportunity for themselves to become teachers: Kafka was already familiar with the British model of the settlement houses from Lehmann's Berlin *Volksheim*; they were based on nineteenth-century community-oriented educational facilities, which encouraged teachers to live with their students at close quarters. This arrangement had proved difficult in Berlin, where the teachers generally lived elsewhere and only came in to teach. But in the youth village Ben Shemen all lived together as a collective. Viktor Kellner visited a few times from the Herzlia Gymnasium, as did Erwin Arnstein, a popular teacher from the Jewish Elementary School in Prague, who had emigrated in 1923, returned to Prague for a year to obtain his doctorate, and later made his home in Jerusalem. As Kafka's niece, Marianne Steiner (1913–2001), recalled:

> Erwin Arnstein was a marvelous teacher and all children, myself included, adored him. His method, for Prague of that time, was revolutionary indeed. The children were asked to call him Erwin (not "Herr Lehrer" as was the custom then); he introduced plasticine and encouraged the children to use their imagination and create models of everyday life: a wedding, a funeral etc. When he left Prague with his fiancée Klara, we children were heartbroken.[49]

Arnstein and Kellner now joined Kafka and Dora at Ben Shemen: all became part of Lehmann's teaching team.

After the Nazi rise to power, Tile Rössler, a good friend of Kafka and Dora, immigrated from Germany to Tel Aviv. Now going by the name of Tehila Ressler (1907–59), she opened one of the first dance studios in Tel Aviv, the "Tehila Ressler School," and inspired the development of free movement dance in the Yishuv, which was now suppressed in Germany. Also in 1933, the writer Arnold Zweig (1887–1968) came to Palestine. Like Kafka, he had Zionist sympathies as a young man, and later began to work for the Zionist newspaper, *Jüdische Rundschau*. Kafka had met Zweig before, and their literary work had once been mentioned in the same column in the Zionist newspaper *Selbstwehr*, but they were not close. In 1938, Martin Buber, too, finally emigrated to Palestine. Through Gershom Scholem's influence, Buber obtained a professorship at the Hebrew University. And it was Buber who ultimately encouraged Kafka to write again. When Kafka began rewriting *Amerika* at Ben Shemen, he changed the title to *Driftwood*, given the desperate situation of European Jews. Some of the children who were "driftwood" and had come to Ben Shemen later became famous. One was Shimon Peres (1923–), later Prime Minister of Israel and recipient of the Nobel Peace Prize in 1994 (together with Rabin and Arafat), who arrived in Tel Aviv in 1934. He left high school in Tel Aviv at the age of fifteen and went to Ben Shemen to continue his education there. Another was the later literary celebrity, Dahn Ben Amotz (1924–89), who came to Ben Shemen in 1938 as an orphan from Poland. Kafka was fifty-five years old when he met Shimon Peres and the fourteen-year-old Ben Amotz. He became their counselor, mentor, and friend. Both students left in 1941; the seventeen-year-old Ben Amotz joined the Palmach (underground elite fighting force of Haganah), while Peres joined the Haganah. Both distinguished themselves in the military, and later enjoyed successful careers in Israeli political and cultural life.

Kafka's novel *Driftwood*, rewritten in the midst of these turbulent political events, took a less optimistic turn and lost much of the light-hearted playfulness of the original *Amerika* novel. While retaining the central character, Karl Rossman (horseman), the novel depicts him as a refugee child at Ben Shemen, who later joins the underground Haganah. As a member of the Guard Corps, we see him patrolling Jewish settlements on his horse, defending and protecting them from Arab invasions. Eventually Karl becomes a spy for Israel/Palestine and discovers many state secrets that destroy the power of the Arabs and enable the Jews to create their own Jewish state much sooner than anyone expected. Yet the ending of *Driftwood* is just as ironic as in the original *Amerika* novel (in which the promising theater of Oklahoma falsely advertised itself as a haven where everyone was welcome and betrayed all who had hope). In *Driftwood*, Kafka transformed this "theater" into the ugly political spectacle during the last phase of the British Mandate, with the British playing the Jews off against the Arabs and vice versa. *Driftwood* depicts both Arabs and Jews as helpless "driftwood," at the mercy of selfish, greedy, and power-hungry authority figures at all levels of society. The novel ends with a highly ironic vision of a soon-to-be-realized Jewish state in 1942, which held out no promise for a peaceful coexistence between Arabs and Jews.

When World War II broke out, Kafka grew even closer to Martin Buber and both became increasingly involved with Brit Shalom. Moreover, Kafka was especially proud of Hugo Bergmann who, since he had become rector of the Hebrew University in 1935, never ceased to emphasize that his university "teaches Arabic, promotes Arab culture and does scientific work in the fields of agriculture and health, [all of which] 'will create new possibilities for future cooperation between Arabs and Jews.'"[50] In 1939, the group formed the League for Arab–Jewish Rapprochement.[51] Arnold Zweig had always been a strong pacifist and at this stage he joined them as well. Through Zweig, Kafka also came to participate in a few political activities advocating peace and understanding.

In 1940 Kafka, Zweig, and the painter Hermann Struck (1876–1944) were invited to Kibbutz Masaryk, to celebrate the renaming of the kibbutz after Tomáš Masaryk (1850–1937), the first President of Czechoslovakia. Arnold Zweig read from his play, *Ritual Murder in Hungary* (1914), for which he had received the Kleist Prize in 1915.[52] Zweig was the attraction of the evening, for his play was about the Hilsner ritual murder trial, which had made Masaryk famous. This was a Czech Dreyfus trial (1894–1906), which also dragged on for years. Like Dreyfus, Leopold Hilsner, a poor Czech Jewish villager, had been wrongly convicted and imprisoned in 1900–18. Hilsner's lawyer Masaryk became the Zola of the Hilsner trial, courageously speaking up against antisemitism at great cost to his personal and professional life. Though Masaryk was initially unable to win Hilsner's release, the case eventually made him very popular and paved the way for his later political career. Moreover, after he became President, his pro-Jewish sentiments set the tone in the country for many years to come. Because he stood by Hilsner unswervingly until the latter was set free by the last Austro-Hungarian Emperor Charles I at the end of World War I, Masaryk was honored by the Kibbutz Masaryk as a righteous gentile. After Zweig's performance, Kafka read excerpts from "The Judgment" and "The Penal Colony," both of which contained echoes of the Beilis ritual murder trial (1911–13).[53] The evening ended with a reading by Hermann Struck, who had immigrated in 1922 and taught at the Bezalel Art School. Struck read from *Das Ostjüdische Antlitz* ("The Face of East European Jewry"), which he had published together with Arnold Zweig in 1920, and afterwards he discussed the lost world of Eastern European Judaism in his own drawings, which he had contributed to the volume.[54]

In 1942, Magnes and Buber, as well as two Hebrew writers, Rabbi Benjamin (Yehoshua Radler-Feldman, 1880–1957) and S. Yitzhar's uncle, Moshe Smilansky (1874–1953), founded the association Ihud (Unity), which supported a binational state.[55] However, these efforts to find peaceful solutions to the Arab–Jewish conflict went largely unnoticed because of other pressing concerns. The war and the Holocaust, news of which had begun to arrive in the Yishuv, were on everyone's minds. Kafka continued his clandestine work in the Haganah and helped refugees who were coming into the country, including his friends Max Brod, Jiři Langer, and the former editor of the Zionist newspaper *Selbstwehr*, Felix Weltsch. Brod and Weltsch managed to get the last train out of Prague in 1939 and eventually were able to establish themselves. Brod found work at the Habima National Theater in Tel Aviv and by 1942 he was already its artistic director; Weltsch became a librarian in Jerusalem. Langer, however, was in very poor health when he arrived in Tel Aviv from Slovakia in 1939. He had been Kafka's most flamboyant friend in Prague. Not only did he "positively reaffirm . . . his Jewishness and his homosexuality," he lived with the Hasidim in Galicia off and on from 1913 to 1916, introduced Brod and Kafka to the wonder rabbis of Grodek and Belz, and was the first to publish his Hebrew poetry in Prague. A scholar and poet, he was also Kafka's Hebrew teacher for years and practiced everyday Hebrew conversation with him long before Kafka emigrated to Palestine. Though Langer's health declined, he continued writing Hebrew poetry in Tel Aviv, and after spending several years translating his Hasidic legends into Hebrew, eventually died in March 1943.[56] Despite desperate personal circumstances and the increasingly worsening political situation, the German émigré community tried to keep their spirits up and founded literary clubs and salons. From 1941 on, Max Brod was a regular visitor at the salon of his brother-in-law Ernst Taussig and his wife, where political and intellectual discussions took place and writers read from their work in German. Kafka accompanied Brod only once: he found the nostalgic, backward-looking German émigré community stifling.

After World War II, Kafka suffered from severe depression when he received the news that most of his family had been killed by the Nazis. He had been informed that all of his three sisters had died in concentration camps: Gabriele ("Elli" [1889–1944?]) and her youngest daughter Hanna (1920–41?), as well as Valerie ("Valli" [1890–1944?]) and her husband Josef Pollak were sent to the Lodz ghetto in 1941 and perhaps died in the Chelmno extermination camp, either in 1941/2 or 1944. Elli's son Felix (1911–40) died in a concentration camp in France. Kafka's youngest sister Ottilie ("Ottla" [1892–1943]) died in Auschwitz-Birkenau. Not long after the war ended, Kafka discovered a little bit more about Ottla's fate. Survivors from Terezin told him that she made her non-Jewish husband divorce her in order to save their two children; thereafter, she was taken to Terezin in 1942, where she attended to a group of severely traumatized Polish orphans from the Bialystock ghetto, who needed special care. Along with fifty others, Ottla had volunteered to accompany these orphans when they were ordered on a transport, supposedly to be exchanged at the Swiss border or in Denmark or Sweden. Yet, their transport was turned back and all of them were sent to Auschwitz and immediately gassed upon arrival.[57] Moreover, word had reached Kafka that his second fiancée Julie Wohryzek had died in Auschwitz in 1944, and his non-Jewish lover, Milena Jesenskà, who had fought courageously in the Czech resistance, had died in the Ravensbrück concentration camp, also in 1944. The Jewish world that he had left behind had collapsed. At first, Kafka believed that only Ottla's two daughters, Vera and Helene, had survived in Prague with their non-Jewish father. He later found out that Valli's daughter, Marianne Steiner (1913–2000), was still alive because she had emigrated with her husband to Great Britain in 1939. There had been no news of Elli's daughter Gerti (1912–72) for the longest time, but Kafka subsequently learned that she was alive as well.

Because of the changing political climate in Israel, Kafka's longtime friend, Arnold Zweig, always a convinced pacifist, openly criticized Israel's nationalistic turn and went back to East Berlin in 1948 "to serve the cause of socialism."[58] Yet Kafka knew that he himself would never return to Europe, though the political future in Israel did not look promising. Kafka's intellectual circle of friends in Brit Shalom tried once again to influence the course of political events. This was Israel's chance to build a democratic foundation for a new Jewish state, grounded in the humanistic values of cultural Zionism. Judah Magnes had become "Buber's most influential and important associate in the struggle for peace during the decade preceding the foundation of the state of Israel."[59] But again their dream failed, as new realities determined Zionism's direction after the war. Faced with the immediate creation of a state, political Zionism triumphed over cultural Zionism. Given the necessity for national security, "the Zionist culture that emerged in Jewish Palestine idealized the New Muscle Jew" and was also "unmistakably gendered; for it was largely the men who claimed the additional mission of national defense."[60] This represented a road not taken, a chance missed.

Perhaps it was because he was emotionally paralyzed by the Holocaust and disappointed about the direction of political events that Kafka gradually rediscovered the urge to write. With hesitation, he turned to his abandoned 1914 novel, *The Trial*, shocked at how many scenes seemed to foreshadow the horrors of war and genocide. He immediately transformed the ethnically unidentifiable protagonist, Joseph K., who was arrested in the original novel without ever having committed a crime, into a Czech Jewish protagonist. This new Josef K. is not only traumatized by the course of events in the late 1930s but has acquired a debilitating illness: he is literally becoming paralyzed when the Germans enter Czechoslovakia in 1938. K.'s "trial" is this mysterious disease, both symbolic and personal, a slow and inevitable process of paralysis, which slowly turns his entire body into stone. Witnessing the deportations around him in 1942, K. is eventually confined to his bed and receives news about the events in Prague and the destruction of the Jewish world only on the radio or from caretakers and friends who visit him. When his friends are deported one by one, his symptoms worsen and he feels his body's rigidity intensify. With no one left to take care of the helpless man, K. is transferred to a local non-Jewish hospital, where this bizarre clinical case becomes a challenge for the medical community in Prague. But no one can find a cure for his mysterious illness.

In September 1940, orders are issued to remove all Jewish patients to a Jewish hospital. K.'s doctors fight this decision for a while, but are helpless in the end. In January 1942, now paralyzed up to his neck, K. is placed on a stretcher to be taken away. After years of confinement, K. is carried one last time through the streets of Prague during daylight. He sees a strange world that he no longer belongs to. Most passersby are afraid to look at him and rush by. Some stare at his strange immobile body and his stony face. No one stops, no one knows him any longer. All of a sudden, K. has a last vision: he witnesses the deportation of a group of little children ahead of him – a few faces seem familiar – as they pass the Jewish Elementary School of Prague, which he himself had helped found in 1920. His sister Valli had been working as a teacher at the school even after the Nazi invasion and his niece Lotte had been one of the first students there. K. tries to get a last glimpse of the group as they are forced onto a truck that he knows will take them to the Terezin concentration camp and from there to Auschwitz. The novel ends with K. straining to move his head one last time when he feels, horrified, that his entire body has now turned to stone and he can no longer move. We never find out what happens to him.

Rewriting this novel was painful and took many years. While Kafka was reworking *The Trial*, other friends also found their voices by addressing the Holocaust. His friend Miriam Singer, still living on Degania Alef, translated the wartime memoirs of Elieser Jerushalmi from Hebrew into German and published them in 1960.[61] *The Trial*, however, was much more than therapeutic release. It became Kafka's seminal work about the Holocaust and earned him international acclaim. When it was published in 1958 it became a worldwide success. As Norman Mailer commented: "Kafka's *Trial* is an emotional *tour de force*. No reader will ever forget Kafka's powerful metaphor of a human being who is slowly turning into stone. This metaphor perfectly captures the inexpressible human suffering of millions who had no voice. A most profound evocation of the holocaust indeed."

Kafka's next novel, *Hordus' Castle*, followed in 1963. This was Kafka's last major work, which helped make him a celebrity around the world. The plot differed significantly from *The Trial*, which had no closure, since the protagonist's fate was deliberately left unknown. *Hordus' Castle* begins with Adolf Hitler's 1939 speech from the Prague Hradcany Castle, proclaiming the creation of the German protectorate of Bohemia and Moravia. The protagonist, Hordus, is a young Zionist who witnesses Hitler's speech. Hordus, the Hebrew name for King Herod, alludes to the legend of Herod the Great, Roman King of Judea, who built, amongst other palaces, the fortress at Masada. For Zionists, Masada always symbolized ultimate Jewish heroism and resistance: as the legend goes, during the Roman siege of Masada in the first century BCE, the Jewish warriors on top of Masada defended themselves valiantly, never giving up, choosing death through mass suicide over surrender. After Hitler's speech at the Prague Castle, Hordus decides to immigrate to Palestine in order to climb the Masada rock in the Judean desert and build his own castle on top of Herod's palace ruins. In Israel, he works as a land-surveyor for many years, surveying the rocky, sandy landscape, working out construction plans to realize his dream of rebuilding Herod's Castle on Masada.

In this highly symbolic novel, which combined Jewish and European history with contemporary Zionist dreams and realities, Kafka used multiple word plays: the German "Schloss" (castle) also carries the meaning of a "lock" in a door, which needs to be opened, while the Hebrew–Aramaic word for the German "Landvermesser" (land-surveyor) ("mashikha") alludes not only to "messiah" but also to "desire."[62] The novel's distinguishing features, in fact, are linguistic playfulness, pervasive irony, and even slapstick comedy, reminding us of the younger Kafka's Chaplinesque humor at the beginning of his *Metamorphosis*, or of some of the hilarious scenes in his original *Trial* or the *Amerika* novel. Most importantly, unlike the struggles of Kafka's previous protagonists, Hordus' relentless pursuit of his goal is not futile: Hordus never loses faith and his struggle is never without purpose. At the end of *Hordus' Castle*, Hordus lays the first stone. The daunting task of resurrecting his castle from the old ruins of Herod's palace on top of Masada has begun.

This last novel received rave reviews. Saul Bellow wrote:

> *Hordus' Castle* is a remarkable contemporary Zionist epic, exploring the fears and anxieties of two generations struggling for a safe home in the midst of political and military upheaval from the British Mandate to the foundation of the Jewish state, to the present Israel now. Playing with multiple allegorical and symbolic meanings drawn from Jewish tradition and history, Kafka has captured the desires and longings of an entire generation that has lived through the War of Independence and the turmoil of the years to come. Kafka has not only found a new voice for himself but truly established himself as an Israeli writer.

Together with Agnon, Kafka was nominated for the Nobel Prize for Literature. In 1966, he became the Nobel laureate and the world's attention turned to Israel, which was increasingly viewed as a bastion of literary brilliance. The Nobel Prize committee announced that:

> This year's Nobel Prize for Literature will be awarded to Israeli writer Franz Kafka as a tribute to his stunning achievement of creating great art out of the ruins of devastation. In his three major novels – *Driftwood*, *The Trial*, and *Hordus' Castle* – Kafka has persistently chronicled important historical and personal events of his time with profound sensitivity and masterly artistic form. The committee believes that Kafka's writings testify to the power and survival of the human spirit. Kafka is truly a literary icon of our times.

Overnight, Kafka had become a celebrity in Israel and around the world. Prior to that point, few of the German émigré writers who had immigrated to Israel had managed to establish themselves within the country's popular literary culture. Kafka knew only one writer who had achieved such a breakthrough, the comedian Sammy Gronemann (1875–1952). In 1943, Kafka accompanied Max Brod to the popular artist café Atara in Tel Aviv to celebrate Sammy's success after his musical comedy, *King Solomon and Shalmai the Shoemaker*, played to a full house in the Ohel ("Tent") Hebrew theater.[63] Now, over twenty years later, Kafka himself had achieved the virtually impossible.

Today, everyone around the world knows the adjective "kafkaesque." In Israel, Kafka first became the idol of the 1960s generation. A few times, he was sighted at the legendary Café Kassit in Tel Aviv, sitting at a table in the company of the old composer, Mordechai Zeira.[64] His former pupil from Ben Shemen, Ben Amotz, was always there, together with Arik Einstein (1939–[2013; editor's note]) and other artists and singers on the political left. Ben Amotz had become a leading left-wing bohemian cult figure of the 1960s. Charismatic and outrageous, he was "a symbol of his generation, the generation of the War of Independence."[65] Projecting his own image of the Sabra, the former Palmach fighter had transformed himself into a bestselling novelist, radio star, and friend of Marlon Brando and other Hollywood stars. He set the tone in Café Kassit – vibrant, flamboyant, intellectual, and critical of contemporary Israeli society and politics. These artists welcomed Kafka into their circle and invited him to share their generation's dreams and visions. After Kafka's death, an original mural by the painter Yosl Bergner (1920–) was dedicated to Kafka and hung in Kassit for many years in the 1970s.[66] Bergner had made his first acquaintance with Kafka at Kassit and acknowledged Kafka's profound influence on his art, stating "it is Kafka who gives me form" and that he used "[Kafka's] writing...[as] a starting place for his own journey."[67] Bergner later created a famous cycle of Kafka paintings.[68] Few older writers were able to connect with this young generation. Kafka's increasing presence in Israeli culture meant that he was right to cling to the hope that "our humanity is our Judaism."[69] For this reason, Israeli novelist and peace activist Amos Oz stressed in 1982 the importance of humanistic cultural Zionism for contemporary Israeli society. "Young people," he wrote, "have rediscovered the secret charm of the original visions" and "there is, at long last...a painful reconsideration of the ideological, ethical and political propositions of the early Zionists, a growing tendency on the part of young Israelis to give a flat no to their parents – and, at the same time, to say 'perhaps' to their grandparents."[70]

214 / Iris Bruce

Kafka's writing is no utopian Herzl *Alt-Neuland* ("Old-New Land," 1902), which already envisioned the peaceful coexistence of Arabs, Jews, men, and women in Palestine. Kafka's alternative vision addresses the complexities and absurdities of contemporary realities beyond our own time and place. He highlights the trials of individual human beings, even if their goals seem out of reach. Many of Kafka's protagonists struggle against all odds and rarely give up. His voice is both new and old. It is heard by many generations around the world and in Israel, too: a modern, secular Jewish voice, questioning certainties, deconstructing truths, continually searching for alternate answers in climates of conflict. Today Kafka's fame in Israel is well established: unlike the diaspora voice of nineteenth-century German Jewish poet Heinrich Heine (1797–1856), whose name is ironically honored by a small dead-end street in Jerusalem, all major Israeli cities have important streets or buildings named after Kafka.

10 WHAT IF THE PALESTINIAN ARAB ELITE HAD CHOSEN COMPROMISE INSTEAD OF BOYCOTT IN CONFRONTING ZIONISM?

Kenneth W. Stein

The Palestinian Arab elite's decision to boycott virtually all British and United Nations overtures made to them during the Mandate period (1920–48) was an egregious miscalculation. It doomed their quest for a state and did not prevent a Jewish state from being established. Officially, Palestinians would not compromise with Zionism. In 1918, the Jewish population of Palestine was only 10 percent of the total. Jewish political organizations in Palestine and lobbying efforts in London were in their infancy. Marginal interest existed among Jews worldwide to take up the Zionist cause. At that moment in the early 1920s, even with the issuance of the Balfour Declaration promising a Jewish national home, Arab leaders could have engaged in political resistance to Jewish growth. They did not. Palestinian Arab leaders said "no" to political participation when repeatedly asked by British officials in the military and civil administrations. The main reason for this resistance was that the Palestinian Arab political community was plagued by enormous internal divisions, especially personal and family feuds. Although a goodly number of moderate Palestinian leaders in the 1920s opposed an absolute boycott of Zionism, their voices were ultimately drowned out by the radical antagonism toward Zionism promoted by Haj Amin Al-Husseini, the Mufti of Jerusalem. Rather than accepting overtures from local British administration officials, Palestinian moderates gradually turned their backs on political engagement.

But what if they had not? If Palestinian leaders had compromised with the Zionists, or with any other power including the British, could they have thwarted the Zionist cause? At first glance, it may seem as if they could have done. During the 1920s in Palestine, Zionism was weak compared to later years. Moreover, most British officials were staunch supporters of Arab rights and were decidedly anti-Zionist in outlook. If Palestinian leaders had pursued a more moderate course in the 1920s, they would have been well positioned to achieve their national aspirations. They could have written laws that severely limited Jewish immigration. They probably could have attained an independent majority state of their own by the late 1920s, even if the British remained in Palestine as imperial tutors, as they did in Iraq. They might even have been able to prevent the creation of a Jewish state – or at least ensure that the eventual state was much smaller geographically. None of these outcomes came to pass, however. For when the British made overtures on behalf of political engagement, the Palestinian Arab elite repeatedly opted for physical resistance, absolutism, and immediacy instead of choosing engagement, compromise, and patience. Concerned that working with the British would undermine their personal, social, and economic control over local politics, they rejected a stance that would have served the greater good of the larger Palestinian community. In the process, the Palestinians' policy of political boycott ironically benefited the Zionist movement.

The road not taken: Tannous, the Mufti, and the Arab debate over boycott

The Palestinian Arab elite chose boycott for a number of reasons. First and foremost, it clearly signaled their principled opposition to the Zionists' goal of establishing a Jewish state in Palestine. Second, they believed that a policy of boycott would forcefully express their frustration with the British government's apparent refusal to establish an Arab state run by Palestinians, and particularly a self-anointed Palestinian political elite. The political elite represented a tiny slice of Palestinian Arab society, numbering less than 1 percent of the entire Arab population during the Mandate. Embracing a strategy of boycott prevented the British from actually granting the Palestinian population self-determination, which the elite feared would be used to challenge their political, economic, and social status. Although it may seem paradoxical, Arab elites throughout the Middle East at the time were not overwhelmingly keen to foster self-determination; they disdained political change, lest it diminish their social influence and standard of living relative to the vast majority of Palestine's poor peasants. Possessing wealth, property, and inherited social status, the elite held enormous economic control over the largely illiterate, massively indebted, and impoverished rural population.[1] The elite traditionally collected rent from the peasants and benefited from their socioeconomic dependency. The Land Registry archives of the Palestine administration and the Palestinian Arab press are full of statements like the one made in 1934 by a Tulkarm landlord, Abdul Latif Tibawi, to the Nablus British district officer, H. M. Foot, complaining that he needed to have his tenants evicted from the land they worked because they threatened him with material loss. Proclaimed Tibawi, "landlords must maintain a high standard of living which would not be fair to compare to that of the tenants."[2] In order to maintain their standard of living and acquire ready cash, some Arab landowners in the late nineteenth and early twentieth century, including those who lived in what was later geographic Palestine, sold off plots of land to newly arrived Jewish immigrants. In the late 1920s and 1930s, however, the older members of the elite slowly gave way to a younger generation of more militant nationalists. Composed of the sons of notables and landowners, many among the Arab elite enjoyed support from their family's income (a portion of which derived from land sales and rents) to assume a more militant stance against the British and the Zionists.[3] Predictably enough, they became leading figures in the policy of boycott. By employing political boycott in their response to the British and the Zionists, they were able to maintain their socioeconomic grasp on other elements of the society, often deflecting social discontent away from themselves and onto the Jews and the British as "foreign" interlopers.

In 1936, Dr. Izzat Tannous, a Palestinian Arab Christian, headed the Arab Center in London, an organization formed to promote support for the Palestinian Arabs. He was also a member of a Palestinian Arab delegation to London in early 1939. The Arab Center's mission was to establish a majority Arab state in Palestine. Tannous was described by Malcolm MacDonald, the British Colonial Secretary at the time, as "a moderate, therefore his influence in Palestine was not very great...he [was] a man capable of reason and some courage...whatever influence he may have had would be exerted on the side of peace."[4] Palestinian Arab delegations journeyed to London half a dozen times between 1920 and 1947 to urge Palestinian Arab self-determination and protest vigorously against the British policy of supporting a Jewish national home, especially the 1917 Balfour Declaration, which called for the "establishment in Palestine of a national home for the Jewish people" while "protecting the civil and religious rights of the existing non-Jewish population." Those among the Arab elite, like Tannous, understood very well that, despite Zionist assurances, a "national home" meant the eventual establishment of a Jewish state. This elite segment was "moderate" insofar as it was willing to tolerate a Zionist presence in Palestine; but it was committed to ensuring that Jews remained a minority.

After World War I, Palestine was administratively and politically separated from Greater Syria by French and British agreement. Paris and London had triumphed over the Ottoman Empire and divided the spoils of the Middle East between them. They created mandates or trusteeships for newly created Arab states, promising them eventual self-rule. Beginning already in 1918, Arabs in Palestine established their own political organizations, separate from those in Syria. These included various Muslim–Christian Associations, which were politically active in urban areas; an Arab Executive Committee, which conducted annual meetings across Palestine; a Supreme Muslim Council in charge of religious policies; individual political parties reflecting diverse opinions and family interests; and an Arab Higher Committee, composed of a small number of unelected representatives. All these organizations embraced an anti-Zionist outlook. And while leaders in the these Arab organizations frequently communicated with British officials, which provided the British administration some access to a narrow slice of Arab political opinion, they never assumed a firm public stance that could have been construed as indirectly accepting Zionism or the British presence.

The most important initial effort to foster British–Arab communication took place in May 1921, when the British appointed a Mufti of Jerusalem. Empowering the Muslim community to govern its own religious affairs enabled the British to avoid criticism from other parts of the British-governed Muslim Middle East – Egypt, Iraq, Transjordan, and along the Persian Gulf coast – that it was intruding into religious matters. Six months after appointing Haj Amin Al-Husseini as the Mufti of Jerusalem, the British established the Supreme Muslim

Council, with Husseini as president. Over time, he came to dominate the Muslim Arab religious community and accumulated enormous political power. Although he derived his legitimacy from the British, he and his peers chose not to participate in any official political activity that sanctioned British rule. The Mufti was also a fierce opponent of Zionism. In the years following the proclamation of the Balfour Declaration, he became increasingly anti-British and virulently anti-Zionist in his outlook. By taking control of the revenues from Waqf property, managing the personnel of religious councils, and controlling the local press, he asserted an increasingly extreme voice in Palestinian Arab politics.[5] In the early 1930s, he vehemently opposed all Jewish immigration and decreed that any Muslim who sold land to Jews would be denied all Muslim burial rights. He frequently used intimidation to silence political opponents and sometimes even had them killed. In 1937, he fled Palestine for refuge in Lebanon. But he continued to advocate violence as the only answer against Jews, Zionists, and the British. Most notoriously of all, during World War II, the Mufti supported Hitler's Final Solution for eradicating the Jews of Europe. Dead Jews, he reasoned, could not immigrate to Palestine.

The Mufti's growing extremism during this period sharpened divisions within the Palestinian Arab elite and rendered it incapable of meeting the Zionist challenge.[6] Before long, the internal weaknesses of the Palestinian national movement allowed it to be taken over by other Arab leaders, such as Jordan's King Abdullah, Egypt's King Farouk, and Azzam Pasha's Arab League, all of whom claimed leadership in the battle against Zionism. The Mufti's destructive impact upon the Palestinian national movement was most visible in his resistance to the 1939 British White Paper. This British policy statement infuriated Zionists because it drastically limited Jewish immigration and virtually halted Jewish land purchase in Palestine. By contrast, the document encouraged Palestinians by proposing the creation of a unitary state in Palestine – one with an Arab majority and a Jewish minority – within ten years. Not long after the British proposed the idea, in March 1939, the moderate Palestinian leader, Izzat Tannous, and fourteen members of the Arab Higher Committee met to discuss this important change in British policy (Figure 21). They deliberated for nearly three weeks at Haj Amin Al-Husseini's residence in Jouneh, a suburb of Beirut. Tannous recorded in his diary that expectations for a "brighter future" were initially high. Yet he subsequently noted with disappointment that the

Figure 21. The Arab Higher Committee featuring Haj Amin Al-Husseini (second from left at the front). What if the Committee had accepted the 1939 British White Paper, which proposed a unitary state in Palestine with an Arab majority and Jewish minority within ten years?

sweet dream did not last long . . . [once we] began to realize that Haj Amin was not in favor of accepting the White Paper. This negative stand, which gradually became more pronounced, made the atmosphere extremely tense . . . The [other] . . . fourteen members [of the Committee] were not only strongly in its favor, but were determined to put an end to the negative policy Arab leadership had been adopting heretofore.

The . . . members knew very well that the acquiescence of Haj Amin . . . was a very essential requisite and that without his blessing, because of his magic influence on the Palestinian masses, the White Paper would not be implemented, a goal which the Zionists were madly seeking to score. Consequently, the sole concern of the Committee was now concentrated on convincing Haj Amin that his negative stand was extremely detrimental to the Arab cause and . . . doing exactly what the Zionists wanted him to do.

Tannous conceded that the White Paper was imperfect, but he insisted that "it had marked a decisive turning point in the history of Palestine" by cancelling "the establishment of a Zionist state recommended by the Royal Commission and adopted by the British Government."[7] Tannous' faction did not rise to the occasion and confront the Mufti's unwillingness to allow for *any* Zionist or Jewish presence in Palestine. In 1939, the Arabs of Palestine were 60 percent of the total population, with Jews numbering 400,000. The Arabs thus held a distinct demographic advantage. This fact notwithstanding, Palestinian leaders turned down the British offer to create a federal state with an Arab majority within a decade. What if the only idea on the table about Palestine's future when it appeared at the United Nations in 1945 had been a federal state? How different would the 1945–8 period have been when Zionist lobbying efforts pushed for the option of a two-state solution? We can never know with certainty. But we do know that the Palestinians' rejectionist policy of resisting Zionism through boycott, intimidation, and violence was destined to fail.

The origins of Arab boycott in the 1920s

The rejectionist strategy displayed by the Mufti in 1939 had been regularly employed by Arab leaders as a normative political tactic since 1920. In July of that year, the British military regime in Palestine was replaced by a civil administration headed by High Commissioner Herbert Samuel, who soon established a small Executive Council and Advisory Council, both consultative bodies with limited power. The Advisory Council was headed by the High Commissioner and consisted of ten British officials and ten nominated nonofficials, including four Muslim Arabs, three Christian Arabs, and three Jews. It created a rudimentary constitution that was to provide for an elected Legislative Council. In 1923, pressure from the Arab Executive led the Arabs to eventually withdraw from the Advisory Council, leaving the Jewish officials with no role, and the Council to be staffed by only British officials for the duration of the Mandate.[8] By the end of the summer of 1921, Samuel tried to establish a Legislative Council, but neither its representation nor its powers were sufficiently attractive to induce Arab participation. The British government told an Arab delegation to London that its policy was to carry out the Balfour Declaration and that it would not concede to a national government. Colonial Office Secretary Winston Churchill hoped that the Arabs would try the Council for two or three years and, if proved not a success, they could put forward their case.⁹ The Legislative Council never became a reality, though it would be earnestly proposed by British High Commissioners in 1930 and again in 1935–6. On both occasions, the refusal of Palestine Arab nationalist leaders to accept British-sponsored overtures prevented the establishment of limited Arab self-government.

Summing up the result of Arab boycott in the early 1920s, a leading authority on early Jewish immigration to Palestine, Moshe Mosek, wrote that the Arabs' "unconditional rejection of the British proposals to set up representative bodies which could give them, if not control, a certain influence over policy, closed for them the door to even token participation in the making of [immigration] policy."¹⁰ In 1923, Samuel asked the Arab political elite to establish an Arab Agency that would regulate immigration and provide constitutional legitimation for British rule in Palestine. The Arab political elite declined, however. They were reluctant to give legitimacy to the Jewish Agency, which was the Zionist representative to the British administration in Palestine; they furthermore feared that the Arab Agency would remain a mere advisory body; the Arab elite were divided among themselves about whether compromising with the British would tacitly strengthen their control over the Mandate. Unsuccessful overtures to the Arab elite to participate in British governance was terribly frustrating for British officials, who dearly wanted the Arabs to take part in running the Mandate, even if its institutions lacked political teeth. In London in 1923, Colonial Office official Sir John Shuckburgh, a civil servant who would deal with Palestine for at least another fifteen years, remarked, "we shall clearly make ourselves ridiculous if we go on making offers to a people who persistently refuse them."¹¹

Ironically enough, each time the Arabs boycotted British overtures, they removed yet another obstacle blocking the Zionists' path to building up a Jewish state. Arab rejectionism allowed the Zionists valuable time to organize, raise funds from the diaspora, create an infrastructure of self-sustaining political entities, establish small industries that focused on the needs of the growing Jewish population, and develop political lobbying skills. It allowed the Zionists to develop a close rapport with British officials, learn about policy changes in a timely manner, and help draft laws on immigration, land, and self-government. In the early 1920s, there were relatively few Jews in Palestine, perhaps 10–15 percent of the total population; the Jewish community, moreover, had not yet successfully rallied diaspora support for the Zionist cause. Most European Jewish immigrants chose North America, South Africa, or South America, rather than going to the economic and political uncertainty of their ancestral home.

Counterfactually speaking, there is little doubt that if the Palestinian Arab "clerical-feudal" political elite had chosen to participate in the working of the Mandate, they would have slowed Zionism's development.[12] If the Arab elites had agreed at the outset of the Mandate to cooperate with the British government's political institutions in Palestine – even those that did not provide them with absolute majority rule – they would have, at a minimum, earned the support of colonial British officials, who were either neutral toward Zionism or opposed to Jewish nationalism. The Arabs could have easily made the Balfour Declaration work to their advantage despite the inclusion of its language in the League of Nation's Mandate for Palestine. Although they hated the declaration and the League of Nations for promising Jews a home in Palestine, it also promised them protection of their civil and religious rights, which they might have systematically expanded into political rights. Had the Arab elites chosen to work within the Mandate, even if that participation fell short of full independence, there was every reason to believe that British officials, at least in the 1920s, would have engaged official Arab participation in the Mandate's operation.

Continued snubs and missed opportunities in the 1930s

The greatest missed opportunity for the Palestinian Arabs to forestall the creation of a Jewish national home came in the 1928–31 period, when British rule in Palestine was handled by the most anti-Zionist and pro-Arab High Commissioner the Palestinian Arabs could have imagined, Sir John Chancellor. Not even the anti-Zionist attitude of British Foreign Minister Ernest Bevin after 1945 offered the political opportunities that Chancellor and his peers provided the Arabs in 1930. This fact notwithstanding, the Arab elite refused to take advantage of this unique chance to advance their cause by engaging with the British.

Not long after he arrived in Palestine in 1928, Chancellor developed considerable sympathy for the Palestinian Arabs and hostility toward the idea of a Jewish national home. These views were largely shaped by the severe Arab riots and disturbances against Jews in August 1929. Not long after the British dispatched inquiry commissions to investigate the causes of the bloody unrest, Chancellor developed a deep disdain for Zionism. His political views of how to limit Zionism strongly influenced the findings of the Shaw Report (March 1930), the Hope-Simpson Report (October 1930), and the Passfield White Paper (October 1930), all policy recommendations or statements indicting Jewish growth in Palestine as one of the underlying causes of Arab disdain for Zionism. In January 1930, Chancellor sent a ninety-page dispatch to the Colonial Office advocating a dramatic turn in the Mandate in favor of the Arab community.[13] He sought a total suspension of Jewish immigration and proposed that the High Commissioner's office be permitted to regulate (and potentially halt) all land sales between Arabs and Jews. Fearing that landless Arabs might become lawless brigands, he proposed immediate legislation protecting tenants and cultivators by preventing their eviction or dismissal from land following the transfer of property.[14] In seeking to regulate land sales between Arabs and Jews, Chancellor sought to draw a clear legal distinction between them; indeed, he wanted to give teeth to the concept of protecting the rights of the non-Jewish population.

Yet while Chancellor's anti-Zionist views made him a natural ally of the Arabs, the Arab elites failed to avail themselves of the golden opportunities that his rule as High Commissioner offered them. Members of the Arab Executive, as well as the Mufti himself, knew that Chancellor wanted to change the Mandate. This fact notwithstanding, they did not reach out to him in any politically significant way to take advantage of his viewpoint or his influence. In March 1930, an Arab delegation traveled to London to discuss Chancellor's proposal for constitutional talks and self-rule. Chancellor tried to convince the Arab elite to change their rejectionist position by establishing a national government in a treaty relationship with Great Britain. Yet since the British declined to give full control to the Arab majority or to the League of Nations for determining Palestine's future, the Palestinian Arab delegation returned to Palestine without a promise for a national government. Because the Arab Executive and the Mufti would not meet the British halfway, there was no change in the Mandate that might have steered it away from promoting the Jewish national home. Hidden beneath the surface for the Arab elite was a distinct fear that self-rule would challenge the self-appointed autocratic control of the Arab elite over Palestinian politics.

Many other officials in the Palestine Administration's bureaucracy, both British and Arab, Muslim and Christian, supported Chancellor's attempt to turn the Mandate against the Zionists. Within the London Colonial Office and Foreign Office as well, staffers were "more than ready to justify Arab opposition to the Jewish claims."[15] Some of the British opposition to Jews was rooted in antisemitism; some of it merely reflected disdain for Zionism. Sir John Hope-Simpson, who shared Chancellor's anti-Zionist views and wrote a critically important report in October 1930 condemning Zionist development in Palestine, noted that "All British officials tend to become pro-Arab, or perhaps more accurately anti-Jew . . . Personally I can quite well understand this trait. The helplessness of the Fellah (peasant) appeals to the British official [with] whom he comes in touch. The offensive self-assertion of the Jewish immigrant is, on the other hand, repellant."[16] Not surprisingly, Zionists feared that Chancellor's ideas, if made into policy, would be the "death knell" for Zionist growth. In the fall of 1930, the Passfield White Paper was issued and the British invited Zionist and Arab leaders to a roundtable conference in London to discuss the proposal to establish a limited representative government under a constitution. Zionist leaders feared the prospect of a representative Palestinian government in which Jews would be greatly outnumbered by Arabs, but the Zionists agreed to participate in the discussion nonetheless. By contrast, Palestinian Arab leaders refused the British invitation to provide their detailed views in London.

As a result, it was only the British and the Zionists who met with one another to discuss the Passfield White Paper's contents in London in November 1930. Significantly, in these discussions, the British capitulated to the Zionists, leaving Chancellor disheartened and his ideas discredited. Gradually, Zionists in London persuaded the British government to write a letter of explanation abandoning the White Paper's contents. The first draft of the so-called MacDonald Letter to Chaim Weizmann, the head of the London Zionist Executive, was written by the British, with little Zionist input. After noting that the Jewish national home would continue, paragraph 11 of the first draft, dated November 29, 1930, said, "It is desirable to make it clear that the landless Arabs were *those Arabs who have been displaced from their lands in consequence of the lands passing into Jewish hands.* It will scarcely be contended that His Majesty's Government have no obligation towards the Arabs so displaced." In reply to this draft, the London Zionist Executive, working with the Jewish Agency in Palestine, pointed out that HMG did not possess definite evidence about the number of persons falling within that landless Arab category. Furthermore, the Zionists insisted that the number of landless Arabs was quite small. Finally, the British accepted the Zionist definition of "landless" to read as those *"Arab cultivators as can be shown to have been directly displaced from their lands in consequence of the lands passing into Jewish hands, and who have been unable to obtain other holdings on which they can establish themselves."*[17]

From 1931 to 1936, therefore, the British administration in Palestine estimated the number of such landless Arabs to be comparatively low, a mere eight hundred.[18] Consequently, the Jewish Agency repeatedly claimed that Jewish land purchase had displaced only a relatively small number of Arabs. This was untrue, of course, as Jewish land purchases had displaced a considerable number of Arab tenants and small Arab owners, many of whom received goodly sums of compensation to leave the lands they or their families had habitually worked. The Zionists were correct that the number was small, but only if the limited definition used to determine landlessness was applied. When discussions with the Zionists concluded in London, British Prime Minister Ramsay MacDonald sent his letter to Weizmann, virtually apologizing for the threat posed to Zionism's growth that had appeared in the Passfield White Paper. On February 12, in the House of Commons, MacDonald affirmed that there had been no change in British policy toward the Balfour Declaration. The purpose of his letter to Weizmann was "to remove misunderstandings but not to make changes of policy." The Prime Minister said that "the obligation to facilitate Jewish immigration and make possible dense settlement of Jews on the land is still a positive obligation of the Mandate, and it can be fulfilled without jeopardizing the rights and conditions of the other part of the Palestine population."

Burying Chancellor's philosophy and political intentions was an enormously important yet quiet victory for the Zionists. It was crucial that the Passfield White Paper died before being implemented. It was equally important that Jewish immigration was exonerated from any responsibility for Arab landlessness. Thanks to the Arabs' boycott of any discussions with the British, the Zionists were able to obliterate

Chancellor's intentions to protect the Arab population. While Chancellor had suggested no less than six different initiatives to help Palestinian peasants – including legislation dealing with mortgage debt forfeiture, usurious loans, agricultural tenants' protection, resettling so-called landless Arabs, and establishment of a development department – the Arab boycott meant that these initiatives were routinely reviewed by Zionist lawyers before being considered for implementation and were ultimately neutralized, eviscerated of content, or rendered still-born. After Chancellor left office in 1931, Jewish economic strength, demographic size, and physical presence grew dramatically. From 1928 to 1939, Jewish-sponsored industrial activity, which provided the major stimulus for the overall Palestinian economy, grew from 44 percent of total output to 70 percent in 1939.[19] From 1930 to 1940, the Jewish population increased from 150,000 to 450,000; by comparison, there were 650,000 Jews in Palestine when the state was established in 1948. In the decade of the 1930s, Jewish land purchases increased from 979,000 dunams to 1,360,000 dunams, a 30 percent increase. By contrast, when Israel was established, Jews had purchased 2 million dunams of land out of the 7 million dunams of registered land in Palestine that would not be later taken by the new Jewish state, Israel, Jordan, or Egypt.[20]

The Arab boycott strategy had other ramifications for the Zionist leadership. After 1930, the Zionists were much more careful about making strategic land purchases and sharing information with British officials about their infrastructure intentions. More attention was devoted to buying lands that were contiguous to existing Jewish land holdings. The collection of data about Arabs who had sold lands to Zionists previously, while never published, was shared quietly with British officials in Palestine and London, sometimes undermining the otherwise positive pro-Arab outlook of British administration bureaucrats. While Zionists won another decade of virtually unimpeded momentum toward the development of a state, the Arab elite chose not to influence British policy, except by angering and frustrating British officials. It is well established that, throughout the Mandate, Arab land sales to Jews were frequent and often in quantities greater than Zionists had the wherewithal to purchase.[21] Moreover, it has also been shown that the Arab landowning elites' demand to limit Jewish land purchases in the 1930s was part of a deliberate ruse to make the sale of land more difficult and thereby drive up its price.[22] Many British officials knew full well that the very population that they supported against Zionism was collaborating with them regularly.[23]

This conclusion is supported by evidence from the Palestinian Arab press. In 1932, one editorial noted that "because the Jews are alert, and our leaders are asleep, the Jews are buying the lands."[24] In November 1934, another opined that:

> those who adopted this profession [land brokers] aim at becoming rich and at collecting money even if they take it from the lives of the country ... Is it human that the covetous should store capital to evict the peasant from his land and make him homeless or even sometimes a criminal? The frightened Arab who fears for his future today melts from fear when he imagines his offspring as homeless and as criminals who cannot look at the lands of their fathers.[25]

Finally, among other examples that could be cited, in January 1936, an Arab editorial noted that "it is on our leader's shoulders that our calamity of land sales lies. They themselves as well as their relatives were guilty of selling lands to the Jews."[26] In June 1940, when Chancellor's 1930 proposed land purchase restrictions were finally applied against the Zionists, British Colonial Office Official Sir John Shuckburgh remarked, "the Arab landowner [needed] to be protected against himself."[27] In November 1945, a British committee looking into how the laws on land sale restrictions to Jews were being routinely circumvented noted that:

> the remedy lies in the hands of the Arabs themselves. Unless they enter into collusion with the Jews to defeat the spirit of the White Paper, Jews will not be able to enter improperly into possession of the land within a restricted area. If the parties whom the law is designed to defend conspire to evade the law, then it is indeed difficult for the authorities to enforce it and to defend them.[28]

Palestine's fourth High Commissioner, Sir Arthur Wauchope, was less stridently pro-Arab than his predecessor. Yet during his tenure from 1931 to 1938, he reached out to the Arab elite in a sincere fashion to seek their participation in governmental operations. Like his predecessors, Wauchope wanted to establish a Legislative Council and organized a series of meetings to that end in 1934–5 with various Palestinian Arab political parties and Jewish leaders. There were to be twenty-eight members of the Council: five British officials, eleven Muslims, seven Jews, three Christians, and two defined as "commercial." Knowing that any community might reject participation in the Council's formation, the High Commissioner retained the prerogative to fill seats on the Council as he saw fit. Selection to the Council was to be by direct election, with other requirements. In August 1935 in Lucerne, Switzerland, the Zionist Congress rejected the idea of a Legislative Council and refrained from participating in any institution where the Arabs and the British High Commissioner would dominate decision-making. The reason was simple: a Legislative Council could have voted to stop Jewish immigration and Jewish development in general. That should have been the very reason why the Arab elite embraced Wauchope's proposal. But instead, in January 1936, the Arab parties rejected the Council idea because it did not provide for the establishment of a national government bound to Great Britain by treaty. Because any direct election might remove the self-appointed members of the elite from office, they criticized the idea for not giving them enough power. In early April 1936, the British Colonial Office again invited the Palestinian Arabs to send a delegation to London to discuss the Legislative Council idea at a time of rising anxiety and political agitation leveled against the Zionists and the British. On April 25, the six main Arab political parties joined together in an outward sign of unity to form the ten-man Arab Higher Committee, presided over by the Jerusalem Mufti, Haj Amin Al-Husseini.

Although the Arab spokesman accepted the Colonial Office's invitation to London, the Arab Higher Committee shortly thereafter called for an Arab General Strike. This decision was meant to end Jewish immigration to Palestine, prevent the transfer of Arab land to Jews, and replace the British Mandate with a national representative government. Soon thereafter, on May 5, 1936, the Arab Higher Committee announced its plan to boycott the London conference. According to British sources, though Arab public opinion in Palestine had reservations about the Council proposal, "a strong section of the [Arab] population" was inclined to accept the British offer of moving toward self-government, and "only a small minority of Arabs rejected the offer unreservedly."[29]

If the Arab leadership had not called for the General Strike and had joined to form the Legislative Council in 1934–6, Palestinian Arabs

(Christians and Muslims) would have controlled immigration to Palestine at the precise moment when Zionist immigration to Palestine was reaching its absolute pinnacle. Precisely at this moment in Palestinian Arab politics, the Mufti was potentially threatened from his "right" by a charismatic leader, Shaykh Izz al-Din al-Qassam, appealing to the agricultural classes with strident militancy. The Mufti could not be seen as moderating his attitude toward the British, lest this charismatic preacher gain more popular prestige. The Arab elite, led by the Mufti, had the same reasons as earlier for remaining unenthusiastic about holding elections in which they would face political challenges to their leadership and potentially not be voted onto the Council. Their immediate personal betterment was more important than a broader initiating of a political process that might wrest control. The boycott tactic continued in 1936–7, when the Arab Higher Committee and Arab political parties refused to give testimony before another British committee looking into Palestine's future. In the assessment of Glubb Pasha, the British advisor to King Abdullah of Jordan, "the Arab struggle in Palestine was haunted by this passion for boycott, which was ultimately to bring them utter ruin."[30]

Boycotting into the 1940s and beyond

Palestinian Arab nonparticipation in critical policy-making decisions about Palestine's future continued unabated into the 1940s and was especially pivotal after World War II, when the British and the UN made key decisions about Palestine's political future. These included the important issues of whether the British should admit 100,000 European Jewish immigrants to Palestine; whether Palestine should remain a British Mandate or trusteeship; whether Palestine's future would be determined by the newly formed United Nations; and whether a single federal state or two separate states should be established in Palestine as a political solution to the competing political claims of Palestinian Arabs and Zionists.

In April 1946, the Anglo-American Committee of Inquiry decided to permit the immediate admission of 100,000 Jews to Palestine. After the decision was announced, the Arabs rejected the idea and stuck to their demand for an immediate halt to all Jewish immigration.[31] In August 1946, the British invited Zionist and Arab delegates to

London. Palestinian Arabs boycotted the conference because the British intention was to strengthen their presence in Palestine, with the High Commissioner retaining control over the entire Mandate in the fields of defense, foreign affairs, immigration, and customs.[32] In December 1946, the newly formed Arab League urged Palestinian Arabs to participate in another London meeting. The Arab Higher Committee put forth its own plan for Palestine's future, which included abrogating the Balfour Declaration and Mandate, ending Jewish immigration, and establishing a Palestinian state on the same footing as other Arab states. Meeting in Basel, Switzerland, the Zionist Congress rejected the notion of provincial autonomy. The Zionists wanted an independent state, free immigration, and land settlement. In February 1947, the British proposed a five-year trusteeship for the purpose of preparing the country for independence.[33] In delaying the creation of a Jewish state, the British hoped to curry favor with Arab leaders and obtain a renewed commitment from the international community to remain in Palestine at least for a while. According to the British Foreign Secretary Ernest Bevin, the British government needed to maintain its economic, financial, and strategic interests in the Middle East. Both Arabs and Zionists impeded British plans, however, by rejecting the proposal.

With the London conference unable to reach an equitable solution for Palestine, the British turned the country's political future over to the newly formed United Nations. The Arab Higher Committee boycotted the ensuing inquiry into Palestine's future, still refusing to accept that it could be determined by the UN or any other authority. On November 29, 1947, the UN voted to accept the proposal that the Mandate should immediately be terminated in favor of independence. By a majority vote, the UN General Assembly proposed the partition of Palestine into Arab and Jewish states, with an economic union between them and a special political status established for Jerusalem (Figure 22). The Zionists rejoiced, while Arab states and the Arab Higher Committee told the UN they would refuse to consider any plan that entailed the loss of Arab sovereignty over any part of Palestine.[34] The next day, civil war erupted and the first large wave of Palestinian Arab refugees left the emerging war zone. True to form, the Arab Higher Committee refused to participate in the UN's Palestinian Conciliation Commission, which was charged with implementing the much-hated decision for partition. Israel declared its independence on May 14, 1948, and after three truce periods with Arab states and

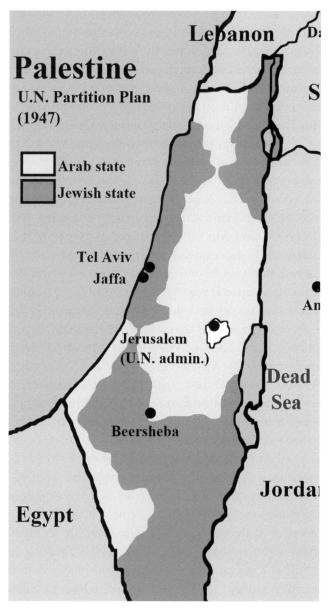

Figure 22. Map of armistice lines in Palestine in 1947 and 1949.

Palestinians, the final armistice agreements halted the fighting in 1949. No peace treaties were signed between Israel and its neighbors.

The rejection of the UN partition plan by Arab states and the Palestinian Arab Higher Committee was consistent with a thirty-year policy of refusing to compromise with Zionism. The Arabs' refusal to adjust their ideology to the pragmatic needs of the moment, particularly in the years 1947–8, like their rejection of Chancellor's embrace in 1930, had disastrous consequences for the Palestinian people for the remainder of the century. Not only did the Palestinian Arabs and Arab states lose the 1947–9 war with Israel, but the Arab refugee flight from Palestine ensued. Moreover, massive numbers of Jews from Arab states fled to Israel over the following five years. If the Arabs had accepted partition, the Zionists would have established their independent Jewish state. And if there had been war between the two new states, the Zionists would have fought with dedication and sacrifice as they did. Above all, the Zionist leaders wanted to control immigration to a Jewish state; if they could have secured that prerogative immediately after having "accepted" partition, it is possible, but not likely, that surrounding Arab states would have accepted it. Already, by 1947, King Abdullah of Jordan was eyeing up all of Palestine for himself, denying the establishment of a Jewish state, even while he negotiated with the Zionists to prevent a state run by the Palestinians. But by rejecting the 1947 partition of Palestine and losing the war, Arab states and the Palestinians lost land to the Zionists that would otherwise have been allocated to the Arab state. By the partition plan, 14,700 square kilometers were to be allotted to the proposed Jewish state, a bit more than half of Palestine. By the end of the 1947–9 war, Israel controlled 20,500 square kilometers.[35]

Conclusion: what ifs?

In assessing the historical significance of the Arab policy of boycott, a provocative counterfactual question may help shed light on the forces that shaped Palestine's political fate: what if the British had never proclaimed the Balfour Declaration in the first place? What if a declaration for Palestine's future had not been written to Lord Rothschild but instead had been penned on November 2, 1917 to Sharif Husayn of Mecca, the same Arab leader who was supported by the British during the war? Suppose that the declaration hypothetically said:

My Dear Sharif Husayn, I have much pleasure in conveying to you, on behalf of His Majesty's Government, the following declaration of sympathy with the aspiration of the Arab people which has been submitted to, and approved by, the Cabinet. His Majesty's Government view with favor the establishment in Palestine of a national home for the Arab people, and will use their best endeavors to facilitate the achievement of this object, it being clearly understood that nothing shall be done which may prejudice the civil and religious rights of existing non-Arab communities in Palestine, or the rights and political status enjoyed by Arabs in any other country that might be established.

How would the Saudis and Rashidis (the other two most powerful tribal families in the Arabian peninsula) have replied to this declaration, while they themselves were struggling with the Hashemites for control over Mecca and portions of the peninsula? By issuing a declaration to one Arab family, the British would have inevitably played favorites, something they had reasoned was not politically sound. The possibility of playing favorites would have angered one or more tribes in the competition for control of the peninsula, and of course for whoever controlled the Holy City of Mecca. For the British, it really did not matter in the end who ruled Mecca; it mattered that whoever was in charge was friendly to British imperial interests. British strategy in the Middle East was to rule through existing elites, rather than imposing changes upon the traditional political and social status quo. Gertrude Bell, the "Oriental Secretary" to the British High Commissioner in Iraq, Sir Percy Cox, certainly advocated maintaining the local status quo when she counseled him about effective British rule there in the early 1920s. Such a British declaration to one family in the Arabian peninsula and not to another would have caused unwanted political fallout in British-controlled Egypt. Moreover, such a declaration would not have been enthusiastically embraced by the French, who had their own imperial designs over Greater Syria at the time. Yet what if the British and French had subsequently decided in 1918 to grant general Arab independence, as they had promised on several occasions after the war? Would such a decision have kept the Zionists from continuing to immigrate and buy land in Palestine? Given the fact that they had been doing both since the 1880s, the likely answer is emphatically no.

There is no evidence that the Zionists were going to be deterred from going to Palestine to create a territory of their own. Of course, it was hardly inevitable that Zionism would have succeeded in building a Jewish state without either the Balfour Declaration or the aftermath of the Holocaust. But Zionism was not just a movement; it was a moment in history when Jews decided to take destiny into their own hands and fight for the right to preserve it. Before World War II, the Zionists were few and underfunded; but they did not lack political skills or a cadre of effective leaders. They had already been on the move to Palestine in small numbers from the 1880s. The Balfour Declaration was an important catalyst, but it was insufficient to catapult Zionism forward. The declaration of international legitimacy ultimately came from the League of Nations. Of course, the Zionists would have moved forward without the League of Nations' declaration, but it made it easier for those wanting a Jewish state. If the British had not sanctioned it in 1917, then perhaps France or the United States might have issued a declaration of similar intended consequences for the Zionists in the 1920s. Certainly, the barriers to European immigration to the US thrown up in 1924 would have redirected Jewish immigration to Palestine as it eventually did anyway. Other countries in the world were vigorously opposed to free Jewish immigration across their own respective national borders in the 1930s. So without a declaration, and with only a British presence in Palestine, it seems likely that a Jewish national home could have developed to one degree or other. This is true, finally, because of the fact that, with or without a declaration of support, Zionist growth in Palestine did not change the personal selfishness of the Palestinian Arab elite. Arabs willingly sold lands to immigrating Jews, thereby helping establish their renewed foothold in Palestine.

A more difficult counterfactual question is whether the British and French declarations favoring Arab independence would have stimulated or suppressed Palestinian national feeling. Without the Balfour Declaration and the promise of a national home in Palestine, it is questionable whether Palestinian Arab nationalism would have emerged as soon after 1918–19 as it did. There is little doubt that Haj Amin Al-Husseini's appointment as Mufti would not have occurred if Sharif Husayn had gladly received the British appointment and passed it on to one of his sons, Abdullah, Ali, Feisal, or Zeid, to head the newly established Arab province or state in Jerusalem. More uncertain, by contrast, is whether the Hashemites would have been even more antagonistic toward Zionism than toward the Mufti's progressively radical and uncompromising policies. As we know from later political interactions, King Abdullah welcomed Zionist overtures in the early 1930s, actually entering into written agreements with them for the option of growing Jewish presence on the east side of the River Jordan. But a significant part of Abdullah's motivation was his antagonism to the Mufti, and he saw the Zionists as an ally.

What is clear, however, is that an explicit British promise to Sharif Husayn to include Palestine as part of an Arab kingdom, province, or state would not have erased Zionist intentions to reestablish a historic Jewish presence in an ancient homeland. The Jewish focus on Eretz Yisrael, the Holy Land of Palestine, was centuries old, despite fleeting thoughts about creating a Jewish homeland elsewhere. Modern Zionism as a national movement for the restoration of a Jewish homeland, a term used by Herzl, was more than half a century old before World War I. No promise to Sharif Husayn or any other Arab notable would have erased concepts, notions, and plans that emerged from the Eastern and Western European writings of Herzl's precursors, such as Alkalai, Pinsker, Hess, Ahad Ha'am, Syrkin, Gordon, and others. The first Zionist Congress in 1897 took place two decades before the actual Balfour Declaration was issued; Herzl, Ussishkin, Nordau, Weizmann, Jabotinsky, and hundreds of others caught the Zionist bug before World War I. In 1882, there were 25,000 Jews in Palestine; by 1918, there were 60,000-plus Zionists there. And, critically, in the period before World War I, Zionist nation-building institutions were already in their infancy, underfunded of course, but including the World Zionist Organization, the Jewish National Fund, the Palestine Office of the Zionist Organization, and settlement activities undertaken by Jewish immigrants. Mayir Verete has argued that the Balfour Declaration was not the start of Zionism, but perhaps a confirmation of what had transpired since European Jewish immigrants trickled into Palestine from the 1880s onward.[36] Jewish nation-building certainly began half a century before Rothschild received the 1917 declaration from Balfour.

It is doubtful, then, that Zionism was going to be suppressed simply because a promise was made to establish an Arab state in Palestine. Zionists would have immigrated to Palestine in the 1920s anyway. They did so illegally at times in the period of late Ottoman rule. They would have brought their personal and political capital to invest in new enterprises different from their previous urban and sometimes cowering existence; and they would have imported newly developing secular varieties of Judaism, while rekindling public use of the Hebrew language. The money they brought to buy lands, with or without a declaration, would similarly have attracted Arab sellers. Future major Jewish land purchases in the Jezreel Valley were negotiated with Arab sellers in Beirut from 1913 onward. We know that from the 1940s laws against Arab land sales to Jews did not stop, but merely reduced, the pace of Zionist land acquisition. British-imposed laws did not deter Arabs from selling their patrimony to Zionists. By the end of World War II, and perhaps as early as 1939, a Jewish state or province lay in Palestine's future one way or another.

It is unlikely, therefore, that a more compromising Arab stance toward the Jews would have prevented the emergence of a Jewish state. What is certain is that the Arab elite's policy of boycott contributed not only to the Zionists building a Jewish national territory, but one strong enough to withstand disorganized Arab forces in 1948–9. Early Palestinian Arab compromise with either the British or the Zionists would have limited the size and scope of a Jewish enclave, canton, or state. There is no doubt that the repeated refusal by the Palestinian Arab elite to engage officially in shaping the Mandate – and thereby shaping their own future – provided Zionists with untold opportunities to build their state's infrastructure, buy land, facilitate immigration, write laws, raise funds, and galvanize Jewish and non-Jewish opinion throughout the world. Zionists fiercely lobbied for their cause of statehood to world leaders, who were often staunchly anti-Zionist or predisposed to give the Arab population an opportunity to run their own affairs.[37] For the Palestinians, the tactic of boycott had enormous historical consequences. It set a precedent that dominated Palestinian Arab policy for seventy years, from the 1917 Balfour Declaration until Yasir Arafat's verbal recognition of Israel in 1988 and written recognition of the state of Israel in September 1993. Now, a quarter-century later, a similarly divided Palestinian Arab leadership remains unwilling to end the conflict with Israel once and for all.

11 WHAT IF MUSA ALAMI AND DAVID BEN-GURION HAD AGREED ON A JEWISH–ARAB STATE?*

David N. Myers

Palestine in crisis: 1936

The sense of mutual understanding and respect was never high between the two sides, but now, in the spring of 1936, Jews and Arabs were caught in another round of convulsive violence in Palestine. The Arab General Strike that began on April 19 set in motion a new policy of confrontation against the Zionists, as well as against the British overlords of the country.

For the Arabs, the rising tide of Jewish immigration to Palestine, some 62,000 people in 1935, indicated that the British were committed to implementing the letter and spirit of the Balfour Declaration of 1917, which recognized the rights of "a national home for the Jewish people" in Palestine, but not their own. Sitting idly by as the Jewish population in Palestine swelled – from some 60,000 in 1918 to over 380,000 in 1936 – was not an option. The momentum in the struggle over control over the land was shifting to the Zionist side, abetted, the Arabs believed, by the British. Decisive action was needed to reverse the trend and reassert their own national priorities.

For the Zionists, immigration was indeed the key issue. If the import of settlement in Erets Yisra'el was clear to them before Hitler's rise to power in 1933, subsequent developments in Europe confirmed

---

* This chapter is a work of fiction. The first section, conveyed in roman type, is based on the established historical record. The second part, rendered in italics, shifts into the realm of the counterfactual.

the need to transport as many of their brethren as possible to Palestine. The Nuremberg Laws of 1935 introduced a harsh regime of racial classification, according to which Jews were deemed inferior to and segregated from Aryans. The Nazis had already demonstrated their willingness to act on their beliefs, setting up concentration camps for political undesirables shortly after taking power. Time was running short for Jews in Europe, and the need for immediate and unlimited *aliyah* was urgent.

Against the background of these rising tensions, on April 17, 1936, David Ben-Gurion, the leading Jewish politician in the Yishuv and member of the governing Zionist Executive, met with George Antonius, a prominent Lebanese-Christian theoretician of the Arab nationalist movement (Figure 23). The meeting was arranged by Dr. Judah L. Magnes, the president of the Hebrew University and longtime advocate of a binational Jewish–Arab state. Despite the deep differences between Magnes and Ben-Gurion, who steadfastly supported a Jewish state in Palestine, the two men got along surprisingly well. Ben-Gurion especially appreciated Magnes' close ties to a range of Arab thinkers, and availed himself of Magnes' connections to them on more than one occasion.

Ben-Gurion began the meeting with Antonius by laying out the two key planks of his platform: unrestricted Jewish immigration to Palestine and the creation of a Jewish state. Antonius responded with deep skepticism, suggesting that it would be impossible to find common ground if the Jews flooded the country. Ben-Gurion countered that a future Jewish state would be affiliated in some fashion with a federation of Arab states in the region. Antonius was unimpressed with Ben-Gurion's formula, and the conversation reached a standstill until Magnes raised the idea of a Legislative Council made up of Arab and Jewish representatives as an interim step. Both sides agreed that it was worth discussing and decided to meet again on April 22 to take up the idea.

In the intervening days, the Arab General Strike broke out in a fit of violence that left sixteen Jews dead in Jaffa. The two subsequent meetings between Ben-Gurion and Antonius on April 22 and April 29 were thus extremely tense. After the third meeting, Antonius came to the conclusion that his fellow Arab leaders, the Lebanese politician Shakib Arslan and the Syrian nationalist Ihsan Bey al-Jabri, had been right in their judgment. They had met Ben-Gurion in Geneva two years earlier, in September 1934, after which they declared that they saw no need for

Figure 23. In the pivotal year of 1936, David Ben-Gurion began a series of important negotiations with Arab political leaders in an effort to resolve the intensifying
Jewish–Arab conflict in Palestine.

further contact. Ben-Gurion, for his part, was struck by Antonius' statement at their second meeting that there was no Arab leader intent on
gaining mutual understanding between Jews and Arabs. It was deeply
depressing for Ben-Gurion to hear that statement, but he knew it not to
be true.

Musa Alami and Ben-Gurion first meet

Shortly before meeting with Arslan and al-Jabri, Ben-Gurion had held
a series of meetings with a thirty-six-year-old Jerusalem lawyer, Musa

Figure 24. Musa Alami, the scion of a renowned Arab family from Jerusalem and a pivotal figure in the eventual creation of a binational Jewish–Arab state in Palestine.

Alami, who was a good friend of Judah Magnes (Figure 24). Several years earlier, the Cambridge-trained Alami had moved from his job as assistant Government Advocate of the British Mandatory government to the post of private secretary to High Commissioner Arthur Wauchope, to whom he was a close confidant. After serving in that capacity for a year, he became chief Government Advocate. Although Zionist officials were concerned by Alami's influence on the British, Ben-Gurion sensed that Alami was interested in mutual understanding with the Jews.

Alami was the scion of a renowned Arab family from Jerusalem. Along with the Husseinis, Khalidis, Nashashibis, and Nusseibehs, the Alamis were major landowners and high-ranking officials in the waning years of Ottoman rule. His father Faidy served as mayor of Jerusalem from 1907 to 1909. Musa was raised in a grand home in the neighborhood of Musrara just outside the Old City. One of the guiding narratives of his life was that his mother gave birth to him at the same time as a boy was born to Jewish neighbors down the street. The local custom in Jerusalem at this time was for the neighboring mothers of two newborns to nurse them interchangeably. As a result, Musa Alami and his Jewish neighbor were deemed "foster-brothers" of sorts and remained friendly until political tensions undid the relationship in the 1920s. And yet Alami was familiar and friendly with Jews throughout his life, in Jerusalem as well as in Britain during his years as a law student.

At the same time, Alami had a strong sense of mission on behalf of the Arab people. He grew up in an environment in which fears of Jewish immigration to Palestine were constant – and ones that he shared. And notwithstanding his immersion in British culture and social norms, he believed that the Balfour Declaration and League of Nations Mandate were deeply biased against Palestine's native Arab population. This conviction did not prevent him from befriending, even while disagreeing with, the first British High Commissioner in Palestine, Sir Herbert Samuel, a devoted Jew and Zionist. Nor did it prevent him from serving under, or giving his professional counsel to, the later High Commissioner, Arthur Wauchope. In the same spirit, Alami believed it better to hear from the Zionists themselves about their plans than to rely on rumor-driven speculation. He thus acceded to David Ben-Gurion's request to meet in April 1934.

The Polish-born Ben-Gurion was marked by the very characteristics that he hoped Zionism would produce in Jews: a willingness to fight for national revival in the ancient homeland, a single-minded devotion to the cause, and unvarnished candor. Ben-Gurion was small of stature, but large in ambition. He sought nothing less than the transformation of Jewish life through the creation of a Jewish majority in a

Jewish state in Palestine. He went about this task with extraordinary discipline and focus, aided by keen powers of analysis and persuasion – if not always refined gentility. In the crowded field of Zionist ideology, one inevitably had to use sharp elbows in order to get ahead. And Ben-Gurion did, whether in contending with his own rivals in the Labor Zionist camp or facing those to the left and right of him.

Unlike his friend Judah Magnes, a Reform rabbi, Ben-Gurion tended not to speak the language of grand spiritual or cultural harmony with the Arab people. He was deeply, indeed inalterably, committed to his Zionist ideology, but he was a pragmatist. He knew that as long as the British maintained the Mandate over Palestine, he had to deal with them. He also knew, as Ahad Ha-am had warned forty-five years earlier, that Palestine was not, as some had said, "a land without people for a people without land." The Arabs were deeply rooted in the soil of Palestine and not inclined to roll over gently.

The leader with whom he would have most liked to meet – indeed, the one with the most authority in the fractious world of Arab politics – was Haj Amin Al-Husseini, the Mufti of Jerusalem and head of the Supreme Muslim Council of the city. The Mufti refused to meet with him, however, and had a reputation as vehemently hostile to Zionists – and Jews, for that matter. Indeed, Zionist officials held him chiefly responsible for the fracas at the Western Wall in 1929 that led to the murder of over 100 Jews.

Lingering resentment from that episode was fanned anew by violence in Arab towns in 1933, as fears of growing Jewish immigration deepened. Against that backdrop, Ben-Gurion was encouraged by his close Zionist associate, Moshe Shertok, to seek out Musa Alami, who was in regular contact with the Mufti (and, in fact, was a brother-in-law of the Mufti's cousin, Jamal Al-Husseini). Ben-Gurion and Alami met for the first time at Shertok's apartment in Jerusalem, where they had a candid exchange of views. Alami expressed his concern that the Jews were interested only in displacing the Arabs from their home in Palestine. Ben-Gurion, for his part, put forward his call for unrestricted Jewish immigration to Palestine culminating in a Jewish state. He added that he was willing to link this state to a larger union of Arab states in neighboring countries. Alami did not dismiss the idea out of hand, but wondered what would happen in the interim. Rather than pursue the British proposal for a Legislative Council, in which Arabs and Jews would serve together (under British control), Ben-Gurion suggested the possibility of a joint Executive in which Jews, Arabs, and the British would share power. The parties agreed to use this point as a basis for discussion.

The pace of discussions picked up over the summer of 1934. Ben-Gurion and Shertok met separately with Lebanese leader Riad al-Sulh and then, through the good offices of Judah Magnes, with Palestinian nationalist leader Auni Abdul Hadi. On August 31 Ben-Gurion met again with Musa Alami, who surprised him by telling him that the Mufti knew of their talks. In fact, the Mufti was astonished to hear that there were Jews interested in achieving mutual understanding with Arabs and listened to Alami's report of Ben-Gurion's ideas with great interest. At some point, it would make sense, Alami proposed, for Ben-Gurion to meet with the Mufti. But in the delicate game of intra-Arab diplomacy, Alami clarified that it was important to meet first with the pan-Arab leaders from Syria, Shakib Arslan and Ihsan Bey al-Jabri (the latter was Alami's father-in-law). The Mufti would want to hear their impressions of Ben-Gurion before proceeding. A meeting was thus scheduled to take place in Geneva when Ben-Gurion was on a European trip.

By Ben-Gurion's account, the discussion at Arslan's apartment on September 23 was exceptionally frank, with differences aired not only between the Zionist leader and the Arabs, but also, subtly, between Arslan and al-Jabri. Ben-Gurion laid out his insistence on a Jewish majority, which Arslan regarded with grave alarm. Arslan cast doubt on the depth of the Jewish connection to Palestine, though al-Jabri was more sensitive to the link. The two sides did not reach agreement on any concrete proposals, though they did agree, at least according to Ben-Gurion, to keep the conversation private in the hope that "the last word had not been spoken." Ben-Gurion was thus upset to read several months later an article in the Lebanese newspaper *La Nation Arabe*, which Arslan and al-Jabri edited, in which they dismissed Ben-Gurion's views as "arrogant and impudent." From that point in late 1934 until the outbreak of the Arab General Strike in 1936, there were various rounds of discussion between Zionist and Arab leaders. But a frustrated Ben-Gurion, who believed that he had been deceived by Arslan and al-Jabri, did not participate. Only in April 1936, as tensions reached a fever pitch, did he meet with George Antonius for their three inconclusive meetings. At the end of them, with Palestine on the verge of a major conflagration, Ben-Gurion decided to turn once more to the most reliable Arab interlocutor with whom he had engaged up to that point, Musa Alami.

Musa Alami returns to the stage: Sunday, September 6, 1936

"Mr. Alami," Ben-Gurion declared in his fluent, though accented English, *"I am delighted to see you after several years. Many thanks for hosting us in your lovely home. You look well, though I'm afraid that the situation around us does not look so good."*

"Good to see you, too, Mr. Ben-Gurion," Alami responded in the elegant lilt of his Cambridge years. *"And yes, like the summer heat of Palestine, the circumstances seem rather oppressive. Thus, rejoining our conversation of two years ago seems most prudent. I should let you know that the High Commissioner has been apprised of this meeting and firmly supports our efforts to achieve understanding."*

"Thank you for letting me know. Mr. Shertok has given me a full report on his meetings with you in May and June. And you may have heard of my meetings with Mr. Antonius."

Shertok, as on previous occasions, sat in on these meetings. Along with the Canadian-born lawyer, Dov Joseph, he had met with Alami on various occasions in the spring and summer of 1936, following Ben-Gurion's conversations with George Antonius.

"Permit me to get right to the heart of the matter, Mr. Alami. Do you think there is any reason to believe that an agreement between Jews and Arabs is possible in Palestine? Mr. Antonius led me to believe that there is not."

"Mr. Ben-Gurion, I do not deign to speak in Mr. Antonius' name, nor is it clear to me that he speaks on behalf of the Arabs of Palestine. But I firmly believe that we do not have the luxury of despair. A vast gulf separates us, indeed. You insist on a Jewish majority as a necessary outcome of negotiations. We look upon such a demand as a denial of the very existence of Arab peoples on the soil of Palestine. And yet we do not desire to have our children and their children and their children's children dwell in a state of perpetual war and bloodshed. We must find a way to understand one another."

"You are right, Mr. Alami. Time is short. Jews in Europe are under increasing attack. The villain Hitler, may his name be erased, makes bolder threats every day. We will need this land to save our

246 / David N. Myers

people. They must be allowed to immigrate without restriction. Otherwise, a catastrophe may occur, and we will all be responsible."

Shertok, who had been sitting silently, interjected without his usual tact: "Where does the Mufti stand, Mr. Alami? You have told us in the past that we cannot do anything unless he permits it. But he seems to be preoccupied now with running a violent rebellion. And he has never acknowledged our presence in Palestine."

Carefully drawing out his words, Alami answered: "Appearances to the contrary, the Mufti is neither naïve nor irresponsible. He is a political leader caught in the midst of a storm, trying to steer his ship in exceptionally rough waters. He not only has to steer clear of the British and the Zionists, but also of many within his own circle. Is it so different from your predicament among fellow Zionists? Under the right conditions, the Mufti would agree to meet with you."

"Would it not make more sense, Mr. Alami, to strengthen the hand of the moderates among you like the Nashashibis or the Khalidis?"

"May I answer your question with a question, Mr. Shertok? Would it not be easier for our side to strike a bargain with Dr. Magnes? Of course, it would. Magnes is not only a close friend, but a widely respected man of humanity and compassion. But we are realistic enough to know that he is not the one with whom to reach an agreement."

Shertok shot a quick smile at Ben-Gurion, nodding in appreciation at Alami's grasp of Yishuv politics. Ben-Gurion then probed: "What would it take to get the Mufti to meet us? Although he is no friend of the Jews, it is not with one's friends that one negotiates. We are prepared to meet him without conditions, assuming that the British don't arrest him first. As far as I can tell – and you may know better – the High Commissioner has tired of his rhetoric, which has become more and more incendiary over the course of the summer."

"Yes, the Mufti is in a tough spot," Alami replied. "But I do not see the British arresting him. What I think we want to avoid, both your side and ours, is a scenario in which the British impose a long-term solution. As you know, they will soon be sending a commission of inquiry to investigate the current state of affairs in Palestine. Perhaps it would be better for us to bring an initiative to the British rather than have them force a plan on us."

"Agreed," Ben-Gurion said. He then proceeded with his customary forcefulness: "What will it take to get the Mufti to the table?

And if he comes, will he only come to complain, as he did in the manifesto he sent to Wauchope in April?"

"The April 26 manifesto of the Mufti," Alami declared, "reflected well our view that, since Balfour, the British have continuously trampled on Arab rights. I understand that you see it differently, but you must recognize our perspective. At the same time, it will serve no good purpose for us to play the victim forever. You Zionists will march steadily toward your goal while we sit in a corner and weep. And so, I will do my best to convince the Mufti that the time has come to sit down with you."

"Thank you again for your assistance, Mr. Alami, and for your hospitality," replied Ben-Gurion. "If there is anything we can do to help, please let me or Mr. Shertok know."

"I will be in touch soon. In the meantime, let us all do our very best to avoid provocative steps."

Ben-Gurion and Shertok nodded in assent, rose, and bade farewell to Alami. Their driver ferried them back from Alami's home in Musrara to the offices of the Jewish Agency building on King George Street.

During the drive, Shertok turned to Ben-Gurion and said: "If Alami is able to deliver the Mufti, you will have to exercise all of your diplomatic skill in dealing with him. Are you up to the task?"

"I have no choice. He is no ohev Yisra'el *[lover of the Jews]. But we are at a crossroads. The Arab General Strike has weakened their cause; the British have lost patience. But we too are in desperate straits: we need the gates of Palestine to be opened to Jews. Let us see if we can break through to the good Mufti. And by the way, inform Magnes of these developments. Given the good will that the Arabs have for him, he should be present at that meeting."*

Musa Alami seeks to persuade the Mufti: Monday, September 7, 1936

Immediately after his guests left, Musa Alami called the Mufti's office and arranged a meeting for the next day. He did not look forward to the encounter. Alami knew Haj Amin Al-Husseini well, perhaps too well. Their families belonged to the same small privileged circle of Jerusalemite Arabs. Both born in 1897, the two were acquaintances and rivals from childhood. As an adolescent, Alami never would have imagined that Amin would follow in the footsteps of his father and brother as Mufti. To this day, he was amused by the fact that Amin was the leading Muslim official in Jerusalem. Amin, after all, was always more interested in politics than religion. From an early age, he was a fervent Arab nationalist and ardent opponent of Zionism. Although he had studied at Al-Azhar in Cairo, he had not been a prominent or even promising religious scholar. In fact, the other candidates for the election to Mufti in the spring of 1921, which included representatives from the well-known Khalidi and Jaralla families, were far more competent as religious authorities. And yet High Commissioner Herbert Samuel intervened in the election and appointed Al-Husseini to the position of Mufti.

Both due to his office and as a result of his personal qualities – he could be, in equal measure, charming and unyielding in support of the nationalist cause – Amin Al-Husseini was the most influential Arab political figure in Palestine. Musa Alami had long considered the Mufti an opportunist, willing to sacrifice principle to his brand of populist politics. But he also knew that he was indispensable. If the Arab side were to secure any guarantee of political rights in Palestine, the Mufti had to be involved.

With a measure of trepidation, Alami arrived at 8:30 the next morning at the Mufti's office on Haram al Sharif, the Muslim holy site overlooking the Western Wall.

"Most Venerable Guardian of Al-Quds, al-Haj Amin, salaam alaikum," announced Alami to his old compatriot with exaggerated formality.

"May peace, mercy, and blessings of Allah be upon you, my dear Musa," replied the Mufti. "It has been far too long. How is Saadiyeh?"

"She is well, Amin. Many thanks for inquiring. I trust that all is well with the Husseinis."

"Praise be to Allah, yes. To what do I owe the honor of your presence?"

"Amin, you know that I am in regular touch with my friend, Dr. Magnes, the president of the Hebrew University who is as sympathetic to the Arabs as any Jew I know. You also know that I have met periodically over the last few years with Ben-Gurion and his associate, Shertok. Our discussions have not led to any agreements, nor could they, since I possess no authority to make a deal. But they have led to a better understanding of the other side."

"Yes, I know, Musa. You and others have kept me informed from time to time. I appreciate your openness to the outside world. It has always been the case with you, even as a young boy. You had your Jewish friends, while the rest of us looked on in astonishment. But I must tell you, Musa, that there are those among us who view your relations with the Jews today with suspicion. They wonder if you truly stand with the Arab nation. I need not tell you that they can be rather impetuous."

"I appreciate the warning, Amin. Of course, I have heard it before. But the moment at which we find ourselves today requires courage. Let me speak to you candidly. Our glorious strike has not served us well at all. Our people cannot sustain the deprivation and lack of livelihood. The British are fed up with us, as I hear from the High Commissioner. And the Jews are more numerous, more powerful, more assertive than ever before. We have little choice but to sit down with them to discuss possible arrangements."

"Musa, you know that the Zionists are devious interlopers who have come to steal our land. How could I, as the custodian of the holy Al-Aqsa Mosque, agree to sit down with them? Your father-in-law did so two years ago with Shakib Arslan, and all they encountered was the intransigence of your friend Ben-Gurion."

"That may well be. But that was then, and this is now. We find ourselves in a different – and I mean weaker – position than before. If we hope to secure any measure of self-determination for ourselves at this point, we must do it with and through the Jews. The British will not grant it to us."

"You understand, Musa, that I would be angering many of our brethren, including my fellow members of the Higher Committee, by meeting with the Jews. And I would be placing myself and my family at great personal risk."

"I do understand, Amin. But that is the mark of a true leader. You have been the model of national steadfastness for the Arabs of Palestine. But the hour now calls upon you to wage a different kind of battle than you have in the past, to extend beyond your hard-earned reputation and sit down with the enemy."

"I will consider it. But you must understand, Musa, that I will never compromise the integrity of our holy Jerusalem, which I have been commanded to safeguard."

"I understand well, Honorable Mufti. I would never ask you to do so."

Ben-Gurion and Shertok consult with Magnes: Monday, September 7, 1936

Following their meeting with Musa Alami on Sunday, Ben-Gurion and Shertok convened in the Jewish Agency offices where the Zionist Executive was housed. Ben-Gurion's election as chairman of the Executive the previous year consolidated his position as the leading political figure in the Yishuv.

This should not lead one to assume that the Jewish population was marked by harmonious coexistence. The spike in violence during the Arab strike had led to some eighty Jewish deaths and widened the chasm between Ben-Gurion's Mapai Party and the Revisionist Zionists of Vladimir Ze'ev Jabotinsky, as well as between their respective paramilitary units, the Haganah and Irgun. The Irgun was unwilling to heed Ben-Gurion's policy of havlagah, *the call for restraint in retaliating against Arab forces following attacks. Ben-Gurion's calculation that restraint served a strategic purpose in inclining the British to favor the Zionists was altogether rejected by the Irgun. For the Irgun's members, the failure to retaliate against Arabs – and, if need be, to attack British forces – replicated the diaspora passivity that Zionism sought to eradicate.*

Ben-Gurion was lost in thought about the problems he faced – the Irgun, the British, and the situation in Europe – when Shertok interjected: "I have called Magnes, and he has agreed to meet with us tomorrow. Let us see what he has to say."

The next morning, Shertok and Ben-Gurion hosted Magnes at the Jewish Agency office. Magnes had been intensely engaged since May with four Jewish colleagues, together known as the Committee of Five, in formulating a document for discussion with Arab leaders regarding the creation of a Legislative Council that would operate "on the basis of equality between the two peoples." The Jewish Agency, including Ben-Gurion and Shertok, had been briefed on it, and rejected the document because it proposed too low a number of Jewish immigrants to Palestine.

"Dr. Magnes, thank you for making time for us on such short notice," Ben-Gurion opened.

"My pleasure, dear Ben-Gurion. Mr. Shertok told me of the interesting prospect before you. As you know, I am always available to assist in matters involving Jewish–Arab reconciliation. At the end of the day, the differences between the two of us are small compared to the perils of obstinacy and inaction."

"Yes, and we have a rare opportunity to talk to someone whose voice matters on the Arab side. If you would be willing, Dr. Magnes, I would like you to join Shertok and me in meeting with the Mufti."

"I will be honored to attend and to serve the interests of the Jewish people. In doing so, I will hope to serve the interests of our Arab cousins as well – and humanity at large. Remember what is etched on the archway of my friend Klausner's home in Talpiot – 'Yahadut ve-enoshiyut' [Judaism and Humanity]. The values of Judaism and of humanity are one. If Klausner, my political opposite, can agree with me about that, then so too can we Jews with the Arabs."

"Inshallah, Dr. Magnes," chuckled Ben-Gurion. "But the devil lies in the details. Your group of five has focused on three key issues: immigration, land, and governance. I do not favor the precise proposals you raised, but I agree on the centrality of these three."

"Let us focus on those issues then," Shertok joined in. "It will be important that we three, divergent as our views may be, present a unified front to Alami and the Mufti. We can begin perhaps by demonstrating our sensitivity to the issue of land."

"Yes, indeed," Magnes responded. "The Arabs feel, and not without cause, that when we buy land in large blocks, we are stripping them not only of their most precious natural resource, but of their very mooring in this country. It is the fellahin, the poor farmers, who are most vulnerable. And so our group of five proposed that for every 75 dunams of land purchased, we commit to preserving 25 for the rural Arab population. We also proposed that we make a major commitment to the economic development of those who remain on the land."

"It has always been a foundation of our position with the Arabs," Shertok noted, "that we make a major investment in their development. Not only will the Jewish Agency contribute. We will also ask our non-Zionist friends – Rothschild and Warburg, for example – to help in that regard. I am confident that we can put together a sizable fund for this purpose."

"Of course, I will be happy to take that up with Warburg, who has been such a generous friend of my university," Magnes added. "He will be delighted to hear of this initiative. But assuming that we can achieve agreement on land, do you believe that we can find common ground on immigration and governance? What do you propose there, Mr. Ben-Gurion?"

"For years, Magnes, I have reiterated my two main goals of creating a Jewish majority in a Jewish state," Ben-Gurion pronounced. "To turn away from either at this point would violate the core of my Zionist convictions."

"But remember that you are about to enter a negotiation, Mr. Ben-Gurion," Magnes stated. "As you said, this is a rare opportunity. It will require not just the appearance of flexibility, but actual evidence of such. You are the leader of the Jewish people in Palestine. History will be your judge."

"Dr. Magnes, I am well aware of the import of the moment," Ben-Gurion responded with a trace of impatience. "Shertok and I will discuss the two issues in the next few days. I promise that I will listen to Alami and the Mufti and demonstrate as much flexibility as I feel I can."

"Well then, I will proceed to contact Mr. Alami and suggest that we focus our conversation around the three issues we just mentioned," added Shertok.

The Zionist leadership meets the Mufti of Jerusalem: Thursday, September 10, 1936

The car carrying Ben-Gurion, Shertok, and Magnes pulled up to Musa Alami's house at the appointed hour of 10:00 a.m. They were greeted cordially at the door by Alami. Before entering the large sitting room, they paused, knowing that they would presently encounter the Mufti of Jerusalem, whose very name evoked fear and revulsion among Jews in Palestine. Magnes led the Jewish delegation into the room and extended his hand to the Mufti. Shertok and finally Ben-Gurion did the same as they announced their names.

The Mufti had been hearing the names of his new acquaintances for years, but had never met them. In fact, he had met relatively few Jews in his life. He now stood face to face with major Zionist figures, the very people who he often said had come to steal his land.

The two key men in the room, Ben-Gurion and the Mufti, towering figures in their respective communities, were of equally diminutive stature. But both radiated a sense of power and importance, creating a palpable sense of tension as they stood a few feet from one another in the middle of Musa Alami's salon. Ben-Gurion proceeded to address the Mufti in his less than perfect French, knowing that this was a common language between them. He thanked him for agreeing *to meet. The Mufti responded that it was a matter of national duty and honor to do so.*

Alami then invited his guests to sit down, as he slowly poured each a demitasse of Turkish coffee. He suggested that he serve as translator, moving between Arabic and English, which would be less of a strain for all. He opened by telling his Jewish guests that he had informed the Mufti of their proposal to focus on three issues and that the Mufti had agreed. It might make sense, he continued, to begin with the issue of land purchases.

As agreed upon by the three Jewish participants, Magnes commenced by acknowledging the sanctity of the Holy Land for Muslims, Christians, and Jews alike, and then quoted a verse from Deuteronomy (16:20) that reflected his most deeply held Jewish credo: "Justice, justice, thou shall pursue." It was his personal mission, he pronounced, to pursue justice for all inhabitants of the Holy Land.

The Mufti appeared unmoved. He parried Magnes' scriptural reference by quoting a Quranic sura (4:58): "Verily! Allah commands that you should render back the trusts to those to whom they are due; and that when you judge between men, you judge with justice." Justice between men, he declared, requires that that which is taken from one unfairly be returned to him.

Shertok stole a quick glance at Ben-Gurion, fearing an angry response. Before either could open his mouth, Musa Alami intervened: "Dear friends, we can all agree on the principle of justice in our religions, as well as the sanctity of the land. Let us turn to the specific issue we agreed to discuss. Mr. Shertok, could you lay out your views on land ownership and purchase?"

"Thank you, Mr. Alami. We come here in the hope of achieving a better understanding of the Arab position. It is in the interests of both groups to find their way to mutual recognition rather than succumb to violence. The view of the Zionist Executive is two-fold: first, Jews should be able to purchase land anywhere in Palestine provided that they do so in conformance with the law of the land and with respect for the well-being of the Arab residents who would be directly affected by a land sale. Second, in the spirit of cooperation and our desire for peaceful coexistence, we are prepared to mobilize the resources of the Zionist movement and its supporters the world over to raise hundreds of millions of dollars for the economic development of Palestine, of which a substantial portion would be directed to the Arab population."

"We appreciate the spirit of cooperation, but the facts on the ground cannot be ignored, Mr. Shertok," Alami retorted in Arabic before repeating the line in English. "The Zionists are not only purchasing land through any means available to them, sometimes legally and often not, but in doing so, they are displacing large numbers of our rural brethren, the fellahin."

"You surely know, Mr. Alami, that many of your urban brethren are willing to sell us their land," Ben-Gurion declared with emphasis. He stared directly at Alami, signaling that he had heard the rumor that Alami had himself sold land from a family estate in the Galilee to Jews. "And why shouldn't they? We only seek legal purchases, and we pay a fair price. That said, we do recognize the logic of the proposal of Dr. Magnes and his friends that it is our obligation to set aside a portion of the property that we purchase for its long-time residents. We propose therefore a 25 percent set-aside on all future land purchases. We also propose a $250 million economic development plan over the next five years, of which half would be directed to the Arab population. That will require a huge effort on our part, but it can be done in the name of peace."

Alami translated Ben-Gurion's words to the Mufti, who listened with evident interest. He did not doubt the ability of the Jews to raise vast sums of capital given their global connections. "How can we be sure that such funds will make their way to our people?" he asked. "And how can we make sure that our land will not be plundered?"

Ben-Gurion sensed a certain pragmatic interest lurking beneath the Mufti's skepticism and responded: "We will establish a joint committee of Arabs and Jews, with British representation as well. Its purpose will be to oversee all land purchases in Palestine to ensure that they are conducted legally and fairly. We will also establish a joint economic development committee to guarantee the equitable distribution of development funds raised abroad."

"Of course, Mr. Ben-Gurion, the question of land cannot be separated from the question of Jewish immigration to Palestine," Alami announced. "Unrestrained immigration will lead to unrestrained land purchases which, in turn, will force the natives of this country off their land. That is unacceptable."

"Mr. Alami, my people are now experiencing one of the darkest chapters in their long history. A brutal German tyrant is threatening to render Europe judenrein, free of all Jews. We believe he is capable of *nothing short of mass murder to accomplish this goal. We must open the gates of Palestine to our brothers and sisters, and we must do so now."*

"Why must the Arab people of Palestine bear the brunt of the Jews' burden elsewhere?" asked the Mufti. "It is not our problem, but we are being asked to pay for it."

"Honorable Mufti, I will not bore you with impassioned professions of our deep connection to the land," Ben-Gurion uttered with characteristic directness. "Rather, I want to mention the careful work of our experts, particularly Professor Arthur Ruppin, an internationally renowned scholar, who has studied the absorptive capacity of Palestine. Quite in contrast to the Hope-Simpson Report that you remember from 1930, he believes that this land can easily absorb millions of new immigrants. We agree entirely. At the same time, we understand that a massive flood of immigrants will overwhelm Palestine's existing infrastructure. We would therefore like to offer an immigration plan beginning this year based on the number of Jewish arrivals last year: 62,000. Should conditions prove hospitable, we would propose to raise the figure by at least 10,000 every year. And if conditions in Europe deteriorate dramatically, we would propose a more significant increase in numbers."

"The Arab people would never accept this," objected the Mufti, upon hearing Alami's translation. "And even if I agreed, I could never win support from the Higher Committee."

"I understand that there are serious risks for you," Ben-Gurion nodded. "I, too, would face fierce opposition from my fellow Zionists for any agreement that we arrive at. But history demands a great deal from the two of us now. Together we have the opportunity to alter the future for the sake of our children. The time is now."

The Mufti looked on pensively, without uttering a word, as Alami joined in: "I appreciate the complexities of your internal situation, Mr. Ben-Gurion. I also understand the delicacy of the situation in Europe. But how can we justify permitting hundreds of thousands of Jews to come into this country and displace our people from their land?"

"I reiterate: We will insist on the preservation of land for the rural Arab population. And we will embark on a massive economic development campaign for both peoples. Mr. Alami, the time is right not only for us, but for you. By all accounts, the British have lost patience

*with the General Strike. We are offering you a compromise. We are not
proposing unlimited Jewish immigration to Palestine, but an incremental plan that balances your interests with ours."*

*"And who will oversee this flood of immigrants?" the Mufti
asked. "What sort of government do you propose? If we share one thing,
it is that we are sick and tired of our British overlords. But we cannot
accept the idea that people who arrived here from Europe no more than
fifty years ago will rule over a majority of the population who have lived
here for millennia."*

*"Here too we are prepared to compromise," Shertok responded.
"Over the past few days, we have had intensive and far-reaching discussions with members of the Zionist Executive. In the past, we have
spoken of our need for a Jewish state. In fact, in previous conversations
with Mr. Alami and others, we have discussed the prospect of linking
such a state to a neighboring Arab federation. However, we are now prepared to raise a different concept, motivated, to no small extent, by our
friend, Dr. Magnes. We are proposing a five-year transition toward self-rule by Jews and Arabs in a state to be known as Filastin-Erets Yisrael.
The mechanisms of government will be: first, a bicameral legislature,
the lower house of which will elect delegates proportionate to the population (and thus will be Arab-controlled for the foreseeable future),
and the upper house of which will be evenly divided between Jewish
and Arab representatives; second, an executive body consisting of four
Arab and four Jewish members led by an Arab first minister and a Jewish deputy first minister; and, third, at the end of the transition period,
after which the British would surrender the Mandate, a ceremonial head
of state to be known as President to be elected by the upper house of
Parliament."*

*Alami translated the details to the Mufti, and the two men sat
in silence. They had come to the meeting expecting to hear once again
the Zionists' insistence on a Jewish state. The new proposal was very
different. It entailed unmistakable compromise on the part of the Zionists, reflecting their urgent need for a place of refuge for European Jews.
It would also require deep compromise on the Arab side.*

*While still processing his thoughts, Alami said: "Thank you
for this proposal, Mr. Shertok. It demands serious attention. I would
like to discuss these ideas with the High Commissioner, whose support
would obviously be needed. Meanwhile, the Mufti will need to speak
with members of the Higher Committee to see if there is any receptivity*

to the proposal. I propose that we be in touch after your Sabbath on Sunday morning."

Alami then translated for the Mufti, who nodded his agreement. The participants stood, shook hands, and parted ways.

The fateful meeting at Magnes' house: Monday, September 14, 1936

When Alami and the Mufti arrived at 10:00 on Monday morning, Ben-Gurion and Shertok were already seated in the living room of Magnes' house in a mixed Jewish–Arab neighborhood in the north of Jerusalem. The Jewish officials rose to greet their Arab counterparts, and then all took their seats.

Alami immediately began: "Dear friends, when we met last at my home, I must confess that I was in a state of near-total despair. The General Strike, about which I always had my doubts, does not seem to be yielding any positive results for the Arab side. Meanwhile, your efforts to bring more Jews to Palestine with the aim of creating a Jewish state are proceeding apace. Tensions between Jews and Arabs are boiling over. It seemed as if all hope was lost. But much has changed since Friday. You have given us a serious proposal. I had a chance to discuss it with the High Commissioner on Friday, and he enthusiastically supports it. He is confident that it will supersede the plan to bring the royal commission to Palestine. He believes that His Majesty's government is prepared to surrender its Mandate over Palestine, assuming that relations between it and the new government of Filastin-Erets Yisrael be strong. I will let the Mufti report on his conversations."

The Mufti turned to face Ben-Gurion and explained: "I have discussed your proposal with my colleagues on the Arab Higher Committee. To recognize you as partners in negotiation would require a major concession on our part. But I am not here to belabor the obvious. What my colleagues and I see is that you are gaining traction in our country, with the support of the British. Although there was not unanimity in the Arab Higher Committee, I have come to believe that we must secure for our people what we can now. Accordingly, I offer you my support to move on to the next phase of negotiation over your plan."

Ben-Gurion looked in astonishment at the Mufti, recalling that a few short months ago his meetings with George Antonius ended with no prospect for further dialogue. In a matter of days, his world – and that of Jews and Arabs in Palestine – had been totally upended: "I am stunned and delighted, sir. We are on the verge of an historic new era, ending a half-century of enmity between Jews and Arabs and offering new hope to our peoples in a time of great need. In that vein, I should add that we have agreed among ourselves that if the negotiations move forward as we hope, we would like to nominate Mr. Alami to serve as the initial first minister in the five-year transition period."

Alami smiled at the suggestion and proclaimed: "I am honored by your confidence, my friends, though hardly deserving of it. I doubt that I am capable of meeting the huge demands of such a job, but I pledge to do all within my powers to help our peoples find their way to peace. And in that spirit, I would like to reciprocate by suggesting here and now that Dr. Magnes be considered for the position of first President of the new state. He has labored tirelessly for peaceful coexistence between our peoples and is an inspiration to Jew and Arab alike."

Magnes was visibly moved by the suggestion, but quickly added: "My dear friend Alami, what an extraordinary privilege that would be! But we are getting ahead of ourselves. We must sell this plan to our respective peoples, and it will be immensely challenging. Even if we succeed in that regard, there would not be a President for five years. Who knows if I will even be around at that point by then, when I will be sixty-five years old? In the meantime, we face the major challenge of crafting instruments of shared governance under British control. But before embarking on that difficult and noble work, let us pause and take stock of this extraordinary moment. The Almighty has made us holy vessels to undertake what I never thought possible – the founding of an Arab–Jewish state in Palestine, a state born in peace and hope rather than in the violence and despair in which we have been so dreadfully mired for decades."

The five men stood up and joined hands in the center of the room. After a minute of silent meditation, they sat down again and began to lay the foundation for the State of Filastin-Erets Yisrael.

12 WHAT IF THE WEIMAR REPUBLIC HAD SURVIVED? A CHAPTER FROM WALTHER RATHENAU'S MEMOIR*

Michael Brenner

It gives me great pleasure to publish an excerpt from Walther Rathenau's forthcoming memoir. As readers will recall, Rathenau died unexpectedly two years ago after retiring from his post as Germany's President (Figure 25). He was nearing the completion of his memoir, which he planned on calling On Bygone Events *("Von vergangenen Dingen"), and had hoped to see it published in time for his seventy-fifth birthday. It was unfortunately not to be. I have therefore taken it upon myself to edit this remarkable book. It would be too much to say that we were companions. But there were many occasions when Rathenau and I shared the same goals and worked for a common cause. We both helped to establish the Deutsche Demokratische Partei and we both were among the supporters of the Deutsche Hochschule für Politik. My admiration for Rathenau grew steadily during the years of his presidency, in which he helped to lead Germany out of political crisis and economic depression. I regarded it therefore both as an honor and as my duty to edit this volume.*

The following excerpts describe Rathenau's reflections on his Jewish background. I was always convinced that Jews contributed much both to the spiritual and economic well-being of Germany. Some of my best students were Jews, among them Franz Rosenzweig, whose dissertation on Hegel remains a work of enduring value to German intellectual history. Unfortunately, Rosenzweig rejected my offer of a university position. He declined to explore the heights of German Protestant

---

* This chapter is a work of fiction.

Figure 25. Portrait of Walther Rathenau by Edvard Munch (1907). Elected President of Germany in 1925, Rathenau helped steer Germany through the crisis of the Great Depression.

culture and instead fled into the world of his blood.[1] *Rathenau was a very different case. Early in his youth, he embraced German Protestant culture, but he struggled most of his life with his Jewishness, at times quite violently. Only when he was accepted as a representative of Germany was he also able to fully embrace his Jewish identity.*

Friedrich Meinecke (1942)

Walther Rathenau, *On Bygone Events* (Berlin: S. Fischer Verlag, 1942)

Chapter 17 The Jewish Question

In contrast to many of my kinsmen (*Stammesgenossen*), I never underestimated the importance of the "Jewish Question." Back in my youth,

I realized that "in the early years of every German Jew, there is a painful moment that can never be forgotten…That is when he first becomes aware that he entered the world as a second-class citizen and that no amount of talent and merit would free him of this status." I first explored my feelings about the Jewish Question in an essay entitled "Hear, O Israel!" which appeared in 1897 in Maximilian Harden's journal, *Die Zukunft*. How often was I called a self-hating Jew after the publication of this essay! Some of my friends, such as Alfred Kerr (who changed his name from Kempner in order to hide his Jewish identity), called me an antisemite. My own father went so far as to buy all the copies of the essay he could lay his hands on – only in order to burn them! To be sure, I meant to be provocative. I even thought initially about writing the essay from an antisemitic perspective. How else could anyone interpret a sentence like this: "Smack in the middle of German life is an isolated exotic race of men, shining and strikingly dressed, hot blooded and constantly in motion. An Asiatic horde on the sands of the Mark Brandenburg…Thus they live in a semi-voluntary, invisible ghetto, not as a living limb of the nation, but as an alien organism within its body."[2]

I was convinced that if we Jews were going to stay in Germany, we had to assimilate. We had to normalize our abnormal situation. We had to adjust our professions, modify our religious practices, and even change our physical appearance. Conversion was not a real solution, but only appeared to change our situation at the most superficial level. I knew early on that "a baptized Jew is never the same as a baptized Christian."

My fellow Jews, however, never understood what I meant. One of the few Jews who recognized the magnitude of our problem was Theodor Herzl. In the same year that I published "Hear, O Israel!," he convened the First Zionist Congress. I happened to learn about the Zionist movement only later, but in retrospect, I discovered that Herzl and I shared common views of the Jewish Question. Herzl also understood that conversion would never solve the Jewish problem. When I raised the question "What needs to happen?" in "Hear, O Israel!," I proposed – like Herzl – "an event without historical precedent." My vision differed substantially from his, however, insofar as I demanded "deliberate training of this race to achieve assimilation, not in the Darwinian sense of 'mimicry'…but by adaptation, in the sense that both good and bad characteristics of the tribe be cast aside and replaced with others if it is evident that they are inimical to their fellow countrymen."[3]

A few years ago, when Herzl's letters were published, I realized that he concurred with my diagnosis, although he rejected my remedy. Thus Herzl wrote about my essay: "If he is advising the Jews to adopt a different bone structure, I will happily accompany him to this future of selective breeding. I am not poking fun at it, as any typical Jew would, but wish to concur with him. It is just that I think that the Jews will only be able to absorb the phosphorus for these new bones from a single source, namely from their own."[4]

I will return later to the success of Herzl's plans. I did not take him seriously at the time, but after the war, I glanced through his book, *The Jewish State*, and realized that his pessimistic prediction about anti-semitism was not entirely wrong. After our defeat in the war, there was a wave of anti-Jewish hatred much worse than I ever had seen before. I quickly came to believe that "antisemitism is the vertical invasion of society by barbarians."[5]

. . .

After I accepted the position of Foreign Minister in 1922, I was warned – not only by my enemies, but also by my friends – to be wary. In March, Albert Einstein, together with the president of the Zionist Federation in Germany, Kurt Blumenfeld, paid me a visit at my home, Schloss Freienwalde. They urged me to step down from my new post, fearing for my safety.[6] They alerted me to something that I already knew full well – even though I had distanced myself from the Jewish community, I was widely reviled as a Jew by right-wing extremists. Einstein and Blumenfeld emphasized this point by recalling an ominous saying that was being recited all over Russia following the October Revolution: "The Trotskys might have tried to turn Russia upside down – the Bronsteins were to pay the price." Our discussion went on for hours, long past midnight. I was not so naïve as to completely dismiss their fears, but I felt that I had no choice but to stay on and fulfill my task. I also knew that my predecessor, the orientalist scholar and diplomat, Friedrich Rosen, was of Jewish descent and had served in the post honorably.

The political climate in 1922 was poisonous, however, and I soon became a target of right-wing groups. The vicious antisemitic forgery, *The Protocols of the Elders of Zion*, was published in many editions, and I was widely accused of being part of a worldwide Jewish conspiracy. One pamphlet, published by the right-wing extremist

Alfred Roth, was called *Walther Rathenau: Der Kandidat des Auslandes*, and claimed that I had worked with other Jews, such as Albert Ballin, to engineer Germany's defeat in the war. The "stab-in-the-back legend" (*Dolchstoßlegende*), which blamed Socialists and Jews for Germany's military defeat, was very much *en vogue*. In the fall of 1921 on the way to my office, I saw a street mob gathering near the Brandenburg Gate, with brownshirts among them. The atmosphere was explosive and I heard many people chanting, "Knock off Walther Rathenau, that goddamned Jewish sow!" The crude slogan was soon embraced by many of the right-wing groups that were starting to gain support during this turbulent period. I still felt safe, however, believing that our democracy could safeguard itself. My closest advisors were less sure. They begged me not to leave the house without armed guards, but I adamantly refused.

On the evening of June 23, 1922, I was in a meeting at the home of the American ambassador Alanson Houghton, together with the industrialist Hugo Stinnes. I explained to them that Germany's ability to satisfy Allied demands was limited and that we had to carefully monitor the growing resistance to the "policy of fulfillment" (*Erfüllungspolitik*) that was officially supported by the German government. A broad coalition of center-right parties was becoming increasingly impatient with what it saw as our overly compliant position with respect to the Allies. I was representing the German people, however, and my own position was irrelevant at this moment. The meeting became increasingly tense, and when we parted long after midnight, we had not reached a consensus.

The next morning, I woke up later than usual and left for my office only at 10:45 a.m. As always, we drove down the picturesque Königsallee, when I suddenly noticed a black car speeding up next to ours. Three young men were in it, and before I was able to comprehend what was happening, I was struck unconscious. When I woke up later on in the hospital, I had no sense of how long I had been there and no recollection of what had happened. Slowly, the image of the car and the three young men returned to me. I was informed by the doctor that I was lucky beyond description. I had survived an assassination attempt. Thanks to a miracle, one of the bullets fired by my assailants went through my jaw but did no lasting damage. Another bullet was deflected by my heroic driver. Unfortunately, his wound was a mortal one and he later died. For their part, my would-be assassins were convinced they had done away with me and quickly fled the scene. In fact, I was in a coma. But after three days, I awoke from it and eventually made a full recovery.

The German public's reaction to my attempted assassination was overwhelmingly sympathetic. It was as if Germany had awakened from a nightmare. Ever since the end of the war, many honorable politicians had been assassinated: among others, the left-wing politicians, Rosa Luxemburg, Karl Liebknecht, and Kurt Eisner; as well as the Catholic Center Party chief, Matthias Erzberger. In addition, the Social Democratic Party official, Philipp Scheidemann, had only narrowly survived a poison attack. Then it was my turn. Following the attack against me, many people began to grasp that right-wing extremists represented a more serious threat to our country's security than any other danger. This became especially clear once it was disclosed that a far right-wing group of rabid nationalists and disgruntled Freikorps soldiers, known as the Organization Consul, was responsible for organizing the assassination attempt against me.

I was still in a coma when my close friend, the Reich Chancellor, Josef Wirth, delivered an impassioned speech in the Reichstag condemning the attack. As I later learned, Wirth paused at the climactic moment of his remarks, pointed dramatically to the right, and exclaimed: "It is there where our enemy stands!" Partly thanks to this speech, many of the right-wing politicians, such as Karl Helfferich, who had been relentlessly attacking me and other liberals, came to be seen as having contributed to the poisonous climate that had led to acts of violence. The public mood now shifted against the right. Ironically enough, the assassins produced the opposite of what they intended. Instead of producing a civil war, they prompted the young Republic to stand up and defend itself. In Berlin, enormous demonstrations, attended by hundreds of thousands of ordinary Germans representing all segments of the population, were held to express solidarity with me and demand tough action against the enemies of democracy. The content of Wirth's speech was widely reprinted on posters and distributed all across the country. More importantly, the Reich President, Friedrich Ebert, immediately decreed emergency laws that safeguarded the Republic and allowed for measures to be taken against its enemies. These laws were crucial for enabling the government to outlaw certain right-wing political parties. Some of my older contemporaries may remember one in particular, the Bavarian-based National Socialist German Workers' Party, which was led by a brash, right-wing fanatic named Adolf Hitler. Thanks to Ebert's laws, Hitler was swiftly sent to prison where he, together with some of his party colleagues, eventually committed suicide.

We knew, of course, that the danger of right-wing extremism would not vanish overnight. The conservative German National People's Party and others like it remained active, but their power diminished as Germany's economy recovered and our reputation within the international community improved. Of course, there remained the serious danger of left-wing extremism (many of us continued to worry about a Soviet-style communist insurrection), but that story is part of another chapter.

Today, it is almost impossible to imagine how virulent the danger of right-wing antisemitism was back then. The last time this poison was part of a national election campaign was in 1925. After the sudden death of President Ebert in February, a new President had to be elected. In the first round, no candidate received the necessary majority. The right-wing German People's Party candidate, Karl Jarres, and the Social Democratic contender, Otto Braun, received the most votes. The extremists Erich Ludendorff, representing the far right, and Ernst Thälmann, representing the far left, received much less support. As a result, a second round of voting had to be held. In order to maximize their chances of success, the various parties adopted different strategies. For its part, the German Communist Party stubbornly stuck with Thälmann as its candidate. The German right, by contrast, abandoned Ludendorff and instead selected the old Field Marshal and World War I hero, Paul von Hindenburg. Significantly, the center-right and center-left parties now tried to identify a candidate who could help forge a new Weimar alliance of moderate political parties. Initially, none of the candidates who had run in the first round proved strong enough to appeal to voters outside their own party. This held true for the Catholic Center candidate, Wilhelm Marx, as well as for the Liberal Party's Willi Hellpach. At the same time, the Prussian Prime Minister, Otto Braun, who had gained a respectable share of the vote in the first round, realized that the Social Democrats would be unable to attract a sufficient number of middle-class votes. This deadlock set the stage for my own return to politics.

On April 7, I received a call from Marx who had decided not to run again, as it became clear that the right-wing parties had picked Hindenburg and that segments of his own party would not stand behind Marx. The Weimar alliance of the Social Democrats, Liberals, and the

Catholic Center had reached an agreement to send me into the race. I was honored to be asked, but I immediately declined. I had left Berlin after the assassination attempt and retreated to Schloss Freienwalde, where I concentrated on writing books. In retrospect I can say that these years between 1922 and 1925 were the happiest of my life. I enjoyed the status of being a political hero without having to suffer the indignities and frustrations of active political service. It was during this period that I completed what I consider to be my main oeuvre, *Zur Funktion der Welt*, in which I tried to address the problems caused by the growing materialism and anonymity of our world by suggesting that only working for the common good provides true personal satisfaction. The satisfaction that I derived from this work led me to ask myself why I would ever want to return to political life at all. Then I recalled the visit that Albert Einstein and Kurt Blumenfeld had paid me several years earlier. I recognized that my failure to follow their recommendation and decline the post of Foreign Minister had nearly cost me my life. But now the times were different. Germany had learned its lesson. Maybe my stubbornness back in the day had actually been worth the price. Maybe my suffering had taught the Germans that the disease of antisemitism could be cured.

When some of my former political colleagues insisted the next day that I should reconsider my stance, my resistance began to weaken. My friend, Count Harry Kessler, begged me to abandon my secluded life for the sake of Germany. Still I hesitated. Could I return to politics only three years after I had nearly lost my life? I decided that no politician could give me honest advice, and so I called on Einstein (Figure 26). At the time, I had no way of knowing that only a few years later he would find himself in a similar position when he was asked to become President of the new state of Judea. Einstein's answer to me was ironic as always: "If you are a successful President," he told me, "the Germans will see you as a German and the French as a European. If you are not successful, the French will see you as a German, and the Germans as a Jew." We laughed but then we became more serious. Einstein told me that he had changed his mind since our talk with Blumenfeld. He thought Germany was now ripe for the right leader, whether he be a Jew or a Christian. This conversation proved decisive for me. I saw no choice but to serve my country.

The election campaign was short but tough. The right wing lined up behind Hindenburg, the Communists behind Thälmann, and

Figure 26. Albert Einstein, who was instrumental in convincing Rathenau to run for the presidency of the Weimar Republic in 1925.

the center behind me. Finally, on April 29, 1925, the people spoke. I knew that Hindenburg and I would not be far apart and indeed the elections were close. I received 48.3 percent, Hindenburg 45.3 percent, and Thälmann 4.6 percent. The decision was a narrow one, but Hindenburg immediately conceded and wished me success. When I ran seven years later during my second campaign, I did not have such strong competition any more. But that, too, is a story for another chapter.

. . .

Einstein proved right again. Just as he had predicted the rise in antisemitism after my initial entry into politics, he was astute enough to note its decline a few years later. Germany had found a cure for one of humanity's worst maladies, Jew-hatred. The fact that, without any of my own doing, I became part of this fight makes me extremely proud. The abominable deed that almost cost me my life had made Germans open their eyes. The right-wing parties slowly vanished from the political spectrum. Ludendorff tried to come back after his stunning defeat in the first race of the 1925 elections, but his *völkisch* party slowly disappeared into oblivion.

I credit the stabilization of the political scene mainly to the consolidation of Germany's economy. In contrast to other politicians, I resisted the severe austerity measures they thought necessary for our recovery. Based on my own experience in economics and my theoretical writings, I recommended a more balanced course to counteract unemployment and at the same time stimulate the economy. Thus, our economy recovered within a decade, while America and some European countries were caught for many years in the Depression.

. . .

As a result, German Jews gradually began to recover from the shock they had experienced in the midst of political crisis. They began to feel more self-confident and less compelled to define themselves in apologetic ways that lacked any basis in reality. For years, German Jews had been secularized, or what Sigmund Freud wittily termed "Staatsbürger jüdischen Unglaubens" (citizens of Jewish unbelief). Yet the important Jewish self-defense organization, the Centralverein, stubbornly clung to its anachronistic view that Jews should regard themselves as "deutsche Staatsbürger jüdischen Glaubens" (German citizens of the Jewish faith). Gradually, though, this view began to change. Already before the First World War, the long-term president of the Centralverein, Eugen Fuchs, admitted that if the organization were established today, it would probably be called "Centralverein jüdischer Deutscher" (The Central Union of Jewish Germans).[7] It was only in the 1930s that the Centralverein finally adopted my own definition of what it meant to be Jewish in Germany. Being Jewish meant being one of Germany's many tribes (*Stämme*). As I had said already during the war, "My people are the

Germans, no one else. The Jews, for me, are a German tribe, just like the Saxons, Bavarians, or Wends."[8]

When Ludwig Holländer, the leading spirit behind the Centralverein, founded the new "League of Jewish Germans" in 1931 with the backing of some of our most outstanding citizens, such as Albert Einstein, Max Liebermann, and Lion Feuchtwanger, I was happy to open their founding event. As the Reich President, I did not want to join, but I felt reunited with my Jewish kinsmen and was happy to give a speech at their inaugural congress. I was satisfied that they admitted who they really were: an ethnic group within Germany, not tied to any particular religious belief and unshakeable in their German patriotism.

. . .

There were some extremists who wanted to exploit my appearance at the League's congress during the election campaign in 1932. They tried to draw connections between our country's economic difficulties and old antisemitic stereotypes about Jewish economic malfeasance. But, as we know, they had little success. The right-wing candidate, Alfred Hugenberg, from the German National People's Party, did not even make it to the second round, and my only serious opponent, the Catholic Center candidate, Heinrich Brüning, avoided the temptation to cater to anti-Jewish resentment.

I always believed that the Jewish tribe had contributed a great deal to German society. Germany has always taken the best from all of its tribes. Our country combines the orderliness of the Prussians, the relaxed manners of the Bavarians, and the slowness of the Frisians. The Jews added their wit. Theodor Fontane recognized this already before the turn of the century in what he called the specific "Berlin-Jewish spirit." For him, such a spirit consisted of "negation, criticism, jest, and sometimes also of joke." Indeed, without the contributions of the writers Heinrich Heine and Ludwig Börne, our culture would not have been the same. It would have lacked its wit. For this reason, I respect the biting satire of Kurt Tucholsky, even if I have sometimes been his target. This perceptive writer may even have played a role in saving our democracy by his fierce struggle against the enemies of the Republic.

. . .

Few people today know that I made a modest contribution to what historians have begun to call the renaissance of Jewish culture in Germany. In 1898, I published a series of Talmudic stories, which, in truth, were allegories of contemporary political events dressed as Jewish legends. After a long period of feeling alienated from Jewish culture, I am once again – in my old age – drawn to the texts of my ancestors. This is due, in large part, to Martin Buber, whose writings I have followed throughout my whole life. Ever since the University of Berlin established the first chair of Jewish Studies in 1933 and awarded it to Buber, we have been in close contact. I did not become religious as a result of our friendship, but I have become increasingly fascinated by the wisdom contained in Jewish texts. Buber established a little study group that I occasionally attended. He calls it by a Hebrew name, which I never remember. I call it the Wednesday Society. Many illustrious scholars regularly attend the group's meetings. Besides Buber, there is the eminent historian Simon Dubnow, who moved from Russia to Berlin in the early 1920s; there is also the young writer, Samuel Yosef Agnon, who moved to Berlin after fire destroyed his house in Bad Homburg. There are also a few younger intellectuals in the group: the writer Arnold Zweig, the philosopher Leo Strauss, and the rabbi Joachim Prinz. He is the rising star in Berlin's Jewish religious establishment. His Friday-evening sermons, on topics ranging from German literature and Jewish history to present-day antisemitism and Zionism, are avidly followed by a large and mainly young audience. Prinz once told me that he was attending a lecture by my friend Ernst Troeltsch at the University of Berlin on the day of the attempt on my life, and that Troeltsch canceled his lecture that day with the words, "This is the beginning of the German tragedy."[9]

. . .

My relationship with Zionism is complex. On the one hand, I have long sympathized with the efforts of Herzl and Blumenfeld to solve the "Jewish Question." On the other hand, I have always been uncomfortable with their methods of doing so. My discomfort became especially pronounced in 1938 with the creation of the state of Judea. To be sure, I was pleased that the League of Nations adopted the recommendation of the British Peel Commission to divide Palestine into separate Arab and Jewish states. But I immediately made it clear that my support of the Jewish state should not put Jews in a position of having to rebut charges of dual loyalty. The British asked me, along with France's Jewish Prime Minister Léon Blum and Italy's Jewish Foreign Minister, Aldo Finzi, to serve as mediator in the ensuing conflict between Jews and Arabs.

Our team arrived in Tel Aviv in October 1938, just when war seemed unavoidable. We made clear to the Arabs that we understood their position and had come to safeguard both Jewish and Arab rights to their respective states. It was only once we were able to convince them that Western European Jews had no reason to emigrate to Palestine, and once we promised to lift immigration restrictions for Eastern European Jewish refugees who wanted to settle in Germany, France, and Italy, that the Arabs were willing to compromise. Unfortunately, our efforts to convince the British government to make its own compromises were initially unsuccessful. But the British eventually accepted partition once they received the promise of a permanent corridor between Jerusalem and Jaffa.

The hardest task was to convince the Zionist leadership, especially David Ben-Gurion and Vladimir Jabotinsky, of the need to forge a deal. Both men insisted on their historical rights, and Jabotinsky continued to lay claim to the land on both sides of the River Jordan. When we reached an agreement on a population exchange between 225,000 Arabs and 1,500 Jews, it helped to reduce their resistance. But had it not been for the increasingly dramatic situation in the Soviet Union, I might not have been able to convince them.

Starting in the late 1930s, Stalin had begun a relentless anti-semitic campaign targeting Jewish intellectuals and doctors. His goal was to remove Jews from high positions in society. The effects were catastrophic. Jews could not emigrate but neither were they safe in Russia. Pogroms began to erupt. The world condemned the Soviet government, but to no avail. These tragic events created a climate of panic among the Zionist movement's leaders and convinced even Jabotinsky to accept a Jewish state in its very restricted borders, stretching from Mount Carmel in the north to Be'er Tuviah in the south. When French Prime Minister Blum succeeded in convincing Stalin to let Soviet Jews emigrate to the future state of Judea, the Zionist leaders had no choice but to accept as well.

On November 27, 1938, the League of Nations voted for partition, and I am proud to say that Germany was the first country to recognize the Jewish state, which was officially founded three weeks later on the eve of Hanukkah. Like the ancient Hanukkah miracle, Jews all over the world celebrated the reestablishment of the state of Judea. It was a wonderful gesture to offer Albert Einstein the presidency of the new state. He hesitated, and this time, he came to me to ask for advice. I told him that I would prefer to see him remain in Germany, but I ultimately recommended that he accept the offer – for the sake of the Jewish state. After long consideration – and especially in view of the fact that the position was mainly ceremonial – he gave in and became Judea's first President.

I accepted Einstein's ensuing invitation to participate in the independence celebrations. It was my first trip to Judea, and I would be lying if I said I was not moved. Like most of my fellow German Jews, I have no desire to settle in the Jewish state and I feel no special attachment to the Orient. But I have to admit that I have a lot of respect for what the small state has already achieved during its brief existence. One of the League of Nations' demands was that neither the Jewish nor the Arab states would have an army. Thus the enormous amount of tax revenue that other states sink into their military budgets is spent in Judea on culture and education. Herzl's utopian agenda of French-style opera houses, English-style boarding schools, and Austrian-style coffee houses have become a reality in Tel Aviv. There is only one significant difference, one that Herzl would not have liked: Hebrew is spoken everywhere. I agree with Herzl, as I could not even buy a train ticket in the Holy Land. Who needs to speak a dead language when so many cultured languages spoken in the civilized world are available!

The tensions between Jews and Arabs did not disappear. But the population exchange, the creation of the British corridor, and the de-militarized status of the two states have all created a viable status quo in which both peoples live side by side in relative peace.

To be sure, Judea today remains dependent on Jewish support from the diaspora. Wealthy German and French Jews help the fledgling middle class in Judea, as do wealthy Jews from Baghdad and Cairo. With the rise of a Jewish state, these ancient centers of Jewish life have flourished and contributed to the well-being of the Arab world as well as to that of the Jewish state. It seems that Zionism is mainly a European movement and that most Arab Jews want to stay in their home countries and are happy to pay occasional visits to Judea.

As long as the region's Jewish population does not grow out of proportion to that of the Arabs, as long as the small state remains viable, conflict can be avoided. When I left office after finishing my second term as Reich President in 1939, the situation in Judea remained stable.

But before long, another of the world's important Jewish communities faced a crisis. With the election of Charles Lindbergh as President of the United States in 1940, American Jews suddenly became uncertain about their future. As we all remember, Lindbergh defeated incumbent Franklin D. Roosevelt by running on a platform opposing any conflict with the Soviet Union. At the time, Great Britain and Jewish organizations in the United States had been calling for immediate action to save the lives of Russian Jews. Roosevelt gave the impression of supporting such action. Lindbergh, however, objected and criticized Roosevelt's position in sharp terms. In so doing, he also gave vent to blatantly antisemitic views, attacking what he described as the overly large Jewish influence in Hollywood, on Wall Street, and in the American press. While Jews lost their jobs and some were even murdered in the streets of Moscow and Kiev, the new American government remained silent. The economic depression further stoked anti-Jewish sentiments in the United States to the great dismay of the big Jewish communities in Berlin, London, Cairo, and Baghdad, where huge street demonstrations protested the US President's antisemitic tendencies.

Europeans never imagined that Lindbergh would defeat President Roosevelt, and when this happened it immediately caused a transatlantic crisis. As I write these lines, the United States Congress is debating whether to enact laws restricting the negative effects of "Jewish influence" on American life. Universities have already introduced anti-Jewish quotas. Racist groups in the South have lynched more than a dozen Jews. And everywhere one hears calls for the boycott of Jewish businesses. The new US government is closely allied with the oil-producing Arab states and has withdrawn its ambassador from Tel Aviv due to Arab pressure. I fear that the American Jewish community, 5 million strong, may eventually have to look for a future in Judea or go back to Europe. My successor as Reich President, the talented Dr. Paul Arnheim, whose policy resembles my own path in almost every respect, has convened an international conference in Montreux and has already offered to grant asylum to 100,000 American Jews in Germany.

Looking back on the twenty years that have passed since the attempt on my life, I am astounded by the unexpected course of Jewish history. Who would have predicted in 1922 that the Jew-hatred that once threatened to spread across Germany would be restricted to an insignificant minority of extremists? Who would have thought that the

Jews would have established their own state in the Middle East? Who would have dared imagine that America, the longtime refuge of Jews fleeing European antisemitism, would itself become vulnerable to the same intolerance? I do not know what the future holds, but if we learn anything from the Jewish past, it is not to be too hopeful when things look right and not to give up hope when things seem wrong.

13 WHAT IF ADOLF HITLER HAD BEEN ASSASSINATED IN 1939?*

Gavriel D. Rosenfeld

YAD VASHEM
The Holocaust Martyrs Remembrance Authority
PO Box 3477
Jerusalem, Israel
Tel.: 026443400

28 November 1959

Mr. Manfred Bühl
Kuhmoosweg 21
78464 Konstanz
Germany

Dear Mr. Bühl,

We are pleased to announce that the Commission for Designation of the Righteous has decided to award the title of "Righteous Among the Nations" to your late father, Johann Georg Elser, for risking his life to help Jews during the period of the Holocaust (Figure 27).[1]

A medal and certificate of honor will be mailed to the Israeli embassy in Berlin, which will organize a ceremony in his honor. Please take into consideration that the process of preparing the award will take at least one month. In the future, his name will be added on the Righteous Honor Wall at Yad Vashem in Jerusalem.

* This chapter is a work of fiction.

Figure 27. Georg Elser, who in 1959 was posthumously awarded the title, "Righteous Among the Nations," by the Israeli Holocaust Martyrs Remembrance Authority, Yad Vashem, for his assassination of Nazi Germany's dictator, Adolf Hitler, in 1939.

Ordinarily, we would request that you forward us documentary materials pertaining to your father, especially photos and letters. But given the special circumstances of your relationship to Mr. Elser, we will forego this request. We respect the fact that it was only recently that you learned the news of your father's existence and, more importantly, his responsibility for the assassination of Germany's dictator, Adolf Hitler, twenty years ago on November 8, 1939.

Like so many other people worldwide, our committee was taken entirely by surprise when we read the sensational report in the *Neue*

Zürcher Zeitung (*NZZ*) last year about Mr. Elser's decision, just before his death at age fifty-five, to reveal to the Swiss press – and to you personally in a separate letter – the story of his historic deed and subsequent years in hiding. His decision to inform you that it was he, and not Hans Bühl – the man you knew as your father – who impregnated your mother, Mathilde Niedermann, in 1930 must have come as a personal shock. How much more so to learn that your father – a man with whom you had never spoken – had probably changed the course of history!

Given the sensitivity of these circumstances, the committee has decided to take the unusual step of sending you a draft of the press release that we have prepared explaining our rationale for honoring your father. Ever since Yad Vashem decided to start recognizing Christian rescuers of Jews several years ago, the committee has emphasized the following criteria: "extending help in saving a life; endangering one's own life; absence of reward, monetary and otherwise; and similar considerations which make the rescuers' deeds stand out above and beyond what can be termed ordinary help."[2] Based on this set of criteria, the committee firmly believes that Mr. Elser fulfills the conditions for our award.

To be sure, we understand that your father was highly conflicted about his deed. As was reported in the *NZZ*, in the years after the assassination, he was plagued by doubts that he had inadvertently made life worse, rather than better, for Europe's Jews. His decision to seek a life of exile and anonymity in the Swiss Alps – while originally motivated by fear of being discovered by the Gestapo – clearly reflected his reluctance to be linked to an act that, however unintentionally, contributed to the death of approximately 1 million Jews. That said, his decision not to leave this earth without taking responsibility for shaping its history ultimately attests to his faith in the rightness of his actions. As the enclosed document makes clear, the committee shares the view that Elser's actions arguably prevented an even worse fate for Europe's Jews.

If you would be so kind as to review the document and send us any comments, we would be grateful. We do hope you are able to attend the ceremony.

Sincerely yours,

Shmuel Shaphat
Director, Department for the Righteous

YAD VASHEM PRESS RELEASE
"Georg Elser recognized as Righteous Among the Nations"
Final Draft: November 1, 1959
(do not circulate or quote without permission)

Preface

Yad Vashem was established in 1947 to perpetuate the memory of the nearly 1 million Jewish victims of the Holocaust. One of Yad Vashem's principal duties is to convey the gratitude of the state of Israel and the Jewish people to non-Jews who risked their lives to save Jews during the Holocaust. This mission was defined by the law establishing Yad Vashem, and in 1958 the Remembrance Authority embarked upon a worldwide project to grant the title of Righteous Among the Nations to those who helped Jews in the darkest time in their history. To this end, Yad Vashem set up a public commission, headed by a Supreme Court justice, which examines each case and is responsible for granting the title. Those recognized receive a medal and a certificate of honor and their names are commemorated on the Mount of Remembrance in Jerusalem.[3]

Text

Johann Georg Elser (1903–58) has been awarded the title of Righteous Among the Nations for his humanitarian courage in assassinating the modern scourge of the Jewish people, Adolf Hitler.

Elser did not undertake his fateful deed on behalf of the Jews. A trained carpenter, he was a proud member of the German working class and shared its general antipathy toward the Nazi dictatorship. Not only did Elser blame Hitler for the economic woes of Germany's laborers, he feared that the Führer was taking the country down the path of war. By 1938, Elser resolved to save his country by eliminating the man who was leading it to ruin. "Through my deed," he wrote in his letter to the NZZ, "I hoped to prevent an even greater spilling of blood."[4]

Elser's plan was to detonate a time bomb in Munich's famous Bürgerbräukeller on the occasion of the annual Nazi Party assembly commemorating the Beer Hall Putsch of November 9, 1923. Over the course of many months, working mostly at night, Elser gathered and assembled the bomb-making materials, placing them inside a hollow column behind the podium where Hitler was scheduled to deliver his address to over one thousand longstanding party members, or *Alte Kämpfer*.

On the fateful evening of November 8, Elser set the bomb to explode at exactly 9:20 p.m., at a point when he knew that Hitler would be in the middle of his speech. A quirk of fate made sure that the bomb found its target. As was later disclosed by the German press, Hitler was originally scheduled to fly back to Berlin immediately after his speech in order to finalize plans for the invasion of France, which he had ordered for November 12. Earlier that day, however, dense fog grounded all flights from Munich's airport in Riem and led Hitler's staff to make new plans for him to travel back to Berlin by train. In order to minimize the lateness of his arrival in the capital, the dictator planned to leave Munich earlier than scheduled by cutting the length of his speech. Had he done so, he would have narrowly escaped the blast. Just before he began to deliver his remarks, however, Hitler received a message that the fog had lifted enough to enable his plane to depart on schedule after all. Buoyed by this fortuitous turn of events, Hitler decided to use his original speech. At 9:20 p.m., with the crowd wildly cheering the dictator's bellicose attacks against Great Britain, the bomb exploded.

Hitler was not the only one killed in the blast. More than one hundred people lost their lives, including some of the NSDAP elite, many of whom, positioned directly in front of the speaker's podium, were crushed to death by the collapse of the Bürgerbräukeller's ceiling. In addition to Hitler, the victims included SS chief Heinrich Himmler, the Führer's deputy Rudolf Hess, the Chief of the Party Chancellery Martin Bormann, DAF head Robert Ley, and the editor of *Der Stürmer*, Julius Streicher. Many others were severely wounded, including Minister of the Interior Wilhelm Frick and party ideologue Alfred Rosenberg. Certain figures, such as Reich Main Security Office (RSHA) chief, Reinhard Heydrich, came away with merely a few scratches. And two key party leaders were spared altogether: Reich Propaganda Minister Joseph Goebbels, who had momentarily stepped away from the gathering to use the bathroom when the bomb exploded; and Luftwaffe chief Hermann Goering, who had remained in Berlin for reasons of security.[5]

The blast immediately sparked chaos in Germany. Because there were no claims of responsibility, wild rumors spread about possible perpetrators. Suspicion immediately fell upon a range of culprits: the

British, the Jews, Bavarian monarchists, and Hitler's rival, Otto Strasser. Heydrich immediately ordered the Gestapo and the SD to cast a wide dragnet in the effort to identify the guilty parties. Thousands of suspects were arrested and interrogated, but to no avail. The Nazis never discovered that the man responsible – Elser – had acted on his own. By the time a Bürgerbräukeller waitress identified him as a possible suspect, five days had passed and he had vanished.

As he recently explained in his letter, Elser slipped undetected from Germany into Switzerland the day before the assassination. He had originally planned to visit his sister, Maria, in Stuttgart on November 6 and then return to Munich the next day to make a final check on the bomb before heading to Konstanz on the German–Swiss border on November 8.[6] After receiving a letter from Maria notifying him that she was sick with a severe case of influenza and would prefer him to delay his visit, however, Elser decided not to go to Stuttgart and left for Switzerland a day early. When he arrived in Konstanz on the morning of November 7, he used the extra time to make a preliminary visit to the border fence where he hoped to cross later that night. This visit proved decisive. Although Elser had remembered the border as lightly guarded when he had last been there in 1938, he now saw that security had been tightened due to the war.[7] He thus took several hours to observe the guards' patrols and locate the best possible crossing point. "Thanks to my surveillance of the scene," Elser recalled, "I was able to plan my escape for the moment when the guards were relieved by replacements and were partly distracted. I used that opportunity to scamper to the fence and quickly cut my way through with a pair of wire cutters." When the bomb detonated the next evening, Elser had already been on Swiss territory for twenty-four hours and had slipped from sight. He was easily able to fall into his familiar itinerant lifestyle, wandering between towns and working on sporadic carpentry jobs for room and board. After amassing some modest savings, he headed into the mountains and disappeared for good.

Before doing so, however, Elser witnessed the consequences of his actions. "Every day," he recalled, "despite being constantly on the move, I sought out newspapers and tried to learn about the Nazis' reaction to Hitler's death (Figure 28). The more I read, the more disturbed I became." Elser's reaction reflected the crisis that engulfed Germany in the assassination's wake. The country's most pressing task after the bombing was to settle the question of leadership. On this question, there

Figure 28. Postage stamp of Adolf Hitler. This commemorative stamp was released by the Deutsche Reichspost shortly after Hitler's death in 1939. Note the SS runes designating his birth and death dates.

was little debate. Ever since 1934, Hermann Goering had been Hitler's officially designated successor. Goering had long been the second most powerful man in Nazi Germany, with considerable influence over the country's economy and military. With Hitler's demise, he swiftly asserted himself as head of state. In his first public speech to the German people, a day after Hitler's death, he vowed to punish the parties responsible for the attack and honor Hitler's legacy by governing in the spirit of the *Führerprinzip*. Despite his assertive stance, however,

Goering was far from secure in power. Behind the scenes, tensions were building between different factions within the Nazi regime. Radicals representing the party and security establishment, such as Goebbels and Heydrich (who succeeded Himmler as the head of the SS), remained committed to pursuing Hitler's ideologically rooted military and political agenda, while representatives of the Wehrmacht preferred to steer a more moderate course. The stage was thus set for a power struggle.

The first step in the struggle was taken by the radicals. Three days after Hitler's death, on November 11, Goebbels delivered a fiery speech before thousands of party members at Munich's Feldherrnhale, in which he blamed the Jews and the British for Hitler's death. Declaring that "a plutocratic cabal of Anglo-Jewish warmongers had descended to a new level of treachery with their killing of the Führer," Goebbels mobilized popular antisemitism to rally Germans behind him and assert his own leadership role in the state. Describing the attack as a "second Jewish *Dolchstoss*," or "stab in the back," Goebbels praised Hitler as a "seeker of peace" and ominously predicted – just as the Propaganda Minister had done on Kristallnacht one year earlier – that "the Jews will once again feel the *Volk*'s anger."

In short order, countless Germans – shocked by the death of the man they had come to view as the nation's most important historical leader – dutifully obeyed and began to avenge themselves on Hitler's alleged killers.[8] Unlike on Kristallnacht, however, Germans this time did not merely target Jewish property (businesses and synagogues having already been laid waste in 1938) but Jewish persons. Across the country, Jews were murdered with impunity. Thousands were arrested by the Gestapo on suspicion of being involved in the assassination plot and sent to concentration camps, where countless numbers were shot by infuriated SS guards. In Munich, many Jews were taken to the Gestapo headquarters at the Wittelsbacher Palais, where they were brutally interrogated and then transported to Dachau where they met their demise. Elsewhere, Jews were attacked in their homes by wild bands of SA men, who beat and shot them to death. In Dresden, the famed diarist Victor Klemperer reported that SA men raided most of the thirty-seven "Jews' homes" (*Judenhäuser*), setting some on fire, and murdering dozens of their inhabitants.[9] Thousands of Jews across the country lost their lives in this manner. The violence lasted several days. But it hardly sated the regime's blood-lust.

Similar violence erupted outside of the *Altreich*. In Austria and the Protectorate of Bohemia and Moravia, Jews were killed by SA and SS men, as well as their local sympathizers. The worst violence, however, was in Poland. Already before Hitler's death, Einsatzgruppen units and Wehrmacht troops had raided Jewish towns and villages, destroying businesses, burning synagogues, and murdering thousands of Jews.[10] Similar atrocities now erupted in the annexed portions of West Prussia, Upper Silesia, and the Warthegau, as well as in the cities of the German-occupied General Government.

This violence was merely a prelude, however, to a more radical policy of mass deportation. Before Hitler's death, in September 1939, leading figures in the SS, such as Himmler and Heydrich, along with Nazi Party leaders such as Alfred Rosenberg, had devised a plan to send Polish Jews from the *Altreich* (as well as from the newly annexed Polish territories) to a "Jewish reservation" in the Lublin district of the General Government. The project, which was also known as the "Nisko Plan" (named after the railway stop from which Jews were sent to the reservation), was intended to house Jews in forced labor camps, where they would be compelled to drain marshes and help build fortifications – for instance, antitank ditches – along the new German–Soviet border. Millions of Jews were envisaged as ending up in the marshy region, where they were expected to die from attrition. Hitler strongly supported the plan and in early October 1939 ordered the deportation of the 300,000 Jews still living in Germany and Austria. (This information comes from the testimony of SS officer, Adolf Eichmann, who, at his recent trial at the Wehrmacht military tribunal in Berlin, confirmed that he himself took the first steps toward implementing Hitler's order by sending nearly 5,000 Jews to Lublin from Vienna, Katowice, and the Moravian town of Ostrava.) Just as soon as the deportations from the *Altreich* commenced, however, they were halted. As Eichmann testified, Himmler decided to prioritize settling ethnic Germans in the newly annexed lands and decreed that, in order to make room for them, the Jews of the region (estimated at around 600,000 people) first had to be deported to the Lublin reservation.[11]

These measures, which began while Hitler was still alive, were expanded and accelerated after his death. Hoping to continue the momentum generated by the upsurge of antisemitism in Germany, in mid November Heydrich ordered the expulsion not only of the Jews of the Warthegau, but of the 300,000 Jews of the *Altreich*, as well as the 350,000 Jews living in the Protectorate and the puppet state of Slovakia. Goebbels publicly explained the policy by invoking Hitler's famous prophecy from January 1, 1939 (in which he predicted the Jews' annihilation in the event of a world war), thundering that they "would now suffer the gradual process of extermination they had planned for us."[12] For its part, the SS swiftly mobilized the Reich's entire transport capacity for the deportation program. The German railway system figured prominently in the effort, with hundreds of passenger and freight trains, each crammed with up to a thousand Jews, heading to the east. Jews were also packed onto buses and driven out of the country.[13] By early January 1940, most of the targeted Jews had been shipped to the transit hub of Nisko. From there, they were forcibly marched to the marshy land outside Lublin. Many died in transit. Others were shot. Those that arrived were left to fend for themselves. Exposed to harsh weather conditions (the winter of 1939–40 was one of the coldest on record), many froze and starved to death.[14] Still others died in work camps established by the chief administrator of the reservation, Odilo Globocnik.[15] Others were killed in spontaneous mob actions organized by ethnic Germans (and some Poles), who bitterly resented the wave of new arrivals.

The death toll of these deportations has never been established with certainty. But of the 1.2 million Jews affected by them, there were probably around three-quarters of a million Jewish victims. The death toll becomes even larger if we include the 50,000 Polish Jewish POWs shot by the Germans and the 100,000 Polish Jews who, after fleeing into Soviet-occupied Poland, perished in Siberia after being deported there by Soviet troops.[16] There were survivors, of course. Many Jews fled from the Lublin reservation into the nascent ghettos of the General Government, most notably that of Warsaw. Others slipped into Soviet territory and successfully evaded capture. On balance, however, the deportations were an unmitigated disaster for the Jews.

The deportation program also had serious repercussions for the Germans. Throughout the fall of 1939, press reports had drawn international attention to the Jews' suffering in Poland and caused a political crisis for Goering's government.[17] Like the world's response to the Kristallnacht pogrom, there was widespread condemnation of the Nazi regime – especially in the United States and Britain – for its excesses against the Jews.[18] At first, Goering claimed that the reports of

Jewish deaths were exaggerated, insisting that they were merely work-ing in labor camps. In doing so, he sought to maintain the support of the SS, whose leaders originally justified the reservation plan as a means of turning the Jews into hostages who could be used to exert "diplomatic pressure against the Western Powers" and compel them to come to an agreement with Germany.[19] By early December, however, Germany's failure to bring Britain and France to the bargaining table led the radi-cals to change course and push ahead with Hitler's goal of launching a military attack in the west. In so doing, they put Goering in a difficult position.

By this time, Goering had become fully aware of the Wehrma-cht's opposition to expanding the war in the west. Ever since 1937–8, many of Germany's leading generals, such as Werner von Blomberg, Werner von Fritsch, Ludwig Beck, Franz Halder, and Erwin von Wit-zleben, together with representatives of the Abwehr (military intelli-gence), such as Wilhelm Canaris and Hans Oster, had been opposed to what they saw as Hitler's reckless warmongering. In the summer of 1938, a group of these men, led by Beck and Canaris, began plotting a coup to remove Hitler from power before he made good on his plan to invade Czechoslovakia. Hitler's unexpected success at the Munich con-ference in September of 1938 forced the plotters to shelve their plan, but they dusted it off again once the Führer, fresh off his victory over Poland, instructed the generals in October 1939 to plan for an immi-nent invasion of France several weeks later. Many of the generals – even loyalists such as Walter von Brauchitsch and Wilhelm Keitel – told Hitler that the army was unprepared for such a major conflict, which they expected to last at least three years. Included among the naysayers was the head of the Navy, Admiral Raeder, who informed Hitler that Germany could not compete with Britain on the seas. None of these protests was able to sway the Führer, however, who remained steadfastly committed to his invasion timetable. As a result, plans for a coup were hatched by yet another group of military men, most notably Halder, General Carl-Heinrich von Stülpnagel, and Lieutenant Colonel Hen-ning von Tresckow. Before they could proceed, however, Elser's bomb exploded in Munich, thereby sparing them the need to act. With Hitler gone, the generals grew more confident about pursuing an end to the conflict with Britain and France.[20]

An important reason for the generals' stance was their aware-ness of Germany's economic weakness. The worsening budgetary situation and shortages of natural resources had already slowed the pace of rearmament by 1939. Germany was spending nearly a quarter of its national wealth on arms, while its Western foes had only begun to tap their spending potential. Hitler's attack on Poland had been timed to make the most of Germany's head start in rearmament, but the generals knew that the country's enemies would soon catch up. The Polish campaign forced the generals to realize that Germany could not compete economically. Ammunition shortages were severe (in the Polish campaign, the consumption of ammunition had outpaced production by a factor of seven). British and French blockades had cut Germany off from world markets and needed resources. Shortages of fuel (caused by transport problems) and workers further sobered up the generals. So did the breakoff of trade negotiations with the Soviet Union following Hitler's death. The only way Germany could afford to fight was by plundering the economies of the nations it defeated. But this required a degree of violence that the generals were loath to sanction.[21]

Indeed, concerns about the crimes committed by German forces in the east also prompted the generals to seek an end to the war. Already during the Polish campaign, high-level military commanders, among them Blaskowitz, Reichenau, Küchler, List, Mackensen, and Stief, along with senior officers, had complained to Hitler about atrocities committed by the SS against Jews and Poles and had ordered investigations and even court martials.[22] To be sure, these protests stemmed less from moral outrage than from concerns about the possible damage to military discipline and the army's overall reputation. The generals also complained that SS actions – especially the Nisko Plan – impeded the Wehrmacht's effort to reimpose order in occupied Poland.[23] These reservations about SS policies merely reinforced the Wehrmacht's longstanding suspicions of the rival organization that dated back to the latter's role in purging leading generals during the Night of the Long Knives in 1934 and the Blomberg/Fritsch scandal of 1938.[24]

For his part, Goering shared many of the generals' views. Although he supported much of Hitler's foreign policy vision and had pushed him to annex Austria in 1938, he was more reluctant to support the Führer's plans to invade Czechoslovakia, Poland, and France.[25] It is true that Goering never supported any of the plots against Hitler and remained loyal to him as long as he lived. But once Hitler was gone, Goering did not find it difficult to switch over to the generals' position. He especially supported their desire to restore order in the occupied eastern territories of Poland. Although Goering was no defender of the Jews, having supported their political disenfranchisement, economic expropriation, and physical expulsion, he also recognized the disruptions caused by the atrocities against them. He had listened sympathetically to the complaints of Hans Frank, the Nazi ruler of the General Government, about the chaos caused by the endless shipments of Jews into his territory. Finally, Goering's responsibility for the Four-Year Plan made him eager to reorient the General Government's purpose from plunder to production, thereby serving the needs of Germany's military.[26]

Yet, despite adhering to such views, Goering had to tread carefully, for any effort to halt the SS's radical agenda was sure to meet with resistance, if not an outright power grab. In short, Goering faced a dilemma similar to the one confronted by Hitler just before the Night of the Long Knives. At that time, the new Chancellor had faced a dual threat: one from below, in the form of party radicals urging him to pursue a "second revolution"; and one from above, in the form of old elites wanting a return to order. Now, six years later, Goering also had a choice to make: between seeking the loyalty of the party radicals and SS by continuing their racial antisemitic vision of war and conquest; or the loyalty of the Wehrmacht leadership, which leaned toward peace. If he sided with the SS, Goering risked a military coup. If he chose the army, he risked an uprising by the SS. He could not do both.

In the end, Goering sided with the Wehrmacht and chose a path of moderation. He knew the chief lesson of the Night of the Long Knives: that it was impossible to rule Germany without the army's support. If this was true in 1934, it was even more so after five years of rearmament. Although the Reichswehr had been limited to 100,000 men by the Treaty of Versailles and was scarcely larger in 1934, by the start of World War II it boasted nearly 5 million men in uniform. This dwarfed the size of the SS, whose armed units (divided between Leibstandarte, Verfügungstruppen, and Totenkopf formations) numbered only around 40,000.[27] Moreover, SS troops lacked anything like the heavy weapons enjoyed by the Wehrmacht.[28] Finally, Goering sided with the generals in order to shore up his own political base. Since August 1934, when the Reichswehr leadership had sworn a personal oath of loyalty to Hitler, the army had been obliged to serve a single individual, not a country. Following Hitler's death, however, the army was released from its oath and regained an important measure of independence. It was not obliged to follow Goering's lead. Because he could not take the Wehrmacht's loyalty for granted and desperately needed its support, Goering had to listen to the generals' increasing concerns about Germany's radical turn under Goebbels and Heydrich.

For all of these reasons, Goering forged a secret agreement with the Wehrmacht in late December 1939 to assume joint control of the government and eliminate the threat posed by the radicals. On January 4, 1940, the Wehrmacht launched its purge. In scenes reminiscent of events that transpired twenty-one years earlier during the Spartacist uprising of 1919, the streets of Berlin were transformed into a battlefield for several days. While regular Wehrmacht troops took up positions in the city center, positioning machine guns at the Brandenburg Gate, elite units, together with *Fallschirmjäger* (paratroopers) belonging to Goering's *Luftwaffe*, surrounded RSHA headquarters on the Prinz-Albrecht-Strasse and moved to arrest the security establishment's leaders. In the firefights that followed, Heydrich and Gestapo chief Heinrich Müller were killed, in addition to lesser figures, such as Ernst Kaltenbrunner. Others, such as Adolf Eichmann, were captured. At the same time, Wehrmacht soldiers raided the Propaganda Ministry in order to arrest Goebbels, but found him dead in his office (reportedly having committed suicide by taking cyanide). Following similar military assaults against SS offices in Vienna and Prague, the security establishment was effectively neutralized. In short order, Canaris and Oster maneuvered the Abwehr to take over the RSHA's responsibilities for domestic and foreign intelligence.

Following the violent events in Berlin, Goering faced the challenging task of explaining the Wehrmacht's actions to the German people. Here again, he took a lesson from Hitler, modeling his explanation on the Führer's rationalization of the SA purge in 1934. In a major speech delivered on January 7 from the balcony of the Reich Chancellery in Berlin to several thousand onlookers, Goering described the rationale for the army's campaign against the RSHA by blaming it for a host of misdeeds. He condemned it as incompetent for having failed to prevent Hitler's assassination and arrest the persons responsible. He accused it of besmirching Germany's international image by unilaterally pursuing crimes against Jewish and Polish civilians in occupied Poland. And he charged it with pushing for a reckless war against France and Britain. He even hinted at the involvement of the SS (along with rogue elements in Hitler's Chancellery) in the killing of mentally and physically handicapped Germans, rumors of which had been circulating in Germany since the fall of 1939.[29] In making these accusations, Goering was careful not to implicate Hitler – who was still beloved by the German people – claiming that "if the Führer had only known" of the crimes committed by his underlings, he would have been furious. Goering further reassured the German people of his commitment to peace, insisting that the last thing Hitler wanted was for Germany to become embroiled in a prolonged war in the west.

On the domestic front, Goering was vague about the nature of Germany's future political order, but he spoke of creating a "true form of National Socialism," purged of all lawless elements and rooted in conservative military traditions. To this end, Goering permanently retired the title of "Führer." He pledged to govern Germany in his capacity as the president of the Reichstag, which he promised to reactivate and have function as an advisory body to his cabinet of generals, which possessed the main decision-making power in the state. He also brought in scattered conservative political leaders, such as Ulrich von Hassell and Carl Goerdeler, to lend his government a veneer of civilian respectability.

Goering's conservative turn was disingenuous and opportunistic, as he himself had supported many of the radicals' policies while Hitler lived. But they were a necessary precondition for pursuing peace negotiations with Britain and France. Goering clearly recognized the need for such a turn, as he had previously been involved in sending out peace feelers via intermediaries toward the two nations prior to the invasion of Poland, as well as following its surrender in October of 1939.[30] At the time, these efforts had been roundly rejected by Britain and France, whose leaders argued that the *sine qua non* for any settlement was "the destruction of Hitlerism."[31] With Hitler gone, however, a new window of opportunity began to open.

It opened fully in February 1940. By this time, the war had reached a pivotal juncture. Since the start of the German–Polish conflict, Britain and France had been at war with Germany only in a technical sense, with hardly any fighting taking place on the ground in Western Europe. On the seas, however, battles had flared between the German and British navies. As it happened, one of these battles provided the opportunity for a diplomatic breakthrough. On February 16, 1940, the British destroyer, HMS *Cossack*, attacked the German oil tanker and supply ship, *Altmark*, in Norwegian waters, freeing 200 British sailors from German captivity. At first, the episode gave a morale boost to the British, angered the Germans, and threatened to inflame hostilities. But behind the scenes peace feelers had been in circulation for weeks, and both nations' military leaders recognized that exploiting the episode for short-term political gain would put them on the slippery slope toward a larger military confrontation on land. Both were particularly afraid of the war spreading to Scandinavia (which was ripe for being pulled into the conflict following the Soviet invasion of Finland in November 1939 and because of Germany's ongoing desire to guarantee its supply of Swedish iron ore). To prevent this from happening, both sides pulled back and decided to negotiate.

The negotiations, which began in Switzerland in April 1940, ultimately led to a peace agreement two months later in June. The Treaty of Zurich involved compromises on all sides. Although Britain and France initially demanded the restoration of independence for Poland and Czechoslovakia (Austria was permitted to stay German), the Western Allies surrendered to the realities on the ground. The Soviet Union's refusal to withdraw from eastern Poland (Stalin rejected the invitation to attend the conference) meant that the *status quo ante* could not be restored in any case. Moreover, the Wehrmacht's refusal to surrender the Polish corridor around Danzig – in addition to the demographic changes caused by the expulsion of Poles and Jews from the annexed territories – made it difficult for the French and British to insist upon the restoration of full Polish sovereignty. (This was especially difficult as the two countries had not actively defended the country in the first place.) Instead, the French and British accepted Germany's withdrawal from the General Government, which created a rump Polish state more or less similar to the kingdom of 1815; they also accepted Germany's withdrawal from Bohemia and Moravia, which created a rump Czech state (Slovakia remained independent). It was an imperfect agreement for both sides, but they preferred it to a direct military confrontation. Tensions between the Germans and their Slavic neighbors remained high in the years that followed, even after the completion of agreed-upon population transfers. But they were somewhat mitigated by British and French economic assistance, which helped facilitate the reconstruction of Polish urban areas and the resettlement of displaced persons.

A far more vexing problem involved the fate of the Jews. Even though the Wehrmacht's purge of the SS brought the direct killing of Jews to a halt in early January, Goering's government did nothing to provide aid to Jewish survivors, who lacked all basic necessities and continued to die of attrition in large numbers until the spring. The death of nearly 1 million Jewish men, women, and children in occupied Poland represented the worst disaster experienced by the Jews in their modern history, exceeding the massacres of Chmielnicki in the mid seventeenth century and Petlura during World War I. The Nazi atrocities, indeed, were widely seen as comparable to the Turks' killing of Armenians in World War I. Among Jews, it gave rise to new terms of designation: "Churbn" (used by Yiddish-speaking Jews) and "Shoah" (used by Hebrew-speaking Zionists). In recent years, the word "Holocaust" has gained prominence in the English-speaking world. Beyond the dead, hundreds of thousands of Jews were stateless refugees and faced little hope of returning to their homes. Immediately following the cessation of hostilities in 1940, relief organizations tried to ameliorate the Jews' plight. The American Committee to Save Central European Jews (modeled after the American Committee for Relief in the Near East, which was devoted to aiding displaced Armenians in 1915) led a relief campaign to tend to the needs of Jewish refugees. But the difficulties faced by the organization merely underscored the need for a comprehensive solution to Europe's Jewish problem.

This was especially true since Jews elsewhere in Europe were also in dire need. Already in the 1930s, Eastern European Jews in Poland, Czechoslovakia, Hungary, Romania, and the Baltic States had suffered increasing persecution, having been subjected to economic discrimination and the revocation of their civil and political rights.[32] A piecemeal solution addressing merely the needs of Jews in Poland was thus inadequate.

Following the Zurich Peace Conference, therefore, Britain, France, and Germany, together with the United States, convened a second conference in August 1940 at the League of Nations headquarters in Geneva to tackle the Jewish Question. Prospects for success were low, especially in view of the international community's failure to help the Jews several years earlier at the Evian Conference in 1938. This time, however, Germany had a greater stake in finding a solution. Like Turkey after World War I, the country faced considerable pressure – both political and moral – to make amends for its crimes. The country was expected, for example, to place the SS officials responsible for the deportation policy on trial. Germany was also expected to offer some form of restitution to the Jews. In 1940, however, the German Reich was in a stronger diplomatic position than Turkey a generation earlier, and it was only willing to go so far to satisfy expectations. While Goering's new Foreign Minister, Ulrich von Hassell (who replaced Joachim von Ribbentrop), officially condemned the SS's radical deportation program, and while he announced plans to prosecute those responsible for it (Eichmann, in particular), he resisted the international call to permit German and Austrian Jews to return to their homes. Germany's military leaders, while no Nazis, believed that it was best for all concerned to find the Jews new places of residence. Pointing to the success of previous population exchanges – for example, those involving Greece and Turkey in the early 1920s – the Germans were able to gain international support for their stance, despite the protests of Jewish organizations.

The conference thus turned its attention to other destinations for Europe's suffering Jews. European diplomats, under pressure from Great Britain, initially proposed sending them to the United States, but American representatives responded with only qualified enthusiasm. In the 1930s, the US had taken in more Jewish refugees than any other nation, but since many Americans had opposed accepting immigrants due to the insecure economic climate of the Depression, Roosevelt's administration saw a political risk in pressing State Department officials to meet the existing quotas, which went unfilled. By 1940, however, a new mood slowly began to dawn. Roosevelt's growing commitment to rearmament (epitomized by his billion-dollar defense program in the spring of that year) promoted a modest economic upswing that slowly eased fears about refugees worsening unemployment.[33] A surge of sympathy for the Jews among the American public following the revelations of the wartime atrocities generated new support for limited immigration reform, as did the waning of isolationist sentiment in the wake of the Zurich Treaty. All of these developments gave Roosevelt a stronger political hand as he faced reelection in the fall of 1940. And so he permitted his representatives in Geneva to commit the US to accepting 100,000 Jewish refugees. (This was later approved by Congress in early 1941 with the passing of an updated version of the previously defeated Wagner–Rogers Bill.)

Yet despite this modest breakthrough, the delegates in Geneva recognized the need for a more sweeping solution, and so attention quickly shifted to British-controlled Palestine. Predictably, British diplomats had little desire to accept any Jewish refugees in the contested territory. In the summer of 1940, the region was once again in turmoil.

Both Arabs and Jews were disenchanted with British rule, the former still bitter about the brutal crushing of the Arab Revolt of 1936–9, the latter newly enraged by the May 1939 proclamation of the White Paper, which had drastically curtailed Jewish emigration, restricted land sales to Jews, and envisioned a permanent Jewish minority in a future independent Palestine. Yet despite the plan's oppressive features, the Zionist leadership did not initially rebel against it. As long as Britain was at war with Nazi Germany, David Ben-Gurion adhered to his pledge that the Jews would fight with Britain against Hitler "as if there were no White Paper."[34] With the arrival of peace in June 1940, however, the Jewish leader altered his pledge by declaring, "now that there is no Hitler, it is time to fight the White Paper."

Ben-Gurion meant the phrase rhetorically, but militant Jews took it literally. In the summer of 1940, the Haganah and Irgun formally abandoned their truce with the British and took up arms against them, launching attacks against British military targets, bombing bases, kidnapping soldiers, and raiding weapons storehouses. In one particularly adventurous gambit, an extreme wing of the Irgun, led by one of its commanders, Avraham Stern, even tried to persuade the Wehrmacht leadership in Germany to provide military aid to help expel the British from the region (he met with no response). At the same time, the Haganah accelerated its program of illegal immigration (*Ha-apala*). In July 1940, just before his death, Revisionist Zionist leader Vladimir Jabotinsky openly proclaimed the need to once more consider adopting his "evacuation plan" of 1936 to transfer 1.5 million Jews from Eastern Europe to Palestine. While the merits of the plan were debated, the Haganah tried to create a fait accompli by organizing dozens of ships to ferry Jewish refugees from Black Sea and Mediterranean ports to Palestine.

The British had difficulty coping with this new rebellion. The army's use of arrests, floggings, and curfews failed to eliminate attacks against its soldiers. And its policy of intercepting and turning back ships carrying Jewish refugees – interning them in Mauritius and Cyprus – earned the country international condemnation. This was especially true in July 1940, after the British tried to make an example of the SS *Exodus*, a ship crammed with more than 4,000 Polish Jews, which was sent back to its port of origin in Danzig. As British public opinion grew impatient with the stream of bad news from Palestine, many politicians began to reconsider the nation's imperial priorities. Concerns over Britain's hold over India, where nationalist feelings were intensifying among Hindus and Muslims, and its possessions in Southeast Asia, which remained threatened by the ongoing Sino-Japanese War, further contributed to the desire to be done with Palestine. All of these considerations made the British realize that the Jewish Question required an international solution and helped motivate them to convene the Geneva conference.

Fortuitously for the Zionist cause, this decision coincided with a change in leadership in Britain. In July 1940, Prime Minister Neville Chamberlain, then dying of cancer, resigned and appointed Winston Churchill as his successor. A longtime supporter of Zionism and an opponent of appeasing Arab militants, Churchill suspended the White Paper, which he had never supported, before the conference and proposed a new territorial solution for Palestine. After initially flirting with the short-lived Philby Plan (which would have established a Jewish state in all of Palestine linked to a larger pan-Arab Federation), he ultimately revived the Peel Commission's plan to partition the territory between the Jews and the Arabs.[35] He also opened up Palestine to renewed Jewish immigration, which he said "should never have [been] . . . stopped before the war."[36] Ben-Gurion welcomed this about-face, but it met with deep hostility from Arab leaders, who immediately resumed attacks against Jewish and British targets. For its part, Germany said the plan did not go far enough, pointing out that the land allotted to the Jews in the Peel Commission plan (15 percent of the total) would be too small to accommodate the number of Jews that needed to be transported out of Europe. As a result, Germany and France, supported by various Eastern European countries eager to expedite the departure of their own Jewish citizens, proposed that the League of Nations form a special committee on Palestine, whose recommendations would be binding on all parties. Britain was reluctant to relinquish the final say over its territory, but its desire to preserve the peace agreement with Germany led it to agree.

The results are well known. In November 1940, the committee recommended partitioning Palestine into Jewish and Arab sections (55 percent for the former, 45 percent for the latter). Shortly thereafter, Britain announced that it would pull out of Palestine within six months. Churchill believed that the expense of stationing 100,000 British troops in the territory was not worth the cost, especially as he was unwilling to employ the brutal tactics that were used to

suppress the Arab Revolt of 1936–9 against Jewish militants, not to
mention against arriving refugees. During this period, multiple waves
of Jewish immigrants arrived in Palestine from all over Europe. Arrang-
ing their transportation was a major logistical challenge and it was
only made possible by the collaboration of the French, German, and
Romanian navies, together with private shipping companies funded by
American Jewish donations. But over the span of two years, they succeeded in transporting nearly 2 million Jews to Palestine. Polish Jewish
refugees who had survived the Nazi onslaught were the most prominent group, with nearly 1 million departing from the General Government. (Only a trickle of Polish Jews from the 1.2 million trapped in the
Soviet zone escaped across the border to join the exodus.) Meanwhile,
nearly 750,000 Jews chose to leave the oppressive circumstances of life
in Central and Eastern Europe. Driven by a mixture of economic despair
and, to a lesser degree, Zionist idealism, this group of immigrants was
made up of Jewish survivors from Germany, Austria, and Czechoslovakia (200,000), Romania (300,000), and Hungary (200,000). Baltic
and Soviet Jews were unable to participate in this migration, and only
a handful of Jews from Western Europe joined in. Nevertheless, the
wave of Jewish emigration was considerable, exceeding the pace set by
Eastern European Jewish immigrants to the United States in the late
nineteenth and early twentieth centuries.

In the face of this swelling tide of humanity, tensions in Palestine
deepened. Having abandoned their policy of interdiction, the British
hastened the withdrawal of their forces, which they increasingly moved
northward to the port of Haifa for the return to Britain. Speeding up
their departure was the eruption of a civil war between Arab and Jewish
forces. This conflict expanded after May 14, 1941, with Ben-Gurion's
declaration of Israel's independence and the Arab coalition's ensuing
declaration of war. For reasons that are familiar, by March 1942, the
war ended with an Israeli victory. The Jewish state's military, though
lacking extensive experience in real combat, was much larger than that
of the Arabs, thanks to the new immigrants, who were quickly trained
and sent into battle (with arms sent by various Eastern European countries). This was the factor upon which the war's outcome hinged. The
very people who contributed so much to Israel's creation contributed
decisively to its survival.

The course of historical events that led to the founding of the
Jewish state cannot be imagined without Georg Elser's assassination of

Adolf Hitler. Indeed, had Elser failed in his deed, we can only imagine the nightmares that might have ensued. Today we know much more about Hitler's real goals than was known at the time. Ever since the political thaw that began in Germany following Goering's death in 1950 and the revelations contained in the famous speech delivered to the nation by his successor, Chancellor Ludwig Beck, we now understand that Hitler was committed to attacking Britain and France as a preliminary step toward invading the Soviet Union. We now recognize that he was bent on plundering the defeated nations of Europe to finance his conquest. And we have come to grasp that he was fanatically obsessed with solving the "Jewish problem" through violent means. The claim that it was rogue elements in the SS who were responsible for the unprecedented crimes of 1939–40 has been exposed as a myth. It was Hitler himself who was responsible. Germans have only recently started to come to grips with these difficult truths and shed their romanticized view of their once-beloved Führer. Too many Germans remain committed to xenophobic and nationalistic ideals. But Jews have long suspected what is now widely recognized: Hitler's death spared them – and probably the world – a worse catastrophe. It is impossible to imagine how a Jewish state would ever have come into being had the Nazis been able to launch a prolonged assault against European Jewry. Without the massive wave of emigrants that left Europe for Palestine in the years 1940–42, the Jewish state that exists today could hardly have been created. Had the war dragged on for years, the Jews of Palestine would have had to ally with the British indefinitely and would never have been able to launch their revolt for independence. Had World War II been a conflict remotely as protracted and destructive as World War I, Israel arguably would never have been created.

Georg Elser surely must have recognized this fact. Although he confessed in his letter that his decision to live in hiding partly reflected a sense of guilt for having indirectly sparked the Nazis' backlash against the Jews in 1939, he cannot help but have recognized that it helped to forge the modern state of Israel. To be sure, the world Elser made is far from perfect. Europe remains mired in ethnic, nationalistic, and religious rivalries; the Soviet Union remains a reclusive cipher; and the Middle East always seems to be on the brink of war. Yet there is hope on the horizon. Germany has slowly begun the process of political reform, having recently held its first free elections and established formal diplomatic relations with Israel. The Jewish state, meanwhile, continues to grow thanks to the continued stream of emigrants from Europe. Although integrating them remains fraught with challenges, they constitute the lifeblood of our young nation. On behalf of them, and on behalf of others who may yet come in the future, Yad Vashem's Commission for Designation of the Righteous recognizes Georg Elser as Righteous Among the Nations.

14 WHAT IF THE NAZIS HAD WON THE BATTLE OF EL ALAMEIN?

Jeffrey Herf

The first and second battles of El Alamein, which were fought between German and British forces in Egypt during the summer and fall of 1942, have long been viewed as pivotal turning points in the history of the Second World War. Recent scholarship has expanded our understanding of the battles' significance by showing how they also shaped the history of the Holocaust. The clashes at El Alamein decisively influenced the Nazi regime's ability to extend the "Final Solution of the Jewish Question" beyond Europe to encompass the approximately 700,000 Jews of North Africa and the Middle East. The ultimate defeat of the Germans by the Allies at El Alamein was crucial for preventing the realization of this nightmare "what if?" scenario. Examining how close Axis forces came to triumphing thus enables us to recognize the significance of one of the more frightening near misses of recent history.

In advancing this argument, I would like to emphasize that my account of the events of 1942 deliberately avoids engaging in explicit counterfactual speculation. Unlike most of the other contributors to this volume, I contend that speculating about the past is a luxury more appropriate for novelists than historians. Indeed, it violates the core mission of the historical profession. When historians hypothesize about events that never happened, they enter a realm of inquiry that is inherently antithetical to their traditional task of gathering and interpreting empirical evidence. Few historians have any training or expertise in crafting alternate paths of historical development. As a result, their imaginative scenarios end up being highly subjective. Most are either upbeat wish-fulfillments or bleak predictions of doom. Regardless of whether they assume the form of fantasies or nightmares, speculative accounts about the past share the trait of being far removed from the realm of fact. The accounts are not alternative "histories," in any meaningful sense of the term, but rather a set of guesses that rest on plausible projections from the established historical record. It is one thing for political leaders or analysts to assess the intersection of means and ends and to think strategically about the likely responses of actors to possible initiatives. Max Weber famously called doing so the "ethics of responsibility." Yet the Weberian assessment was focused on what should be done in the present and near future. Winston Churchill's genius and excellent political judgment in the late 1930s, for instance, did not stem from his ability to speculate about what Hitler might do. Rather, it was the result of his unflinching gaze at the most inconvenient and unpleasant facts about what Hitler actually believed at the time. As the political scientist Karl Dietrich Bracher pointed out long ago, too many other leaders of those years underestimated Hitler because they hoped he was not serious about what he was writing and saying.[1] Of course, historians should examine the contingencies of past moments and the decisions that led to one outcome rather than another. Doing so stands at the center of historical interpretation and keeps us from embracing the deterministic belief that historical events had to transpire as they did. Yet to go beyond this and invent imaginary pasts out of whole cloth pushes the legitimate concern with contingency beyond all plausible connections of fact and evidence.

A second problem with counterfactual speculation is its involvement in worrisome global cultural trends. Since the advent of the internet, high-technology corporations with deep financial interests have peddled the mendacious notion that everything we need to know is available on the world wide web. The growing acceptance of this idea has had a variety of adverse consequences for objective historical knowledge. It has contributed to the growing separation of facts from verifiable sources of evidence; to the proliferation of wild conspiracy theories; and to the ease of forging photographic and video evidence. All of these trends pose serious challenges to the discipline of history, especially our belief that we can separate truth from lies, fact from fiction. The contempt for fact and evidence has been most infamously apparent in Holocaust denial, which, having originated among fringe extremist groups on the right and left in the 1970s, has increasingly gained mainstream status in the form of official government sponsorship in states like Iran and widespread distribution on Islamist websites throughout the Middle East.[2] But even in less extreme examples, the disregard for the past's facticity has become a growing problem. Unfortunately, counterfactual speculation, by being similarly unmoored from genuine facts, has encouraged this worrisome trend.

It is with these caveats in mind that I have produced my account of the battles of El Alamein in 1942. Without engaging in recklessly speculative leaps of imagination, I recount the actions taken by the key political actors of the time and survey the historical interpretations offered by subsequent scholars in order to illuminate the pivotal importance of the two battles for the fate of the Jews of North Africa and the Middle East during the Holocaust.

On February 16, 1942, the American diplomat and head of the American Legation in Cairo, Alexander Kirk, wrote a memo to United States Secretary of State Cordell Hull in which he expressed the "concern of the United States regarding effect of Axis military advance into Egypt."[3] Kirk understood that the Roosevelt administration was focused on the aftermath of the attack on Pearl Harbor in the Pacific and on the devastating German submarine attacks in the Atlantic on American shipping just off the eastern and southern US coastline. But he nevertheless made the case for prioritizing the defeat of Fascist Italy and Nazi Germany in the Mediterranean, North Africa, and the Middle East. Kirk believed that the British and their allies lacked the resources to win the war in a theater whose importance was not yet adequately understood in Washington. He pointed out that if the Axis seized control of the Suez Canal and the oil fields of the Middle East, it would prove disastrous for Britain's ability to continue the war. Preserving Allied access to both, he added, was a precondition not only for defeating the Axis in North Africa and the Middle East, but for establishing a base for a future invasion of Axis-occupied Europe from the south. Winning the war in this region, he concluded, was essential for winning what had become a truly *world* war. The growing sense of the region's geostrategic centrality among American officials ultimately led President Franklin Roosevelt to send additional military materials to British forces in northern Africa and to lay the groundwork for Operation Torch, the American invasion of the region in November 1942. Similarly, it was the sense of North Africa's geostrategic centrality – not any concern for the fate of its Jews – that led Churchill and Roosevelt to order the military intervention that had the additional consequence of thwarting the extension of Hitler's anti-Jewish policies in the Middle East.

On November 28, 1941, the radical Palestinian Arab nationalist and Grand Mufti of Jerusalem, Haj Amin Al-Husseini met with German Foreign Minister Joachim von Ribbentrop in Berlin (Figure 29).[4] He stressed that:

> the Arabs were naturally friends of Germany because both were fighting three common foes: the English, the Jews, and the Bolsheviks. It had been a great deed on the part of Germany to have proceeded against these three enemies. The Arabs hoped that Germany would also help them in their fight on these three fronts. They thought that victory in this battle was important not only for the Arabs, but also for their own people.

Husseini went on to add that the Arabs were prepared to "do everything" to help in the fight, including undertaking acts of sabotage and creating an "Arab Legion" to fight with Axis forces. The Arabs in Palestine, he explained, "were on the best of terms with the centers of the Moslem faith" and would try to influence Muslims in India and Indian prisoners of war to rally to the Axis cause. He also repeated his request that the Axis swiftly issue a declaration supporting Arab independence. Ribbentrop acknowledged Husseini's comment about "the three common foes of the Arabs and the German people" and he observed that Russia was "as good as beaten," declaring that "the political power of Bolshevism was almost broken." He further assured Husseini that "as a sworn enemy of the Jews, Germany understood the troubles of the Arabs in this field." And he added that "the war against England was another bond uniting the Axis and the Arabs." Yet Ribbentrop cautioned Husseini that, in view of the recent setback suffered by Axis-supported forces at the hands of the British in Iraq, it was necessary to proceed "very cautiously and prudently." Ribbentrop did not think that the time for a declaration had arrived. It needed to be "made at the proper time." Now it was "better to wait until the guns did the talking." Given the German advance into the Soviet Union and the Caucasus, the Black Sea would become a German base of operations "in the near future." The "right moment for the declaration," he concluded, would come only when the Germans "had advanced to the areas of the Near East."[5]

Husseini responded by reiterating his demand for an immediate German declaration in order to counter English appeals to the
Arabs, but again Ribbentrop demurred. The Foreign Minister pointed
to all the "trouble" that the Arabs had experienced with Jews and
doubted that the Arabs would ally with Britain after "all the English
had done to them." Husseini replied that while anti-British sentiment was strong among Palestinian Arabs, unnamed "others" thought
differently. Ribbentrop nevertheless repeated that a declaration now
would be harmful, "particularly since it was not a question of years
but could only be a matter of months before intervention in the
Near East was possible." He also did not want to place German
sympathizers in the Arab world at risk of being suppressed by the
English.[6] German diplomats further urged caution out of a desire not
to antagonize Italy and France, both of which had intentions toward
the Arabs that conflicted with complete independence. The exchange
between Husseini and Ribbentrop illustrated the connections between
the course of the war in Europe and political events in the Middle East.
The Mufti made clear that that realization of Arab aspirations was
inseparable from the military success of the Axis powers, especially Nazi
Germany.

Later on that same November day, Husseini met with Hitler.[7]
The photo of the meeting appeared in the German and world press
and was later reproduced in German propaganda materials distributed
throughout the Middle East. The Nazi dictator now personally experienced what the memos of his diplomats had previously indicated,
namely that Husseini was a true comrade-in-arms and ideological soul-
mate. Husseini told Hitler that the Führer was "admired by the entire
Arab world." He thanked him for the sympathy he had shown to
the Arab and especially the Palestinian cause. He was convinced that
Germany would win the war and that, as a result, the Arab cause would
prosper. As he had emphasized to Ribbentrop, Husseini told Hitler that
"the Arabs were Germany's natural friends because they had the same
enemies as had Germany, namely the English, the Jews, and the Communists." Therefore, speaking for "the Arabs," he said that they were
prepared to cooperate with Germany with all their hearts and stood
ready to participate in the war, not only negatively by the commission
of acts of sabotage and the instigation of revolutions, but also positively by the formation of an "Arab Legion" that would fight alongside the German army. The Arabs could be useful allies due to their

Figure 29. Haj Amin Al-Husseini with Adolf Hitler (1941).

geographical location and "because of the suffering inflicted upon them by the English and the Jews." They also had "close relations with all the Moslem nationals, which they could make use of on behalf of the common cause." An Arab Legion composed of prisoners of war from Algeria, Tunisia, and Morocco was feasible. "The Arab world" was convinced that Germany would win the war, "not only because the Reich possessed a large army, brave soldiers, and military leaders of genius, but also because the Almighty could never award the victory to an unjust cause." In their struggle for independence and for the unity of Palestine, Syria, and Iraq, the Arabs had the fullest confidence in the Führer and looked to his help to soothe the "wound which had been inflicted upon them by the enemies of Germany." Husseini then mentioned a previous German statement (of April 8, 1941) recognizing Arab aspirations for independence and freedom and supporting "the elimination of the Jewish national home." A public declaration of that nature "would be very useful for its propagandistic effect on the Arab peoples at this moment. It would rouse the Arabs from their momentary lethargy ... give them new courage" and facilitate Husseini's secret efforts to organize an Arab revolt, which he would unleash "at the right moment and only strike upon an order from Berlin."[8]

Hitler's reply was more interesting than Husseini may have anticipated, as it included his first hint that he intended to extend the Final Solution of the Jewish Question beyond the borders of Europe. He said that Germany stood for an uncompromising war against the Jews. That naturally included active opposition to the Jewish national home in Palestine. Hitler made it clear to Husseini that his private views matched his public pronouncements, noting that:

> Germany was at the present time engaged in a life and death struggle with two citadels of Jewish power: Great Britain and Soviet Russia. Theoretically there was a difference between England's capitalism and Russias communism; actually, however, the Jews in both countries were pursuing a common goal. This was the decisive struggle; on the political plane, it presented itself in the main as a conflict between Germany and England, but ideologically it was a battle between National Socialism and the Jews. It went without saying that Germany would furnish positive and practical aid to the Arabs involved in the same struggle, because platonic promises were useless in a war for survival or destruction in which the Jews were able to mobilize all of England's power for their ends.[9]

Hence, Hitler continued, "the Mufti could not but be aware . . . that the outcome of the struggle going on at present [in Europe] would also decide the fate of the Arab world."[10]

Hitler subsequently approved issuing the declaration requested by Husseini, but not in November 1941. As Germany was now fighting in the Caucasus, he did not want to antagonize the French with a declaration about Syrian independence, which would be seen as an effort to break up France's colonial empire. However, the Nazi dictator then made a striking promise to Husseini, "enjoining him to lock it in the uttermost depths of his heart." He promised to "carry on the battle to the total destruction of the Judeo-Communist empire in Europe." German armies fighting on the Eastern Front at some moment in this struggle would "reach the southern exit" from the Caucasus. At that point, Hitler would give the Arab world the assurance that its hour of liberation had arrived. Germany's objective would then be solely the destruction of the Jewish element residing in the Arab sphere under the protection of British power. In that hour, the Mufti would be the most authoritative spokesman of the Arab world. It would then be his task to set off the Arab operation which he had secretly prepared. When that time had come, Germany could also be indifferent to French reaction to such a declaration.[11]

With these words, Hitler effectively told Husseini that if his armies should succeed in defeating the armed forces of the Soviet Union, and if they were thereafter able to move south from the Caucasus, the "destruction of the Jewish element" would then be extended to Jews living in Egypt, Palestine, Iraq, and Trans-Jordan. Given the fact that only a few months earlier, in the summer and fall of 1941, the Nazi leadership was finalizing plans for a European-wide plan to murder the Jews, the implications for the Jews of North Africa and the Middle East were clear.[12]

Hitler's comments to Husseini on November 28, 1941 indicated that, given the opportunity, he wanted to extend the Final Solution outside Europe. For him, doing so was the logical corollary to the idea that an international Jewish conspiracy was waging war against the Third Reich. If so, then the German counterattack – in the form of the Final Solution – would be no less international. The battles in the Caucasus in the fall and winter of 1941, in addition to the subsequent fighting in North Africa, were thus not only significant events in the history of World War II. Their outcome would determine whether the approximately 700,000 Jews living in the Middle East and North Africa would also become victims of the Holocaust.

In order to achieve his genocidal aims, Hitler first had to accomplish his military objectives. In early 1942, he sent General Erwin Rommel and the Afrikakorps to North Africa to deliver a devastating blow to the British (Figure 30). The chief goal was to seize control of the Suez Canal and gain access to the oil fields while denying them to Great Britain. In the spring of 1942, Rommel's forces advanced from Tunisia into Egypt. On June 21, 1942, following almost a month-long siege of the British base in the port city of Tobruk in eastern Libya, the Germans and their Italian allies defeated the British Eighth Army and captured

Figure 30. General Erwin Rommel in North Africa.

28,000 mostly Australian and British soldiers, as well as large quantities of war materials. These were among the grimmest days of the war for the Allies. By the end of June, Axis forces had invaded Egypt and reached a point 66 miles west of the port city of Alexandria. Apart from British forces in El Alamein, there were no significant military forces blocking the Afrikakorps' path to Cairo and Palestine. The first battle of El Alamein (July 1–27) between Axis and British forces ended in a stalemate.

During these weeks, Nazi Germany's Arabic-language propaganda effort, conveyed in the form of short-wave radio broadcasts coming from powerful European transmitters and in leaflets distributed by agents in Rommel's forces in North Africa, urged Arabs to support the German troops, who were described as coming to save them from the oppressive rule of the British and the nefarious plans of the Zionists.[13] The broadcasts became increasingly incendiary to the point of urging Arab and Muslim listeners to "kill the Jews before they kill you."[14] Due to the proximity of Rommel's forces, the British fleet withdrew from Alexandria on June 30. In the first week in July, American Embassy personnel and prisoners of war were transferred from Egypt to Palestine. Throughout these months and indeed throughout the war, Nazi

Arabic-language broadcasts claimed that a victory for the Axis powers would represent a victory for Arabs and Muslims, while a victory for the Allies would mean Zionist domination of the entire Middle East. American intelligence officials in the region reported that the Nazi propaganda campaign against the Allies and the Jews was striking a chord among Arab audiences, due to their desire to support the war's expected winner and their ideologically colored opposition to Zionism.[15]

The proximity of the Nazi danger was apparent to David Ben-Gurion, the leader of the Mapai Party and the leading political figure of the Jewish population in Palestine. On October 25, 1942, two days after the beginning of the second battle of El Alamein, he spoke to a Mapai Party meeting at the Kfar-Vitkin *moshav* north of Netanya. Following the victory of Rommel's Afrikakorps over British forces at Tobruk in the spring of 1942, Ben-Gurion had written to President Roosevelt to express his fears for the fate of the Jewish population in Palestine. Though the first battle of El Alamein had blocked Rommel's immediate advance to the east – and thus toward Palestine – the Nazi menace remained intact. Moreover, in the fall of 1942, as Germany's Sixth Army was approaching Stalingrad, the Allies faced the possibility of a giant German pincer movement in which Axis forces moved south into the Middle East following a possible victory in the southern Soviet Union. In Kfar-Vitkin, Ben-Gurion told his colleagues that "the Nazis are not far away, but we are being threatened not only by Rommel in North Africa. We are also in danger of invasion from Syria and even Iraq and Turkey."[16]

Recent historical research has shown how acute the danger really was.[17] Following the first battle of El Alamein, which had ended in a draw, Winston Churchill appointed Bernard Montgomery to replace Claude Auchenlick as the commanding general of the British Eighth Army. The second battle of El Alamein, which was fought between October 23 and November 11, 1942, resulted in a decisive Allied victory. Ever since the end of World War II, the battle has been viewed by historians as a major turning point in the conflict. It represented the Western Allies' first decisive victory over the Germans since the beginning of the war in 1939. And it ended the Axis threat to Egypt, the Suez Canal, and the oil fields of the Middle East and Iran. Yet more than anyone at the time understood (at least outside the highest offices of the Nazi regime), the victory at El Alamein in November 1942 was the first and only time during World War II that Allied military policy had the additional consequence of blocking the implementation of Nazi anti-Jewish policy.

Military and diplomatic historians have long sought to understand the relationship between events in North Africa and Europe during the Second World War.[18] In 1966, Lukasz Hirszowicz's study, *The Third Reich and the Arab East*, presented an enduring synthesis of military, diplomatic, and political history.[19] He established the chronology and key causal arguments concerning the prospects of victory for, and the reasons for the ultimate defeat of, Fascist Italy and Nazi Germany in the region, especially in Iraq and Egypt. Since then, subsequent historians in West and East Germany have further elaborated on the military and diplomatic dimensions of Nazi Germany's wartime policies toward the Arab countries.[20] In 2005, two German historians, Klaus Michael Mallmann and Martin Cüppers, broke new ground in their important study, *Nazi Palestine: The Plans for the Extermination of the Jews in Palestine*.[21] They drew on records of the Nazi regime that had been declassified in the four decades since Hirszowicz's classic study. During that time, the place of the Holocaust in the history of the war had become more important. This shift was evident in Mallmann and Cüppers' careful work in the archives of the German military as well as the SS. They documented plans by the SS to send an Einsatzgruppen unit to Egypt following the expected victory of German forces at the battle of El Alamein. After a meeting between Hitler and SS Reichsführer Heinrich Himmler on July 1, 1942, Karl Wolff, Himmler's chief of staff, contacted the Army's Supreme Command (OKH). The deployment guidelines sent on July 13, 1942 read, in part, as follows:

> With the approval of the Reichsführer-SS and the chief of the German policy, the deployment of the SS unit with Afrika Korps will be regulated as follows: (1) The SS Einsatzkommando receives its technical instructions from the chief of the security policy and SD and carries out its assignments under its own responsibility. It is entitled, within the scope of its mission, to take executive measures against the civilian population on its own authority.[22]

A week later, SS-Obersturmbannführer Walter Rauff flew to Tobruk to receive the "necessary instructions for the deployment" from Field Marshal Rommel. Mallmann and Cüppers conclude that "the deployment was thus imminent."[23] The unit, which was composed of seven

SS officers and seventeen noncommissioned officers, flew from Berlin to Athens on July 29 to prepare for transfer to Egypt. From there, it would proceed to Palestine to engage in the mass murder of the Jewish population. Drawing on reports by German diplomats and intelligence agents in the region, Mallmann and Cüppers conclude that "a vast number of Arabs... were ready to serve as willing accomplices of the Germans in the Middle East... The central task of Rauff's Einsatzkommando – the implementation of the Holocaust in Palestine – would have been quickly put into action with the help of those collaborators."[24]

Fortunately, it was never meant to be. As a result of the indecisive outcome of the first battle of El Alamein and then the Allied victory in the second battle in October and November, Rauff's unit never made it to Egypt or Palestine. While the Nazi occupation of Tunisia and Libya brought suffering to the Jews there, a full-scale murder campaign envisaged in the orders of July 1942 was never implemented. German intelligence reports reached conclusions comparable to those coming to American and British policy-makers, namely that, in the face of Rommel's military victories and Nazi propaganda, there was "broad support for Nazi Germany and its Führer" in the Middle East in the summer of 1942 and that anti-Jewish sentiment intensified during the German advance. The Germans expected that the victory of the Afrikakorps would lead to "widespread readiness to support the arrival of the Germans and the expulsion of the British" in Egypt and possibly in Iraq and Syria as well.[25]

Mallmann and Cüppers conclude that "the situation in the Middle East during the summer of 1942 was therefore very reminiscent of that of the previous year in Eastern Europe, and there is no reason to believe that the antisemitic potential of Lithuanian, Latvian, or Ukrainian nationalists was any different than that of the Arab awaiting the German Wehrmacht."[26] The reports of American and British intelligence regarding Arab sentiments, while paying more attention to those Arabs who had decided to fight with, not against, the Allies, came to similar conclusions about the impact of German military victories combined with the success of German propaganda in fanning anti-British and anti-Jewish sentiment. American assessments of the immediate postwar months and years found considerable evidence of the enduring impact of the enthusiasm for Nazi Germany, especially in organizations such as the Muslim Brotherhood. Husseini's success in restoring his political career as the leader of Palestinian nationalism after his return to the region in 1946 offered yet further evidence of a positive reception of Nazism's messages among some important and politically active groups and individuals such as Hassan al Banna and Sayyid Qutb.[27]

Historians in recent years have confirmed the worst fears voiced by David Ben-Gurion in October 1942. If the armed forces of Nazi Germany had won the battles at El Alamein that month, Hitler would have been able to carry out his intention to extend the Holocaust to the Jews of North Africa and the Middle East. In view of the paucity of Allied armed forces in the region, the limited arms at the disposal of the Jews of Palestine in 1942, and the willingness of vocal and active groups of Nazi sympathizers in the Arab countries, it is likely that the Einsatzgruppe Egypt, operating behind the lines in conjunction with the Afrikakorps, would have been able to perpetrate crimes against the Jews of the region comparable to those inflicted by the Einsatzgruppen on the Jews of Eastern Europe at the very same time. It is impossible to know how events would have transpired from this point. But in all likelihood, the interaction between Nazis, Arabs, and Jews would have followed the same patterns of behavior visible among perpetrators, victims, bystanders, collaborators, rescuers, and resisters in Europe. There is no need to speculate. The result would have been catastrophic for the Jews of Palestine.

In the end, the chief significance of the battles of El Alamein lies in the realm of real history not counterfactual history. The battles have long been famous as turning points in the global history of the Second World War. We now know that they were also turning points as well in the history of the Holocaust. As was also true in Europe, the great battles of World War II in the Middle East were deeply intertwined with Nazi Germany's war against the Jews. Recent scholarship allows us to better appreciate Alexander Kirk's strategic awareness of Nazi anti-Jewish policies in the Middle East, the decisions of Winston Churchill and Franklin Roosevelt regarding the Mediterranean theater, and the courage, skill and sacrifice of Allied soldiers who fought at El Alamein. Taken together, the Allies in North Africa did far more to save Jewish lives than most of them probably realized at the time and more than historical scholarship and public memory understood in the postwar decades.

15 WHAT IF THE FINAL SOLUTION HAD BEEN COMPLETED?: NAZI MEMORY IN A VICTORIOUS REICH

Dirk Rupnow

If the Nazis had won the Second World War and completed the Final Solution of the Jewish Question, how would they have tried to shape the memory of their genocidal crimes against the Jews?[1] In recent years, scholars and writers have explored this question in different ways. Aleida Assmann, Christoph Münz, and Harald Weinrich, for instance, have argued that the term "genocide" would have been inadequate for describing the Nazis' goals and have instead proposed alternative concepts, such as "mnemocide," "memorycide," and "memory-murder." These terms suggest that the Nazis did not only seek to physically exterminate the Jews but "remove them from history and memory" by eliminating the evidence of their existence and of the atrocities perpetrated against them.[2] In a sense, the Nazis were bent on committing a "double murder."[3] They did not merely want to kill the Jews but prevent their survival in remembrance. Various writers of popular fiction have explored this idea in recent works of alternate history. Robert Harris's novel *Fatherland* (1992) describes a victorious German Reich in the early 1960s, one in which all traces of the death camps have been eliminated and even leading SS officials know nothing of the Final Solution. Similarly, Brad Linaweaver's novel, *Moon of Ice* (1988), depicts how, in the wake of the Germans' nuclear destruction of the extermination camps, subsequent Nazi Party leaders have no knowledge of the events that transpired there. Only the elite SS preserves the memory of the events in their initiation rites.[4]

The notion that the Nazis would have pursued an official policy of amnesia toward the crimes of the Holocaust is, at first glance, eminently plausible. There was ample precedent for regimes seeking to expunge the memory of their alleged adversaries. Ever since antiquity, the promotion of amnesia has been advanced for political purposes, a practice epitomized by the Roman tradition of "damnatio memoriae," according to which statues of condemned leaders were toppled and their names erased from coins in order to efface their political legacy. Given the Jews' reputation as the proverbial "people of memory," it is highly likely that the Nazis would have sought to eradicate their cultural heritage along with their physical existence. This seems especially true in light of the well-established dictum that history is written by the victors. Already during the Second World War, many Jews suspected that the Nazis were planning to expunge them from the historical record. The Polish Jewish historian Ignacy Schiper (1884–1943) said as much prior to his deportation from the Warsaw ghetto, noting, "All that we know of vanished peoples is what their killers have wanted to say about them. If our killers will win the war, if they will write its history . . . they can also decide to blot us out completely from the memory of the world as if we had never existed."[5]

Schiper's observation can be read as a powerful confirmation of the Nazis' desire to render the Jews forgotten, yet it is also notable for pointing out that they had a choice about whether to do so or not. In fact, the Nazis' pursuit of amnesia with respect to the Holocaust is only part of the story. Had they won the war and completed the Final Solution, they arguably would have pursued a more nuanced policy straddling the line between forgetting and remembrance.

To be sure, proving such a speculative claim is quite difficult, given the many interpretive challenges that come with studying the Third Reich. First, there is the fact that the Nazi regime only existed for twelve years and was unable to fully realize its goals. Any hypothetical reconstruction of what might have been is thus, by definition, counterfactual and unverifiable. Then there is the complexity of the power relations within the polycratic Nazi state. Since there were numerous rivalries within the regime between moderate and radical factions, and since, as a result, there were countless competing initiatives and dynamics in play at any given time, it is difficult to determine which would have been successful in the long run. Above all, imagining the consequences of a German *Endsieg*, or "final victory," in World War II is made difficult by the emotional and moral challenges of doing so. To be sure, no confrontation with the Third Reich's extermination policies can proceed without contending with what Hannah Arendt described as "dwelling on horrors."[6] Yet there is the danger that counterfactual speculation might allow for the evasion of difficult moral questions. Only by directly confronting them, eliciting discomfort in readers, challenging prevailing views, and exposing ambiguities, can the task of historical analysis truly be fulfilled.

Nazi memory: between erasure and representation

There is considerable evidence that the Nazis sought to render the crimes against the Jews invisible. One of the best examples was a secret program known as Special Action 1005. Decreed in 1942 and directed by SS Captain Paul Blobel, it ordered the exhumation of corpses from the main killing sites.[7] The program's goal was to prevent incriminating evidence of the regime's racial and political persecution from falling into the hands of the Allies before the end of the war. Another famous example of the Nazis' desire to "murder memory" was Heinrich Himmler's notorious Posen speech of October 4, 1943. This speech, which openly admitted to the mass killings of Jews while insisting on the unviolated "decency" of the SS perpetrators, culminated in the well-known claim that the regime's actions were to be an "unwritten and *never to be written* page of glory of our history."[8] But only two days later, Himmler delivered a subsequent speech at the same location, in which he seemed to qualify the need to keep the Final Solution of the Jewish Question secret. In this speech, the SS leader noted the difficulty of deciding "to make this people [the Jews] disappear from the earth" and implied that, at least in the short term, it would be advisable to take "the secret with us to the grave." But he left open the possibility that "maybe a long time hereafter, one may think about whether the German people are to be told more about it."[9]

Himmler's remark suggests that while the Nazis were committed to eradicating the signs of their crimes in the present, they might be willing to remember them in the future. This possibility has also been floated by Saul Friedlander, who hypothesized that a victorious Reich would have produced numerous "comic emplotments" of the Jews' elimination.[10] Significantly, the Nazis' dilemmas involving remembering and forgetting intensified over the course of the extermination process. In August of 1942 in Lublin, following what Kurt Gerstein claimed was an official inspection of the extermination facilities, a brief conversation took place between Hitler, Himmler, his friend and confidant, and local Lublin SS leader and head of the notorious Aktion Reinhardt murder campaign, Odilo Globocnik, along with Reich Interior Ministry Official and T4 "Euthanasia" program planner, Herbert Linden. In this meeting, the eyewitness who documented it, SS officer Kurt Gerstein, recalled that Linden asked,

> "Mister Globocnik, do you think that it is proper to bury the bodies instead of burning them? One day we might be succeeded by a generation that does not understand our actions." Globocnik [replied]: "Gentlemen, if ever a generation succeeds us that is so weak and feeble that it fails to understand our great task, yes, in that case, National Socialism in its entirety will have been for nothing. However, it is actually my opinion that we should bury bronze plaques in the ground to honor the courage we have shown in performing this grand and necessary work." To this, the Führer replied: "Right, Globocnik, that's exactly what I think we should do."[11]

Even if Gerstein's recollections are not entirely accurate, they nevertheless show, as do Himmler's remarks, that the perpetrators were highly ambivalent about their actions. German historian Hans Mommsen has aptly summed up this feeling in noting that the very same task that the Nazis "stylized into a world historical mission was simultaneously supposed to be kept secret from the world."[12] In mulling over the conflicting goals of self-glorification and secrecy, Himmler ultimately came down in favor of silence, which served to underscore the SS's elite character. By contrast, Globocnik favored a more calculated form of eventually commemorating what he and others considered to be a heroic accomplishment. These differences within the Nazi leadership show that the perceived need for secrecy did not entirely preclude more open and direct forms of commemoration.

The victims initially played no visible role in Himmler's and Globocnik's considerations. Yet the need to represent them eventually became a necessary component of transforming the Nazis' crime into a "world historical task." Nazism was a bipolar ideology that could not function without a constitutive "other." This was already recognized during the war. Franz Neumann, in his study of the structure and practice of Nazism, argued that the domestic political value of antisemitism could never permit the "complete extermination of the Jews." As he put it, "the foe cannot and must not disappear; he must always be held in readiness as a scapegoat for all the evils originating in the socio-political system."[13] Around the same time, the Polish Jewish historian Emanuel Ringelblum, writing in the straitened circumstances of the Warsaw ghetto, expressed the belief that the Nazis would have to allow at least some Jews to live, for without them they would lose their "Jewish argument."[14]

Even ordinary Germans who supported the Nazis' anti-Jewish policies were aware of this problem. In 1942, a letter sent to the anti-semitic journal, *Der Stürmer*, pointed out that:

> the number of people on the street who are wearing the yellow Star of David and the word "Jew" have fortunately been declining in recent days. In the process, however, the younger generation is being denied the repellant visual impression that that Jew makes in daily life. I therefore suggest that, next to the monkey cages in the zoo, a second roomy cage should be established, one part of which can house a Jewish family with typical Jewish traits: flat feet, hooked noses, black hair, bent posture, throbbing lips, a concealed glance, thick eyelids; the other part of which can house a family that is Jewish but does not look like it. Further strategies of separation according to gender could also be undertaken. A plaque would point out that all types of gradations appear between the two groups.[15]

This private suggestion insisted that the only way to compensate for the effects of the Nazis' deportation program was to keep a small number of Jews alive as negative examples for ordinary Germans.

In so doing, the suggestion implied that, at least to some degree, Nazi antisemitism was ultimately tactical in function. This belief dates back to Hermannn Rauschning's conversations with Hitler from the 1930s. Responding to Rauschning's question as to whether the Jews should be destroyed, Hitler allegedly answered in the negative, declaring "then we would have to invent them. One requires a visible enemy, not an invisible one."[16] Similarly, Jean-Paul Sartre declared in his famous essay about antisemitism that "if the Jew did not exist, the antisemite would invent him." "The antisemite," he insisted, "is in the unhappy position of having a vital need for the very enemy he wishes to destroy."[17]

Such observations help clarify some of the functional aspects of Nazi ideology, but they fail to explain the larger question of why, if antisemitism was merely tactical, it ultimately resulted in a systematic program of mass murder. In answering this question, it is important to recognize that the Nazis sought, at one and the same time, to preserve the Jews in memory while physically exterminating them. This paradoxical reality was demonstrated by many projects in the Third Reich that were closely linked to the regime's policies of persecution, theft, expulsion, and extermination.

The Nazis remember the Jews: museums, scholarship, and film

One of the most significant of these projects was the Jewish Central Museum in Prague.[18] This institution – in particular, the policies that its Jewish staff and SS overseers devised with relation to collection, preservation, and exhibition – does not merely represent an esoteric, absurd, or even Kafkaesque sidelight to the Holocaust, it actually leads us into the heart of the Final Solution itself.

Already in 1906, as part of a larger movement within the European and North American Jewish communities, a Jewish museum was founded in Prague. The immediate occasion for its creation was the urban renewal of the old Prague ghetto, which city officials deemed necessary for reasons of hygiene and city planning. During the renovation process, three major synagogues were demolished and their collections of Judaica rendered homeless. The museum was thus envisioned as a repository that could house and exhibit the valuable ceremonial objects, which could no longer be used in religious services. When the museum found its first permanent home in 1912, it was housed in the headquarters of the Jewish community's Burial Society in the old Jewish cemetery. Despite serving an obvious need, however, the Jewish Museum was never more than a modest success. The many visitors that initially visited the institution in the 1920s quickly ebbed during the economically depressed 1930s. Following the German occupation, moreover, the museum was taken over by the Jewish religious community and was effectively shut down.

It was only in 1942, following the first deportations of Jews and the closing of the synagogues in the Nazi-occupied Protectorate of

Bohemia and Moravia, that the idea was conceived to establish a central Jewish museum in Prague. There are two competing explanations for this turn of events. The first claims that Jewish communal leaders came up with the idea of collecting the Czech Jewish community's cultural treasures from across Bohemia and Moravia in a central location in Prague in the hope of eventually returning them to their rightful owners (or otherwise preserve them for posterity) after the war. Knowing that these large kinds of collection projects could never be completed without the knowledge of the Nazi occupiers (especially the Central Office for Jewish Emigration, controlled by Adolf Eichmann's Sub-Department IV B4 within the Reich Security Main Office), the Jewish community tried to make it palatable to them. The second explanation argues that SS officials within the Central Office for Jewish Emigration forced Jewish personnel employed at the Nazis' "Trustee Agency" in charge of confiscating Jewish property to establish the Jewish museum ostensibly under the purview of the Jewish community but ultimately under German control.

The documentary record does not allow any clear conclusions, but the actions of the museum personnel are revealing. In April 1942, as deportations were accelerating, Jewish communal officials recognized that transporting the movable artifacts of the provincial communities to Prague was an obvious solution to the problem of where to house the now homeless treasures. The growth of the collection in Prague directly mirrored the deportation of the Protectorate's Jewish communities. To be sure, this task represented an exceptional form of musealization, in the sense that it was compulsory rather than voluntary. The cultural artifacts were snatched directly from people who used them on a daily basis – just as their lives would soon be snatched from them as well.

At the beginning of July 1942, SS Lieutenant Karl Rahm, the deputy director of the Central Office of Jewish Emigration in Prague and later commander of the Theresienstadt ghetto, instructed the Jewish community to transform the local Klaus synagogue into a "Jewish Museum, Department Province." Around the same time, he ordered them to turn the women's prayer hall in Prague's medieval Altneuschul into an exhibition space for its own artifacts. Shortly thereafter, the first mention of a Jewish Central Museum appeared in Jewish communal discussions as a possible exhibition site for textiles. On the same day, Rahm visited the old Jewish Museum and the surrounding synagogues. Simultaneously, a bank account was opened with 30,000 Czech korunas for financing the museum, while the Pinkas synagogue was insured against fire and vandalism (a highly ironic turn of events given the Nazis' recent destruction of synagogues on Kristallnacht). With these decisions, the Nazis made a commitment to preserving not only Jewish objects, but Jewish buildings, including the old cemetery. Looking at the photographs of the museum's wartime exhibits today, one does not get the impression of a Nazi propaganda project, but rather of a legitimate Jewish institution. The exhibits were organized according to art historical criteria and, notably enough, lacked the kinds of derogatory features that marked other Nazi projects like the infamous propaganda exhibition "The Eternal Jew." In the first exhibit in the Hoch synagogue organized in November 1942, various items of Judaica, rare prints, and historic documents attesting to special Jewish privileges were displayed in simple wooden cabinets. Most were objects that reflected the Jews' distinct traditions (instead of assimilation and living together) and made them appear to conform to the stereotype of the foreign "people of the book." By all accounts, SS officials were highly satisfied with the exhibit.

In the Klaus synagogue, meanwhile, other ceremonial objects were displayed in the effort to document Jewish religious rites. A Seder table with five life-sized mannequins representing three generations of a Jewish family was set up along with a separate mannequin holding a Torah scroll (Figure 31). For its part, the Pinkas synagogue exhibition was supposed to tell the story of Bohemia and Moravia's Jews up through the modern era. Dioramas were planned as part of this larger narrative project. Due to instructions of the Central Office for Jewish Emigration, however, work on the Pinkas synagogue was broken off before it could be completed. Work resumed in 1944, when a "Prague Ghetto Museum" was set up in the building of the Prague Burial Society. But the public was not allowed in to view any of the exhibits prior to the war's end.

Jewish experts working under the Jewish community's authority assembled the exhibits under SS supervision. Yet despite cooperating with the Germans, the Jews were unable to prevent their own murder. Paradoxically, the interests of Jews and Germans dovetailed at the Central Museum: the former wanted to preserve something of their history, while the latter sought to humiliate, rob, and destroy their victims. The

Figure 31. Mannequin of Jew holding Torah scroll in the Klaus synagogue, Prague.

collection project, oscillating as it did between theft and preservation, united two diametrically opposed interests. The victims reckoned with the ultimate defeat of the perpetrators, while the perpetrators were confident about their ultimate victory over the victims.

It is unclear how the ensemble of synagogues, exhibits, and the old Jewish cemetery in Prague would have been used in a world in which the Nazis won World War II and completed the Holocaust. There is no record of considerations being devoted to the museum's future in such a world. Indeed, it is possible that no such documents exist at all. This lack of planning for the future may reflect the fact that the museum (despite being quite large with some 200,000 objects in eight buildings and fifty warehouses at the war's end) was ultimately a local project devised by regional SS authorities instead of a national project coordinated with higher-ups in Berlin.

Still, there are many questions we might ask about how the museum would have been used following a Nazi "final victory." Would the old Prague ghetto have served as an antisemitic Disneyland? Would it have been a featured destination for "Strength Through Joy" tourists, schoolchildren on fieldtrips, and soldiers pursuing adult education opportunities? Would the exhibits have been made accessible to the public as they were originally fashioned by their Jewish creators? Or would the perpetrators have adjusted them to fit the antisemitic require- ments of Nazi propaganda? How would the Nazis have incorporated the film footage they took of Jewish religious rituals in early 1944 (including footage of a prayer service and circumcision) in the museum exhibit? Would the footage have been shown as part of the exhibit's larger narrative? Or would it have been edited and distributed through- out the Reich for didactic purposes?

None of these questions can be answered with any finality, but one thing is certain: the Jewish Central Museum in Prague would not have been the only site in the Nazi Empire where the perpetrators would have displayed their narrative of Jewish history and culture. Indeed, the museum was not even intended to have a central role in the Great German Reich, merely in the Protectorate. There is no evi- dence that the Nazis meant the Prague museum to be the only such Jewish museum in Europe. This is confirmed by the ways in which the Nazis dealt with Judaica in other museums during the years of the Third Reich.

One well-documented example can be found in the small town of Schnaittach in Franconia. Home to a significant Jewish community since the sixteenth century and a well-known Yeshiva since the seven- teenth century, Schnaittach today boasts one of the most comprehen- sive collections of rural Judaica in all of south Germany. Local historic preservation officials "Aryanized" the synagogue in 1938 and turned it into a local history museum (*Heimatmuseum*). Various items of Judaica were incorporated into some of the museum's exhibits and presented in neutral fashion, as is shown by photographs from the period. It is unknown to what extent the artifacts were situated into an antisemitic context during the obligatory guided tours. As in Prague, the ceremonial objects, together with the synagogue, were able to survive until the war came to an end. It is impossible to know whether or not the museum's use of Jewish gravestones as steps in its main staircase was deliberately meant to be a symbolic insult. It is obvious, however, that the exhibit communicated some sense of the Jews' role as an integral component of regional culture and history.

The same can be said about the representation of the Jews in the regional museum of Braunschweig. In 1925, the entire interior furnishings of an abandoned eighteenth-century synagogue from the nearby town of Hornburg were transferred to the National Museum (*Vaterländisches Museum*) in Braunschweig. Together with ritual objects from the Braunschweig Jewish community and private donors, the items were displayed in the museum's main exhibition galleries. Despite the Nazi Party's entry into Braunschweig's state government in 1930 and Hitler's rise to power in 1933, the museum's display of the synagogue interior and its Judaica collection remained untouched. To be sure, the Nazis subsequently moved to transform the museum into a "national political education center" and added a denunciatory plaque at the synagogue describing it as a "foreign element within German culture." But the synagogue and the other Jewish artifacts were not removed from the museum; they were merely repositioned within it. Thanks to the Nazis' policies of theft and expulsion, in short, even non-Jewish museums in the Third Reich came to acquire items of Judaica and integrate them into their larger collections.

The Nazis' musealization of Jewish life also extended to cemeteries. Prague's Jewish cemetery would not have been the only one preserved in a German-dominated Europe. Typically, the Nazis dealt with Jewish cemeteries pragmatically, with most remaining intact due to the failure to adapt burial laws to the regime's antisemitic principles. Many deteriorated in the wake of deportations, however, while others were subjected to vandalism; gravestones, fences, and gates were looted for their valuable metals. To be sure, some communities strove to raze Jewish cemeteries and utilize their sites for new purposes.

At the same time, however, local historic preservation authorities often tried to preserve certain cemeteries (for example, in Vienna, Eisenstadt, and Mattersburg) for the purposes of antisemitic research and propaganda.[19] In certain cases, the removal of anthropological remains was permitted as long as the cemetery's appearance remained unaltered. In Mattersburg in the Burgenland, renovation work at the old Jewish cemetery, which authorities wanted to transform into a public park, led to the excavation of several graves. Viennese anthropologists wanted to disinter the skeletons and place them in the Natural History Museum. The same thing happened at the Jewish cemetery in Vienna-Währing, where construction work on an air raid shelter led to similar efforts to exhume Jewish remains and use Jewish gravestones for genealogical research. In 1943, a Natural History Museum official described the dissection and scientific handling of the skeletons as "crucial for scholarly, curatorial, and political reasons" and concluded that they "represented a valuable addition to the museum's collection."[20]

For the Nazis, it was but a short leap from disinterring Jewish corpses in cemeteries to killing Jews in extermination camps in order to get their skeletons for research and preservation purposes. The most famous proponent of this ghoulish practice was anatomist August Hirt at the Reich University of Strassburg, who was part of the SS *Ahnenerbe* (Racial Heritage) program. He justified collecting Jewish bones by claiming that a shortage of them impeded the pursuit of necessary research projects. It was not Hirt, however, but SS captain and racial anthropologist Bruno Beger who came up with the idea of compiling an "anthropological collection of foreign races."[21] In contrast to the artificially manufactured Jewish mannequins displayed in the Prague Central Museum, the bones collected by Hirt and Beger were the real material remains of murdered Jews. Hirt's program represented an extreme form of appropriating and preserving remnants of the perceived enemy by taking advantage of opportunities offered by the regime's extermination policies. In 1943, 115 people (nearly all of them Jews) were selected at Auschwitz, subjected to evaluation, and transported to the Natzweiler concentration camp in Alsace, where they were murdered in the gas chamber especially for Hirt's purposes. Had the Nazis won the war, Jewish skeletons would have been widely displayed in Germany's many natural history museums alongside prehistoric skulls and other physical remains. How they would have been described with accompanying texts is unknown. But we can assume that, as in Braunschweig, they would have been portrayed as a racially inferior, foreign element whose disappearance represented a welcome development for the German *Volk*.

In addition to these museum projects, various research institutions were established to compensate for the absence of the indispensable Jewish enemy. These institutions, which were initially created to legitimize the regime's antisemitic policies, promoted the research of non-Jewish scholars into Jewish history and culture and helped to create a new scholarly field of Nazi "Jewish Studies" (*Judenforschung*).[22] This field sought to solidify itself in the Third Reich with an array of institutes, academic journals, and conferences. It was in no way identical to the disciplines of racial science or anthropology, even if such racially informed studies were sponsored under its auspices. Rather, it was a field led by historians, theologians, philosophers, literary scholars, and legal thinkers, who focused on questions of political, social, and cultural history.

Within a short period of time, there was a veritable wave of institutes founded in Nazi Germany, including the Institute for the Study of the Jewish Question in Berlin (1935), the Research Department on the Jewish Question in the Reich Institute for History of the New Germany in Munich (1936), the Institute for the Study and Eradication of Jewish Influence on German Church Life in Eisenach (1939), and the Institute for Research on the Jewish Question in Frankfurt am Main (1941). Similar institutes were founded during World War II in Nazi-occupied Europe. There was a Department for Jewish Research in the Institute for German Work in the East in Cracow, an Institute for the Study of the Jewish Question in Paris, and similar institutions in Milan, Florence, Trieste, Bologna, and Budapest. Scientifically grounded research projects on Jewish history and culture were also undertaken in the context of security police activities within the Reich Security Main Office under the category of "enemy research." Dissertations were also produced in various academic fields at many German universities. While most studies addressed different aspects and the history of the "Jewish Question" in different countries, their focus was quite broad, as was made clear by such sample titles as: "The Development of the Ghetto Within the Context of Jewish Law in Medieval Germany," "Jewish Characters on the German Stage," "The Jewish Policies of the Frankish-German King and Kaiser," and "Anti-Jewish Trends within German Catholicism." Plans to establish professorships in Nazi Jewish

Studies were also pursued at universities in Tübingen, Vienna, Berlin, and Frankfurt.

One of the main goals of Nazi Jewish Studies was to "dejudaize" a field of scholarly research that had been pioneered by Jewish scholars. The representatives of the new Nazi field sought to counter the older Jewish tradition of the "Science of Judaism," which had never been admitted into mainstream German academia, while exploiting its scholarly findings for their own purposes. The anti-Jewish scholarship should be understood as an appropriation and distortion of existing themes, ideas, sources, resources, and materials. Jews were only permitted to be the passive objects of research, not active subjects pursuing it in their own right. The allegedly dominant Jewish view of Jewish history was to be replaced by a non-Jewish German perspective. Jewish scholars were denied the capacity to objectively study Jewish history. At the same time, Jews were covertly employed as forced laborers in the Nazi plundering of Europe's libraries and their expertise exploited for the sake of Nazi scholarship.

The antisemitic scholars were themselves aware of the paradox of studying and preserving the legacy of an ostensibly inferior enemy. They recognized the perils of neglecting to study their own allegedly more valuable history. In order to prevent any threat to the ideologically mandated hierarchy, Nazi Jewish Studies (*Judenforschung*) was defined as the "history of the Jewish Question" and distinguished from the "Study of the Jews" (*Judenkunde*), which focused more on Jewish history, practices, and traditions. The study of these internal Jewish subjects was dismissed as superfluous and deemphasized in favor of studying "the intersection of German and Jewish social milieus." The "Jewish Question" was thus understood as an integral feature of German history. The promoters of Nazi "Jewish Studies," therefore, did not only work to construct an image of the "other," but helped to forge a sense of German identity.

Within the field of Nazi Jewish Studies, history became the leading discipline, since the Final Solution both enabled and necessitated the historicization of the "Jewish Question." Research into previous attempts to solve the "Jewish Question" served to establish its prehistory and legitimize the Nazis' more radical policies. There were many efforts to show how previous failures to solve the question in the past might provide lessons for doing so in the present. There were also efforts to study contemporary anti-Jewish policies. Dissertations focused on the problem of Jewish emigration from Germany, the "Aryanization" of German economic life, and foreign countries' reactions to Germany's anti-Jewish policies. The Nazis' version of Jewish Studies thus represented an affirmative approach to studying antisemitism and the Holocaust.

On March 16, 1941 in Frankfurt am Main, Nazi ideologue Alfred Rosenberg marked the opening of his Institute for Research on the Jewish Question (Figure 32) by noting the longterm importance of studying Jewish history from a Nazi perspective. He declared:

> Once the Jewish Question in Germany – and in all of Europe – is solved, there may come a generation after us that may not be able to give an account of what transpired in these decades. Our grandchildren, freed from Jewish influence, might fall susceptible to dreamy ideas and lose sight of the potency that Jews still possess in Europe today. Peoples' memories are short and it may take a mere thirty or fifty years for the most difficult experiences to be deleted from popular consciousness. For this reason, we cannot remain content with the experiences of the last decade, with the books and speeches emerging from the immediate struggle, but must complement the experienced khowledge, which was already in part rooted in deep insights, with a comprehensive program of research.[23]

It is difficult to know how the Nazis' version of Jewish Studies would have developed in a victorious Reich. But the study of Jewish history and culture would have been firmly anchored both in universities and independent research institutions. It would have been defined by professorships, graduate students, dissertations, journals, conferences, and all the other familiar accoutrements of academic life. Even the regime's antisemitic and exterminationist policies would have been the subject of scholarly research, albeit from an affirmative perspective that validated them as key components of a world historical deed grounded in the lessons of history.

The Nazis did not merely seek to preserve an image of the Jews in museums and scholarship, but in visual media as well. Joseph Goebbels' Reich Propaganda Ministry used film to document Jewish life beyond expulsion and destruction. Fritz Hippler, the director of the Film Department in the Propaganda Ministry, wrote about these efforts in his memoirs in a chapter entitled "Jewish Footage for the Archive." In it, he recalled that:

Figure 32. Nazi ideologue Alfred Rosenberg, who opened the Institute for Research on the Jewish Question in Frankfurt am Main in 1941.

as I was presenting the raw cut of the latest German *Newsreel*, Goebbels said to me, "Go see for yourself how these Jews live at home. Take footage of life in the Polish ghettos. Travel to Litzmannstadt (Lodz) tomorrow with a pair of cameramen and film everything you can get a hold of – the bustle on the streets, the trading and haggling, the rituals in the synagogue, especially the ritual slaughter of animals. We have to document all of this on site since there will soon be no more Jews. The Führer wants to resettle them all to Madagascar or some other area. We therefore need these cinematic documents for our archives."[24]

Hippler instructed the German authorities in Lodz to open the city's shuttered great synagogue and approve the otherwise banned ritual slaughter practice for the sake of his film. After his return, he showed Goebbels the footage and recalled that the Propaganda Minister

tried to show me how someone with the correct view of the Jewish Question would react. He responded to practically every major scene with catcalls of aversion and disgust; he even cursed certain figures so vigorously as if to call forth reactions from the screen; when the ritual slaughter scenes appeared, he pressed his hands in front of his face and moaned.

At the conclusion, he decreed that the footage did not belong in the archive but should be incorporated into a full-length feature film. He wanted to send cameramen back to the ghetto after speaking to them first. Dr. Taubert from the Institute for Research on the Jewish Question was to produce the film's script. Goebbels and his colleagues worked on this film for an entire year, presenting rough versions to countless committees and ordering numerous edits before permitting it for public presentations.[25]

The film that emerged from Hippler's footage was perhaps the most notorious and aggressive antisemitic work of cinema produced in Nazi Germany, *The Eternal Jew* (1940). The film was used throughout occupied Europe to support anti-Jewish measures, whether the mandated wearing of the Jewish Star or mass deportations. Apart from its short-term propaganda function, however, the film footage was also inspired by the Nazis' need to document for the future what they themselves were in the process of destroying in the present. Had the Nazis won the Second World War, this footage would probably have become a reservoir of material for future propaganda work. It might even have provided a basis for subsequent German television documentaries about the heroic implementation of the Final Solution and the disappearance of the Jews.

Indeed, in crafting the official memory of the Jews and their eventual destruction, the Nazis would have embraced an explicit narrative portraying the necessity of their disappearance. Party officials might have followed Himmler's example from his Posen speech of 1943 and legitimized the SS killers' brutal actions while praising their ability to preserve their "decency." It is also possible that, in the years following the Wehrmacht's final victory, German publishing houses would have eventually published a stream of perpetrator autobiographies and memoirs detailing the hard, but decent, work they completed on behalf of the German people. Eric Norden's alternate history novel, *The Ultimate Solution* (1973), provides a vivid sense of how memory might have evolved in a world in which a victorious Reich succeeded in murdering the entirety of the Jewish people. One scene in the novel portrays how an extermination camp outside of New York City – one in which 4 million American Jews have been killed – is transformed into a "national shrine," a tourist destination, and a "studying camp for administration and extermination techniques." The site even partakes in the commercialization of memory, with an entry sign to the camp reading:

> Welcome to Croton-on-Hudson. Home of the Final Solution. Visit the Frederick Barbarossa Death Camp, 1 mile ahead, first right. Admission 35 marks, children free. No dogs allowed. Picnic areas adjacent.[26]

Revealingly, the novel portrays the camp's commandant as having become the museum's curator and archivist, busily writing his memoirs of the heroic war years.

It is impossible to know whether Norden's nightmarish vision would have come to pass. One can just as easily imagine the Nazis trying to keep the German public from learning about all the grisly details of the killings. Indeed, they might have followed the real historical example of Germany after 1945 and spared the German people any serious confrontation with guilt and responsibility. At the same time, it is easy to hypothesize that, in a victorious Reich, countless perpetrator memoirs would have been published, complete with explicit photographs of mass shootings and extermination sites. After all, in real history, many German perpetrators copiously documented their killings in contravention of official prohibitions. Had the Nazis won the war, the so-called Auschwitz Album and Stroop Album ("The Jewish quarter of Warsaw is no more!") might have been published as popular books portraying Germans efficiently carrying out their orders – whether sending Hungarian Jews to Birkenau's gas chambers or crushing the Warsaw ghetto uprising.

The future of Holocaust memory in a Nazi-ruled world would have also been shaped by the regime's ultimate ambitions. Hitler's longterm foreign policy goal was not merely to assert German dominance in Europe, but on the larger global stage. Given Hitler's recognition that accomplishing this goal might take several generations, the Nazis probably never would have been content to solve the Jewish Question merely in a European context. Until they could achieve a global solution, they would have continued to disseminate antisemitic propaganda – if need be, worldwide – as a crucial means of achieving their larger ends. As the German historian and antisemite, Wilhelm Grau, resolutely declared in 1941:

> In our generation, the Jewish Question will remain a great
> spiritual and political question that will be wrestled with around
> the world. Having relocated their spiritual and scientific power
> centers to the American continent, Jewry will continue to wage an
> ideological fight against the new European solution to the
> question... It will prefer to fight on the turf of science, where it
> imagines itself to be particularly well-armed and respected.
> Germany, which has thrown the Jew to the ground at home, is
> committed to spiritually attacking and defeating him wherever he
> appears.[27]

As indicated by Grau's observation, the Nazis' fight against the eternal Jew was itself destined to be eternal.

In attempting to determine how history would have been different if the Nazis had completed the Holocaust, it seems unlikely that there would have been a "Final Solution of Memory" comparable to the "Final Solution of the Jewish Question." Instead, the Nazis probably would have "Aryanized" remembrance, instrumentally utilizing it for the purposes of their larger political ideology. In his important novel about wartime and postwar Prague, *The Invisible Wall* (1989), the Holocaust survivor and writer, H. G. Adler, portrayed an SS official bluntly telling some of the Jews working in the city's Jewish Museum, "You must exist, even when you no longer exist."[28] In their own perverse way, the Nazis needed the Jews, even as they fanatically fought to get rid of them.

To be sure, remembrance in a Nazi-ruled world would have lacked dissenting voices: above all those of the victims. We can only speculate about what would have happened had the Nazis discovered the Jews' efforts to document their sufferings and their perspective on their own history, whether in the milk bottles hidden by Emanuel Ringelblum's Oneg Shabbat group in the Warsaw ghetto or the writings of the historians of the Jewish Sonderkommando in Auschwitz-Birkenau. Would the perpetrators have destroyed these documents or preserved them in their archives? Would they have made use of them for their own purposes and published them in some kind of manipulated form? No one can say for sure, but one thing is certain: the Nazis' portrayal of the victims would have been fundamentally inauthentic.

That said, the Nazis' approach to remembering the Holocaust would have paradoxically possessed jarring similarities to our own ways of remembering the event today. In the same way that the Western world has embraced an extensive, state-supported, and institutionally grounded culture of Holocaust consciousness in recent decades, a similar culture would have taken shape in a Nazi-ruled world as well. In establishing a rich network of museums, research institutes, and monuments devoted to chronicling the history, culture, and disappearance of the Jews, the Nazis clearly demonstrated their commitment to remembering their wartime fate. To be sure, Nazi memory would have had a totally opposite moral valence from that which exists in our own world. Rather than being viewed as representing the nadir of modern civilization, the crimes of the Holocaust would have been celebrated in a victorious Reich as a heroic deed of world historical importance. This fact more than anything else should serve as a profound reminder of the discomfiting ambiguities of remembrance.

What, finally, would have been the longterm fate of Holocaust memory under a victorious Nazi regime? Here, there may be a surprising answer. We are used to thinking of totalitarian states such as Nazi Germany as all-powerful entities that brooked no opposition. But, in the same way that historians have shown the existence of dissent within the interstices of Germany's regimented society, so too might counter-memories have existed as well. While it is true that the Nazis' official narrative about the history, culture, and ultimate disappearance of the Jews would have been predictably propagandistic, it may eventually have been open to revisionist correctives. The alternate history novels, *Fatherland* and *Moon of Ice*, plausibly show the Nazis' policies of amnesia to be vulnerable to challenges from below, with skeptics questioning official orthodoxies and searching for deeper historical truths. These fictional scenarios confirm a fundamental fact: memory is ultimately uncontrollable. As has been shown by the countless controversies that have erupted in recent years over divisive historical legacies in our own world, the past never settles into a completely ossified form and is always potentially contestable. Even in a victorious Nazi Empire the triumphalistic representation of the Holocaust may eventually have been challenged by revisionist counter-narratives. What they would have claimed, whether they would have been able to chip away at the official orthodox narrative, and whether they would have come closer to what we know as the truth of the Holocaust, is unknowable. What is clear, however, is that memory has always been, and always will be, in flux.

16 WHAT IF THE HOLOCAUST HAD BEEN AVERTED?

Jeffrey S. Gurock

It was an emotional expression of collegial brotherhood that brought even the stiffest upper-lipped members of the British Parliament to cheers and tears. On October 1, 1938, Prime Minister Neville Chamberlain returned from the diplomatic summit in Munich and reported to the House of Commons on the breakdown of negotiations over the Sudetenland, the ethnically mixed region of Czechoslovakia so coveted by Adolf Hitler. Chamberlain had spent many weeks prior to the summit trying to broker a "peace in our time" via shuttle diplomacy, but when push came to shove, he and French Premier Édouard Daladier refused to abandon the Czechs. Dismissing fears that opposition to Nazi aggression might soon lead to an attack against the British Isles, he recognized that the balance of armaments was still in the Western Allies' favor and sensed that it was still possible to stand up to Germany's unbridled malevolence. Critically, Chamberlain had in the back of his mind – as well as his back pocket – a military analysis projection that indicated that as of January 1, 1939, London and Paris together possessed 200,000 more soldiers, 2,000 more airplanes, and far more battleships, cruisers, and destroyers than Germany. Now was the time to stand strong – perhaps even more for the sake of his own people's future than for the Czechs. The summit broke up after Chamberlain warned that "invasion of the Sudetenland meant war."[1]

Upon his return to London, Chamberlain had to reassure fearful Britons that they were not going to have to spend the coming months "digging trenches and trying on gas masks," but Winston Churchill believed that the Prime Minister had shown impressive courage.[2] The

Member of Parliament who, until Munich, had been one of the most outspoken critics of the Conservative government, asserted to all within earshot that "your steadfastness has set in motion consequences of which will travel far with us along our road and when weighed in the balance over the length of time will be judged both correct and courageous." Churchill and Chamberlain, the new comrades-in-arms, then spontaneously embraced in the well of the House of Commons to a standing ovation from both sides of the chamber.[3]

Back in Germany, the Führer was infuriated that "these weaklings" had stood up to him. It was a new experience for the German leader, who, until that time, had succeeded in bullying his way in foreign affairs as he rearmed his country, reoccupied the Saar, built up the German air force (Luftwaffe), reintroduced conscription, remilitarized the Rhineland, and annexed Austria. Determined to teach the Czechs and the world a lesson, Hitler, who had wanted to attack the Czechs since 1937, moved the Wehrmacht across the border and ignited a new European war. The Nazis initially succeeded in their aggression. The Tenth Army broke through Czech opposition as their forces moved rapidly from Bavaria to the Bohemian plain. But they soon paid a heavy price. The German army had superior weaponry and sent more men into battle. But the Czechs were worthy opponents, fighting on their own home turf with a spirited regular army supplemented by committed reserve units and relying on their stockpile of armaments.[4]

Even more important was the decision of France and Britain to fulfill their treaty obligations to the Czechs and join the battle against the Nazis. For the next six years, the conflict raged back and forth across the German and French borders. Periodically, ceasefires halted the carnage, only to have the warring sides rearm and resume the blood-letting. In many places, stalemate was the order of the day – as in the Great War of 1914–18 – and the Germans were never able to strike a decisive blow. Hitler never fulfilled his dream of watching his troops march triumphantly down the Champs-Élysées. The war ended only in 1944 when German High Command officers, fearful that a vulnerable Central and Western Europe would be ripe for a Soviet invasion, found negotiating partners among anticommunist British and French military leaders and sued for peace. The chief condition for the ensuing armistice was the removal of the Nazi regime's entire leadership, which was made easier after Hitler was assassinated by a cabal of Wehrmacht officers.

The new "Allies" were right to fear the Soviets. As early as 1939, Stalin watched the Wehrmacht descend into disarray and determined that he did not need a nonaggression pact with Hitler. Acting independently, he moved Soviet forces against Poland and in six weeks brought it into the communist sphere. The Russian dictator had hated the Poles since 1920, when they had succeeded in repelling the Bolshevik attack against Warsaw, thereby impeding the new regime's goal of spreading radical revolutions worldwide. Soviet comrades would have to be content in the 1920s and 1930s to build "Socialism in One Country." But now, at the end of the 1930s, the prospects for an international communist revolution seemed brighter than ever. The occupation of Poland was a first step in that direction, even as it immediately served as a territorial barrier between the Motherland and the equally hated Third Reich.[5]

The Wehrmacht's military difficulties did not only benefit the Soviets but also German and Austrian Jews, who now gained a new lease on life. Although Hitler continued to insist that the Jews were the chief source of Germany's troubles, he had larger problems to deal with as a result of the worsening military situation. The German people had not been prepared properly for war. Until 1938, all of the regime's territorial successes had been achieved without the loss of German life. With war and all of its privations now upon the German citizenry, however, naysayers began to appear on the scene. Initially, they merely whispered, but as the war dragged on they began to openly express, words of "defeatism." In the late fall of 1938, with Hitler coming under increasing internal criticism, the energies of the Gestapo and the SS were redirected from dealing with the Jewish Question to suppressing internal dissent.[6]

On November 9, 1938, SS officer Adolf Eichmann was notified that the regime's priorities had changed when he received a directive from SS head Heinrich Himmler, ordering him to halt his Jewish emigration efforts (which he had been responsible for in annexed Austria) and begin rounding up critics of the regime. Any plans to accelerate German Jewish emigration by unleashing a terror campaign against them in the form of a national pogrom were now put on hold. Eichmann was reluctant to shut down his highly praised emigration processing center, but he did his duty and followed orders. The Jews of Vienna were relieved, as were co-religionists elsewhere in the Reich, when a week later Hitler designated Hjalmar Horace

Figure 33. Hjalmar Schacht, seen here with Adolf Hitler, helped promote German Jewish emigration to Palestine through the so-called Transfer Agreement.

Greeley Schacht head of a new Commission on the Jewish Question (Figure 33).

Schacht was not a Nazi Party member and regularly appeared at official occasions in civilian attire instead of jackboots and uniform.

Appointed Economics Minister in 1934, he was a realist on the "Jewish Question." Before assuming his position, he had the gumption to make his attitudes clear to Hitler. Not intimidated in the least, Schacht inquired, in his typically straightforward, fearless manner, "before I take office, I should like to know how you wish me to deal with the Jewish Question." He took Hitler's reply – "in economics, carry on exactly as you have in the past" – to mean that nothing should be done to the Jews that would stymie recovery.[7]

Upon assuming his new post five years later, Schacht again asked the Führer to explain how he planned to address the Jews' future in the Reich. The minister's question sent Hitler into one of his frequent rages. "My struggle is to win a war against the Jews for the German people and for the survival of the world," he sputtered. "But at this precise moment in human history, I must concern myself with their surrogates, the British and the French, and those within the Reich who would keep me from my destiny." Calming himself, Hitler took Schacht aside and instructed him to "Do as you see fit."

Schacht now put all of his energy into updating a plan that he had developed back in September 1933 to send Jews to Palestine. The so-called Transfer Agreement was a remarkable trade pact between unlikely allies – Zionists and Nazis – that was designed to boost the ailing German economy while also meeting Jewish needs. The pragmatic plan reflected both sides' complementary ideological views of one another. The Nazis perceived the Zionists to be uniquely honest Jews, since they denied that Germany was their homeland and supported Jewish emigration from Europe. The Reich leadership, especially Schacht, furthermore believed the initiative would improve Germany's balance of trade. German Zionists, meanwhile, believed they could look beyond the Nazi regime's malevolent antisemitism and deal with it on the basis of rational, mutual self-interest. They further needed the hard goods that the Germans could provide and were eager to boost Jewish immigration to the Yishuv in Palestine. A deal was therefore struck in which Jews who left Germany for Palestine were allowed to leave their resources in escrow accounts in Germany. When the Yishuv purchased goods from the Reich, it paid only half of the costs from its own resources. The remainder was borne by the monies from those German Jews who resided freely in Palestine. The Zionist trust company, in turn, compensated the new arrivals with half of the amount from their previously frozen bank accounts, thereby helping them get a new start in life in the Jewish homeland.[8]

As the architect of the plan, Schacht was convinced that more could be done to accelerate migration. Fortunately for the Jews, and for the success of Schacht's mission, Chamberlain's turn away from appeasement enabled Palestine to reemerge as a viable option for Jewish migrants. A reversal of fortune was now afoot in the Middle East. Among diplomats, the talk was no longer of partitioning the territory or turning it over to the Arabs. The newly resolute British were ready to remain in Palestine on a more permanent basis. While Jewish immigration would be closely monitored, there was the potential down the road of a future Jewish commonwealth in Palestine. Such a scenario had been discussed seriously just a year earlier, in 1937. It was now back on the diplomatic table, starting in the British Foreign Office.

From the time the British were granted legal control over Palestine in the early 1920s, their policy had been one of "equality of obligation." The Mandatory power sagaciously played Jewish aspirations and Arab fears off against one another in the hope of buying time for moderate voices and attitudes to emerge from the two antagonistic parties. This strategy had enjoyed a reasonable chance of success through the 1920s, at a time when limited Jewish immigration to Palestine did not endanger the territory's "absorptive capacity." Yet as the Jewish settlement became more politically sophisticated and as the Arabs began to respond to it with violence – as in the riots of 1929 – the British policy showed serious signs of vulnerability.

Hitler's rise destroyed the British fantasy definitively. The Jews needed Palestine as a refuge and the Arabs saw themselves as victims for the sins of European antisemitism. In 1933, some 30,000 Jews chose to go to Palestine, three times the number that had fled there just a year earlier. Moreover, additional Jews were on the way: 42,000 in 1934 and 62,000 in 1935. By 1936, the Arabs had seen enough. Encouraged by their religious and political leaders, they unleashed a massive revolt, thereby forcing the British to reevaluate their policies. The subsequent Peel Commission hearings in London determined that Jews and Arabs could no longer live together in any semblance of peaceful coexistence. The only hope for quiet in the region was to divide the land into Zionist and Arab national entities. Neither of the warring sides was happy with the proposal. For the Jews it was a betrayal of their understanding of the 1917 Balfour Declaration, which had promised them a national home in Palestine. They were being pushed to accept a reduced presence in Zion and, more importantly, limited Jewish migration from Europe. The Arabs, for their part, would not agree to any concessions that would legitimize the Jews' claims. But for all of their fulminations, the Arabs felt that time was on their side. Looking ahead to a possible world war in the early 1940s, they knew that the Jews would have to support the British against Hitler. They were free agents. The about-face of the British and French at Munich and the subsequent problems that the Nazis faced in trying to defeat the Czechs, however, changed the geopolitical picture fundamentally.[9]

The British Foreign Office determined that an alliance between the Nazis and the Arabs of Palestine was not particularly troubling. In charting their new course, the Chamberlain government recognized that a conscious return to a true "equality of obligation" policy would not play well on the Arab street. Realpolitik in this critical area meant that the British needed good relations with both the Egyptians, who controlled access to the Suez Canal, and the Iranians, who sat on millions of gallons of oil needed by British armed forces. Great Britain was likewise the global master of 20 million Muslim subjects, whose opinions could not be totally ignored. But in its post-appeasement mode of behavior, Britain's leaders felt that another twist in Mandatory policy would not egregiously raise the hackles of the Muslim world. In effect, the British were signaling that they would not leave Palestine in the foreseeable future. Moreover, Britain's strategic experts sensed that the Egyptians, Iranians, and the others – for all their lip service to anti-Zionism – were far from fully committed to the Palestinian Arab cause. So the old game of attempting to be "all things to all peoples" resumed. The Chamberlain government spoke strongly within Arab earshot that Jewish immigration to Palestine had to be curtailed. But in practice, to the tacit satisfaction of Zionists and the utter relief of oppressed Jews everywhere, the doors remained open.

Chamberlain now dusted off a plan that his new friend Churchill had broached to the House of Commons in 1937. The British would expend the energies necessary to put a lid on lawlessness in Palestine. The numbers of Jews to be allowed into Palestine would be fixed "at a certain number." However, Chamberlain was quick to point out that whatever that exact figure would be, it would not displace, or otherwise endanger, Arab life in the land. The Prime Minister used figures provided by Churchill that indicated that the Arab population had increased during the Zionist migration to a degree "almost as great as that of the Jewish population." The newcomers had provided employment and other opportunities to the Arabs of the land.

Chamberlain also let Churchill address the question of Arab intransigence. Proud that his plan was becoming policy, Churchill asserted that the Arabs were to be told "quite plainly that unless they accept within a reasonable period of time a fair offer and cease to wage war upon Britain, we shall have to carry out our plan." Their uprising was cast not only as an attack against Jews but against Britain as well. The British government was now determined to proceed "not without regard to their rights but without any sense of special obligation."[10]

Haj Amin Al-Husseini, the Grand Mufti of Jerusalem, the religious and political head of the rejectionist Palestinian Arab front against Zionism, was outraged over this ominous development. He was a scion of an aristocratic Jerusalem family with an abiding hatred for Zionists as invaders who had brought to his world not only a Jewish, but a hated European style of life. His supporters had credited him with inspiring Arab uprisings against the Zionist invaders in 1921, 1929, and 1936. In 1937, he had made his opposition to the Peel Commission recommendations abundantly clear at a pan-Arab conference when he called for the scrapping of the Balfour Declaration, the end of the Mandate, and the quick establishment of an Arab state in Palestine. He promised only that the civic and religious rights of "minorities" – Christians and Jews – would be "guaranteed." He warned belligerently that "Great Britain must choose between our friendship and the Jews. Britain must change her policy in Palestine or we shall be at liberty to side with other European powers whose policies are inimical to Great Britain."[11]

The Mufti now rushed to Berlin in the hope of forging an alliance with the Nazis. Al-Husseini banked on Hitler making good on a recent proclamation of behalf of the "defenseless Arabs in Palestine." What the Mufti and the Aryan Führer had in common was "hatred of the Jews and of the British." Politics now trumped "scientific racism" as the Semite, Al-Husseini, received a respectful hearing in Berlin. His ensuing meetings with Nazi officials, however, left him frustrated. Since Schacht declined to meet with him, Husseini returned to the Middle East without any formal alliance with the Third Reich. This did not keep him and his followers from subsequently stirring up trouble, however.[12]

While the Munich disagreement bolstered the morale of German and Austrian Jews, Stalin's capitalizing upon the start of the new European war brought misery to the world's largest Jewish communities. Since the 1920s, more than 6 million impoverished Jews had been forced to live under oppressive Eastern European regimes. In Poland, old-style religious Jew-hatred, coupled with "a virulent form of nationalism that was influenced by fascist models," undermined Jewish life. In the 1930s, outbreaks of violence against people and property exceeded that seen early on in Nazi Germany. In Soviet Russia, antisemitism was officially outlawed, even as folk-based Jew-hatred persisted. But communist ideology and policies constantly endangered Jewish religious and cultural life. Moreover, like all denizens of the Soviet Union, Jews suffered from Stalin's failed economic impositions. Now, the Jews of Poland, Lithuania, Ukraine, and the Russian heartland were "unified" – albeit under the merciless hand of the Soviet dictator. Millions of Jews hunkered down and did their best to survive the deprivations that became their unhappy lot for years to come.[13]

For American Jews, meanwhile, Britain's stand at Munich and Hitler's ill-fated war against the Czechs came at a most opportune time. It provided a welcome respite for a harried community that, for much of the 1930s, felt insecure in America, uncertain of its status among its fellow citizens, and fearful, for good reason, of growing antisemitism. American Jews had been the quintessential internationalists, while the majority of Americans – both those in the cities, where most Jews lived, as well as those in the heartland, where few of them resided – wanted little part of foreign problems. Making the situation more acute, the Jew-haters among them had twisted American Jews' support for their overseas brethren into conspiracy theories by branding them as warmongers willing to sacrifice American lives for their own selfish purposes.[14]

There were allegations that a Semitic cabal was manipulating President Roosevelt, whom it was said the Jews controlled first through imposing a socialist New Deal upon the nation and then through instigating American involvement in unnecessary conflicts far away from its shores. The most notorious prophet of an endangered America was Father Charles Coughlin. From his radio pulpit in Royal Oak, Michigan, he preached to millions of attentive Americans. As early as 1936, he spoke derisively of "Roosevelt and Ruin ... because the money changers" – implying Jews – "had not been driven out from the temple" – the government in Washington. In July 1938, two months before Munich, he showed his true colors when he began publishing in his newspaper *Social Justice* chapters from the *Protocols of the Elders of Zion*, the scurrilous forged document that alleged a nefarious Jewish plan not only to gain control over the United States but also to bring the whole world to its knees.[15]

With a new reality afoot late in 1938, however, American Jewish leaders stood down from their previous battles against restrictionists and sought to improve their reputation in the halls of Congress and on the streets of America. The circumstances were hopeful. America was at peace and did not seem likely to become embroiled in any foreign conflicts. In fact, in 1941, while European armies slogged back and forth between German and Western European battlefields, a crucial world-changing decision was made in Tokyo war rooms to forego attacking the Philippines and other US possessions as part of Japan's push to establish an Asian empire for itself. While Japanese militarists pushed for a quick strike that would force a disabled America to agree to an armistice, moderates insisted that an aroused enemy, even if temporarily wounded, had sufficient resources to resist signing a dishonorable peace and would fight on. As the moderates constituted the majority faction within the Japanese regime, General Hideki Tojo realized that he would have to remain content with dominating China and seizing the Asian possessions of Britain, France, and the Netherlands. The United States was thus spared active involvement in both the European and Asian theaters of military operations. The latter struggle would end up lasting until the late 1940s. On Sunday, December 7, 1941, sailors on the USS *Arizona* sunned themselves on the deck of their battleship as they were wont to do in a serene Hawaii.[16]

With the United States free of foreign entanglements, American Jews pursued a policy of "American Jewry First." Following the retirement of President Franklin D. Roosevelt in 1941 after two terms in office, his successor, isolationist Republican Robert Taft, entered the White House. American Jewish "foreign policy" was limited to succoring the remaining Jews in the German Reich, mostly the aged, infirm, and naïvely optimistic. The American Jewish Joint Distribution Committee attended to their needs and to those of Eastern European Jews under Soviet control. Back in the United States, American Jews showed great concern for the well-being of the nearly 150,000 German and Austrian Jews who made it to American shores despite the country's enduring immigration quotas. No one wanted these refugees to under-mine the Jews' reputation in the US. Combating antisemitism rose to the top of the community's agenda.

In response – and in spite of the Depression – philanthropic organizations energetically assisted German and Austrian newcomers. With the implementation of New Deal social welfare measures, needy immigrants also now had the government on their side. Further miti-gating the problems of transplantation and adjustment was the proud resourcefulness of former German Jews who put down their roots in America. In New York in the mid to late 1930s, Jews from the Reich were not billeted in the mostly dilapidated hub of the Lower East Side. Rather, they took full advantage of a glut in the real estate market in Washington Heights, in the northwest corner of Manhattan, where affordable housing was available in an unblighted area of town. Once a foothold was secured, a chain migration ensued. By the late 1930s, Washington Heights had acquired the moniker of the "Fourth Reich," speaking to the visible presence of German Jewish refugees.[17]

But while the refugee issue was now coming under control, American Jews still faced daunting personal and communal dilemmas. Most were unhappy with their place in America. They obsessed over discrimination and prejudice while their religious leaders worried about the community's spiritual future. Even if the palpable negativity toward their advocacy of interventionism were to dissipate, the problem that galled them most was that so many Americans simply did not like Jews and did not want to associate with them. Social antisemitism in the United States reached its peak in the 1930s. Most Americans, to be sure, were unwilling to take to the streets against Jews; but they consistently excluded them from the best schools, finest residential areas, the most coveted jobs, and the most favored prestigious clubs.

Examples of discrimination were everywhere. Paltry numbers of Jewish admissions to Ivy League colleges in the 1920s and 1930s chilled the dreams of many high school valedictorians. Jews were not wanted because they were seen as unable to fit in. Devoted students they might be, but they were outsiders who did seem to resemble the elite gentlemen these schools were dedicated to producing. Even if an ambitious and cagy youngster changed his name on his application and fibbed about other personal information, a photograph that revealed his "Semitic features" was a dead giveaway to attentive admissions officers that he was Jewish. The situation was deplorable even at Columbia, the Ivy League school in New York – the nation's largest Jewish city – where discrimination reduced the percentage of Jewish students from 40 percent in the early 1920s to 22 percent ten years later.[18]

Law schools of almost every rank accepted more Jewish applicants. But prestigious law firms felt it was improper to have Jews represent their clients. Perhaps there was room for scholarly Semites in the research department buried under a stack of legal tomes, but they were not wanted as the outfit's public face at trials or in conference rooms. Jews likewise felt that they were outsiders when they ventured away from Jewish neighborhoods on vacations, only to be turned away red-faced from inns that posted signs reading "No Jews or dogs allowed." Other establishments discriminated more subtly, advertising that they catered to "selected clientele."[19]

In this climate of discrimination, the Jews in the United States craved an opportunity to prove their mettle to their fellow citizens. As Americans, they felt blessed that their soldiers were not fighting overseas. As concerned Jews, they were grateful that the refugee issue was under control. Yet they realized, with some degree of regret, that the country's peacetime stability denied them the opportunity to advance the goal of social integration. Serving in the military and being able to fight shoulder to shoulder with one's countrymen was a time-honored way of gaining acceptance in a free society. It was said that in America's earliest war, Jews advanced because of their participation, a fact that the Jewish War Veterans Association publicized widely, with detailed statistics of the numbers of Jews in uniform. More recently, World War I had started well for Jews. But in the aftermath of the 1917 Russian Revolution, questions were raised about Jews on the political left. With Americans now sitting on the sideline during the new Great War, Jews had no chance to prove their patriotism. There would be no Stars of David intermingled with Crosses on iconic battlefields to capture the public's imagination. There would be no growing sense of respect for religious diversity rising out of shared wartime sacrifice. Rather, in a still highly intolerant America, Jews courted public approbation with extensive gestures that bespoke 100 percent Americanism.

In 1939, Warner Brothers made the most dramatic effort to turn the tide of popular feelings about the Jews when they produced *Sons of Liberty* featuring Claude Rains who had previously played Robin Hood on the silver screen. This film biography lauded the contribution of Haym Salomon, who was projected as the financial savior of the American Revolution. It was said that in 1781 this Polish Jew had lent George Washington the necessary funds to keep the battle against the British alive. Seeking to connect this eighteenth-century hero to present-day American realities, screen writer Crane Wilbur was instructed in no uncertain terms to have Salomon say at the end of the film: "From this day forward, Jews in America will harbor no allegiance to any foreign power or movement. We have come to believe – and we will teach our children and our children's children – that America is our eternal homeland. We pray that the tolerance we have earned today in this blessed country will continue forever."[20]

While this movie and other apologetic moves did not appreciably change perceptions of American Jews, they created a growing division between them and the Jews of Palestine. This development left American Zionists adrift. Originally, back in the 1930s, Hitler's rise to power had made Zionism popular in America as Jews expressed their concerns about the frightening developments in Germany and Austria. The sudden news out of Munich in 1938 and the ensuing British reconsideration of its Middle Eastern policies, however, ironically had a negative effect on American Zionism. The general sense among American Jews was that the refugee crisis was finally under control. They now believed that Jewish nationalism was only for Palestinian Jews and migrants from Europe, whose future was now more secure. More importantly, there was a lurking wariness "of political agitation" for the Zionist cause "that might give credence to the image of the 'international Jew.'" The canard that Jews were guilty of "dual loyalty" was a favorite of antisemites like Henry Ford, who in the 1920s first brought the *Protocols of the Elders of Zion* to America, and, of course, Father Coughlin.[21]

American Jews' loyalty to the Jewish national movement was severely tested in the late 1940s, when the World Zionist movement increasingly began to demand formal sovereignty for the Yishuv. This move put them at loggerheads with an unsympathetic President and State Department. Unlike the situation before the Munich summit, there was no talk in the late 1940s of stranded Jewish refugees and murderous Nazis; as a result, there was no humanitarian sympathy for a Jewish homeland. A little-known Missouri senator, Harry S. Truman, asserted that, "if hundreds of thousands of Jewish lives were indeed in existential danger, I would be a supporter of Zionism. But the situation has not yet reached such a critical moment."

In this milieu of conflicting Palestinian Jewish and US agendas, American Jews retreated from their brethren, causing an enduring rift between the two communities. The bombing of Jerusalem's King David Hotel in 1947 by the Palestinian underground that killed scores of British officers and American advisors sparked fears of an antisemitic backlash among American Jews (Figure 34). Especially when their fellow citizens turned a jaundiced eye against the Zionist cause and questioned their patriotism, American Jews sought to distance themselves from their Palestinian co-religionists.

American soldiers ultimately had ended up in harm's way in Palestine due to the Taft administration's reversal of policy. The same fears of Soviet aggression that had limited the Western European blood bath eventually forced the President away from isolationism toward championing anticommunism in a volatile Europe. In the year 1944 – with the British, French, and Germans still fighting their debilitating war – the Soviets began to mass troops on their side of the Polish–German border in preparation for an expected invasion. But they ultimately refrained from launching an attack after learning that the United States had developed a mysterious "wonder weapon." Stalin's stand-down did not end the conflict in the Pacific, however. The British still fought a ceaseless battle against the Japanese. While London struggled to salvage its Far Eastern empire, fears of future Russian infiltration into Asia Minor convinced the British to turn to the United States for assistance in Palestine. The Americans thus became embroiled in the turmoil in the Middle East.

The Americans and the British were unable to control violence in the region and the dispute made front-page news in the US when Jewish terrorists attacked American peace-keeping forces and installations. A *New York Daily Mirror* headline shouted, "Palestine's Jews at War with America." American Jews were disturbed by what their outraged fellow citizens were saying about "Jews everywhere" and felt compelled to declare where their loyalties lay in no uncertain terms.

Shaken by the tabloid headlines, the president of the American Jewish Committee (AJC), Judge Joseph Proskauer, called for a "unity conference" among leading Jewish groups. In May 1947, he sent telegrams to every "responsible" Jewish leader, calling on them to gather

Figure 34. Ruins of the King David Hotel, Jerusalem. The bombing of the hotel by the Palestinian underground in 1947 caused numerous American deaths and created a backlash against American Jews in the United States.

at the Biltmore Hotel in Manhattan to publicly reaffirm "American Jewish patriotism." In innumerable private conversations, he explicitly opined that "distance must be put between us and those Palestinian troublemakers who are providing antisemites in this country with the opportunity to accuse American Jews of 'dual loyalty.'" To friends and confidants, Proskauer averred that "the Committee had to be the unerring mouthpiece for the unalterable position that in the United States as in all other countries, Jews, like others, are devoted nationals of their countries and no others."[22]

The Biltmore Platform pledged American Jewry's "unequivocal devotion to the cause of democratic freedom and international justice to which the government of the United States has long been dedicated." It called upon American Jews to desist completely from "aiding those within our own religious group who would undermine a fair and just peace." While American Zionists were quick to refer to Biltmore as "perfidy," one spokesman declared that ultimately "the greatest tragedy is not so much Proskauer's play on the status fears of American Jews but that so many of our people do not care to be part of an unparalleled moment that could change the destiny of the Jewish people."

Somewhat later, in early October 1947, a troubling State Department memorandum was forwarded to President Taft. Military analysts who had studied the turmoil in Palestine now estimated that to "lock down Arab violence against the outnumbered Jews would require 400,000 US combat troops." Such a move "would quite inevitably throw the majority of the Arabs into the arms of Soviet Russia." Massive American intervention, it also was predicted, would "virtually concede the loss of American access to Middle East oil." Consulting political experts conceded that a full-fledged embrace of the Arabs would infuriate American Jews in some key electoral geographical areas, "whose power, money and influence should not be gainsaid." But Taft was approaching the end of his administration and would not have to endure "ballot box scrutiny." The State Department's advice was for the administration to disengage from Palestine and to convince the British to do as well. Weeks of testy deliberations between Washington and London over the American desire to "get out of the Middle East" raised the hackles of British politicians and diplomats. But they ultimately recognized that without US support, they could not "go it alone" in Palestine. The British therefore resolved to remove all of their troops from the region by May 1948.[23]

As Jews and Arabs battled in Palestine in the months before the Anglo-American withdrawal, additional American advisors – "heroic peace keepers" in the words of the tabloids – died in the crossfire.[24] To make matters worse, various reports suggested that Russian-made armaments were being used in some of these "killings of innocents." When an FBI raid on an upstate New York bullet factory yielded rabbinical students from Yeshiva College and the Jewish Theological Seminary, American "patriotic" organizations picketed these Jewish institutions, demanding that they "show their true colors." School leaders tried to answer charges of disloyalty by disassociating their institutions from the bullet makers, who were expelled. On religious matters, President Samuel Belkin of Yeshiva and Chancellor Louis Finkelstein of the Seminary were often at loggerheads with each other. But on this "defense" concern, they acted as one. In a joint statement they condemned "these radicals who acted willfully and totally without institutional authorization. They have unconscionably placed a blot on our well-earned reputation as good Americans." The popularity of Zionism reached a new low among the masses of American Jews, who did little to help the embattled nationalist movement. They remained deeply concerned about their reputations in the United States.[25]

On May 14, 1948, with British soldiers and American advisors preparing to depart, the Jewish Agency for Palestine was meeting in a theater in Tel Aviv when its chairman David Ben-Gurion declared the creation of the state of Israel. Almost immediately, Andrei Gromyko, the Foreign Minister of the Soviet Union, proclaimed the "right of Jews to enjoy self-determination" and recognized the new political entity. Ben-Gurion did not publicly thank the Soviets for their approbation. He understood the political ramifications of a perceived friendship with Stalin's regime. But he was disappointed that the United States and Great Britain did not immediately extend a comparable welcome to Israel. American assent to the Jewish state came several weeks later, after the President had tested the political waters and determined that animosity toward "Jewish terrorists" had subsided. Ben-Gurion was also deeply put off by the tepid response of American Jewry to what he saw as "the culmination of 2,000 years of Jewish exile and anguish." Most were waiting to see how their gentile neighbors reacted to the creation of the new Jewish state before they responded themselves. Advocates for Zionism in America ended up tabling plans for a massive "Salute to Israel" rally at Madison Square Garden in late May 1948. They were apprehensive both about not filling the 20,000 seat arena and about possible protests against Zionism in the streets near 50th Street and 8th Avenue.

In the months that followed – and against all odds – the new Jewish state succeeded in holding off the Arabs. In the early weeks of the war, superior firepower gave the Arabs the upper hand. But an absence of unity within Arab circles and a "lack of staying power" eventually undid their efforts. The Yishuv also benefited from the fact that the Soviets, pursuing their own cynical version of "even-handedness," sold arms to both sides. By the summer of 1948, Israel had secured its northern boundaries and its most aggressive commanders were looking to move beyond the conquered Negev and drive the Egyptians out of the Sinai Peninsula.[26]

The magnitude of the Israeli battlefield turnabout was unsettling to foreign policy strategists. Israel was becoming a new regional power without the help of the United States. State Department prognosticators did not fear an Israeli alliance with the Soviets. Kremlinologists felt that Stalin's personal antisemitism and the tradition of Jew-hatred among his subjects would never permit such a compact. However, Washington worried that there would be a substantial decline in American influence in the region, given "an ungrateful, unaligned" Israel.

In the months that followed, the question of "Who Lost Palestine?" became a major issue during the presidential campaign. The Democratic Party pilloried the Taft administration for its "incoherent policies that had undermined American power." Its nominee for the White House, General George C. Marshall, spoke incessantly about the administration's "misadventures, first involving the country in that tinderbox, then cutting and running, leaving the Jews and Arabs to battle without Christian restraints, rendering the territory open for Soviet chicanery, and now witnessing the Jewish State demonstrate a lack of respect for a nation that had long served as a haven for oppressed Jews the world over." The Republican nominee, Thomas A. Dewey, was hard-pressed to defend Taft, with whom he was widely identified.

A career army officer of the highest echelon, Marshall was the designated point man in 1944 when the Taft administration faced down the Soviet threat to Central and Eastern Europe. Marshall was widely honored for his "strength and preparedness." These sterling characteristics became the ubiquitous slogans of his presidential run.

Marshall argued that "with the world in flux, there has been a lack of clarity in American objectives; an opaqueness seen most sadly in the Middle East. The present administration failed to understand our most basic needs. We have alienated our oil-rich Arab friends. What would we do if war came again to Europe and the Muslim states starved us of oil?" When confronted by reporters about this "pro-Arab stance," Marshall bristled and replied that, "it is a specious argument that the Jewish state, this so-called bulwark of democracy, is an effective military ally of the West. The Arabs are as much anticommunist as the Jews and the Jews took arms from our enemies." The general's eyes narrowed as he argued passionately that the "history of American support for the Jews' nationalism is nothing more than a poorly disguised ploy to garner 'New York votes.' In the past few months, Israelis have not shown loyalty to us. America must do what is best for Americans."[27]

For the first time in US history, a serious candidate for the presidency had made the Jews a central issue for the White House. Though Marshall and his surrogates repeatedly denied that they were antisemites, Jews noted that the Democrat had conflated Jews with Zionism and that "New York votes" really meant New York Jewish votes. What made matters worse was that American Jewish leaders believed that too many Americans knew exactly what the candidates meant. Too many thought that Jews were "Zionists and not Americans in their heart of hearts."

In the weeks after Marshall won the White House in November of 1948, anxious meetings were held in many Jewish quarters. Joseph Proskauer declared that new ways had to be found to "restore American Jewish credibility." At a gathering of officials from the two oldest self-defense organizations, the American Jewish Committee and the Anti-Defamation League of the B'nai B'rith (ADL), Proskauer canvassed the room for "men of wealth with sterling American reputations, no connections with offensive Zionist organizations, and no history of even a hint of leftist feeling to stand up for our religious group in America."

Ultimately, these leaders decided on a two-pronged approach. They first formed an American Jewish Public Affairs Committee (AJPAC) to work the halls of Congress and try to convince the administration of their good will. They also organized a "Jewish Loyalty Day" rally at Los Angeles' Hollywood Bowl to "show where we stand." The news of this conference received a tepid reaction from Marshall as he assumed office. He told his Defense Department designee, James

Forrestal, that he would take "a wait and see attitude towards America's Jews." Marshall made clear that "no group in this country should be allowed to influence our policy to the point it could endanger our national security."

Meanwhile in Jerusalem, David Ben-Gurion was apoplectic when he heard about Proskauer's initiatives and learned that Zionists were barred from participating by "those self-appointed leaders who serve only themselves and presume to speak for American Jewry." A long battle then ensued – lasting a generation – between Israeli officials and those whom they derided as the "American Jewish establishment" over issues of political allegiance and group identity. Proskauer and David Blaustein, the new president of the American Jewish Committee, were outraged when Ben-Gurion stated that:

> this cowardly establishment has committed itself to "isolationism," to envisioning that the fate of American Jews lies elsewhere than with the world Jewish community centered in Palestine. In their desperation to garner complete acceptance, they have adopted the worst American tradition in foreign policy, believing that they will live well if they only abandon their ties to their brethren. Perhaps, these fearful Jews will mitigate antisemites. But I predict that they will not survive culturally as Jews in America. We must target American Jewish young people who may be saved by migration en masse from their empty US shells to live in Israel. Even if their parents object, they must come to where they can really be Jewish.[28]

Time would tell whether Judaism would survive in America "devoid of a Zionist spirit," as one dispirited American Zionist put it as he boarded a boat to Palestine. What became certain, however, was that as the early 1950s unfolded, American Jewish declarations of patriotism went largely unrequited. Though President Marshall spoke of the United States as "One Nation under God and indivisible" – as a rhetorical answer to atheistic communism – there was no sense of unity in the land. Absent from social discourse was the "common purpose" that might have come out of wartime social mobilization and cooperation. On one battlefield, Jews still had to block allegations that they were not "one with America." A most vexing problem was the widely held belief that Jews were associated with the political left and somehow connected to the feared Soviet threat.

In 1954, the tercentenary of the arrival of the first Jews in New Amsterdam provided Jewish community leaders with another opportunity to distance themselves from suspicions about Jewish patriotism. An AJC "Committee of 300" organized a nationwide series of exhibits and lectures that were dedicated to highlighting "the past 300 years of our participation in America and how committed we remain to civic responsibility and the strengthening of democracy." Strict editorial controls were placed on the many books and essays that chronicled "our heroic history in America." Much attention was again devoted to the figure of Haym Salomon, while little was said about the Jews who supported the British side. These texts also marginalized the history of Jewish labor unions and ignored the saga of Jewish radicalism on the Lower East Side. Proskauer insisted in a letter to the Committee of 300 that he wanted "the troubling history of Zionism in America to be kept out of our story. Why possibly raise the hackles of the Administration with whom we have worked so hard to bring over to our side?" While the Committee did not formally respond to Proskauer, the consensus was that "our feelings towards Israel are thankfully at the moment not being strongly challenged in America. But our radical past still puts us in a bad light. Works that would show how notable Jews, like Justice Louis Brandeis, had contributed so much to America while promoting democracy in the Palestine of the 1910s–1930s could be sponsored."[29]

But in response to the "threat of Communism in our midst," Frank Goldman, president of the B'nai B'rith, argued that "every organization must clean their houses of any employee or professional with past or present ties with communist or socialist groups." He also directed the ADL research group to voluntarily turn over its files on Jewish leftist activities to congressional leaders who were looking at the communist threat to America. "They," Goldman asserted emotionally, "are not part of us."[30]

The high point of the commemoration was the National Tercentenary Dinner on October 20, 1954 at New York City's Waldorf Astoria. Organizers were thrilled that President George Marshall – anxious to show that he "liked the right types of Jews" – gave the keynote address and praised the community for its "history of patriotism." The Committee closely scrutinized the guest list to "prevent embarrassment to our community through affirming in any way, shape or form anti-Americanism." However, there was little afterglow from the Committee's effort. Few Americans paid attention to the commemorative events, which did little to change attitudes on Main Street.

On the "home front," Jews also felt a cold shoulder. In 1954, a troubling ADL study exposed the fact that "Christians were still saying that they did not like Jews and did not want to live next to them." Even in the new suburbs where there were fewer restrictions in place, American Christians did not subscribe to a "get along with Jews attitude." "Truth be told," said one respondent to the ADL survey, "we really do not know Jews intimately, like the way men in barracks who face a common foe get to appreciate the other fellow." Although Jews did not fear that violence would be used against them and their property, they remained unsettled by the general climate of unfriendliness.

In 1948, author Laura Z. Hobson wrote an expose of social antisemitism called *Gentleman's Agreement*. In this novelistic treatment of this enduring form of discrimination which so many Jews faced, she imagined a gentile writer for a major American magazine posing as a Jew to "experience first-hand what it meant to be unwanted in polite circles." Sadly for Hobson, she spent a decade searching for a publisher to bring her work to the public. Unbeknownst to her, one of her problems was that the AJC and the ADL undermined her effort. These defense organizations conducted a whispering campaign against Hobson, making it known to all concerned that she came from an "un-American socialist background." Their answer to the persistence of genteel Jew-hatred was "self-policing": making sure that Jews "behaved well in a nonostentatious way while we await better times in America."[31]

Such was the environment that stymied Jewish life in America as this skittish minority group continued to face many social barriers. America's elite colleges and universities persisted in excluding Jews from their academic communities. Because quotas continued until the late 1950s, many qualified Jewish applicants had to contend with a discriminatory glass ceiling and faced limited career prospects. Only at the end of the decade were steps taken to dismantle the quota system. In 1959, presidential candidate Joseph P. Kennedy Jr. responded to the Soviet Union's launching of the first satellite into space two years earlier by declaring "that the largest task before us is to unleash the power of the best and the brightest from among us to show that the American democratic way of life is the path toward a better future for all peoples worldwide." After he was elected President in 1960, Kennedy enacted policy changes that cleared the way for Jewish applicants to gain wider admission to colleges and universities. Many Jews quietly rejoiced at the dawn of a new era of acceptance based on merit. In their own circles they crowed that their youngsters were indeed among the country's best and the brightest. As Jewish students began to populate America's most prestigious campuses, they hoped it signaled the possibility they were becoming accepted into the American mainstream.

However, this new acceptance came at a great cultural cost. The most influential American universities had moved from being preserves of Anglo-Saxon conformity to melting-pot cauldrons. Missing, however, was a commitment to cultural pluralism. Essentially, America wanted Jewish brains but rejected Jewishness as such. Jewish college students understood the bargain that had been struck, as they proudly wore their freshman beanies through the "quad" or "yard" – head-coverings that certainly would never be confused with yarmulkes. Scattered voices within the Jewish community argued that, for America to be truly great, its best and brightest had to draw on the dignity of their ancestral past in contributing to the country's advancement. But few Americans and few American Jews were listening.

Surveying this troubling scene, a young, outspoken American Zionist leader, Rabbi Arthur Hertzberg, offered a dystopian vision of American Jewry's future. Mincing few words, this vice-president of the American Jewish Congress editorialized mournfully in its *Monthly*:

We are reaping the whirlwinds of a generation of parental fears of "dual loyalty" unmitigated neither by American humanitarian concerns over endangered European Jews nor by comradeship with us as allies in a grand fight for our country's survival. Carefully orchestrated Loyalty Day events have had no impact upon our fellow citizens. In this unfavorable environment, our intimidated community has failed to embrace an organic connectedness between Jews of the American diaspora and our spiritual center home in Eretz Yisrael. We have been tried and have failed to assure community continuity. Our young people have no pride in being Jewish. And America has not granted them the right to affirm their distinctiveness. Now that they are welcomed with half-opened arms into gentile realms, the majority will – more than ever – drift away from identification with their people's future. Such has become our unhappy fate.

NOTES

Introduction: Counterfactual history and the Jewish imagination

1. The exact passage appears in Exodus 16:3. David Lieber (ed.), *Etz Hayim: Torah and Commentary* (New York: Jewish Publication Society, 2001), p. 414.

2. Among the most important titles are Niall Ferguson's edited volume, *Virtual History: Alternatives and Counterfactuals* (New York: Basic Books, 1997); Robert Cowley's edited volumes, *What If? Military Historians Imagine What Might Have Been* (New York: Berkley Trade, 1999), *More What If?: Eminent Historians Imagine What Might Have Been* (New York: Putnam, 2001), and *What Ifs? of American History* (New York: Berkley Trade, 2003). See also Andrew Roberts (ed.), *What Might Have Been: Imaginary History from Twelve Leading Historians* (London: Phoenix, 2004); Philip E. Tetlock, Richard Ned Lebow, and Geoffrey Parker (eds.), *Unmaking the West: "What-If?" Scenarios That Rewrite World History* (Ann Arbor: University of Michigan Press, 2006); Jeremy Black, *What If?: Counterfactualism and the Problem of History* (London: Social Affairs Unit, 2008); Richard J. Evans, *Altered Pasts: Counterfactuals in History* (Lebanon, NH: Brandeis University Press, 2014). Journalists have also embraced the genre, as is shown by Jeff Greenfield's books, *And Then Everything Changed: Stunning Alternate Histories of American Politics: JFK, RFK, Carter, Ford, Reagan* (New York: Putnam, 2011), and *If Kennedy Lived: The First and Second Terms of President John F. Kennedy: An Alternate History* (New York: Putnam, 2013).

3. There are nearly as many definitions of counterfactual history as there are synonyms for the term itself. Counterfactual history been called many things by scholars in recent years, including "virtual history," "allohistory," and

"alternate history." See Ferguson, *Virtual History*. The word allohistory (and the useful adjective, allohistorical) comes from the Greek root, "allo," meaning "other." For an introduction, see Gordon Chamberlain, "Afterword: Allohistory in Science Fiction," in Charles G. Waugh and Martin H. Greenberg, *Alternative Histories: Eleven Stories of the World as it Might Have Been* (New York: Garland, 1986), pp. 281–300. For a discussion of other terms, see Karen Hellekson, *The Alternate History: Refiguring Historical Time* (Kent State University Press, 2001), p. 3.

4. Scholars have used different terms to distinguish between the two types of narrative. Jörg Helbig refers to "discursive" and "narrative" alternate histories. Jörg Helbig, *Der parahistorische Roman: Ein literarhistorischer und gattungstypologischer Beitrag zur Allotopieforschung* (Frankfurt: Peter Lang, 1987), pp. 108–9. I myself have differentiated between "analytical" and "dramatic" counterfactual narratives. See Gavriel D. Rosenfeld, *The World Hitler Never Made: Alternate History and the Memory of Nazism* (Cambridge University Press, 2005), p. 4.

5. The terms "counterfactual history" and "alternate history" are largely synonymous, though they differ in the sense that the practitioners of the former pose "what if?" questions primarily to understand the origins of historical events, while the practitioners of the latter do so to imagine the consequences of their alteration. To cite an example, practitioners of counterfactual history would be interested in assessing the importance of Archduke Franz Ferdinand's assassination in leading to the outbreak of World War I by imagining him escaping death and then determining whether the war still would have happened due to other factors. Practitioners of alternate history, by contrast, would prefer to imagine the ways in which the Archduke's survival would have led history to turn out differently. Often, those who employ the first approach are historians and other scholars, while those utilizing the second are novelists and other fiction writers. There is frequent overlap between the two approaches, however, and so there is little point in trying to draw overly strict boundaries. To simplify matters, this volume uses counterfactual history as the broadest descriptive term for "what if?" narratives and reserves the term "alternate history" for its more literary versions.

6. The inclusion of a "point of divergence" is what distinguishes alternate history from other related literary genres, such as historical fiction, "secret histories," and "future histories." For a short discussion of the differences, see the "Introduction" on the Uchronia website: www.uchronia.net/intro.html.

7. Counterfactual histories may also portray the historical record turning out more or less the same. These scenarios are known as "reversionary counterfactuals" and usually show how history snaps back to its original trajectory after being temporarily sidetracked by the alteration of a particular event. See Philip Tetlock and Geoffrey Parker, "Counterfactual Thought Experiments," in Tetlock *et al., Unmaking the West*, p. 19.

8. Richard Ned Lebow, "Counterfactuals, History and Fiction," *Historical Social Research* 2 (2009), p. 57. This claim reflects the influence of Jacques Derrida's notion of deconstruction which, based on the idea of supplementarity, has shown how meaning is always forged through negation. Applied to history, it reveals that we can never truly understand what happened in the past without knowing what did not.

9. See Niall Ferguson's introduction to *Virtual History*. The increasingly mainstream status of counterfactual history has been seen as a function of the anti-deterministic mood of the decades since 1989. That said, even deterministically inclined thinkers can employ "what if?" reasoning in the form of "'reversionary' counterfactuals." For instance, the Russian Marxist Georgi Plekhanov described the "what if?" potential of individual actions as the "instrument[s] of . . . necessity" determined by "social relations." Cited in Ferguson, *Virtual History*, pp. 39–40.

10. Demandt writes that alternate history is based upon "private conjecture, which reveals more about the character of the speculator than about the probable consequences [of a different historical scenario]." Alexander Demandt, *History that Never Happened: A Treatise on the Question, What Would Have Happened If . . . ?* (Jefferson, NC: McFarland, 1993), p. 5.

11. Nightmare scenarios can also express a critique of the present, with imagined dystopias in the past serving as allegories for present-day problems.

12. Gingrich co-wrote three novels with William Forstchen: *Gettysburg: A Novel of the Civil War* (New York: St. Martin's Press, 2003), *Grant Comes East* (New York: St. Martin's Press, 2004), and *Never Call Retreat. Lee and Grant: The Final Victory* (New York: Thomas Dunne Books, 2007). For a critical discussion of the first two novels, see Thomas J. Brown and Elisabeth Sifton, "Against Appomattox," *The New Republic*, September 6, 2004.

13. Yongle Zhang documents forty counterfactual observations in Herodotus' account of the Persian Wars. Yongle Zhang, "Imagining Alternate Possibilities: Counterfactual Reasoning and Writing in Graeco-Roman Historiography" (Ph.D. dissertation, University of California, Los Angeles, 2008), p. 18.

14. *The History of Herodotus: A New English Version*, vol. IV, trans. George Rawlinson (London: J. Murray, 1880), p. 113.

15. Stewart Flory, "Thucydides' Hypotheses about the Peloponnesian War," *Transactions of the American Philological Association* 118 (1988), p. 45.

16. *The Annals of Tacitus, Books I–VI*, trans. G. G. Ramsay (London, 1904), pp. 171–2.

17. This remark comes in Book 9, section 17 of *The History of Rome by Titus Livius*, vol. II, trans. George Baker (Boston: Wells & Lilly, 1823), p. 249.

18. This is the argument of Ruth Morello, "Livy's Alexander Digression (9.17–19): Counterfactuals and Apologetics," *Journal of Roman Studies* 92 (2002), pp. 77–80.

19. Zhang's "Imagining Alternate Possibilities" provides the best survey of counterfactual historical thought in antiquity.
20. The passage is in Genesis 3:22. Lieber, *Etz Hayim*, p. 23.
21. Genesis 18:31. Ibid., p. 104.
22. Exodus 4:1. Ibid., p. 332.
23. Exodus 19:5. Ibid., p. 437.
24. Deuteronomy 8:19. Ibid., p. 1042. See also Deuteronomy 4:25–6 and 11:26–8.
25. Berakhot 8.7. *The Mishnah*, trans. Herbert Danby (London: Clarendon Press, 1933), p. 9.
26. Peah 2.7. Ibid., p. 12.
27. *The Prophets: A New Translation of the Holy Scriptures According to the Masoretic Text* (Philadelphia: Jewish Publication Society, 1978), p. 612.
28. "The Holy One, blessed be He, wished to appoint Hezekiah as the Messiah, and Sennacherib as Gog and Magog; whereupon the Attribute of Justice said before the Holy One, blessed be He: 'Sovereign of the Universe! If Thou didst not make David the Messiah, who uttered so many hymns and psalms before Thee, wilt Thou appoint Hezekiah as such, who did not hymn Thee in spite of all these miracles which Thou wroughtest for him?' Therefore it [i.e. the mem] was closed." The text can be found at: www.come-and-hear.com/sanhedrin/sanhedrin_94.html.
29. Sanhedrin 94a: www.dafyomi.co.il/sanhedrin/insites/sn-dt-094.htm.
30. *The Prophets*, p. 466.
31. This is also true of the Talmudic story in Sanhedrin 99b about the origins of the Israelites' nemesis, Amalek. He was conceived by the royal princess, Timna, who married Esau's son, Eliphaz, after she was turned away by the patriarchs, Abraham, Isaac, and Jacob, after seeking them out so that she could convert to Judaism. The Talmud states: "From her Amalek was descended who afflicted Israel. Why so? – Because they should not have repulsed her." This statement contains an implied counterfactual: that if Timna had been allowed to convert, Amalek and Jewish suffering would not have come into the world. This story has been interpreted as containing the (disturbing) moral lesson that Jewish bigotry toward Timna, who was a foreigner from the nation of Seir, helped give rise to anti-Jewish bigotry. The parable appears to be a plea for tolerance. Joshua Cohen, "The Remembrance of Amalek: Tainted Greatness and the Bible," in Nancy Anne Harrowitz (ed.), *Tainted Greatness: Antisemitism and Cultural Heroes* (Philadelphia: Temple University Press, 1994), pp. 296–7.
32. Numbers 14:2. Lieber, *Etz Hayim*, p. 845.
33. *The Prophets*, p. 13.
34. *The Writings: A New Translation of the Holy Scriptures According to the Masoretic Text* (Philadelphia: Jewish Publication Society, 1982), p. 172.

35. The passage is in Chapter 5, Section 2. *The Jewish War of Flavius Josephus: A New Translation by Robert Traill*, vol. II (London: Houlston & Stoneman, 1851), p. 80.

36. Arnaldo Momigliano wrote that after *The Jewish War*, Josephus essentially turned into "a Greek historian." Arnaldo Momigliano, *The Classical Foundations of Modern Historiography* (Berkeley: University of California Press, 1992), p. 22. He adds that "historiography of the Greek type never became a recognized part of Jewish life," p. 25. See also Michael A. Meyer, *Ideas of Jewish History* (Detroit: Wayne State University Press, 1974), pp. 10–11.

37. Ibid., pp. 2–4; Amos Funkenstein, *Perceptions of Jewish History* (Berkeley: University of California Press, 1993), pp. 52–7.

38. This is not to say that the Greek view of history was cyclical, a claim long made by many scholars. Momigliano dismisses the view of cyclical or circular time shaping Greek historical consciousness. Arnaldo Momigliano, "Greek Historiography," *History and Theory* (February 1978), pp. 8–9. He cites, as an exception, Polybius' cyclical view of constitutions. See also Funkenstein, *Perceptions of Jewish History*, p. 13.

39. Meyer, *Ideas of Jewish History*, p. 8.

40. Funkenstein, *Perceptions*, p. 12; Momigliano, "Greek Historiography," pp. 4–7.

41. Momigliano stresses, however, that Jewish chronicles broke with the Oriental model by focusing less on "individual kings and heroes" than on the history of "a political community." Momigliano, *The Classical Foundations of Modern Historiography*, p. 17.

42. Funkenstein, *Perceptions*, p. 16. This fact challenges E. H. Carr's famous assertion that "in a group or a nation which is riding in the trough, not on the crest, of historical events, theories that stress the role of chance or accident in history will . . . prevail. The view that examination results are all a lottery will always be popular among those who have been placed in the third class." E. H. Carr, *What Is History?* (New York: Knopf, 1962), p. 132.

43. Amram Tropper, "The Fate of Jewish Historiography after the Bible," *History and Theory* (May 2004), p. 187; Momigliano, *The Classical Foundations of Modern Historiography*, pp. 20–4.

44. Ibid., p. 189; Meyer, *Ideas of Jewish History*, p. 71.

45. Funkenstein, *Perceptions*, p. 54.

46. Meyer, *Ideas of Jewish History*, p. 75.

47. This was true even if, as Funkenstein argues, halakhic rulings preserved a sense of historical consciousness. Funkenstein, *Perceptions*, pp. 17–18.

48. Robert Bonfil, "Jewish Attitudes Toward History and Historical Writing in Pre-Modern Times," *Jewish History* (Spring 1997), p. 13.

49. Yosef Hayim Yerushalmi, *Zakhor: Jewish History and Jewish Memory* (Seattle: University of Washington Press, 1996), p. 36.

50. Robert Bonfil, "How Golden was the Age of the Renaissance in Jewish Historiography?" *History and Theory* (December 1988), pp. 83–6. Bonfil rejects the contention of Yerushalmi and other scholars that the sixteenth century was a momentous period for Jewish historiographical productivity, noting that the number of historiographical texts amounted perhaps to "half a dozen works . . . over a period of almost two hundred years." This compares with "hundreds of non-Jewish works." Ibid., p. 86. Johannes Heil's essay, "Beyond 'History and Memory': Traces of Jewish Historiography in the Middle Ages," suggests that fragments of lost Jewish historical narratives can still be seen in non-Jewish historical sources – a phenomenon he calls "interlinear history-writing." *Medieval Jewish Studies Online*, 2007/8, available at: www.medieval-jewish-studies.com/Journal/Vol1/PDF/Article02_Heil_History_Memory.pdf.

51. Bonfil, "How Golden was the Age?," p. 90.

52. David Myers, *Re-inventing the Jewish Past: European Jewish Intellectuals and the Zionist Return to History* (Oxford University Press, 1995); Moshe Rosman, *How Jewish Is Jewish History?* (Oxford: Littman Library of Jewish Civilization, 2007), pp. 47–55.

53. Rosman, *How Jewish Is Jewish History?*, pp. 51–3.

54. Isaak Markus Jost, *Geschichte des Judenthums und seiner Sekten: Viertes und fünftes Buch*, vol. II (Leipzig: Dörffling und Franke, 1858), p. 79.

55. Isaak Markus Jost, *Geschichte der Israeliten: Theil 6* (Berlin: Schlesinger, 1826), p. 150.

56. Heinrich Graetz, *History of the Jews*, vol. I (London: David Nutt, 1891), p. 331.

57. Heinrich Graetz, *History of the Jews*, vol. II (New York: Cosimo Inc., 2009), p. 234. He also observed that "the Jewish community of [medieval] England might have developed peacefully . . . had not the fanaticism kindled by Thomas à Becket included them among its victim," and he claimed that, following "the discovery of America, the Jews might have lifted Spain to the rank of the . . . most prosperous and enduring of states . . . But Torquemada would not have it so." Heinrich Graetz, *History of the Jews*, vol. IV (New York: Cosimo Inc., 2009), p. 353; Heinrich Graetz, *History of the Jews*, vol. III (New York: Cosimo Inc., 2009), pp. 409–10.

58. Simon Dubnow, *History of the Jews in Russia and Poland*, vol. I (Philadelphia: Jewish Publication Society of America, 1918), p. 487.

59. Salo Baron, *A Social and Religious History of the Jews*, vol. I (New York: Columbia University Press, 1952). He added that the religion would not have "remained intact . . . had it not been suited to the people's objective conditions

of life." Ibid., p. 41. In a separate comment about medieval Spanish Jewry, Baron speculated that "the Marranos could have continued their struggles for many more years had it not been for the repeated interventions of Charles V with the pope." Salo Baron, *A Social and Religious History of the Jews*, vol. XIII (New York: Columbia University Press, 1969), p. 51.

60. Ferguson, *Virtual History*, pp. 8–9, 32–3. See also Robert E. Sullivan, *Macaulay: The Tragedy of Power* (Cambridge, MA: Harvard University Press, 2010), p. 281. Burckhardt speculated about France failing to suppress the Reformation and Frederick the Great of Prussia failing to win the Seven Years War in his mid-nineteenth-century book, *Das Zeitalter Friedrichs des Grossen* (Munich: Beck, 2012), pp. 69, 14. Treitschke made numerous counterfactual comments in his *History of Germany in the Nineteenth Century* (New York: Robert M. McBride & Co., 1919). In his volume *The Methodology of the Social Sciences* (which collected essays written in the years 1903–6), Weber speculated about the battle of Marathon and the Revolution of 1848 transpiring differently. Max Weber, *The Methodology of the Social Sciences* (Glencoe, IL: Free Press, 1949).

61. The aversion of historians to counterfactual speculation was further bolstered by the deterministic leanings of certain nationalistic historiographical traditions, especially that of the Prussian and Whig Schools.

62. Geoffroy-Château's novel was a fantasy written by an adoptive son of Napoleon Bonaparte, which describes Napoleon's creation of a universal monarchy that brings peace and tranquility to the earth. Méry's novella (recently translated as *The Tower of Destiny*) imagines Napoleon being able to triumph against the British at the siege of Acre on the coast of Palestine in 1799. Renouvier's novel (whose full title was *Uchronie (l'utopie dans l'histoire): esquisse historique apocryphe du développement de la civilisation européenne tel qu'il n'a pas été, tel qu'il aurait pu être*) was originally written in 1857 but only published two decades later. It was intended as a liberal critique of Catholicism during the rule of Napoleon III.

63. See the list at www.uchronia.net/bib.cgi/oldest.html.

64. Michael Weingrad asserts that Jewish thought has a basic aversion to fantasy, based in the genre's roots in Christian thought. Michael Weingrad, "Why There Is No Jewish Narnia," *Jewish Review of Books* (Spring 2010), pp. 16–20. See also D. G. Myers, "The Golem of Prague and the Jewish Aversion to Fantasy," *Commentary*, November 7, 2011, available at: www.commentarymagazine.com/2011/11/07/golem-of-prague-and-jewish-fantasy/.

65. In a fascinating exception, however, the very first Jewish alternate history to appear in this period was penned by none other than Herzl himself: a short story, published in 1900, entitled *Der Unternehmer Bonaparte* ("Bonaparte the Entrepreneur"). It explores how history would have been different had

there never been a French Revolution (among other things, Napoleon becomes a businessman). See http://zeek.forward.com/articles/116672/.

66. Rosenfeld, *The World Hitler Never Made*, pp. 6–10.

67. Turtledove also has a Ph.D. in history from UCLA (in Byzantine history).

68. Andrew Roberts, *What Might Have Been: Imaginary History from Twelve Leading Historians* (London: Weidenfeld & Nicolson, 2005); Black, *What If?*; Tetlock *et al.*, *Unmaking the West*. See also Richard Ned Lebow, *Forbidden Fruit: Counterfactuals and International Relations* (Princeton University Press, 2010).

69. Henry Turner, *Hitler's Thirty Days to Power* (New York: Basic Books, 2003); Frank Harvey, *Explaining the Iraq War: Counterfactual Theory, Logic, and Evidence* (Cambridge University Press, 2012); Peter Bowler, *Darwin Deleted: Imagining a World Without Darwin* (University of Chicago Press, 2013).

70. An exception is Jeffrey Gurock's *The Holocaust Averted: An Alternative History of American Jewry, 1938–1967* (New Brunswick, NJ: Rutgers University Press, 2015).

71. The appeal of counterfactual speculation for Israeli writers is predictable given their country's turbulent history since 1948. See the Uchronia website for a full list of Hebrew-language essays.

72. Myers writes that Jewish historians have displayed an "unreflexive impulse" in contrast to the "self-contextualization" shown by non-Jewish scholars. He adds that Jewish scholarship "offers almost no parallels to twentieth-century histories of historiography" and notes that Jewish scholars have been unwilling "to relent on the steadfast claim to objectivity," for fear that "to acknowledge extra-'scientific' considerations in the production of historiographical work" would undermine "the scholar's quest for truth." David Myers, "Introduction," in David B. Ruderman (ed.), *The Jewish Past Revisited: Reflections on Modern Jewish Historians* (New Haven, CT: Yale University Press, 1998), pp. 2–3.

73. See, among others, Rosman, *How Jewish Is Jewish History?*; David Biale, *Cultures of the Jews: A New History* (New York: Schocken Books, 2002); Vincent Brook, *You Should See Yourself: Jewish Identity in Postmodern American Culture* (New Brunswick, NJ: Rutgers University Press, 2008); David Biale, Michael Galchinsky, and Susannah Heschel (eds.), *Insider/Outsider: American Jews and Multiculturalism* (Berkeley: University of California Press, 1998); Ruth Ellen Gruber, *Virtually Jewish: Reinventing Jewish Culture in Europe* (Berkeley: University of California Press, 2002); Daniel Boyarin, *Unheroic Conduct: The Rise of Heterosexuality and the Invention of the Jewish Man* (Berkeley: University of California Press, 1997).

74. Michael Brenner, *Prophets of the Past: Interpreters of Jewish History* (Princeton University Press, 2010), p. 198. To be sure, the postmodern agenda of challenging all metanarratives is itself a metanarrative.
75. Rosman, *How Jewish Is Jewish History?*, p. 186.

Chapter 1 What if the Exodus had never happened?

1. Robert Silverberg, *Roma Eterna* (New York: Harper Voyager, 2003).
2. See, for example, J. M. Miller and J. H. Hayes, *A History of Ancient Israel and Judah* (Philadelphia: Westminster, 1986), pp. 67–8. The view has become so influential that it has been embraced by Reform and some conservative rabbis. See Rabbi D. Wolpe, "Did the Exodus Really Happen?," published on the website *Beliefnet*: www.beliefnet.com/Faiths/Judaism/2004/12/Did-The-Exodus-Really-Happen.aspx. For some recent attempts to salvage something historical in the Exodus story, see Baruch Halpern, "The Exodus from Egypt: Myth or Reality?," in H. Shanks *et al.*, *The Rise of Ancient Israel* (Washington, DC: Biblical Archaeology Society, 1992), pp. 87–113; R. Hendel, *Remembering Abraham: Culture, Memory and History in the Hebrew Bible* (Oxford University Press, 2005), pp. 57–73.
3. Yosef Yerushalmi, *Zakhor: Jewish History and Jewish Memory* (Seattle: University of Washington Press, 1982).
4. Sara Japhet, *The Ideology of the Book of Chronicles and its Place in Biblical Thought* (Frankfurt am Main: Peter Lang, 1989), pp. 379–86.
5. See J. Geoghegan, "The Abrahamic Passover," in R. Friedman and W. Propp (eds.), *Le David Maskil: A Birthday Tribute for David Noel Freedman* (Winona Lake, IN: Eisenbrauns, 2004), pp. 47–59.
6. For the Greek text and English translation of Hecateus, see Menachem Stern, *Greek and Latin Authors on Jews and Judaism*, vol. 1 (Jerusalem: Israel Academy of Sciences and Humanities, 1974), pp. 26–9.
7. Michael Walzer, *Exodus and Revolution* (New York: Basic Books, 1985).
8. See Marshall Sklare and Joseph Greenbaum, *Jewish Identity on the Suburban Frontier: A Study of Group Survival in the Open Society* (New York: Basic Books, 1967), who explain the high rate of Passover observance among modern American Jews by noting the ways in which it helps them balance between adaptation to American culture and maintaining a distinct identity. See also Joel Gereboff, "With Liberty and Haggadahs for All," in J. Kugelman (ed.), *Key Texts in American Jewish Culture* (New Brunswick, NJ: Rutgers University Press, 2003), pp. 275–92. For feminist reinterpretations of the Exodus story, see Judith Plaskow, *Standing Again at Sinai: Judaism from a Feminist Perspective* (New York: HarperCollins, 1990); and Athalya Brenner

(ed.), *Exodus to Deuteronomy: A Feminist Companion to the Bible* (Sheffield Academic Press, 2000).

9. For an attempt to grapple with the Exodus story in light of the Holocaust, see Emil Fackenheim, *God's Presence in History: Jewish Affirmations and Philosophical Reflections* (New York University Press, 1970), pp. 3–34.

10. Barry Kosmin, *American Religious Identification Survey 2001* (New York: Graduate Center of the City University of New York, 2001).

11. Liora Gubkin, *You Should Tell Your Children: Holocaust Memory in American Passover Ritual* (New Brunswick, NJ: Rutgers University Press, 2007).

12. Geraldine Brooks, *People of the Book* (New York: Viking Press, 2008).

13. Joshua Cohen, *Witz* (Champaign and London: Dalkey Archive Press, 2010).

Chapter 2 What if the Temple of Jerusalem had not been destroyed by the Romans?

1. Sulpicius Severus, *Chronica* 2.30.6, in Tacitus, *Histories, Books 4–5*, trans. C. H. Moore, Loeb Classical Library 249 (Cambridge, MA: Harvard University Press, 1931).

2. See the examples in A. Giovannini, "Die Zerstörung Jerusalems durch Titus: Eine Strafe Gottes oder eine historische Notwendigkeit?," in P. Barceló, *Contra quis ferat arma deos? Vier Augsburger Vorträge zur Religionsgeschichte der römischen Kaiserzeit* (Munich: Ernst Vögel, 1996), pp. 24–5.

3. Tacitus, *Histories, Books 1–3*, trans. C. H. Moore, Loeb Classical Library 111 (Cambridge, MA: Harvard University Press, 1925), 3.72.

4. Josephus, *Bellum Iudaicum* 1.152–3; *Antiquitates Iudaicae* 14.72. Cf. Tacitus, *Historiae* 5.9.1.

5. Josephus, *Bellum Iudaicum* 1.179; *Antiquitates Iudaicae* 14.105–9.

6. Sulpicius Severus, *Chronica* 2.30.6.

7. See the classic study by J. Bernays, "Über die Chronik des Sulpicius Severus, ein Beitrag zur Geschichte der classischen und biblischen Studien," in J. Bernays, *Gesammelte Abhandlungen*, vol. II, ed. H. Usener (Berlin: Hertz, 1885 [1861]), pp. 81–200, which, however, did not remain unchallenged: see H. Montefiore, "Sulpicius Severus and Titus' Council of War," *Historia* 11 (1962), pp. 156–70, and, more recently, E. Laupot, "Tacitus' Fragment 2: The Anti-Roman Movement of the Christiani and the Nazoreans," *Vigiliae Christianae* 54 (2000), pp. 233–47.

8. Y. Lewy, "Titus' Justification with Regard to the Destruction of the Temple According to Tacitus (Hebrew)," in Y. Lewy, *Studies in Jewish Hellenism* (Jerusalem: Bialik Institute, 1969), p. 192, suspected that in Tacitus the "root"

(which would be removed) referred to the Temple and the "offspring" (which would easily perish) to the Jewish people: with the destruction of the Temple, the Jews would come to an end. Orosius, a contemporary of Sulpicius Severus, also reports how Titus, after deliberation, concluded that the Temple should be destroyed (*Historiae* 7.9.5–6).

9. Josephus, *Bellum Iudaicum* 6.241, trans. H. St. J. Thackeray, Loeb Classical Library 210 (Cambridge, MA: Harvard University Press, 1928).

10. Ibid., 6.252, 254. See Z. Yavetz, "Reflections on Titus and Josephus," *Greek, Roman and Byzantine Studies* 16 (1975), pp. 411–32.

11. For Josephus see, for example, M. Goodman, *Rome and Jerusalem: The Clash of Ancient Civilizations* (New York: Vintage, 2008), pp. 420–3; for Sulpicius Severus see, for example, Giovannini, "Die Zerstörung Jerusalems durch Titus," p. 32. Both versions of Titus' military council, that of Josephus as well as that of Sulpicius Severus, are of course literary constructs of what might have actually happened.

12. Montefiore, "Sulpicius Severus and Titus' Council of War," p. 180. See on this question also the discussion in J. Rives, "Flavian Religious Policy and the Destruction of the Jerusalem Temple," in J. Edmondson *et al.* (eds.), *Flavius Josephus and Flavian Rome* (Oxford University Press, 2005), pp. 145–66.

13. Giovannini, "Die Zerstörung Jerusalems durch Titus," pp. 21–2.

14. Josephus, *Bellum Iudaicum* 7.218. See M. Goodman, "Nerva, the *Fiscus Iudaicus* and Jewish Identity," *Journal of Roman Studies* 79 (1989), pp. 40–4.

15. See F. Millar, *The Roman Near East: 31 BC–AD 337* (Cambridge, MA: Harvard University Press, 1993), p. 76.

16. Josephus, *Bellum Iudaicum* 7.5.

17. See F. Millar, "Last Year in Jerusalem: Monuments of the Jewish War in Rome," in Edmondson *et al.*, *Flavius Josephus and Flavian Rome*, pp. 101–28.

18. Josephus, *Bellum Iudaicum* 7.148–50.

19. Ibid., 7.158–62.

20. Cf. the reconstruction of the inscription by G. Alföldy, "Eine Bauinschrift aus dem Colosseum," *Zeitschrift für Papyrologie und Epigraphik* 109 (1995), pp. 195–226; Millar, *The Roman Near East*, pp. 117–19.

21. J. Price, *Jerusalem under Siege: The Collapse of the Jewish State 66–70 C.E.* (Leiden: Brill, 1992), pp. 171–4.

22. Josephus, *Bellum Iudaicum* 6.420, speaks of 97,000 prisoners and 1.1 million victims.

23. Cf. J. Klawans, *Purity, Sacrifice, and the Temple: Symbolism and Supersessionism in the Study of Ancient Judaism* (Oxford University Press, 2006).

24. Moses Maimonides, *Guide for the Perplexed*, 3.32.

25. G. Stroumsa, *The End of Sacrifice: Religious Transformations in Late Antiquity* (University of Chicago Press, 2009), p. 63: "The Jews should no doubt pay thanks to Titus, for having destroyed their temple for the second time, for imposing on them the need to free themselves from sacrifice and its ritual violence, before any other society."

26. Isaiah 1.11, 1.17 trans. *The New Oxford Annotated Bible*, (2010).

27. When the Roman soldiers destroyed the Antonia fortress (on 17 Tammus of the year 70) the daily sacrifices were stopped: Josephus, *Bellum Iudaicum* 6.93–4.

28. Matthew 9.13, 12.7 trans. *The New Oxford Annotated Bible*. On the complexity of these passages, see U. Luz, *Matthew 8–20: A Commentary* (Minneapolis: Fortress, 2001); and on rabbinic parallels citing Hosea 6.6, H. L. Strack and P. Billerbeck, *Das Evangelium nach Matthäus erläutert aus Talmud und Midrasch*, vol. 1 (Munich: Beck, 1922), pp. 499–500.

29. On the difficult question of to what extent Jesus criticized the temple, see G. Theissen, "Jesus im Judentum: Drei Versuche einer Ortsbestimmung," in G. Theissen, *Jesus als historische Gestalt: Beiträge zur Jesusforschung* (Göttingen: Vandenhoeck und Ruprecht, 2003), p. 50: "Either he wanted to end sacrificial dealings and through a cleansing of the temple eliminate the abuse or he wanted to abolish sacrifice and turn the temple into a synagogue through reform or, as a prophet, he wanted to herald the destruction of the temple" (author's translation from the German original). The Qumran community distanced itself from the Temple cult in Jerusalem (*Damascus Document* (CD), pp. 6.11–16; Josephus, *Jewish Antiquities* 18.19). There is no archaeological evidence for sacrifices from the site of Qumran. According to Philo, the Essenes did not offer animal sacrifices (*Quod omnis probus liber sit* 75). On Qumran and the Temple, see L. H. Schiffman, "Community Without Temple: The Qumran Community's Withdrawal from the Jerusalem Temple," in B. Ego *et al.* (eds.), *Gemeinde ohne Tempel: Community without Temple* (Tübingen: Mohr Siebeck, 1999), pp. 267–84.

30. Jonathan Z. Smith, *Map Is Not Territory: Studies in the History of Religions* (University of Chicago Press, 1978), p. 128.

31. Ibid., p. 187.

32. P. Brown, *The World of Late Antiquity* (London: Thames and Hudson, 1971), pp. 102–3, cited ibid., pp. 186–7.

33. On the complexity of this shift, see the critical remarks in R. S. Boustan, "Confounding Blood: Jewish Narratives of Sacrifice and Violence in Late Antiquity," in J. Wright Knust and Z. Várhelyi (eds.), *Ancient Mediterranean Sacrifice* (Oxford University Press, 2011), pp. 265–86; see also C. Auffarth, "Le rite sacrificiel antique: la longue durée et la fin du sacrifice" (review of Maria-Zoe Petropolou, *Animal Sacrifice in Ancient Greek Religion, Judaism,*

and *Christianity 100 BC–AD 200* [Oxford University Press, 2008]), *Kernos*
25 (2012), pp. 300–1; and, for Egypt, D. Frankfurter, *Religion in Roman
Egypt: Assimilation and Resistance* (Princeton University Press, 1998).

34. Late antique Christian and Jewish approaches to the sacrifice were certainly
diverse. With regard to Judaism, see more recently (with further literature)
Boustan, "Confounding Blood," and M. D. Swartz, "Liturgy, Poetry, and the
Persistence of Sacrifice," in D. R. Schwartz and Z. Weiss, *Was 70 CE a
Watershed in Jewish History? On Jews and Judaism Before and After the
Destruction of the Second Temple* (Leiden: Brill, 2012), pp. 393–412.

35. Theophrastus, *On Piety*, fr. 2–19, ed. W. Pötscher (Leiden: Brill, 1964); Varro
in Arnob. 7.1: *Dii veri ea neque desiderant neque deposcunt*; see W. Burkert,
*Homo Necans: The Anthropology of Ancient Greek Sacrificial Ritual and
Myth* (Berkeley: University of California Press, 1986), p. 8, n. 36.

36. *Codex Theodosianus* 16.10.2. See Stroumsa, *The End of Sacrifice*, p. 57. On
the wider context of this passage, cf. J. Hahn, "Gesetze als Waffe? Die
kaiserliche Religionspolitik und die Zerstörung der Tempel," in J. Hahn (ed.),
*Spätantiker Staat und religiöser Konflikt: Imperiale und lokale Verwaltung
und die Gewalt gegen Heiligtümer* (Berlin: De Gruyter, 2011), pp. 205–6.

37. Cf. E. S. Gruen, *Diaspora: Jews amidst Greeks and Romans* (Cambridge, MA:
Harvard University Press, 2002), pp. 3, 232–3. According to Strabo (first
century BCE/CE) the people of the Jews had "already made its way into every
city, and it is not easy to find any place in the habitable world which has not
received this nation and in which it has not made its power felt." Cited by
Josephus, *Antiquitates Iudaicae* 14.115, trans. R. Marcus, Loeb Classical
Library 489 (Cambridge, MA: Harvard University Press, 1943).

38. As is indicated by the Theodotus inscription which is usually dated pre-70 CE;
see A. Runesson *et al.*, *The Ancient Synagogue from its Origins to 200 C.E.:
A Source Book* (Leiden: Brill, 2008), pp. 52–4. Josephus reports on (pre-70)
synagogues in Caesarea (*Bellum Iudaicum* 2.285–92) and Tiberias (*Vita* 277).

39. Burkert, *Homo Necans*, p. 8.

40. At the end of the war the Romans closed the Jewish temple in Leontopolis:
Josephus, *Bellum Iudaicum* 7.420–36. I am not discussing the particular case
of the Samaritans and the temple on Mount Gerizim. On the current status of
research on the Samaritans, see M. Mor and F. V. Reiterer (eds.), *Samaritans,
Past and Present: Current Studies* (Berlin: De Gruyter, 2010), and on all three
temples J. Frey, "Temple and Rival Temple – The Cases of Elephantine,
Mt. Gerizim, and Leontopolis," in Ego *et al.*, *Gemeinde ohne Tempel*,
pp. 171–203.

41. Philo, *De Specialibus Legibus* 1.76.

42. Ibid., 1.69.

43. L. Levine, "Temple, Jerusalem," in J. J. Collins and D. C. Harlow (eds.), *The Eerdmans Dictionary of Early Judaism* (Grand Rapids: Eerdmans, 2010), p. 1290.

44. Philo, *De Providentia* 2.64.

45. This is very much the point of J. Leonhardt-Balzer, "Priests and Priesthood in Philo: Could He Have Done Without Them?," in Schwartz and Weiss, *Was 70 CE a Watershed?*, pp. 127–53.

46. Cf. W. K. Gilders, "Jewish Sacrifice: Its Nature and Function (According to Philo)," in Wright Knust and Várhelyi, *Ancient Mediterranean Sacrifice*, pp. 94–105.

47. Philo, *In Flaccum*, 41–53, 121–4; *Legatio ad Gaium* 132–9; Philo, *De Vita Mosis* 2.216.

48. Josephus, *Bellum Iudaicum* 1.9–12.

49. Josephus, *Contra Apionem* 2.193; 1.38–40 (on scripture). See J. Barclay, *Flavius Josephus: Against Apion* (Leiden: Brill, 2007), p. 279. In *Bellum Iudaicum* 5.184–237 Josephus includes a detailed *ekphrasis* of the Temple (using the past tense); cf. also *Bellum Iudaicum* 7.148–50 (spoils from the Temple are presented at the Flavian triumph in Rome) and *Contra Apionem* 2.102–9, 119; and on this R. Bauckham, "Josephus' Account of the Temple in Contra Apionem 2.102–109," in L. H. Feldman and J. R. Levison, *Josephus' Contra Apionem: Studies in its Character and Context with a Latin Concordance to the Portion Missing in Greek* (Leiden: Brill, 1996), pp. 327–47.

50. On this cf. R. Bloch, *Moses und der Mythos: Die Auseinandersetzung mit der griechischen Mythologie bei jüdisch-hellenistischen Autoren* (Leiden: Brill, 2011), pp. 30–49.

51. On Josephus' diaspora Judaism, see now M. Tuval, *From Jerusalem Priest to Roman Jew: On Josephus and the Paradigms of Ancient Judaism* (Tübingen: Mohr Siebeck, 2013). Tuval observes a profound change during Josephus' tenure in Rome: "by the time he produced *AJ* [*Jewish Antiquities*], he wanted to convey to his readers that the Temple was a memory and Torah was his present life" (p. 12). For a different reading of Josephus' understanding of the Temple, see J. Klawans, *Josephus and the Theologies of Ancient Judaism* (Oxford University Press, 2012), pp. 180–209.

52. For Judea, N. Sharon, "Setting the Stage: The Effects of the Roman Conquest and the Loss of Sovereignty," in Schwartz and Weiss, *Was 70 CE a Watershed?*, pp. 415–43, notes a continuous withdrawal from the Temple in Judea, starting with the loss of sovereignty in 63 BCE.

53. Cf. W. Eck, *Rom und Judaea: Fünf Vorträge zur römischen Herrschaft in Palaestina* (Tübingen: Mohr Siebeck, 2007), pp. 115–55; P. Schäfer (ed.), *The Bar Kokhba War Reconsidered: New Perspectives on the Second Jewish*

Revolt Against Rome (Tübingen: Mohr Siebeck, 2003); and the good survey by H. Eshel, "Bar Kokhba Revolt," in Collins and Harlow, *The Eerdmans Dictionary of Early Judaism*, pp. 421–5.

54. P. Perkins, "If Jerusalem Stood: The Destruction of Jerusalem and Christian Anti-Judaism," *Biblical Interpretation* 8 (2000), p. 195, arrives at the same conclusion.

55. On Julian and the Jews, see M. Stern, *Greek and Latin Authors on Jews and Judaism*, vol. II: *From Tacitus to Simplicius* (Jerusalem: Israel Academy of Sciences and Humanities, 1980), pp. 502–72; J. Lewy, "Julian and the Rebuilding of the Temple" (in Hebrew), in Lewy, *Studies in Jewish Hellenism*, pp. 221–54; M. Avi-Yonah, *The Jews under Roman and Byzantine Rule: A Political History of Palestine from the Bar Kokhba War to the Arab Conquest* (Jerusalem: Magnes Press, 1984), pp. 185–207; N. Belayche, "Sacrifice and Theory of Sacrifice During the 'Pagan Reaction': Julian the Emperor," in Albert I. Baumgarten (ed.), *Sacrifice in Religious Experience* (Leiden: Brill, 2002), pp. 101–26.

56. Julianus, *Contra Galilaeos* 306B: "the Jews agree with the Gentiles, except that they believe in only one God. That is indeed peculiar to them and strange to us, since all the rest we have in a manner in common with them – temples, sanctuaries, altars, purifications, and certain precepts. For as to these we differ from one another either not at all or in trivial matters," trans. W. C. Wright, Loeb Classical Library 157 (Cambridge, MA: Harvard University Press, 1923).

57. Ephraem Syrus, *Contra Iulianum* 1.16, 2.7; and Rufinus, *Historia Ecclesiastica* 10.38. See Avi-Yonah, *The Jews under Roman and Byzantine Rule*, pp. 193–4.

58. Avi-Yonah, *The Jews under Roman and Byzantine Rule*, p. 197; Stern, *Greek and Latin Authors*, pp. 506, 511.

59. Ammianus Marcellinus, *Res Gestae* 23.1.2–3. See J. Hahn, "Kaiser Julian und ein dritter Tempel? Idee, Wirklichkeit und Wirkung eines gescheiterten Projektes," in J. Hahn (ed.), *Zerstörungen des Jerusalemer Tempels: Geschehen – Wahrnehmung – Bewältigung* (Tübingen: Mohr Siebeck, 2002), pp. 237–62.

60. Avi-Yonah, *The Jews under Roman and Byzantine Rule*, p. 204.

61. Matthew 22.7; see U. Luz, *Matthew 21–28: A Commentary* (Minneapolis: Fortress, 2005), p. 54: "the destruction of Jerusalem is understood to be the punishment for the rejection, mistreatment, and murder of the prophets and Jesus' emissaries... After the destruction of the city of those murderers the king seeks new guests for the wedding feast of his son."

62. Mark 12.9; see J. Marcus, *Mark 8–16: A New Translation with Introduction and Commentary* (The Anchor Yale Bible) (New Haven, CT: Yale University

Press, 2009), pp. 813–14. Cf. also Luke 19.42–4, and Perkins, "If Jerusalem Stood," p. 196.

63. Cf. John 2.21: "But he [Jesus] was speaking of the temple of his body."

64. Ruth A. Clements, "70 CE After 135 CE – The Making of a Watershed?," in Schwartz and Weiss, *Was 70 CE a Watershed?*, pp. 520–1 (pp. 525–33 on Justin Martyr); J. Frey, "Temple and Identity in Early Christianity and in the Johannine Community: Reflections on the 'Parting of the Ways,'" ibid., pp. 447–507; *Letter of Barnabas* 16, in F. R. Prostmeier, *Der Barnabasbrief* (Göttingen: Vandenhoeck und Ruprecht, 1999), pp. 501–25.

65. See R. Bloch, "Iosephus Flavius (Flavius Josephus), Bellum Iudaicum," in C. Walde (ed.), *The Reception of Classical Literature* (Leiden: Brill, 2012), pp. 191–2.

66. See Perkins, "If Jerusalem Stood," p. 203. Would the "delocativization" of religion which we mentioned above still have happened if Christianity had developed in a different way? It probably would. The move from public to private forms of religion was not simply a Christian phenomenon, but part of a wider development. On a possible change from cult to a more interiorized form of religion in Rome, see Stroumsa, *The End of Sacrifice*, p. 87 with further literature.

67. See www.nobelprize.org/nobel_prizes/literature/laureates/1966/agnon-speech .html.

68. Stroumsa, *The End of Sacrifice*, pp. 63–4.

69. Mishna, *Taanith* 4.6, trans. H. Danby (London: Clarendon Press, 1933). Beth-Tor (Bethar) and the ploughing of the city refer to the end of the Bar Kokhba revolt. On rabbinic responses to the destruction of the Temple, see G. Stemberger, "Reaktionen auf die Tempelzerstörung in der rabbinischen Literatur," in Hahn, *Zerstörungen des Jerusalemer*, pp. 207–36.

70. Thus the tractate *Tamid* describes the daily life in the Temple, the tractate *Middot* describes in great detail its architecture. See S. Safrai, "Jerusalem and the Temple in the Tannaitic Literature of the First Generation after the Destruction of the Temple," in A. Houtman *et al.* (eds.), *Sanctity of Time and Space in Tradition and Modernity* (Leiden: Brill, 1998), pp. 135–52.

71. G. Stemberger, *Einleitung in Talmud und Midrasch*, 9th fully rev. edn (Munich: Beck, 2011), pp. 78–84.

72. S. J. D. Cohen, "The Judean Legal Tradition and the Halakhah of the Mishna," in C. E. Fonrobert and M. S. Jaffee (ed.), *The Cambridge Companion to the Talmud and Rabbinic Literature* (Cambridge University Press, 2007), p. 131.

73. See S. Schwartz, *Imperialism and Jewish Society, 200 B.C.E. to 640 C.E.* (Princeton University Press, 2001). According to Schwartz, "the rabbis did not have any officially recognized legal authority until the end of the fourth century" (pp. 103–4).

74. M. Hadas-Lebel, *Jerusalem Against Rome* (Leuven: Peeters, 2006), pp. 152–7.
75. G. Stemberger, *Die römische Herrschaft im Urteil der Juden* (Darmstadt: Wissenschaftliche Buchgesellschaft, 1983), pp. 69–73.
76. See Schwartz and Weiss, *Was 70 CE a Watershed?*

Chapter 4 What if the "ghetto" had never been constructed?

1. On the term "ghetto" see Cecil Roth, "The Origin of Ghetto: A Final Word," *Romania* 60 (1934), pp. 67–76, reprinted in *Personalities and Events in Jewish History* (Philadelphia: JPS, 1961), pp. 226–36; Giuseppe Sermoneta, "Sull'origine della parola 'gheto,'" in E. Toaff, *Studi sull'Ebraismo italiano in memoria di Cecil Roth* (Rome: Barulli, 1974), pp. 185–202; the very illuminating piece by Sandra Debenedetti-Stow, "The Etymology of 'Ghetto': New Evidence from Rome," *Jewish History* 6 (1992), pp. 79–85; Benjamin Ravid, "From Geographical Realia to Historiographical Symbol: The Odyssey of the Word Ghetto," in David B. Ruderman, *Essential Papers on Jewish Culture in Renaissance and Baroque Italy* (New York University Press, 1992), pp. 373–85, and the many studies cited at the end; Kenneth R. Stow, "The Consciousness of Closure: Roman Jewry and its Ghet," in Ruderman, *Essential Papers*, pp. 386–400.
2. On the complex history of the Nazi ghetto and its relation to the earlier model, see Dan Michman, *The Emergence of Jewish Ghettos During the Holocaust* (Cambridge University Press, 2011).
3. On the connotations of "ghetto" and its equivalents in German, English, French, and Italian, see "Ghetto" in Christian Topalov *et al.* (eds.), *L'Aventure des mots de la ville* (Paris: Robert Laffont, 2010), pp. 524–44.
4. For this approach, see the various essays of Hayden White – for example, the introduction to his *Metahistory: The Historical Imagination of the Nineteenth Century* (Baltimore, MD: Johns Hopkins University Press, 1973), or "The Question of Narrative in Contemporary Historical Theory," in *The Content of the Form: Narrative Discourse and Historical Representation* (Baltimore, MD: Johns Hopkins University Press, 1987), pp. 26–57.
5. Here I follow the terminology of Raymond Williams whose sense of puzzlement about, and his subsequent drive to investigate and define, the changed academic terminologies he encountered upon returning to university after World War II can be applied to Jewish Studies as any other field. See, for example, the introduction to Raymond Williams, *Keywords*, rev. edn (Oxford University Press, 1985). As Williams points out: "Academic subjects are not eternal categories" (p. 14).
6. *The Menorah Journal* 14 (1928), pp. 515–26. On the context of the article, see David N. Meyers, "Introduction," in David N. Meyers and William V. Rowe (eds.), *From Ghetto to Emancipation: Historical and Contemporary*

Reconsiderations of the Jewish Community (University of Scranton Press, 1997).

7. Jacob Katz, *Out of the Ghetto: The Social Background of Jewish Emancipation, 1770–1870* (Cambridge, MA: Harvard University Press, 1973), ch. 2, p. 9.

8. Howard M. Sachar, *The Course of Modern Jewish History* (New York: Vintage, 1990; first published 1958), p. 3.

9. Michael Goldfarb, *Emancipation: How Liberating Europe's Jews from the Ghetto Led to Revolution and Renaissance* (New York: Simon & Schuster, 2009). Goldfarb imagines that "almost all aspects of life were different inside the ghetto, and it was the opening of the ghetto gates that remarkably led to a quick Jewish assumption of leadership roles in general society" (p. xv).

10. To take an example more or less at random, Ari Elon speaks of his own traumatic transition from religious traditionalist to skeptic and secular activist:

> In those days I felt that the Jewish nation had willingly relinquished the "certificate of exemption" [*te'udat shihrur*] offered by the Zionist revolution and chose to retreat into the pre-Emancipation ghetto. That [i.e. the ghetto age] was an era when the national identity certificate required a membership card in the rabbinic cult.

Alma Di (Tel Aviv: Yedi'ot Aharonot, 2011), p. 30.

11. Anne Fuchs and Florian Krobb (eds.), *Ghetto Writing: Traditional and Eastern Jewry in German-Jewish Literature from Heine to Hilsenrath* (Columbia, SC: Camden House, 1999); Gabriele von Glasenapp, *Aus der Judengasse: Zur Entstehung und Ausprägung deutschsprachiger Ghettoliteratur im 19. Jahrhundert* (Tübingen: Niemeyer, 1996), and see her brief overview of "Jewish Emancipation Processes and Cultural Change in the Light of German Ghetto Tales," *Jewish Studies* 39 (1999), pp. 43*–53*; Irene Stocksieker Di Maio, "Berthold Auerbach's *Dichter und Kaufmann*: Enlightenment Thought and Jewish Identity," *Lessing Yearbook* 19 (1988), pp. 265–84. Josephine Donovan, *European Local-Color Literature: National Tales, Dorfgeschichten, Romans Champêtres* (New York: Continuum, 2010), provides a broader, pan-European context for this type of literature.

12. The quote is from the 1893 introduction to the third edition, reprinted in *Selected Works of Israel Zangwill: Children of the Ghetto, Ghetto Comedies, and Ghetto Tragedies* (Philadelphia: Jewish Publication Society, 1938). Similar usage can be found in many other works of ethnographic fiction of the time; see, for example, Karl Emil Franzos' attitude to the "Podolian ghetto" in his preface to the English translation of *Jews of Barnow* (New

York: D. Appleton, 1883). Hutchins Hapgood sought to counter the negative images of poverty, dirt, ignorance, and immorality associated with Yiddish-speaking New York when he described *The Spirit of the Ghetto* (New York: Funk and Wagnalls, 1902).

13. I use the now-popular term "social construct" in the sense given by the *Oxford English Dictionary*: "something based on the collective views developed and maintained within a society or social group; a social phenomenon or convention originating within and cultivated by society or a particular social group, as opposed to existing inherently or naturally." Google's Ngram viewer attests to the rapid rise in popularity of the term since it first emerged at the beginning of the twentieth century. With particular relevance to the "reading" of the cultural significance attached to changing spatial arrangements, architectural historians have adopted the related phrase: "constructed meaning." See, for example, Eleftherios Pavlides and Susan Buck Sutton (eds.), *Constructed Meaning: Form and Process in Greek Architecture* (Minneapolis, MN: University of Minnesota Press, 1995).

14. Though Polish historians have, in a nationalist vein, often downplayed the primacy of German settlers and German law in the development of Polish cities, it is still clear that the thirteenth-century *locatio civitatis* (legal privilege of location) and the concomitant recognition of Magdeburg law were necessary triggers for the expansion of urban life in Cracow as elsewhere in the region. See, for example, Aleksander Gieysztor, "Le origini delle città nella Polonia medievale," in *Studi in onore di Armando Sapori* (Milan: Istituto Editoriale Cisalpino, 1957), pp. 127–45; and "Foreign Colonization and the Introduction of German Law in the Thirteenth Century," in Nora Berend (ed.), *The Expansion of Latin Europe, 1000–1500*, vol. v: *The Expansion of Central Europe in the Middle Ages* (Farnham and Burlington, VT: Ashgate Variorum, 2012), pp. 399–425. In "Urban Changes in Poland in the 12th and 13th Centuries," in *La Pologne au XIIe Congrès International des Sciences Historiques à Vienne* (Warsaw: Polish Academy of Sciences, 1965), pp. 7–30, citing current Polish scholarship, Gieysztor makes the case for the gradual emergence of the Polish city and of the legal independence of urban residents from direct ducal authority even before the introduction of German law. He concedes, however, that "former changes of quantity" became "new qualities in the 13th and 14th centuries" (p. 20). For patterns specifically in Cracow, see p. 23. As part of his argument, Gieysztor stresses the early appointment of a separate "market judge" or *iudex fori* and the general development of an autonomous merchant law (*ius fori*), a pattern he finds in other areas of Middle Europe as well (p. 17). Though beyond the scope of the present study, this is, I suspect, of relevance to developing claims for Jewish legal and institutional autonomy, the jurisdictional expression of the spatially defined ghetto.

15. On the medieval settlement, see Hanna Zaremska, "Jewish Street (Platea Judeorum) in Cracow: The 14th–The First Half of the 15th C.," *Acta Poloniae Historica* 83 (2001), pp. 27–57. Boguslaw Krasnowolski's 2006 paper cited by Michał Galas and Antony Polonsky, "Introduction" to "Jews in Kraków since 1772" (Part I of *Jews in Krakow*), *Polin: Studies in Polish Jewry* 23 (2011), pp. 3–48 at 5–7, was unfortunately not available. Hanna Zaremska, *Żydzi w Średniowiecznej Polsce Gmina Krakowska* (Warsaw: Instytut Historii PAN, 2011), deals with the transfer to Kazimierz on pp. 493–504. My thanks to Alicja Maślak-Maciejewska for her help in identifying and translating the relevant passages for me in this book as well as in the study mentioned in the following note.

16. Majer Bałaban, *Toldot ha-Yehudim be-Krakov u-ve-Kazimiez 1304–1868*, vol. I (Jerusalem: Magnes Press, 2002), edited by Jacob Goldberg from the expanded second Polish edition, *Historia Żydów w Krakowie i na Kazimierzu 1304–1868* (Cracow: KAW, 1991; first published 1931); see especially chapters 5, 7, and 12. The term "ghetto" does appear as early as 1637 to refer to the Jewish quarter: see the letter from Jan Tęczyński, *wojewod* of Cracow, about an attack on Jews in the "Giet" cited in Bałaban, p. 147 (Hebrew) and p. 184 (Polish). Interestingly, the reference is not to Kazimierz but to a Jewish commercial area in Cracow. Bałaban realizes the oddity of this usage, marks it "sic!," and feels required to translate it in a footnote. The term "vicus judaicus," quite common in the documents of the time, can also be found as "oppidum judaeorum," as in the engraving of Cracow and Kazimierz in Georg Braun and Franz Hogenberg, *Civitates orbis terrarium*, vol. VI (Cologne, 1617). A high-quality scan of the image is available at http://historic-cities.huji.ac.il/poland/krakow/maps/braun_hogenberg_VI_43_b.jpg. See the fuller treatment of Jews in towns in historic Poland in Maria and Kazimierz Piechotkowie, *Oppidum judaeorum: Żydzi w przestrzeni miejskiej dawnej Rzeczypospolitej* (Warsaw: Wydawnictwo Krupski i S-ka, 2004), pp. 6–7.

17. Bałaban, *Toldot ha-Yehudim be-Krakov*, vol. I, ch. 5, p. 50 (Hebrew) and p. 57 (Polish).

18. Ibid., pp. 52 ff. (Hebrew) and pp. 60 ff. (Polish). It is not insignificant that this crucial trade agreement survives in the archives in Hebrew, Latin, and German versions.

19. Bożena Wyrozumska, "Did King Jan Olbracht Banish the Jews from Cracow?," in Andrzej Paluch (ed.), *The Jews in Poland*, vol. I (Cracow: Jagiellonian University, Research Center on Jewish History and Culture in Poland, 1992), pp. 27–37. Wyrozumska argues that references in government records to Cracow's Jews, Jewish elders, or *kahal* after 1494 cannot refer to the Jews living in Kazimierz since the two urban areas were legally separate until 1800 (p. 33). It seems to me more likely that these referred collectively

to all Jews of the conurbation under the name of the larger zone which was, after all, the name of the original settlement. The uniform terminology reflected the jurisdictional reality of the single united community (a theme of some relevance to our discussion). Nevertheless, Wyrozumska is certainly correct that some Jews did receive special license to live in Cracow itself, that Jews continued to rent and perhaps own commercial property in the city, and that Jewish businessmen (from craftsmen and peddlers to large-scale merchants) continued to compete for custom in Cracow's market, much to the ongoing frustration of the Christian businessmen there. See also Wyrozumska's collection of municipal records, *Żydzi w Średniowiecznym Krakowie* ("The Jews in Mediaeval Cracow") (Cracow: Polska Akademia Umiejętności, 1995), and the references in Jan M. Malecki, "Cracow Jews in the 19th Century: Leaving the Ghetto," *Acta Poloniae Historica* 76 (1997), pp. 85–96 at p. 85. The question is taken up again by Hanna Zaremska, "Crossing the River: How and Why the Jews of Kraków Settled in Kazimierz at the End of the Fifteenth Century," *Polin* 22 (2010), pp. 174–92.

20. Bałaban, *Toldot ha-Yehudim be-Krakov Historia*, ch. 12: "The Hundred Years War Over the *Vicus Judaicus* and over Commercial Rights in Kazimierz (1533–1655)," Hebrew translation, pp. 148–63; Malecki, "Cracow Jews in the 19th Century," p. 85; Bogusław Krasnowolski, *Ulice i Place Krakowskiego Kazimierza Z dziejów Chrześcijan i Żydów w Polsce* (Cracow: Universitas, 1992), p. 17. In personal correspondence (through Alicja Maślak-Maciejewska, November 19, 2013), Professor Krasnowolski wrote that "movements of Jews and Christians in both directions – from and into the Jewish town – were absolutely possible and nobody controlled them during the day. At night Jews served as guards at the gates, opening and closing them." So far as I have been able to determine, there were no special restrictions placed on Jews' mobility outside of their area at night as was the case in Venice or, as we shall see, Rome. Bałaban records complaints from the Christian city council that the Jews were not maintaining the city's defensive perimeter, allowing sewage drainage to undermine the wall in their quarter. The phrase "de non tolerandis Christianis" appears in a footnote in the Hebrew Bałaban, p. 153, and Polish, p. 194. The Jews in Poznan received a similar privilege in 1633.

21. Location is not just a commercial question. Urban anthropologists have long understood that the spatial arrangements and architectural forms in a city are part of a system of "legibility," a means of expressing the power and legitimacy of the ruling elite relative to other urban groups. See, for example, the comments of Bierman on Venetian and Ottoman Crete in "The Ottomanization of Crete," in Irene A. Bierman *et al.* (eds.), *The Ottoman City and its Parts: Urban Structure and Social Order* (New Rochelle, NY: Aristide D. Caratzas, 1991), pp. 53–75 at pp. 57 ff., and Donald Preziosi,

"Power, Structure, and Architectural Function," ibid., pp. 103–5. In this chapter, however, we must restrict ourselves to the phenomenon of segregation itself.

22. On the immigration of Czech Jews into Cracow see Bałaban, *Toldot ha-Yehudim be-Krakov*, p. 81. On the Jewish demographics of Ukraine and the number of Jews killed in the uprising, see now Shaul Stampfer, "What Actually Happened to the Jews of Ukraine in 1648?," *Jewish History* 17 (2003), pp. 207–27.

23. Heinrich Graetz, *Geschichte der Juden*, 3rd edn, vol. IX (Leipzig: O. Leiner, 1891), p. 39: "In Venedig wurde zuerst unter allen italienischen Stadten, wo Juden wohnten, ein besonderes Judenquartier, Ghetto, für sie eingeführt (März 1516), eine Nachahmung der deutschen Gehässigkeit gegen sie."

24. Richard Sennett, *Flesh and Stone: The Body and the City in Western Civilization* (New York: W. W. Norton, 1994), ch. 7: "Fear of Touching," pp. 212–51. He republished most of this chapter almost unchanged in *The Foreigner* (London: Notting Hill Editions, 2011).

25. Ibid., p. 248, and compare *The Autobiography of a Seventeenth-Century Venetian Rabbi: Leon Modena's "Life of Judah,"* trans. and ed. Mark R. Cohen (Princeton University Press, 1988), p. 144. Sennett's dramatic invention was picked up unquestioned by scholarly reviewers (Marina Warner in the *London Review of Books* 16[23], December 8, 1994, available at: www.lrb.co.uk/v16/n23/marina-warner/magic-zones) and authors (Jeremy Brent, *Searching for Community: Representation, Power and Action on an Urban Estate* [Bristol: Policy Press, 2009], p. 208).

26. A detailed analysis of the various stages of the settlement of Jews in Venice was laid out in Brian Pullan, *Rich and Poor in Renaissance Venice: The Social Institutions of a Catholic State, to 1620* (Cambridge, MA: Harvard University Press, 1971), part III: "Venetian Jewry and the Monti di Pietà," especially pp. 431–509; Benjamin Ravid, "The Legal Status of the Jews in Venice to 1509," *Proceedings of the American Academy for Jewish Research* 54 (1987), pp. 169–202, and many other studies; Reinhold C. Mueller, "Les prêteurs juifs de Venise au Moyen Age," *Annales ESC* 30 (1975), pp. 1277–1302; Reinhold C. Mueller, "Charitable Institutions, the Jewish Community, and Venetian Society: A Discussion of the Recent Volume by Brian Pullan," *Studi Veneziani* 14 (1972), pp. 37–82.

27. Patricia Anne Allerston, "The Market in Second-Hand Clothes and Furnishings in Venice c. 1500–c. 1650" (Ph.D. dissertation, European University Institute, Florence, 1996). Dr. Allerston and her work are featured in the documentary film, *Venice, A Second-Hand City*, sponsored by the Open University (Princeton, NJ: Films for the Humanities and Sciences, 2003). Though it may have been uniquely developed in Venice, the market in second-hand clothing and its offshoots, both legal and illegal, were important

everywhere in early modern Europe as is becoming clear from the investigations of scholars such as Laurence Fontaine and the contributors to her edited volume, *Alternative Exchanges: Second-Hand Circulations from the Sixteenth Century to the Present* (New York: Berghahn, 2008).

28. Ravid, "Legal Status of the Jews in Venice," mentions complaints in the Venetian Great Council in 1498 about Jews coming to the city to sell *strazzaria* and actually renting facilities to store their goods there. Legislators were sure that this was a new situation; Jewish dealers in *strazzaria* had formerly come into the city only during fairs but then immediately departed (pp. 194 f.).

29. Pullan, *Rich and Poor*, p. 482. The following year, when ghettoization was proposed, one of Anselmo del Banco's arguments against it was that these shops had already been set up; ibid., p. 487.

30. On abuses related to the older system of registering loan contracts in Mestre and elsewhere, see Mueller, "Charitable Institutions," p. 66.

31. Brian Pullan, "Jewish Moneylending in Venice: From Private Enterprise to Public Service," in Gaetano Cozzi (ed.), *Gli ebrei e Venezia: Secoli XIV–XVIII* (Milan: Edizioni Comunità, 1987), pp. 671–86 at p. 675, as well as the list of allowed interest rates provided in Mueller, "Charitable Institutions," p. 82.

32. The finances of the banks and the subsidy system in Venice were explained by David Joshua Malkiel, *A Separate Republic: The Mechanics and Dynamics of Venetian Jewish Self-Government, 1607–1624* (Jerusalem: Magnes Press, 1991), ch. 5, "Communal Finances."

33. The literature on the admission of the merchant groups is enormous and the considerations were not unique to Venice. See, for example, Bernard Dov Cooperman, "Venetian Policy Towards Levantine Jews in its Broader Italian Context," in Cozzi, *Gli ebrei e Venezia: Secoli XIV–XVIII*, pp. 65–84, and Benjamin Ravid, "A Tale of Three Cities and Their Raison d'État: Ancona, Venice, Livorno, and the Competition for Jewish Merchants in the Sixteenth Century," *Mediterranean Historical Review* 6 (1991), pp. 138–62.

34. A lengthy passage from the colloquial shorthand notes in Sanudo's *Diarii* is reproduced in Robert Bonfil, *Gli ebrei in Italia nell'epoca del Rinascimento* (Florence: Sansoni, 1991), and carefully translated by Anthony Oldcorn in the English version: *Jewish Life in Renaissance Italy* (Berkeley and Los Angeles: University of California Press, 1994), pp. 39–43. Parts of the text are also translated in Pullan, *Rich and Poor*, pp. 489–90.

35. A separate residential area for Jews had already been considered once before when, in 1385, the Venetian Senate had experimented with a ten-year license allowing a small number of Jewish bankers to live in the city proper. Legislation at that time had specified "that the said Jews . . . will be provided by us with a place of their own, so that they can live together for their convenience, paying the usual rent." Apparently, the authorities never got

around to assigning this place, and by 1388 the Jews' housing situation was deemed unacceptable – why and from whose perspective, we unfortunately cannot tell. But "for the honor of the state" the Senate demanded "that the Jews live together by themselves and separated from the others in some suitable and adequate place." Benjamin Ravid, "The Establishment of the Ghetto Vecchio of Venice, 1541," *Proceedings of the Sixth World Congress of Jewish Studies*, vol. II (Jerusalem: World Union of Jewish Studies, 1975), pp. 153–67 at p. 154; Ravid, "Legal Status," pp. 176–9. Ambiguities in the motivations for spatial segregation are cited in the notes to both articles.

36. Among recent studies of the physical layout of the ghetto, see Dana E. Katz, "The Ghetto and the Gaze in Early Modern Venice," in Herbert L. Kessler and David Nirenberg (eds.), *Judaism and Christian Art: Aesthetic Anxieties from the Catacombs to Colonialism* (Philadelphia: University of Pennsylvania Press, 2011), pp. 233–62, and Ennio Concina, Ugo Camerino, and Donatella Calabi, *La Città degli ebrei. Il Ghetto di Venezia: architettura e urbanistica* (Venice: Albrizzi, 1991).

37. This is the approach, for example, of Shlomo Simonsohn, *The Apostolic See and the Jews: History, Studies and Texts*, vol. CIX (Toronto: Pontifical Institute of Mediaeval Studies, 1991), pp. 133–56.

38. Julius Aronius, *Regesten zur Geschichte der Juden* (Berlin: L. Simion, 1902), §274, pp. 301–3 at p. 302. The circumstances under which this edict was issued are not at all clear. It may have been a clerical response to the pathbreaking extension of trade and residential privileges to Jews by Bolesław, duke of nearby Kalisz, in 1264; cf. Phillip Bloch, *General-Privilegien der polnischen Judenschaft* (Posen: J. Jolowicz, 1892), p. 2. According to Davies and Moorhouse, the synod decree was issued in reaction to a *Schutzprivilegium* (Protection Privilege) granted to Jews in Wroclaw itself in 1267; Norman Davies and Roger Moorhouse, *Microcosm: Portrait of a Central European City* (London: Jonathan Cape, 2002), p. 92.

39. I have used the felicitous translation of Friedrich Heer, *The Medieval World: Europe 1100–1350* (London: Cardinal, 1974), p. 312, as quoted in Davies and Moorhouse, *Microcosm*, p. 92. The latter authors tread gingerly, as do many modern historians, around Jewish–Christian relations, trying to spread the blame as evenly as possible but, in so doing, it seems to me that they draw false equivalencies and misrepresent the thrust of Church rulings. Thus they speak without proof of "Jewish law ... forb[idding] Jews to live in close proximity to Gentiles, so physical segregation would have been the norm," and then add that "segregation, of course, well suited the prejudices of the Christian majority" (p. 92).

40. Simonsohn, *The Apostolic See and the Jews*, p. 146, acknowledges that segregationist policies were generally not enforced by the popes in medieval Italy but does not explore why this ostensibly universally shared

religious principle was ignored at the administrative heart of Catholic
Christianity.

41. On the reversal in policy toward *conversos* see Bernard Dov Cooperman,
"Portuguese Conversos in Ancona: Jewish Political Activity in Early Modern
Italy," in Cooperman (ed.), *In Iberia and Beyond: Hispanic Jews Between
Cultures* (Newark: University of Delaware Press, 1998), pp. 297–352.

42. Kenneth R. Stow, *Catholic Thought and Papal Jewry Policy 1555–1593* (New
York: Jewish Theological Seminary, 1977). In an interesting exploration of
the back-and-forth of papal Jewry policy in subsequent decades, Stow
speculatively pushes back Roman Jews' sense of the finality of their isolation
to 1589 and the reign of Sixtus V; Stow, "The Consciousness of Closure."

43. For the argument over Stow's translation of the Latin decree, see David
Berger, "Cum Nimis Absurdum and the Conversion of the Jews," *Jewish
Quarterly Review* 70(1) (1979), pp. 41–9, and Stow's brief response in *Jewish
Quarterly Review* 71(4) (1981), pp. 251–2. Stow is certainly justified in
emphasizing the conversionist efforts of Carafa and his successors; the
question is only whether that was the purpose of the ghetto.

44. On the early part of the century, see the summary in Bernard Dov Cooperman,
"Ethnicity and Institution Building among Jews in Early Modern Rome," *AJS
Review* 30(1) (2006), pp. 119–45, especially 128–31, and the sources cited
there, as well as Kenneth Stow, *Theater of Acculturation: The Roman Ghetto
in the Sixteenth Century* (University of Washington Press, 2015), pp. 25, 62 f.,
136, n. 11, and 168 f., nn. 74 and 78. Some 3,500 Jews are reported in Rome
at the end of the sixteenth century according to Jean Delumeau, *Vie
économique et sociale de Rome dans la seconde moitié du XVIe siècle*, vol. 1
(Paris: E. de Bocard, 1957), pp. 214–17 and, more recently, by Claudio
Schiavoni, "Introduzione allo studio delle fonti archivistiche per la storia
demografica di Roma nel '600," *Genus* 27 (1971), pp. 357–403 at p. 384.
Paul Rieger, *Geschichte der Juden in Rom*, vol. II (Berlin: Meyer & Müller,
1895–6), p. 427, cites a seventeenth-century report that mentions 4,500 Jews
in the ghetto – presumably a round number indicating that the ghetto seemed
very crowded. Despite an enlargement of the ghetto under Sixtus V, the
quarter would have held some 400 people per acre – essentially the same
figure given for the Warsaw ghetto at its most crowded at the very start of
World War II, but without the equivalent number of high-rise buildings.

45. For example, Paul III, elected October 13, 1534, confirmed the privileges of
the Jews of Rome on November 22, and then again after payment of the
vigesima tax on June 13, 1536; Simonsohn, *Apostolic See*, §1678 (p. 1911)
and §1792 (p. 2037). The latter text appears also in Kenneth Stow, *Taxation,
Community, and State: The Jews and the Fiscal Foundations of the Early
Modern Papal State* (Stuttgart: Anton Hiersemann, 1982), p. 84, and is
summarized on p. 59. Stow mentions two other almost identical privileges

from 1543 and 1548. Compare also the privilege to the Jews of Ancona issued June 5, 1535; Simonsohn, *Apostolic See*, §1748, p. 1983.

46. For the Jews' residential spread beyond the *rione* Sant'Angelo already in the 1520s, we have the often-cited residential city survey of 1526–7, discussed now in the illuminating study by Pierina Ferrara, "La struttura edilizia del 'Serraglio' degli ebrei romani (secc. XVI–XIX)," *Roma Moderna e Contemporanea* 19(1) (2011), pp. 83–102, who includes (p. 86) a graphic representation from Italo Insolera, *Roma: Immagini e realtà dal X al XX secolo* (Rome and Bari: Laterza, 1980), p. 96.

47. Simonsohn, *Apostolic See and the Jews*, §2566 (November 11, 1545) and §2625 (August 18, 1546), though note also §2704 (August 1, 1547) and §2721 (November 26, 1547), the special exemption issued to the well-connected banker, Elias Corcos.

48. *Il Ghetto di Roma* (Rome: Stabilimento Typografico della Tribuna, 1887), p. 2. It is interesting to note that Rome's then-Chief Rabbi Elio Toaff cited Natali in his own introduction to Salvatore Fornari, *La Roma del Ghetto* (Rome: Fratelli Palombi, 1984), pp. 7–8, but could not help adding that the area was nevertheless among the most interesting and picturesque complexes, not least because of the unusual height of the buildings and superstructures erected to supply more housing space for the growing population. Toaff agreed that the area needed to be improved but regretted that it was totally razed, referring his readers to significant examples of Baroque and neoclassical architecture described in Carla Benocci's study, *Il Rione S. Angelo* (Rome: Edizioni Rari Nantes, 1980), p. 93.

49. Umberto Cassuto, *Gli Ebrei a Firenze nell'età del Rinascimento* (Florence: Olschki, 1965; first published 1918). For Medici tolerance see, for example, p. 55; for their practical appreciation of the Jews' value for the state, for example, p. 80. The quote is from p. 88. The privilege to Levantines is published as Appendix, document 54, and discussed on pp. 173 ff.

50. Ibid., p. 94, and the documents in the Appendix.

51. The term "ghetto", and the detailed regulations for its administration, including the appointment of someone to open and close the ghetto gates at the appropriate hour, were actually formalized a year later on July 31, 1571. Cassuto, *Gli Ebrei*, pp. 114–17. The same policy was introduced in the Sanese, where Jews were required henceforth to live in a ghetto in Siena.

52. Stefanie B. Siegmund, *The Medici State and the Ghetto of Florence: The Construction of an Early Modern Jewish Community* (Stanford University Press, 2006), p. 6. Siegmund emphatically rejects "the presumption that ghettos by and large formalized a separation between Jews and Christians that already existed naturally," noting that "the presumption of an inevitable and progressive persecution of Jews in the premodern world ... [is] not supported by the documents [she has studied] in the archives of Tuscany" (p. xvi).

53. Cassuto, *Gli Ebrei*, p. 410, emphasis added. We do not know if this separate zone was requested by the Levantines or imposed by the Medici. To my knowledge, no such separate zone of Jewish housing was ever actually established for the Levantines.

54. In subsequent years, moreover, Levantines and perhaps other Jews who lived in Florence were sometimes licensed to live outside the ghetto.

55. Francesca Trivellato, *The Familiarity of Strangers: The Sephardic Diaspora, Livorno, and Cross-Cultural Trade in the Early Modern Period* (New Haven, CT: Yale University Press, 2012).

56. Concerning the Ashkenazic Jews who could not live in Hamburg proper and therefore resided in nearby Altona, see, for example, *The Memoirs of Glückel of Hameln*, ed. Marvin Lowenthal (New York: Schocken Books, 1977), pp. 5–10.

57. *Goethes Werke*, vol. IX, ed. Erich Trunz (Hamburg: Wegner, 1950), pp. 149–50, trans. R. O. Moon (Washington, DC: Public Affairs Press, 1949), p. 125, cited in Klaus L. Berghahn, "Patterns of Childhood: Goethe and the Jews," in Klaus L. Berghahn and Jost Hermand (eds.), *Goethe in German-Jewish Culture* (Rochester, NY: Camden House, 2001), pp. 3–15, at pp. 9 ff.

58. Alfred Kazin, *A Walker in the City* (New York: Harcourt Brace Jovanovich, 1951), p. 5.

Chapter 6   What if Russian Jewry had never been confined to the Pale of Jewish Settlement?

1. Nathan Hanover, *Abyss of Despair*, trans. Abraham J. Mesch (New York: Transaction Books, 1983), p. 110.

2. Jean-Jacques Rousseau, *The Government of Poland*, trans. Willmoore Kendall (Indianapolis: Hackett Publishing Company, 1985), p. 2.

3. Ibid., p. 11.

4. Ibid., p. 14.

5. "A letter to Lord ****," in Edmund Burke, *A Vindication of Natural Society; or, a View of the Miseries and Evils arising to Mankind from every Species of Artificial Society*, ed. Frank N. Pagano (Indianapolis: Liberty Fund, Inc., 1982), p. 20.

6. Cited in Artur Eisenbach, *The Emancipation of the Jews in Poland, 1780–1870*, trans. Janina Dorosz (Oxford: Basil Blackwell, 1991), p. 71.

7. Cited in Theodor R. Weeks, *From Assimilation to Antisemitism: The "Jewish Question" in Poland, 1850–1914* (Dekalb: Northern Illinois University Press, 2006), pp. 19–20.

8. Rousseau, *The Government of Poland*, p. 6.

Chapter 7   What if a Christian state had been established in modern Palestine?

1. Richard Ned Lebow, "Counterfactual Thought Experiments: A Necessary Teaching Tool," *The History Teacher* 40 (2007), pp. 153–76.

2. A counterfactual thought experiment, even a whimsical one, is a crucial first step toward drawing vivid, empirical comparisons between different countries at different times. As Martin Bunzel has argued, "lacking a laboratory, the next best thing for historians to resort to is comparative history," which can demonstrate how "changes in antecedents would have been compatible with the same outcome." Martin Bunzel, "Counterfactual History: A User's Guide," *American Historical Review* 109 (2004), pp. 31, 34.

3. Cited in John Canup, *Out of the Wilderness: The Emergence of American Identity in Colonial New England* (Middletown, CT: Wesleyan University Press, 1990), p. 82.

4. Ibid., p. 219.

5. E.g. Donald Harman Atkensen, *God's Peoples: Covenant and Land in South Africa, Israel and Ulster* (Ithaca, NY: Cornell University Press, 1992); Uriel Abulof, *'Al pi tehom: umah, eimah, umusar ba-siah ha-tsioni* (forthcoming from the University of Haifa Press); Uriel Abulof, *The Morality and Mortality of Nations* (Cambridge University Press, 2015). Abulof has also written many articles on what he calls "the existential uncertainty of small peoples."

Chapter 9   What if Franz Kafka had immigrated to Palestine?

1. Franz Kafka, *Letters to Felice*, ed. Erich Heller and Jürgen Born, trans. James Stern and Elisabeth Duckworth (New York: Schocken, 1973), pp. 500–1.

2. Max Brod, "Franz Kafka und der Zionismus," *Emuna* 10(1–2) (1975), p. 34.

3. Franz Kafka, *The Diaries of Franz Kafka, 1910–1913*, ed. Max Brod, trans. Joseph Kresh (New York: Schocken, 1948), p. 272.

4. *Selbstwehr* (Unabhängige jüdische Wochenschrift) (Prague), Zionist newspaper, May 13, 1910, p. 6.

5. Ibid., September 22, 1911, p. 2.

6. Hugo Bergmann, *Jawne und Jerusalem: Gesammelte Aufsätze* (Berlin: Jüdischer Verlag, 1919), p. 38.

7. Martin Buber, *The Letters of Martin Buber*, ed. Nahum N. Glatzer and Paul Mendes-Flohr (New York: Schocken, 1991), p. 172.

8. Iris Bruce, *Kafka and Cultural Zionism: Dates in Palestine* (Madison: University of Wisconsin Press, 2007), pp. 119–24, 173–7.

9. Franz Kafka, *The Diaries of Franz Kafka 1914–1923*, ed. Max Brod, trans. Martin Greenberg, with Hannah Arendt (New York: Schocken, 1949), pp. 287–315.

10. Kafka, *Diaries, 1910–1913*, p. 263.

11. Franz Kafka, *Letters to Milena*, trans. Philip Boehm (New York: Schocken, 1990), p. 217.

12. Kafka, *Letters to Felice*, p. 500.

13. Ibid., p. 522.

14. Buber, *Letters*, pp. 171–2.

15. Franz Kafka, *Letters to Friends, Family, and Editors*, trans. Richard and Clara Winston (New York: Schocken, 1977), pp. 142, 453, nn. 35, 120.

16. Iris Bruce, "Kafka's Journey into the Future: Crossing Borders into Israeli/Palestinian Worlds," in Stanley Corngold and Ruth V. Gross (eds.), *Kafka for the Twenty-First Century* (Rochester, NY: Camden House, 2011), pp. 223, 234, n. 7. For an excellent discussion of "Jackals and Arabs" within the Zionist context, see Dimitry Shumsky, "Czechs, Germans, Arabs, Jews: Franz Kafka's 'Jackals and Arabs' between Bohemia and Palestine," *AJS Review: The Journal for the Association for Jewish Studies* 33(2) (2009), pp. 71–100.

17. See Corngold and Gross, "Introduction," in *Kafka for the Twenty-First Century*, pp. 6, 21, n. 18; Reiner Stach, *Kafka: Die Jahre der Erkenntnis* (Frankfurt am Main: S. Fischer Verlag, 2008), pp. 240, 277.

18. Franz Kafka, *Briefe 1902–1924*, ed. Max Brod (Frankfurt: Fischer, 1975), p. 510, n. 3; Kafka, *Letters to Friends, Family, and Editors*, p. 239; Kafka, *Briefe*, p. 512, n. 14.

19. Kafka, *Letters to Milena*, pp. 213, 216; Kafka, *Letters to Friends, Family, and Editors*, p. 257.

20. Kafka, *Letters to Friends, Family, and Editors*, p. 370.

21. Hugo Bergmann, "Erinnerungen an Franz Kafka," *Universitas: Zeitschrift für Wissenschaft, Kunst und Literatur* 27(7) (1972), p. 746.

22. Max Brod, *Der Prager Kreis* (Frankfurt: Suhrkamp, 1979), p. 116.

23. Bruce, *Kafka and Cultural Zionism*, pp. 166–7, 177–80.

24. Niels Bokhove, "'The Entrance to the More Important': Kafka's Personal Zionism," in Mark Gelber (ed.), *Kafka, Zionism, and Beyond* (Tübingen: Max Niemeyer Verlag, 2004), p. 47.

25. Kafka, *Letters to Friends, Family, and Editors*, p. 374.

26. Ibid., pp. 394, 390.

27. Kafka, *Diaries, 1914–1923*, p. 197. For pictures from the film, see the slides reproduced in Hanns Zischler, *Kafka geht ins Kino* (Reinbeck: Rowohlt, 1996), pp. 148–53.

28. Felix Salten, *Neue Menschen auf Alter Erde* (Berlin: Paul Zsolnay Verlag, 1925), p. 72.

29. Kafka, *Letters to Friends, Family, and Editors*, p. 313; Franz Kafka, *Wedding Preparations in the Country and Other Posthumous Prose Writings* (London: Secker & Warburg, 1954), p. 119.

30. Kafka, *Letters to Friends, Family, and Editors*, p. 261; Bokhove, "Kafka's Personal Zionism," p. 48; Roger Hermes, Waltraud John, Hans-Gerd Koch and Anita Widera (eds.), *Franz Kafka: Eine Chronik* (Berlin: Verlag Klaus Wagenbach, 1999), p. 156; Alena Wagnerová, *Die Familie Kafka aus Prag* (Frankfurt: Fischer, 1997), pp. 164, 167; Kafka, *Letters to Friends, Family, and Editors*, pp. 226–8, 467, n. 9; ibid., p. 389.

31. Bokhove, "Kafka's Personal Zionism," p. 49.

32. "An Interim Report on the Civil Administration of Palestine, during the period 1st July, 1920 – 30th June, 1921." Available at: http://unispal.un.org/ UNISPAL.NSF/0/349B02280A930813052565E90048ED1C.

33. See my discussion of *Bambi* as a Zionist text: Iris Bruce, "Which Way Out? Schnitzler's and Salten's Conflicting Responses to Cultural Zionism," in Dagmar C. G. Lorenz (ed.), *A Companion to the Works of Arthur Schnitzler* (Rochester, NY: Camden House, 2003), pp. 103–26.

34. Bruce, *Kafka and Cultural Zionism*, pp. 81–4, 188–95; Kafka, *Diaries, 1914–1923*, pp. 202–3.

35. Shlomo Zemach, *Jüdische Bauern: Geschichten aus dem neuen Palästina* (Vienna: R. Löwit Verlag, 1919).

36. Derek Penslar, *Israel in History: The Jewish State in Comparative Perspective* (New York: Routledge, 2006), pp. 156–7.

37. Salten, *Menschen*, pp. 54, 55, 57–8, 61, 63.

38. Ibid., pp. 64, 68, 70, 77, 79.

39. Ibid., pp. 84, 85, 89. Many thanks to Ruthie Unz from Tel Aviv for generously sharing her extensive knowledge of the history and geography of "this little piece of land" (Israel).

40. Salten, *Menschen*, p. 23.

41. See Bathja Bayer, "Zeira, Mordechai," in *Encyclopaedia Judaica* (2007). Available at: www.encyclopedia.com.

42. Buber, *Letters*, p. 32.

43. Ibid., p. 33.

44. Zemach, *Jüdische Bauern*, pp. 15, 17; Kafka, *Letters to Felice*, p. 420. For Bloch see Hans Bloch, "Die Legende von Theodor Herzl," in K. Z. V. (ed.), *Der Zionistische Student* (Berlin: Jüdischer Verlag, n.d. [1912?]), pp. 51–62.

45. Buber, *Letters*, p. 22.

46. Bruce, *Kafka and Cultural Zionism*, p. 61; Sander Gilman, *Franz Kafka, the Jewish Patient* (New York: Routledge, 1995), pp. 102–3, 154.

47. Allan Arkush, "The Jewish State and its Internal Enemies: Yoram Hazony versus Martin Buber and his Ideological Children," *Jewish Social Studies* 7(2) (2001), p. 173.

48. Buber, *Letters*, p. 50.

49. I am grateful to Kafka's niece, the late Marianne Steiner, for this information (letter to the author, March 16, 1995).

50. See www.jta.org/1937/03/25/archive/dr-bergmann-hebrew-u-rector-honored-at-dinner-here.

51. Buber, *Letters,* p. 51.

52. Arnold Zweig, *Ritualmord in Ungarn* (Berlin: Hyperionverlag, 1914).

53. See Arnold Band, "Kafka and the Beiliss Affair," *Comparative Literature* 32 (1980), pp. 168–83; Bruce, *Kafka and Cultural Zionism,* p. 59.

54. Arnold Zweig and Hermann Struck, *Das Ostjüdische Antlitz* (Wiesbaden: Fourier Verlag, 1988; first published 1920).

55. Buber, *Letters*, p. 51.

56. Bruce, *Kafka and Cultural Zionism,* pp. 85–7, 178–9. See also Shaun Halper, "Mordechai Langer (1894–1943) and the Birth of the Modern Jewish Homosexual" (unpublished Ph.D. dissertation, University of California, Berkeley, 2013), p. 76, n. 217. Many thanks to Shaun Halper for sharing his fascinating Ph.D. thesis with me. For Langer's writings cf. Georg (Jiří) Langer, *Nine Gates to the Chassidic Mysteries,* trans. Stephen Jolly (New York: Behrman House, 1976; first published 1961), as well as his scholarly study, *Die Erotik der Kabbala* ("Eroticism of the Kabbalah") (Munich: Eugen Diederichs Verlag, 1989; first published 1923).

57. For dates of Kafka's family members, see Anthony Northey, *Kafka's Relatives: Their Lives and his Writing* (New Haven, CT: Yale University Press, 1991); for information about the concentration camps and the Bialystock orphans, see Kathi Diamant, *Kafka's Last Love: The Mystery of Dora Diamant* (New York: Basic Books, 2003), pp. 262–3. For Julie Wohryzek, see Bruce, *Kafka and Cultural Zionism,* p. 10; Diamant, *Kafka's Last Love,* p. 317; and especially Northey, "Julie Wohryzek, Franz Kafkas zweite Verlobte," *Freibeuter* (April 1994), p. 15.

58. Buber, *Letters*, p. 21.

59. Ibid., p. 50.

60. Tamar Mayer, "From Zero to Hero: Nationalism and Masculinity in Jewish Israel," in *Israeli Women Studies: A Reader* (New Brunswick, NJ: Rutgers University Press, 2005), p. 105.

61. Elieser Jerushalmi, *Das jüdische Martyrerkind: Nach Tagebuchaufzeichnungen aus dem Ghetto von Schaulen 1941–44,* trans. from the Hebrew by Miriam Singer (Degania/Israel), drawings by Abram Ameraut (Mizza/Israel) (Darmstadt-Eberstadt: Oekumenische Marienschwesternschaft, 1960).

62. Shaun Halper writes in relation to Jiří Langer's poetry that he plays on the word "mashakh" twice as the root for "messiah" and "desire." Halper, "Mordechai Langer (1894–1943) and the Birth of the Modern Jewish Homosexual," p. 76, n. 217. See also Suchoff in regards to the Hebrew root for "messiah" and "land-surveyor," and Langer's claim that "Kafka took comic pleasure in such coinages when he spoke Hebrew in Prague," in David

Suchoff, *Kafka's Jewish Languages: The Hidden Openness of Tradition* (Philadelphia: University of Pennsylvania Press, 2012), pp. 170, 171, 252, n. 10.

63. Hanni Mittelmann, *Sammy Gronemann: Ein Leben im Dienste des Zionismus* (Berlin: Hentrich & Hentrich Verlag, 2012), pp. 49, 57. Many thanks to Derek Penslar for informing me of Gronemann's literary success in Israel.

64. "Café Society." Available at: www.haaretz.com/culture/arts-leisure/cafe-society-1.292252.

65. Ze'ev Chafets, "A Shock in the Mirror," *The Jerusalem Report*, January 23, 1992, p. 20. See http://theawarenesscenter.blogspot.ca/1992/01/case-of-ben-amotz.html.

66. See www.eretzmuseum.org.il/e/199/117.htm.

67. Frank Klepner, *Yosl Bergner: Art as a Meeting of Cultures* (New York: Macmillan, 2004), pp. 130, 133.

68. Yosl Bergner, *Paintings to Franz Kafka* (Tel Aviv: Shva Publishers, 1990).

69. Bergmann, *Jawne und Jerusalem*, p. 38.

70. Amos Oz, "Has Israel Altered its Visions?" (1982), in Oz, *Israel, Palestine and Peace: Essays* (San Diego: Harcourt Brace & Company, 1994), pp. 16, 18.

Chapter 10 What if the Palestinian Arab elite had chosen compromise instead of boycott in confronting Zionism?

1. Taysir Nashif, "Palestinian Arab and Jewish Leadership in the Mandate Period," *Journal of Palestine Studies* 6(4) (1977), pp. 113–21. See Kenneth W. Stein, "Palestine's Rural Economy, 1917–1939," *Journal of Israeli History* 8(1) (1987), pp. 25–49, and Kenneth W. Stein, "Rural Change and Peasant Destitution: Contributing Causes to the Arab Revolt in Palestine, 1936–1939," in John Waterbury and Farhad Kazemi (eds.), *Peasants and Politics in the Modern Middle East* (Miami: Florida International University Press, 1989), pp. 143–70.

2. Abdul Latif Tibawi to H. M. Foot, Nablus Assistant District Commissioner (later Lord Caradon who helped draft UN Resolution 242 of November 1967), November 16, 1934, Land Registry Files, Box 3922, Israel State Archives, Jerusalem.

3. *Sepher Toldot Ha-Haganah (History of the Haganah)* (Tel Aviv: Israel Ministry of Defense, 1971), vol. B, part I, pp. 446–7.

4. For more information, see Malcolm MacDonald's "Discussion on Palestine" (August 21, 1938), which details Tannous' meetings with MacDonald in August 1938. British Cabinet Papers 190 (1938) and Foreign Office Record Group 371/file 21863, The National Archives, Kew.

5. See Uri Kupferschmidt, *The Supreme Muslim Council: Islam under the British Mandate* (Leiden: Brill, 1987).

6. See Issa Khalaf, *Arab Factionalism and Social Disintegration, 1939–1948* (Albany: State University of New York Press, 1991).

7. Izzat Tannous, *The Palestinians' Eyewitness History of Palestine* (New York: Igt Co., 1988), pp. 309–10.

8. *A Survey of Palestine Prepared in December 1945 and January 1946 for the Information of the Anglo-American Committee of Inquiry*, vol. 1 (London: Government Printer, 1946), p. 22.

9. Bernard Wasserstein, *The British in Palestine* (London: Royal Historical Society, 1978), pp. 113–15.

10. Moshe Mosek, *Palestine Immigration Policy under Sir Herbert Samuel: British, Zionist and Arab Attitudes* (London: Cass, 1978), p. 155.

11. Minute by Sir John Shuckburgh, October 15, 1923, CO 733/50/92, The National Archives.

12. See Ghassan Kanafani, *The 1936–39 Revolt in Palestine* (New York: Committee for Democratic Palestine, 1972).

13. Sir John Chancellor to Secretary of State for the Colonies, January 17, 1930, Cabinet Papers 108 (1930)/file 20835; also found in Great Britain, Colonial Office files, CO 733/183/77050, Part 1, The National Archives.

14. Sir John Chancellor to his son, Christopher, January 15, 1930, The Chancellor Papers, CP Box 16/3, Rhodes House, Oxford, UK.

15. Esco Foundation for Palestine, *Palestine: A Study of Jewish, Arab, and British Policies*, vol. II (New Haven, CT: Yale University Press, 1947), p. 660.

16. Remarks by Sir John Hope-Simpson to Lord Passfield, August 18, 1930, Cabinet Papers 24/215, The National Archives.

17. See Jewish Agency Memorandum, "Definition of Arab Landlessness," November/December 1930, Record Group S25/file 7587, Central Zionist Archives, Jerusalem.

18. Many Arabs did not find alternative holdings but did not submit claims to be classified as homeless because they found alternative jobs working either for Zionists or for the British in the building trade or the citrus industry.

19. Jacob Metzer and Oded Kaplan, "Jointly but Severally: Arab/Jewish Dualism and Economic Growth in Mandatory Palestine," *Journal of Economic History* 45(2) (1985), p. 11.

20. It is a total misrepresentation to say that the remaining area of Palestine under the Mandate was owned by Arabs; more than half of Palestine reflected no ownership by anyone (the Negev and Dead Sea area wilderness and large portions of the Galilee). Key for the Zionists was their ability to acquire land for strategic needs to create demographic contiguity; Arab sellers repeatedly gave the Zionists broad purchase options to fulfill strategic requirements, like the Upper Galilee to be adjacent to the River Jordan's sources around Acre and Haifa because of their importance to the port of Haifa and the outlet of

the pipeline from Mosul on the Jaffa–Jerusalem road, so that there would be a Jewish land connection between Jerusalem and the bulk of Jewish-purchased land along the coastal plain. In their willingness to sell lands to Jews, the Arabs did not boycott the Zionists; rather, in this realm, they engaged Jews willingly, and not merely large landowners, but peasant owners with smaller parcels to sell, particularly in the early 1930s. See Kenneth W. Stein, *The Land Question in Palestine, 1917–1939* (Durham: University of North Carolina Press, 1982 and 2003), pp. 173–92.

21. See ibid.; Yossi Katz, *The Battle for the Land: The History of the Jewish National Fund (KKL) before the Establishment of the State of Israel* (Jerusalem: Magnes Press, 2005), and Kenneth W. Stein, "The Jewish National Fund: Land Purchase Methods and Priorities, 1924–1939," *Middle Eastern Studies* 20(4) (1984), pp. 190–205.

22. See Jacob Metzer, *The Divided Economy of Palestine* (Cambridge University Press, 1988).

23. For a lucid account of Palestinian Arab collaboration, see Hillel Cohen, *Army of Shadows: Palestinian Collaboration with Zionism, 1917–1948* (Berkeley: University of California Press, 2008).

24. *Al-Jami'ah al-Islamiyyah*, August 21, 1932.

25. *Al-Difa'*, November 5, 1934.

26. *Al-Jam'iah al-Islammiyah*, January 22, 1936.

27. Remarks by Sir John Shuckburgh, June 14, 1940, CO 733/425/75872, Part 2, The National Archives.

28. The Palestine Administration, *Land Transfer Inquiry Committee,* November 1945. The original draft reports are housed at the Israeli State Archives in files SF/215/1/40 and LS 249/file 4.

29. Palestine Royal Commission, *Memoranda Prepared by the Government of Palestine*, memorandum no. 23, "Brief Account of Recent Legislative Council Proposals and of the Reception, including Reference to the Various 'Pledges' and Statements," London, 1936, pp. 84–93, The National Archives. See also J. C. Hurewitz, *The Struggle for Palestine* (New York: W. W. Norton, 1950), pp. 67–8.

30. Glubb Pasha, *Britain and the Arabs: A Study of Fifty Years, 1808–1958* (London: Hodder and Stoughton, 1959), p. 151.

31. Christopher Sykes, *Crossroads to Israel 1917–1948* (Bloomington: Indiana University Press, 1973), pp. 283, 288–94, and Hurewitz, *The Struggle for Palestine*, pp. 236–45.

32. Ibid., pp. 262–3.

33. Haim Levenberg, *The Military Preparations of the Arab Community in Palestine 1945–1948* (London: Cass, 1993), pp. 76–81.

34. Sykes, *Crossroads to Israel*, pp. 318, 323–5; Hurewitz, *The Struggle for Palestine*, pp. 285–90.

35. Shalom Reichman, "Partition and Transfer: Crystallization of the Settlement Map of Israel Following the War of Independence," in Ruth Kark (ed.), *The Land That Became Israel: Studies in Historical Geography* (Jerusalem: Magnes Press, 1990), p. 320.

36. Mayir Verete, "The Balfour Declaration and its Makers," *Middle Eastern Studies* 4 (1970), pp. 48–76.

37. The list of pro-Arab and anti-Zionist British officials in London, Palestine, or elsewhere in the Middle East is lengthy, beginning with the British officials who were not enamored with political Zionism, including Lord Curzon and Edwin Montagu in the World War I period and the generals who ran the British military administration from 1918 to 1920, such as General Arthur Money. A brief list of the more notable personalities who opposed Zionism includes Gertrude Bell, Ernest Richmond, Sydney Moody, Walter Shaw, John Hope-Simpson, John Chancellor, Sidney Webb (Lord Passfield), Lewis French, George Rendel, Sir Miles Lampson, and Ernest Bevin. Then there were the overwhelming number of British officials who were not rabid in their antagonism toward Zionism but certainly held either pro-Arab viewpoints or middle-ground positions about the legitimacy of both nationalisms, including John Shuckburgh, William Ormsby-Gore and all of Palestine's High Commissioners: Herbert Samuel, Herbert Plumer, Arthur Wauchope, Harold MacMichael, John Vereker, and Alan Cunningham.

Chapter 12 What if the Weimar Republic had survived?

1. *Historische Zeitschrift* 142 (1930), p. 220.

2. "Höre, Israel!," in *Impressionen* (Leipzig: S. Herzel, 1902), p. 4. "Inmitten deutschen Lebens ein abgesondert fremdartiger Menschenstamm, glänzend und auffällig staffirt, von heißblütig beweglichem Gebahren. Auf märkischem Sand eine asiatische Horde . . . so leben sie in einem halb freiwilligen, unsichtbaren Ghetto, kein lebendes Glied des Volkes, sondern ein fremder Organismus in seinem Leibe."

3. Ibid., pp. 4, 10.

4. March 16, 1897 – Herzl to Harden, in Theodor Herzl, *Briefe und Tagebücher*, vol. IV, ed. Alex Bein, Hermann Greive, Moshe Schaerf, and Julius H. Schoeps (Berlin: Propyläen, 1990), p. 205.

5. "Der Antisemitismus ist die vertikale Invasion der Gesellschaft durch die Barbaren."

6. Kurt Blumenfeld, *Erlebte Judenfrage: Ein Vierteljahrhundert deutscher Zionismus* (Stuttgart: Deutsche Verlags-Anstalt, 1962), p. 142.

7. Eugen Fuchs, *Um Deutschtum und Judentum*, ed. Leo Hirschfeld (Frankfurt: Kauffmann, 1919), p. 237.

8. Walther Rathenau, *Briefe*, vol. 1 (Dresden: Reiss, 1926), p. 220. "Mein Volk sind die Deutschen, niemand sonst. Die Juden sind für mich ein deutscher Stamm, wie Sachsen, Bayern oder Wenden."
9. Michael A. Meyer (ed.), *Joachim Prinz, Rebellious Rabbi: An Autobiography – The German and Early American Years* (Bloomington: Indiana University Press, 2008), p. 53.

Chapter 13   What if Adolf Hitler had been assassinated in 1939?

1. The text of this letter is based on a sample letter sent by Yad Vashem. See Harry Benjamin, "Elli's Saviours now Righteous Among the Nations," *J-Wire*, March 13, 2012. Available at: www.jwire.com.au/news/ellis-saviours-now-righteous-among-the-nations/23532.
2. Walter Laqueur and Judith Tydor Baumel (eds.), *The Holocaust Encyclopedia* (New Haven, CT: Yale University Press, 2001), pp. 569–70.
3. See "The Righteous Among the Nations" on the Yad Vashem website at: www.yadvashem.org/yv/en/righteous/program.asp.
4. This is the opening quotation on the authoritative Georg-Elser-Arbeitskreis Heidenheim website: www.georg-elser-arbeitskreis.de/gestart.php.
5. Scholars disagree about whether Himmler was present. Hellmut G. Haasis claims he was absent. See Hellmut G. Haasis, *"Den Hitler jag' ich in die Luft": Der Attentäter Georg Elser, Eine Biographie* (Berlin: Rowohlt, 1999), pp. 9–10. Peter Koblank convincingly argues that Himmler was present. See his web article from 2009: "Wenn das Elser-Attentat Erfolg gehabt hätte," available at: www.mythoselser.de/elser-folgen1.htm. Himmler was present in Munich on the night of the assassination.
6. Haasis, *"Den Hitler jag' ich in die Luft,"* p. 18.
7. Ibid., pp. 23–7.
8. Joachim Fest famously claimed that "if Hitler had succumbed to an assassination...at the end of 1938, few would [have] hesitate[d] to call him one of the greatest of German statesmen." Joachim Fest, *Hitler* (New York: Harcourt, Inc., 1974), p. 9.
9. There were already thirty-seven Jewish houses in Dresden by the end of 1939. See http://dresden.stadtwiki.de/wiki/Judenhäuser.
10. In real history, an estimated 7,000 Polish Jews had been killed by the end of 1939. Alexander B. Rossino, *Hitler Strikes Poland: Blitzkrieg, Ideology, and Atrocity* (Lawrence: University of Kansas Press, 2003), p. 234. Rossino adds that in this same period of time, the Nazis killed some 50,000 Polish Christians.
11. Christopher Browning, *The Origins of the Final Solution: The Evolution of Nazi Jewish Policy, September 1939 – March 1942* (Lincoln: University of Nebraska Press, 2004), pp. 36–54. J. Noakes and G. Pridham (eds.), *Nazism,*

1919–1945, vol. III: *Foreign Policy, War, and Racial Extermination* (Exeter University Press, 2001), pp. 442–51. Himmler's desire to prioritize the resettlement of ethnic Germans reflected his early October appointment to the directorship of the new Reich Commissariat for the Strengthening of Germandom (RKFDV). Still, by the end of 1939, some 87,000 Jews had been deported from the Warthegau to the General Government. Noakes and Pridham, *Foreign Policy, War, and Racial Extermination*, p. 449.

12. Toby Thacker, *Joseph Goebbels: Life and Death* (Houndmills: Palgrave Macmillan, 2010), p. 239.

13. Richard J. Evans, *The Third Reich at War* (New York: Penguin, 2008), p. 70.

14. This is what happened to the roughly 1,200 Jews expelled from Stettin to Lublin in February of 1940 (they were deported to make room for ethnic Germans arriving from the Soviet-annexed Baltics). Of the 1,200, over 200 died in the harsh conditions. Browning, *The Origins of the Final Solution*, pp. 64–5.

15. Joseph Poprzeczny, *Odilo Globocnik, Hitler's Man in the East* (Jefferson, NC: McFarland, 2004). Globocnik began creating work camps in late 1939 and had over thirty in operation by the summer of 1940 (ibid., p. 160).

16. Evans, *The Third Reich at War*, pp. 53, 46.

17. Western newspapers and journals published news of the reservation in the fall and winter of 1939–40. Reports addressed the fact that 45,000 Jews were already working under the supervision of SS Death's Head troops and that the reservation was ultimately to hold nearly 2 million Jews. Poprzeczny, *Odilo Globocnik*, pp. 149–50; Browning, *The Origins of the Final Solution*, pp. 64–5.

18. See Deborah Lipstadt, *Beyond Belief: The American Press and the Coming of the Holocaust, 1933–1945* (New York: Free Press, 1993), ch. 4.

19. Noakes and Pridham, *Foreign Policy, War, and Racial Extermination*, p. 448. John Lukacs, *The Last European War: September 1939 – December 1941* (New Haven, CT: Yale University Press, 2001), p. 433.

20. Evans, *The Third Reich at War*, pp. 112–13. See also Theodore Hamerow, *On the Road to the Wolf's Lair: German Resistance to Hitler* (Cambridge, MA: Harvard University Press, 1997).

21. Adam Tooze, *The Wages of Destruction: The Making and Breaking of the Nazi Economy* (New York: Viking, 2006), pp. 326–32.

22. Browning, *The Origins of the Final Solution*, pp. 73–5; Noakes and Pridham, *Foreign Policy, War, and Racial Extermination*, pp. 330–3; Evans, *The Third Reich at War*, pp. 24–5; Rossino, *Hitler Strikes Poland*, p. 118.

23. Noakes and Pridham, *Foreign Policy, War, and Racial Extermination*, p. 445.

24. Peter Longerich, *Heinrich Himmler* (Oxford University Press, 2012), p. 181.

25. Klaus Hildebrand, *The Foreign Policy of the Third Reich* (Berkeley: University of California Press, 1973), pp. 88–90; Evans, *The Third Reich at War*, p. 113. Richard Overy stresses that Goering was interested in a general war against these enemy states, but only once Germany was economically and militarily prepared by the middle of the 1940s. Richard Overy, *Goering: Hitler's Iron Knight* (New York: I. B. Tauris, 2012), pp. 86–7.

26. Browning, *The Origins of the Final Solution*, p. 107. In real history, the generals' complaints stopped with the May 10 invasion and the subsequent defeat of France. This victory allowed the Nazis to shift course in their treatment of the General Government, which they now decided to Germanize instead of rebuild.

27. Longerich, *Heinrich Himmler*, pp. 249, 427.

28. Until 1941, these militarized SS units (which were known as the Waffen SS in 1940) lacked their own weapons procurement power and were dependent on the Wehrmacht for their weapons supply. The Waffen SS grew to around 100,000 troops around the same time. George H. Stein, *The Waffen SS: Hitler's Elite Guard at War, 1939–1945* (Ithaca, NY: Cornell University Press, 1984), pp. 50–5.

29. The crimes of the so-called T4 euthanasia campaign were approved in October of 1939. Gassings began in Brandenburg in January 1940. Noakes and Pridham, *Foreign Policy, War, and Racial Extermination*, pp. 401–3, 411–12.

30. Goering had sent out private peace feelers to the British via a Swedish intermediary, Birger Dahlerus. Gerhard Weinberg, *The World at Arms: A Global History of World War II* (Cambridge University Press, 2005), pp. 89–90.

31. Neville Chamberlain rejected Hitler's peace feeler on October 12, 1939. Ibid., p. 91.

32. See Ezra Mendelsohn, *The Jews of East Central Europe Between the World Wars* (Bloomington: Indiana University Press, 1983).

33. The unemployment rate in the United States fell from 17.2 percent in 1939 to 14.6 percent in 1940 to 9.9 percent in 1941. *Historical Statistics of the United States, Colonial Times to 1970*, part 1 (Washington, DC: US Dept. of Commerce, Bureau of the Census, 1975), p. 126.

34. Klaus-Michael Mallmann and Martin Cüppers, *Nazi Palestine: The Plans for the Extermination of the Jews in Palestine* (New York: Enigma Books, 2010), p. 143.

35. Gerhard Weinberg, *Visions of Victory: The Hopes of Eight World War II Leaders* (Cambridge University Press, 2005), p. 157. If the Peel plan had been carried out, it would have involved the transfer of up to 225,000 Arabs and 1,250 Jews.

36. Martin Gilbert, *Churchill and the Jews: A Lifelong Friendship* (New York: Henry Holt, 2008), p. 270. This quote was from 1948.

Chapter 14   What if the Nazis had won the battle of El Alamein?

1. On this point, see Jeffrey Herf, *The Jewish Enemy: Nazi Propaganda during World War II and the Holocaust* (Cambridge, MA: Harvard University Press, 2006). For the classic statement, see Karl Bracher, "The Role of Hitler: Perspectives of Interpretation," in Walter Laqueur (ed.), *Fascism: A Reader's Guide* (Berkeley and Los Angeles: University of California Press, 1976), pp. 211–25.

2. Richard Evans has eloquently come to the defense of the discipline of history in *In Defense of History* (New York: W. W. Norton, 2000). Also see his *Lying About Hitler: History, Holocaust and the David Irving Trial* (New York: Basic Books, 2002). On Holocaust denial in France, see Valerie Igounet, *Histoire du negationnisme en France* (Paris: Seuil, 2000). On denial in the Arab countries, see Meir Litvak and Ester Webman, *From Empathy to Denial: Arab Responses to the Holocaust* (New York: Columbia University Press, 2009). For an early work on Holocaust denial see Deborah Lipstadt, *Denying the Holocaust: The Growing Assault on Memory and Truth* (New York: Plume, 1994).

3. On Kirk's memo to Hull of February 16, 1942, see Jeffrey Herf, *Nazi Propaganda for the Arab World* (New Haven, CT: Yale University Press, 2009), p. 97. For full text see Kirk to Secretary of State (February 16, 1942), "Concern of the United States regarding Effect of Axis Military Advance into Egypt; Plans for Evacuation of American Diplomatic and Consular Personnel from Egypt," in *Foreign Relations of the United States (FRUS), Diplomatic Papers 1942*, vol. IV: *The Near East and Africa* (Washington, DC: US Government Printing Office, 1962), pp. 71–3.

4. On Husseini's meetings with Ribbentrop, see Herf, *Nazi Propaganda for the Arab World*, pp. 74–6. Also see "No. 514, Record of the Conversation of the Grand Mufti with the Foreign Minister in Berlin on November 28, 1941," in *Documents on German Foreign Policy (DGFP) Series D (1937–1945)*, vol. XIII (Washington, DC: US Government Printing Office, 1956–64), pp. 876–81.

5. Ibid., p. 75.

6. Ibid.

7. On the meeting with Hitler, see Herf, *Nazi Propaganda for the Arab World*, pp. 76–8. For the official transcript see "No. 515, Memorandum by an Official of the Foreign Minister's Secretariat, Record of the Conversation between the Führer and the Grand Mufti of Jerusalem on November 28, 1941, in the Presence of Reich Foreign Minister and Minister Grobba in Berlin," Berlin (November 30, 1941), in *DGFP Series D (1937–1945)*, vol. XIII, pp. 881–5. Also see Lukasz Hirszowicz, *The Third Reich and the Arab East* (London: Routledge and Kegan Paul, 1966), pp. 218–21.

8. Cited in Herf, *Nazi Propaganda for the Arab World*, p. 76.

9. Ibid., p. 77.

10. Ibid.

11. Ibid., pp. 77–8.

12. On Holocaust decision-making and public pronouncements in summer and fall 1941, see Christopher Browning, *The Origins of the Final Solution: The Evolution of Nazi Jewish Policy, September 1939–March 1942* (Lincoln: University of Nebraska Press, 2004), and *Fateful Months: Essays on the Emergence of the Final Solution* (New York: Holmes and Meier, 1991); Saul Friedlander, *The Years of Extermination: Nazi Germany and the Jews, 1939–1945* (New York: HarperCollins, 2007); and Herf, *The Jewish Enemy*.

13. See Herf, *Nazi Propaganda for the Arab World*, pp. 102–26.

14. "Kill the Jews before They Kill You," broadcast by the *Voice of Free Arabism* on July 7, 1942, transcribed by the staff of the American Embassy in Cairo. Cited in Herf, *Nazi Propaganda for the Arab World*, pp. 125–6.

15. Zionism inspired by secular anti-imperialism or "pan-Islamist" religious ideology. Ibid., pp. 138–40.

16. Tuvia Friling, *Arrows in the Dark: David Ben-Gurion, the Yishuv Leadership and Rescue Attempts during the Holocaust*, trans. Ora Cummings (Madison: University of Wisconsin Press, 2005), pp. 64–5. Robert Satloff has recently described policies of antisemitic persecution and the establishment of harsh labor camps during the North Africa occupation by Nazi Germany, Vichy France, and Fascist Italy. Yet as terrible as these policies were, the Nazis and their allies were unable to implement plans to engage in mass murder either in the region or via deportation to death camps in Europe. See Robert Satloff, *Among the Righteous: Lost Stories from the Long Reach of the Holocaust into Arab Lands* (New York: Public Affairs, 2006).

17. See, in particular, Klaus Michael-Mallmann and Martin Cüppers, *Nazi Palestine: The Plans for the Extermination of the Jews in Palestine* (New York: Enigma Books, 2010), translation of *Halbmond und Hakenkreuz: das Dritte Reich, die Araber und Palästina* (Darmstadt: Wissenschaftliche Buchgesellschaft, 2005); and Herf, *Nazi Propaganda for the Arab World*.

18. For recent examples, see Gerhard Weinberg, *A World at Arms: A Global History of World War II* (Cambridge University Press, 1994); and Horst Boog et al., *The Global War: Widening of the Conflict into a World War and the Shift of the Initiative, 1941–1943*, trans. Ewald Osers (Oxford University Press, 2001). German original: Horst Boog et al., *Das Deutsche Reich und der Zweite Weltkrieg*, vol. VI: *Der Globale Krieg: die Ausweitung zum Weltkrieg und der Wechsel der Initiative, 1941–1943* (Stuttgart: Deutsche Verlags-Anstalt, 1990).

19. Hirszowicz, *The Third Reich and the Arab East*.

20. See Heinz Tillmann, *Deutschlands Araberpolitik im Zweiten Weltkrieg* (Berlin: Deutsche Verlag der Wissenschaften, 1960); Philip Bernd Schröder,

Deutschland in der Mittlere Osten im Zweiten Weltkrieg (Göttingen: Musterschmidt, 1975); Robert Lewis Melka, "The Axis and the Middle East: 1930–1945" (unpublished doctoral dissertation, University of Minnesota, 1966); Josef Schröder, "Die Beziehungen der Achsenmächte zur Arabischen Welt," in Manfred Funke (ed.), *Hitler, Deutschland und die Mächte: Materialien zur Außenpolitik des Dritten Reiches* (Dusseldorf: Droste Verlag, 1976), pp. 365–82; and Wolfgang Schwanitz, *Germany and the Middle East, 1871–1945* (Princeton: Markus Wiener Publishers, 2004).

21. It was originally published as Mallmann and Cüppers, *Halbmond und Hakenkreuz: Das Dritte Reich, die Araber und Palästina.*

22. Memo from Supreme Command of the Army to Joint Operations Staff, "OKW/WFSr/Qu.I to Dr. Gen.b.HQu.It.Wehrm," July 13, 1942, RW 5/690, Bundesarchiv-Militärarchiv, Freiburg; cited by Mallmann and Cüppers in *Nazi Palestine*, p. 117.

23. Ibid.

24. Ibid., pp. 124–5.

25. Ibid., pp. 126–38.

26. Ibid., p. 139.

27. Herf, *Nazi Propaganda for the Arab World*, especially "Postwar Aftereffects," pp. 233–66.

Chapter 15 What if the Final Solution had been completed?

1. For more on the topic, see Dirk Rupnow, *Vernichten und Erinnern: Spuren nationalsozialistischer Gedächtnispolitik* (Göttingen: Wallstein, 2005), and "Annihilating – Preserving – Remembering: The 'Aryanization' of Jewish History and Memory during the Holocaust," in Peter Meusburger, Michael Heffernan, and Edgar Wunder (eds.), *Cultural Memories: The Geographical Point of View* (Knowledge and Space 4) (Dordrecht: Springer, 2011), pp. 189–200.

2. James E. Young, *Writing and Rewriting the Holocaust: Narrative and the Consequences of Interpretation* (Bloomington: Indiana University Press, 1988), p. 189.

3. Avishai Margalit, *The Ethics of Memory* (Cambridge, MA: Harvard University Press, 2004), p. 21.

4. See Gavriel D. Rosenfeld, *The World Hitler Never Made: Alternate History and the Memory of Nazism* (Cambridge University Press, 2005).

5. Quoted in Jay Winter and Emmanuel Sivan (eds.), *War and Remembrance in the Twentieth Century* (Cambridge University Press, 2000), p. 126.

6. Hannah Arendt, *The Origins of Totalitarianism* (New York: Schocken, 2004), p. 441.

7. Jens Hoffmann, *"Das kann man nicht erzählen." Aktion 1005: Wie die Nazis die Spuren ihrer Massenmorde in Osteuropa verwischten* (Hamburg: KVV konkret, 2008); Shmuel Spector, "Aktion 1005 – Effacing the Murder of Millions," *Holocaust and Genocide Studies* 5 (1990), pp. 157–73.

8. "Der Prozess gegen die Hauptkriegsverbrecher vor dem internationalen Militärgerichtshof, Nürnberg, 14. November 1945 bis 2. Oktober 1946," Dok. PS-1919, pp. 64ff. (emphasis added).

9. Bradley F. Smith and Agnes F. Peterson (eds.), *Heinrich Himmler: Geheimreden 1933 bis 1945 und andere Ansprachen* (Frankfurt am Main: Propyläen, 1974), pp. 170f.

10. Saul Friedlander, "Introduction," in Saul Friedlander (ed.), *Probing the Limits of Representation: Nazism and the "Final Solution"* (Cambridge, MA: Harvard University Press, 1992), p. 10.

11. "Augenzeugenbericht zu den Massenvergasungen (Dokumentation)," ed. Hans Rothfels, *Vierteljahrshefte für Zeitgeschichte* 1(2) (1953), p. 189.

12. Hans Mommsen, "Die Realisierung des Utopischen: Die 'Endlösung der Judenfrage' im 'Dritten Reich,'" in Hans Mommsen, *Der Nationalsozialismus und die deutsche Gesellschaft: Ausgewählte Aufsätze* (Reinbek b. Hamburg: Rowohlt, 1991), p. 186.

13. Franz Neumann, *Behemoth: The Structure and Practice of National Socialism* (New York: Ivan R. Dee, 2009), p. 125.

14. Emanuel Ringelblum, *Notes from the Warsaw Ghetto*, ed. Jacob Sloan (New York: McGraw-Hill, 1958), p. 325.

15. E39, 2326/1, Stadtarchiv Nürnberg.

16. Hermann Rauschning, *Gespräche mit Hitler* (Vienna: Europa, 1947), p. 223.

17. Jean-Paul Sartre, *Anti-Semite and Jew* (New York: Schocken, 1965), pp. 13, 28.

18. On the Jewish Central Museum, see Dirk Rupnow, *Täter-Gedächtnis-Opfer: Das "Jüdische Zentralmuseum" in Prag 1942–1945* (Vienna: Picus, 2000); Dirk Rupnow, "'Ihr müßt sein, auch wenn ihr nicht mehr seid': The Jewish Central Museum in Prague and Historical Memory in the Third Reich," *Holocaust and Genocide Studies* 16 (2002), pp. 23–53; Dirk Rupnow, "From Final Depository to Memorial: The History and Significance of the Jewish Museum in Prague," *European Judaism* 37(1) (2004), pp. 142–59.

19. Letter from Reichsstatthalter Niederdonau to Bürgermeister Eisenstadt, o.D. [1943], Bundesdenkmalamt Wien, NS-Materialien/K4: Jüdische Friedhöfe und Grabsteine; Konzept an das Gau-Kulturamt/Jölli, 19.1.1939, Bundesdenkmalamt Wien, NS-Materialien/K3: Jüdische Friedhöfe. See also Bundesdenkmalamt Wien, Akt Wien IX., Jüdischer Friedhof/Seegasse 9.

20. Memorandum, February 17, 1943, Naturhistorisches Museum Wien/Anthropologische Abteilung, Korrespondenz 1943, p. 333.

21. Letter from Sievers to Hirt, Berlin, September 8, 1942, NS 21/904, Bundesarchiv Berlin.

22. On Nazi Jewish Studies, see Dirk Rupnow, *Judenforschung im Dritten Reich: Wissenschaft zwischen Politik, Propaganda und Ideologie* (Historische Grundlagen der Moderne/Autoritäre Regime und Diktaturen im 20. Jahrhundert IV) (Baden-Baden: Nomos, 2011); Dirk Rupnow, "Racializing Historiography: Anti-Jewish Scholarship in the Third Reich," *Patterns of Prejudice* 42(1) (2008), pp. 27–59; Dirk Rupnow, "'Arisierung' jüdischer Geschichte: Zur nationalsozialistischen 'Judenforschung,'" *Leipziger Beiträge zur jüdischen Geschichte und Kultur* 2 (2004), pp. 349–67; Nicolas Berg, Dan Diner, and Dirk Rupnow (eds.), "'Judenforschung' – Zwischen Wissenschaft und Ideologie," *Jahrbuch des Simon-Dubnow-Instituts/Simon Dubnow Institute Yearbook* 5 (2006), pp. 303–538; Alan Steinweis, *Studying the Jew: Scholarly Antisemitism in Nazi Germany* (Cambridge, MA: Harvard University Press, 2006).

23. Alfred Rosenberg, "Nationalsozialismus und Wissenschaft," *Weltkampf: Die Judenfrage in Geschichte und Gegenwart* 1–2 (1941), p. 5.

24. Fritz Hippler, *Die Verstrickung. Auch ein Filmbuch . . .* (Düsseldorf: Mehr Wissen, 1981), p. 187.

25. Ibid., p. 189.

26. Eric Norden, *The Ultimate Solution* (New York: Warner Paperback, 1973), p. 71.

27. Wilhelm Grau, "Das Institut zur Erforschung der Judenfrage," *Weltkampf* 1–2 (1941), p. 19.

28. H. G. Adler, *Die unsichtbare Wand* (Vienna: p. Zsolnay, 1989), p. 413.

Chapter 16 What if the Holocaust had been averted?

1. On the deliberations that actually took place in Munich and the projected balance of military forces as of January 1939, see Niall Ferguson, *The War of the World: Twentieth-Century Conflict and the Descent of the West* (New York: Penguin, 2006), pp. 360–8.

2. For Chamberlain's fearful remarks to the British people about poison gas, see Richard Evans, *The Third Reich in Power* (New York: Penguin, 2005), p. 672.

3. Churchill's fictitious speech is the obverse of his actual attack on Chamberlain's policies. See Williamson Murray, "The War of 1938: Chamberlain Fails to Sway Hitler," in Robert Crowley (ed.), *The Collected What If?: Eminent Historians Imagine What Might Have Been* (New York: Penguin, 1999), p. 660.

4. This account is my extension of Murray's own projections of the possible dilemmas for the Nazis of an early start to the Second World War. For his account, see Crowley, *The Collected What If?*, pp. 655–80.

5. On the history of Soviet foreign policy toward Poland, see Adam B. Ulam, *Expansion and Coexistence: Soviet Foreign Policy, 1917–1973*, 2nd edn (New York and Washington: Praeger, 1974), pp. 282, 287.

6. The work of Karl Schleneus informs this scenario. He has argued that from 1933 to 1939, there were many turns in Nazi policies toward the Jews: a path that ultimately led to their physical destruction with the start of World War II. He often emphasizes the exigencies of office that Hitler faced early in his regime that did not involve the consummate enemy, the Jews, and the relatively late direct involvement of the SS in the Jewish Question. Similarly, he notes how Schacht was given a free hand in developing the German economy even if his moves ran counter to ideological views of Jews. See below for the reference to specific sections of his *The Twisted Road to Auschwitz: Nazi Policy towards German Jews, 1933–1939* (Urbana: University of Illinois Press, 1970).

7. Evans, *The Third Reich in Power*, pp. 343, 347, 358, 360, 370, 384–5; Schleneus, *The Twisted Road to Auschwitz*, pp. 137–8, 145–6, 151–2.

8. For the most comprehensive history of the evolution of this plan, which focuses much on the conflicts within the Zionist camp over this deal, see Edwin Black, *The Transfer Agreement: The Untold Story of the Secret Agreement between the Third Reich and Jewish Palestine* (New York: Macmillan, 1984). For insights specifically into Schacht's role, see ibid., pp. 113, 115, 373; see also Schleneus, *The Twisted Road to Auschwitz*, pp. 197–8.

9. On the actual policies of the British, including the negotiations of the Peel Commission and the subsequent White Paper of 1939 (which in my version of history did not take place), see Christopher Sykes, *Crossroads to Israel, 1917–1948* (Bloomington: Indiana University Press, 1973), especially pp. 153–200.

10. In my iteration of Churchill's actual proposal in 1937, his plan is adopted and not rejected by the British. See, on this subject, Martin Gilbert, *Churchill and the Jews: A Lifelong Friendship* (New York: Henry Holt, 2007), pp. 144–5, 151–3.

11. Sykes, *Crossroads to Israel*, p. 177.

12. On the Grand Mufti's relations with the Nazis and his pro-Nazi, anti-Jewish statements and plans, see Walter Laqueur and Barry Rubin (eds.), *The Israel–Arab Reader: A Documentary History of the Middle East Conflict*, 3rd edn (New York: Penguin, 1976), pp. 79–84; Joseph B. Schechtman, *The Mufti and the Fuehrer* (New York: Thomas Yoseloff, 1965), pp. 15, 76–85 and *passim*; Klaus Geniscke, *The Mufti of Jerusalem and the Nazis: The*

Berlin Years (London and Portland, OR: Valentine-Mitchell, 2011), pp. 20, 32–4.

13. Andrew Roberts, *The Storm of War: A New History of the Second World War* (New York: HarperCollins, 2011), pp. 25–6. See also Ulam, *Expansion and Coexistence*, p. 289.

14. For conflicts between Jews and their neighbors in cities over the question of international affairs see, for example, Ronald H. Bayor, *Neighbors in Conflict: The Irish, Germans, Jews and Italians of New York City, 1929–1941* (Baltimore, MD: Johns Hopkins University Press, 1978); Robert L. Fleegler, "Theodore G. Bilbo and the Decline of Public Racism, 1938–1947," *Journal of Mississippi History* (March 2006), p. 10; David Brody, "American Jewry: The Refugees and Immigration Restriction (1932–1942)," *Publications of the American Jewish Historical Society* (June 1956), pp. 220–3.

15. Charles J. Tull, *Father Coughlin and the New Deal* (Syracuse University Press, 1965), cover text.

16. This scenario, articulated by military people of both the US and Japan, many of whom point to Japan focusing its aggression on East Asia and not attacking Pearl Harbor, is derived and interpolated from Jim Bresnahan (ed.), *Refighting the Pacific War: An Alternative History of World War II* (Annapolis, MD: Naval Institute Press, 2011), pp. 2–3, 12, 23, 25, 31, 33–5, 37, 39, 40.

17. Beth Wenger, *New York Jews and the Great Depression: Uncertain Promise* (New Haven, CT: Yale University Press, 1996), ch. 5; Steven M. Lowenstein, *Frankfurt on the Hudson. The German-Jewish Community of Washington Heights, 1933–1983: Its Structure and Culture* (Detroit: Wayne State University Press, 1989), pp. 45, 46, 50; see also p. 45 on chain migration as applied to this community's growth.

18. Stephen Steinberg, *The Academic Melting Pot: Catholics and Jews in American Higher Education* (New York: McGraw-Hill, 1974), pp. 20–1; Marcia Graham Synott, *The Half-Opened Door: Discrimination and Admissions at Harvard, Yale and Princeton, 1900–1970* (Westport, CT: Greenwood Press, 1979), pp. 158, 195. See also Dan A. Oren, *Joining the Club: A History of Jews and Yale* (New Haven, CT: Yale University Press, 1985), pp. 143–51.

19. Heywood Broun and George Britt, *Christians Only: A Study in Prejudice* (New York: Vanguard Press, 1931), p. 256.

20. While Warner Brothers did produce its film about Salomon starring Rains, the final speech is fictitious. See Beth Wenger, *History Lessons: The Creation of American Jewish Heritage* (Princeton University Press, 2010), p. 204.

21. On the fluctuations of popular support for Zionism in America during the 1920s and 1930s, see Naomi W. Cohen, *American Jews and the Zionist Idea* (New York: KTAV Publishing House, 1975), pp. 31–2, 43.

22. On Proskauer's actual anti-Zionism statements and activities, see Samuel Halperin, *The Political World of American Zionism* (Detroit: Wayne State University Press, 1961), pp. 15, 127, 128. See also Thomas A. Kolsky, *Jews Against Zionism: The American Council for Judaism, 1942–1948* (Philadelphia: Temple University Press, 1990), pp. 41–2, and Naomi W. Cohen, *Not Free to Desist: The American Jewish Committee, 1906–1966* (Philadelphia: Jewish Publication Society, 1972), pp. 305–6.

23. On the British position on the Palestine question in 1948, including a last attempt at partition, see Sykes, *Crossroads to Israel*, pp. 310–11.

24. The account of a pre-May 1948 battle over Palestine was derived from Benny Morris's analysis of the actual "civil war" in the future Israel of those months. See Benny Morris, *1948: The First Arab–Israeli War* (New Haven, CT: Yale University Press, 2008), especially pp. 394–402.

25. On the various activities – legal and illegal – that American Jewish groups undertook to assist Israel, see Leonard Slater, *The Pledge* (New York: Simon & Schuster, 1971).

26. This account of a post-May 14 War of Independence was likewise interpolated from Morris's study, *1948*, especially pp. 400–4.

27. The geopolitical positions ascribed to candidate Marshall were derived from an examination of his statements and those of other anti-Zionists in the State Department and military on Zionism, Israel, and American policies. See Joseph W. Bendersky, *The "Jewish Threat": Anti-Semitic Politics of the U.S. Army* (New York: Basic Books, 2002), pp. 378–80, and Ed Cray, *General of the Army: George C. Marshall, Soldier and Statesman* (New York: W.W. Norton and Co., 1990), pp. 656–8.

28. In actuality, in 1949 Ben-Gurion publicly stressed the value of large-scale immigration of American Jewish youth to Israel, even over parental objections, and projected Israel as spokesman for world Jewry. After heated exchanges between Ben-Gurion, Blaustein, and Proskauer, the Prime Minister backed down, declaring reports on his position to have been "unauthorized." A contretemps was thus averted. See Charles S. Liebman, "Diaspora Influence on Israel: The Ben-Gurion–Blaustein Exchange and its Aftermath," *Jewish Social Studies* 36(3–4) (1974), pp. 271–80.

29. For a discussion of the Committee of 300 and its actual activities, which operated with a different tone from my alternative history description, see Arthur A. Goren, "A 'Golden Age' for American Jews: 1945–1955," *Studies in Contemporary Jewry* 8 (1992), pp. 10–14.

30. During the McCarthy era, the ADL did clean house, ridding itself of some professionals who had leftist backgrounds or presumed leanings, and files were turned over to the government. See Deborah Dash Moore, *B'nai B'rith and the Challenge of Ethnic Leadership* (Albany: State University of New York Press, 1981), pp. 197, 226.

31. On the publication of *Gentleman's Agreement* as a book and as a movie, which in an increasingly tolerant America received Academy Award acclaim, see Rachel Gordan, "When 'Gentleman's Agreement' made Jewish Oscars History: Fascinating Back Story Behind 1948 Academy Award Winner," *Jewish Daily Forward* (February 22, 2013), on-line edition.

INDEX

Abdullah, King of Jordan, 219, 233, 235

Abraham, iii, xi, 8, 30, 31, 32, 38, 62, 64, 69, 107, 168, 358, 363, 381

Aegyptiaca, 36

Afrikakorps, 305, 307, 309, 310

Afrikaners, 152, 154, 155, 156

Agnon, Samuel Yosef, 55, 185, 203, 212, 270

Al-Husseini, Haj Amin, 215, 229, 235, 243

Alami, Musa, vi, viii, 22, 238, 240, 241, 242, 243, 244, 245, 246, 247, 248, 250, 251, 252, 253, 254, 255, 256, 257, 258

Alexander I, Tsar, 125, 134

alternate history, 4, 16, 17, 18, 25, 26, 29, 33, 167, 311, 328, 331, 356, 357, 361

Antiochus IV, 49

antisemitism, 143, 145, 150, 160, 162, 193, 198, 207, 262, 265, 266, 268, 270, 274, 282, 283, 315, 316, 325, 336, 337, 340, 342, 349, 353

apartheid, 154, 155, 156, 157, 158, 160, 185

Arab Executive Committee, 218

Arab Revolt, 293, 386

Ashkenaz, 14, 73, 79

Auerbach, Berthold, 107, 112, 118, 119, 372

Augustus, 8, 43, 87

Auschwitz, 208, 210, 322, 329, 330, 398

Baer, Yitzhak, 15

Balfour Declaration, 145, 146, 147, 192, 215, 218, 219, 221, 223, 226, 231, 233, 235, 236, 237, 238, 242, 338, 339, 389

Bar Kochba revolt, 15, 189

Baron, Salo, 15, 16, 82

"Beardlings," 128

Beck, Ludwig, 285, 296

Begin, Menachem, 179, 180

Ben-Gurion, David, vi, viii, 22, 238, 239, 240, 242, 243, 244, 245, 246, 247, 248, 249, 250, 251, 252, 253, 254, 255, 257, 293, 294, 295, 307, 310, 348, 351, 394, 400

Bergmann, Hugo, 189, 190, 192, 193, 194, 196, 204, 206

Bialik, Chaim, 198, 200, 201

Blobel, Paul, 313

Blumenfeld, Kurt, 262, 266, 270, 389

Bonaparte, Napoleon, 17, 150, 361

Brod, Max, 189, 192, 193, 204, 208, 213

Bronstein, Lev, 139

Buber, Martin, 190, 197, 201, 202, 203, 204, 205, 206, 207, 209, 270, 382, 383, 384, 385

Burke, Edmund, 125, 126, 381

Canaan, 10, 24, 28, 30, 34, 36

Catherine the Great, 21, 123, 133

Centralverein, 268, 269

Chamberlain, Neville, 294, 332, 333, 337, 338, 339
Chancellor, Sir John, 223, 224, 225, 226, 227, 228, 233
Chmielnicki, 59, 72, 291
Chronicles, 29, 30, 31, 33, 34, 36, 37, 38, 39, 41
Churchill, Sir Winston, 222, 294, 299, 300, 307, 310, 332, 338, 339, 392, 397, 398
Cohen, Hermann, 103, 106, 113, 121
Coughlin, Father Charles, 340, 344, 399
counterfactual history, 3, 4, 5, 6, 7, 16, 17, 18, 19, 20, 310, 355, 356, 357
Cracow, vii, 84, 85, 86, 87, 88, 91, 92, 373, 374, 375, 376
Crassus, 44, 47
Cyrus, King, 32

da Costa, Uriel, 107
Daladier, Édouard, 332
David, King, 10
"Dayenu," 3, 10, 38
Degania Alef, 193, 194, 197, 199, 200, 201, 202, 204, 211, 385
diaspora, 13, 21, 50, 51, 52, 55, 57, 175, 180, 186, 214, 250, 354, 367, 368, 381, 400
Divre Hayyamim, 29
Dubnow, Simon, 15, 16, 270, 360, 397
Dymant, Dora, 194

Edict of Tolerance (1781), 134
Egypt, 1, 2, 3, 10, 13, 21, 24, 25, 26, 27, 28, 29, 30, 31, 32, 33, 36, 51, 64, 150, 161, 218, 219, 227, 234, 298, 300, 305, 306, 307, 308, 309, 310, 363, 367, 393
Eichmann, Adolf, 283, 292, 317, 334
Einsatzgruppen, 283, 308, 310
Einstein, Albert, viii, 204, 213, 262, 266, 267, 268, 269, 271, 272
El Alamein, battle of, vi, 22, 181, 298, 300, 306, 307, 308, 309, 310
Elijah, 129
Elser, Georg, viii, 22, 275, 276, 277, 278, 279, 280, 285, 295, 296, 390
Enlightenment, 20, 82, 112, 126, 128, 129, 134, 136, 372

Evian Conference (1938), 291
Exodus, i, v, 1, 3, 8, 9, 10, 24, 25, 26, 28, 29, 30, 31, 32, 33, 34, 35, 36, 37, 38, 39, 40, 41, 293, 355, 358, 363, 364

Faisal IV, King of Iraq, 167
Farouk, King of Egypt, 219
Frankfurt, 83, 101, 323, 325, 326, 356, 363, 383, 384, 389, 396, 399

Genesis, 8, 28, 30, 32, 358
Gerstein, Kurt, 314
ghetto, v, vii, 81, 82, 83, 87, 88, 89, 92, 93, 95, 121, 208, 312, 315, 318, 320, 323, 329, 330, 371, 372, 375, 376, 378, 379, 380, 385, 389, 396
Globocnik, Odilo, 284, 314, 391
Goebbels, Josef, 279, 282, 284, 288, 325, 327, 391
Goering, Hermann, 279, 281, 284, 285, 286, 287, 288, 289, 290, 292, 296, 392
Graetz, Heinrich, 15, 89, 360, 376
Grau, Wilhelm, 329, 397

Haganah, 204, 206, 208, 250, 293, 386
Haggadah, vii, 26, 27, 35, 38, 40, 41
Hasidim, 129
Hecateus, 36, 37, 363
Heine, Heinrich, vii, 112, 117, 118, 214, 269, 372
Herodotus, 7, 12, 13, 357
Herzl, Theodor, 17, 144, 145, 147, 165, 168, 169, 170, 171, 173, 175, 178, 182, 190, 197, 202, 214, 236, 261, 262, 270, 272, 361, 384, 389
Hess, Moses, 107, 112, 120
Heydrich, Reinhard, 279, 280, 282, 283, 288
Hezekiah, 9, 31, 358
Himmler, Heinrich, 279, 282, 283, 308, 313, 314, 328, 334, 390, 391, 392, 396
Hindenburg, Paul von, 265, 266
Hirt, August, 322

Hitler, Adolf, i, vi, viii, 19, 22, 178, 181,
    211, 219, 238, 245, 265, 275, 276,
    278, 279, 280, 281, 282, 283, 285,
    286, 287, 288, 289, 293, 296, 299,
    301, 302, 303, 304, 305, 308, 310,
    314, 315, 321, 329, 332, 333, 334,
    335, 336, 337, 339, 340, 344, 356,
    362, 390, 391, 392, 393, 395, 396,
    397, 398
Holocaust, vi, 3, 20, 22, 23, 40, 41, 124,
    148, 156, 159, 160, 162, 208, 210,
    211, 235, 275, 276, 278, 291, 298,
    299, 300, 305, 308, 309, 310, 311,
    312, 316, 320, 325, 329, 330, 332,
    364, 371, 390, 391, 393, 394, 395,
    396
Hope-Simpson, Sir John, 225
Hope-Simpson, Report, 224, 255
Hourwitz, Zalkind, 128

Irgun, 250, 293
Isaac, 30, 32
Isaiah, 10, 12, 33, 49, 366
Israelites, vii, 1, 2, 3, 8, 10, 24, 25, 26, 27,
    28, 29, 30, 31, 32, 33, 34, 36, 39, 40,
    41, 152, 358

Jabotinsky, Ze'ev (Vladimir), 170, 171,
    172, 173, 174, 176, 177, 178, 179,
    181, 182, 184, 236, 250, 271, 293
Jacob, 28, 30, 32
Jesus, 24, 40, 49, 50, 54, 55, 110, 117,
    366, 369, 370
Jewish Central Museum, Prague, 316,
    317, 320, 396
Joselewicz, Berek, 128, 140
Joseph, 26, 28, 30
Joseph II, Emperor of Austria, 134
Josephus, vii, 10, 11, 45, 47, 52, 54, 359,
    364, 365, 366, 367, 368, 370
Jost, Isaak Markus, 15, 360, 381
Julian, 52, 53, 369

Kabbalah, 77, 198, 385
Kafka, Franz, vi, viii, 17, 22, 173, 187,
    188, 189, 190, 191, 192, 193, 194,
    195, 196, 197, 198, 199, 200, 201,
    202, 203, 204, 205, 206, 207, 208,
    209, 210, 211, 212, 213, 214, 382,
    383, 384, 385, 386

Kazimierz, 84, 85, 86, 87, 88, 101, 374,
    375
kehilles, 126, 129, 131, 132, 133
Kennedy, John F., 5
Kennedy, Joseph P., 353, 355
Kenya, 166, 168, 184
Kenyatta, Jomo, 184
Kessler, Harry, 266, 378
Kikuyu, 168, 182, 184
King David Hotel, 345, 346
Kirk, Alexander, 300, 310, 393
Klatzkin, Jakob, 103, 105, 106, 108
Klausner, Joseph, 113, 121, 122, 251
Kook, Abraham Isaac, Chief Rabbi,
    121
Kook, Hillel, 177
Kościuszko, Tadeusz, 128, 140
Kristallnacht, 282, 284, 318

League of Nations, 147, 177, 179, 223,
    224, 235, 242, 270, 271, 272, 291,
    294
Lehmann, Siegfried, 204
Libya, 305, 309
Lindbergh, Charles, 7, 273
Lithuania, 21, 88, 126, 132, 140, 309
Livorno, 95, 97, 99, 100, 101, 377, 381
Louis de Bourbon, Prince of Condé, 113
Luzzatto, Samuel David, 112, 116,
    117

Maasai, 168, 177, 182, 184, 186
MacDonald, Malcolm, 217
MacDonald, Ramsay, 225, 226, 386
Magnes, Judah L., 204, 207, 209, 239,
    241, 243, 244, 246, 247, 248, 250,
    251, 252, 253, 254, 256, 257, 258,
    374, 377, 388
Maimonides, Moses, 14, 48, 365
marranos, 74, 110, 361
Marshall, George C., 349, 350, 351
Maskilim, 136, 140
Mather, Cotton, 152
Medici, Cosimo d', 97
Mehmed IV, Sultan of Turkey, 59, 60
Mendelssohn, Moses, 112
Montgomery, Bernard, 307
Moses, 1, 2, 8, 10, 16, 24, 25, 30, 31, 35,
    36, 37
Moulay Ismail, 59, 75

Moulay Rashid, 59, 62, 75
Musafia, Benjamin, 107, 113, 115

New Judea, vii, viii, 22, 165, 166, 167,
    168, 169, 170, 173, 174, 176, 177,
    178, 179, 180, 181, 182, 184, 185,
    186
Nicholas I, Tsar, 136
Night of the Long Knives, 286, 287
Nisko Plan, 283, 286
Nordau, Max, 168, 171, 172, 173, 176,
    177, 179, 180, 181, 191, 192, 236
Notkin, Nota Khaimovich, 134

Operation Torch, 300
Ottoman Empire, 59, 75, 92, 147,
    218

Pale of Jewish Settlement, vi, 123, 124,
    125, 134
Palestine, i, vi, viii, 3, 22, 51, 121, 124,
    142, 143, 144, 145, 146, 147, 148,
    149, 150, 152, 153, 155, 156, 158,
    161, 162, 163, 167, 171, 172, 173,
    174, 176, 180, 184, 187, 189, 190,
    191, 192, 193, 194, 195, 196, 197,
    198, 201, 202, 203, 204, 205, 206,
    208, 209, 211, 214, 215, 216, 217,
    218, 219, 220, 221, 222, 223, 224,
    225, 226, 227, 228, 229, 230, 231,
    232, 233, 234, 235, 236, 238, 239,
    240, 241, 242, 243, 244, 245, 246,
    247, 248, 249, 250, 252, 253, 254,
    255, 256, 257, 258, 270, 271, 292,
    293, 294, 295, 296, 301, 303, 304,
    305, 306, 307, 308, 309, 310, 335,
    336, 337, 338, 339, 344, 345, 347,
    348, 349, 351, 352, 361, 369, 382,
    383, 386, 387, 388, 389, 392, 394,
    395, 398, 400
Palestinians, 142, 143, 152, 153, 161,
    162, 164, 189, 215, 216, 219, 221,
    233, 237, 387
Passover, 3, 10, 25, 26, 27, 30, 31, 38, 40,
    41, 42, 176, 363
Peel Commission, 270, 294, 337, 339,
    398
Peres, Shimon, 185, 189, 206
Pharaoh, 1, 26, 27
Philo of Alexandria, 51, 56

Pinsker, Leo, 163, 169, 236
Poland, 59, 67, 68, 71, 73, 76, 77, 94,
    123, 125, 126, 127, 128, 129, 132,
    133, 134, 140, 141, 179, 180, 206,
    283, 284, 285, 286, 288, 289, 290,
    291, 334, 340, 360, 373, 374, 381,
    390, 398
Pompey, 44
Pope Paul IV, 94, 95
Proskauer, Joseph, 345, 347, 350, 351,
    352, 400
Protocols of the Elders of Zion, 262, 341,
    344
Puritans, 151, 152

rabbinic Judaism, 21, 54, 55, 56
Rahm, Karl, 317
Rathenau, Walther, viii, 22, 259, 260,
    263, 267, 390
Rauff, Walter, 308, 309
Ribbentrop, Joachim von, 292, 301, 302,
    303, 393
Rishon LeZion, 198
Rome, vii, 8, 16, 43, 44, 46, 53, 55, 64,
    67, 73, 82, 93, 94, 95, 96, 97, 98,
    101, 105, 120, 357, 365, 368, 369,
    370, 371, 375, 379, 380
Rommel, Erwin, viii, 181, 305, 306, 307,
    308, 309
Roosevelt, Franklin D., 180, 181, 273,
    292, 300, 307, 310, 340, 341
Rosenberg, Alfred, viii, 279, 283, 325,
    326, 397
Rousseau, Jean-Jacques, 125, 126, 140,
    141, 381
Russian Empire, 133, 134

Salten, Felix, 197, 198, 199, 200, 201,
    383, 384
Samuel, Herbert, 221, 222, 242
Schacht, Hjalmar, viii, 335, 336, 337,
    339, 398
Schmitt, Carl, 162, 163
Scholem, Gershom, 203, 204, 205
"Science of Judaism," 324
Second Temple, 3, 13, 21, 39, 56, 367
Sejm (Polish parliament), 126, 127,
    130
Sharif Husayn of Mecca, 233, 234, 235,
    236

Shertok, Moshe, 243, 244, 245, 246, 247, 248, 250, 251, 252, 253, 254, 256, 257

South Africa, 150, 151, 154, 155, 156, 157, 158, 160, 168, 178, 185, 190, 223, 382

Spinoza, Baruch, v, vii, 21, 103, 104, 105, 106, 107, 108, 109, 110, 111, 112, 113, 114, 115, 116, 117, 118, 119, 120, 121, 122

Stalin, Joseph, 180, 271, 290, 334, 340, 345, 348, 349

Strauss, Leo, 270

Sulpicius Severus, 43, 45, 364, 365

Tacitus, 7, 44, 45, 357, 364, 369

Taft, Robert, 341, 345, 347, 349

Tannous, Izzat, 216, 217, 219, 221, 386, 387

Templers, 148

Thucydides, 7, 12, 13, 357

Titus, Emperor, vii, 43, 44, 45, 46, 47, 48, 55, 56, 357, 364, 365, 366

Tobruk, 305, 307, 308

Truman, Harry S., 344

Trumpeldor, Josef, 176, 177, 179, 180, 182, 199

Tuscany, 97, 98, 99, 380

United Nations, 142, 150, 156, 186, 215, 221, 230, 231

Ussishkin, Menahem, 171, 172

Venice, 67, 73, 81, 82, 84, 88, 89, 90, 91, 92, 95, 97, 101, 375, 376, 377, 378

Vespasian, Emperor, 44

Wauchope, Sir Arthur, 228, 241, 242, 247, 389

Wehrmacht, 181, 282, 283, 285, 286, 287, 288, 290, 293, 309, 328, 333, 334, 392

Weizmann, Chaim, viii, 144, 145, 146, 147, 225, 226, 236

Wise, Stephen, 179

World War I, 22, 145, 147, 174, 207, 218, 236, 265, 291, 296, 343

World War II, 5, 17, 22, 162, 164, 180, 187, 206, 208, 219, 230, 237, 287, 296, 305, 307, 310, 312, 320, 323, 371, 379, 392, 393, 394, 398, 399

Yerushalmi, Yosef Hayim, 14, 20, 25, 360, 363

Yishuv, 22, 147, 155, 159, 205, 208, 239, 246, 250, 336, 344, 349, 394

Zangwill, Israel, 83, 166, 169, 173, 175, 176, 372

Zedekiah, King, 9

Zemach, Shlomo, 198, 202, 384

Zionism, iii, vi, 17, 20, 22, 104, 121, 142, 143, 144, 145, 147, 148, 150, 152, 155, 158, 159, 160, 161, 173, 189, 190, 191, 192, 193, 197, 201, 204, 209, 213, 215, 216, 218, 219, 221, 223, 224, 225, 226, 228, 233, 235, 236, 242, 248, 250, 270, 272, 294, 307, 338, 339, 344, 345, 348, 350, 352, 382, 383, 384, 385, 386, 388, 389, 394, 399, 400

Zunz, Leopold, 15

Zweig, Arnold, 205, 207, 209, 270